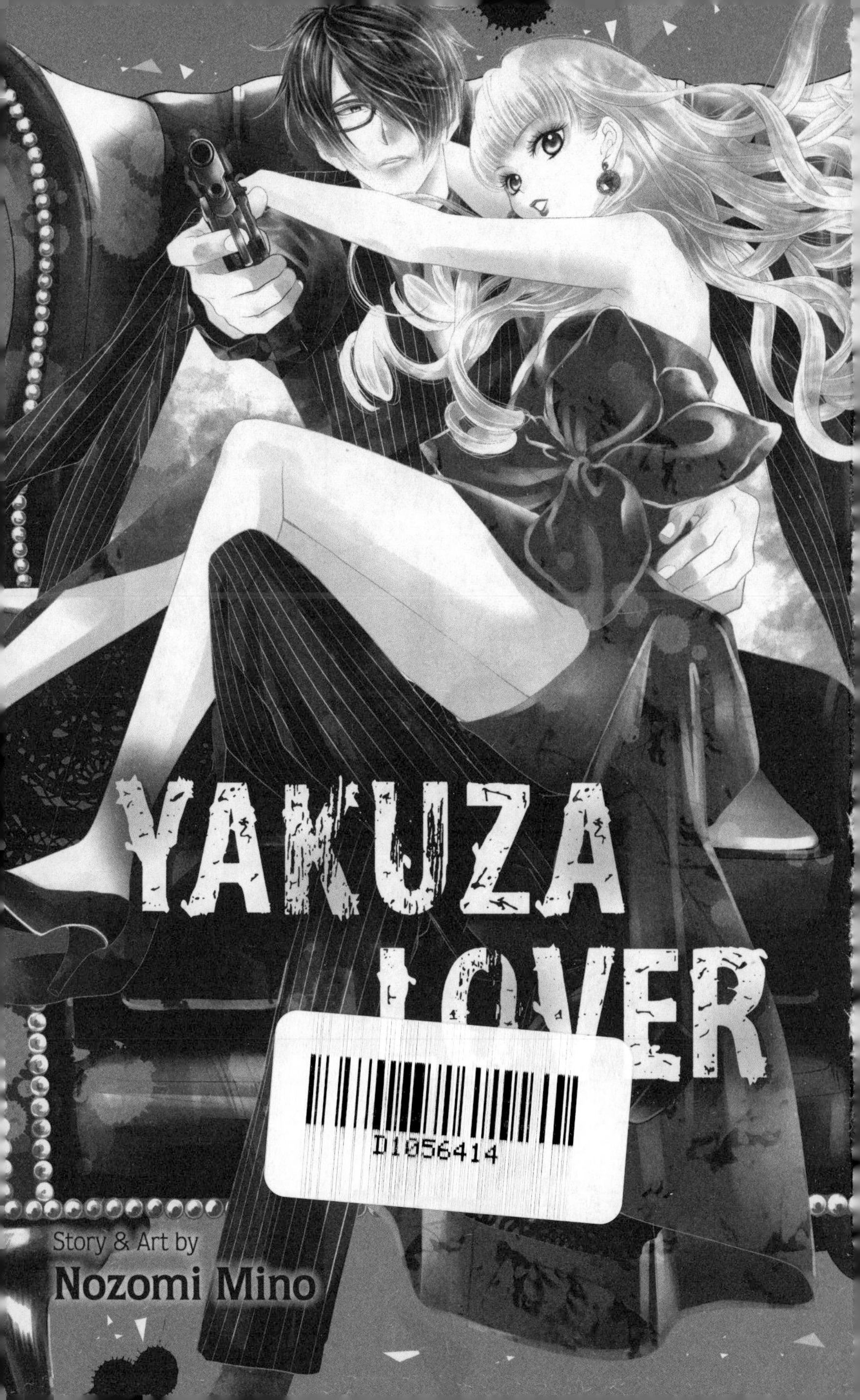
YAKUZA
LOVER
Story & Art by
Nozomi Mino

Contents

Toshiomi Oya
Underboss
Underboss of the Oya yakuza syndicate. He's a gentle man with a heart of gold—yet no mobster would dare defy him.

Yuri
College Student
A college student with a strong sense of integrity who cares deeply about her friends. Thanks to her former days as a basketball player, she is very confident in her stamina.

Story

Feisty college student Yuri's life is turned upside down when drug dealers attack her at a party and Toshiomi Oya, the underboss of a yakuza syndicate, swoops in to save her. Yuri and Toshiomi are instantly drawn to each other—Toshiomi to Yuri's strength and Yuri to Toshiomi's sweet, gentle nature.

After an attempt on Toshiomi's life, Yuri prepares herself for the reality of becoming a yakuza's lover and all that it entails. Toshiomi lives life on the edge with no promise of tomorrow, and Yuri finds herself swept up in their passionate, all-consuming love affair.

The new couple decides to take a trip to Shanghai for what is supposed to be a weeklong, romance-filled romp. But instead, they're accosted by Russian mobsters. Luckily, the mobsters back down when confronted with Toshiomi's power, but not before injuring Yuri.

The thrilling climax of the Shanghai trip awaits...

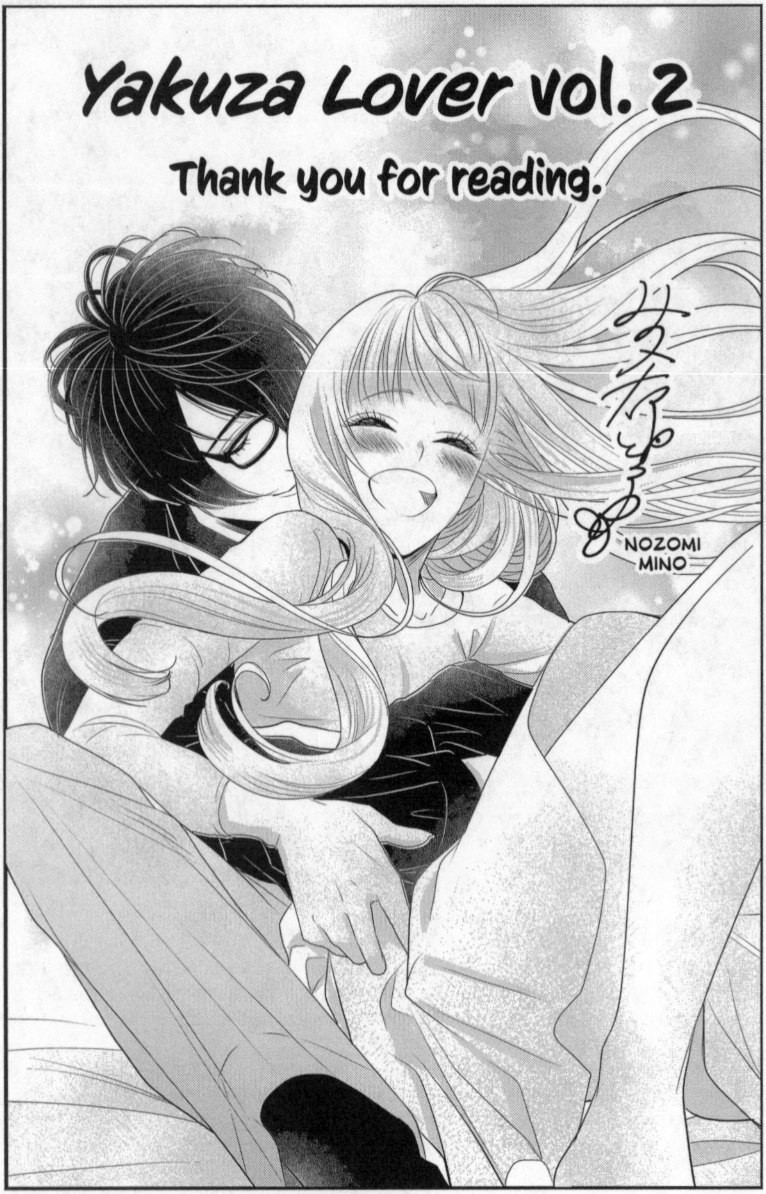

Yakuza Lover vol. 2
Thank you for reading.
みのりのぞみ
NOZOMI MINO

bullet 05

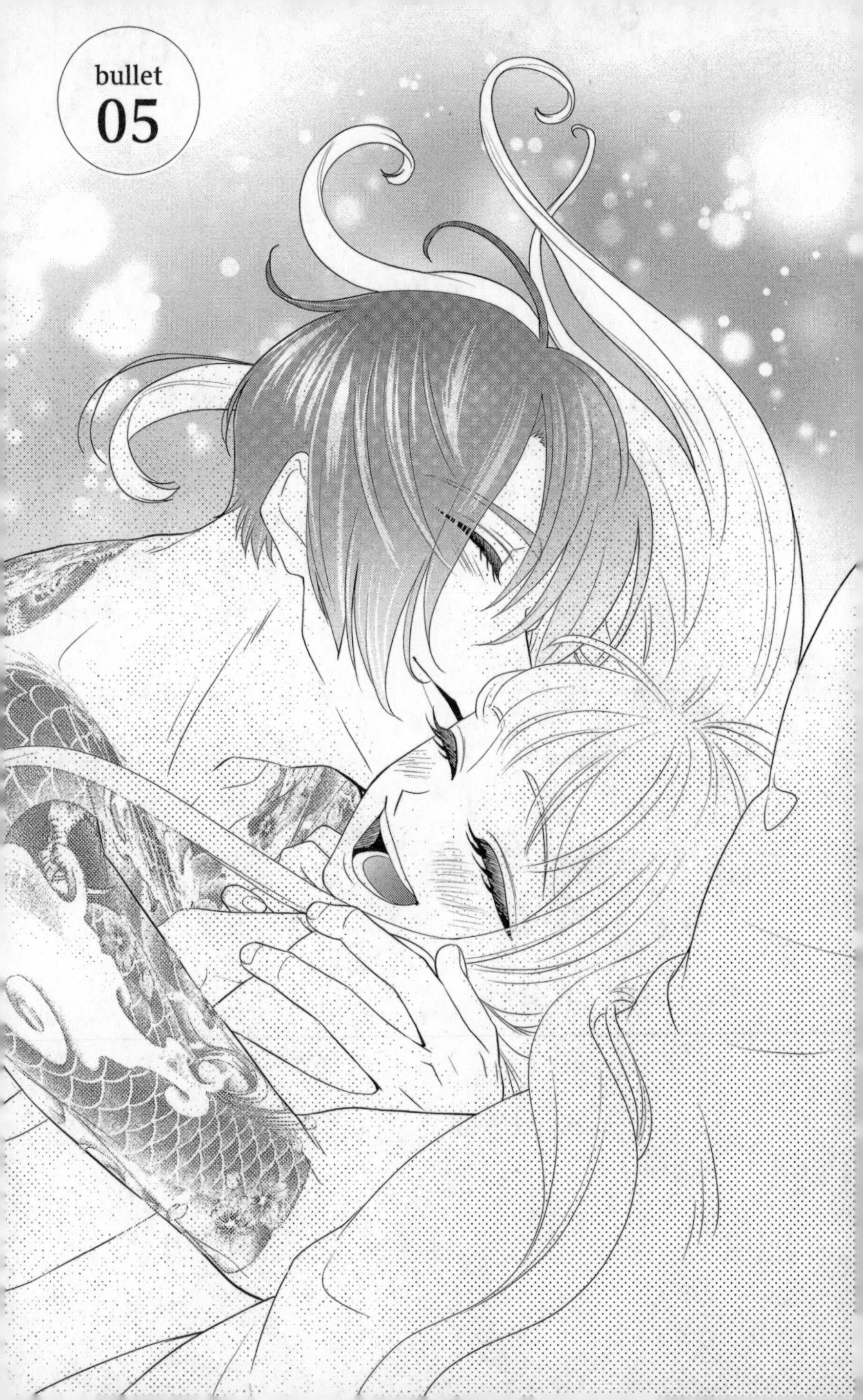

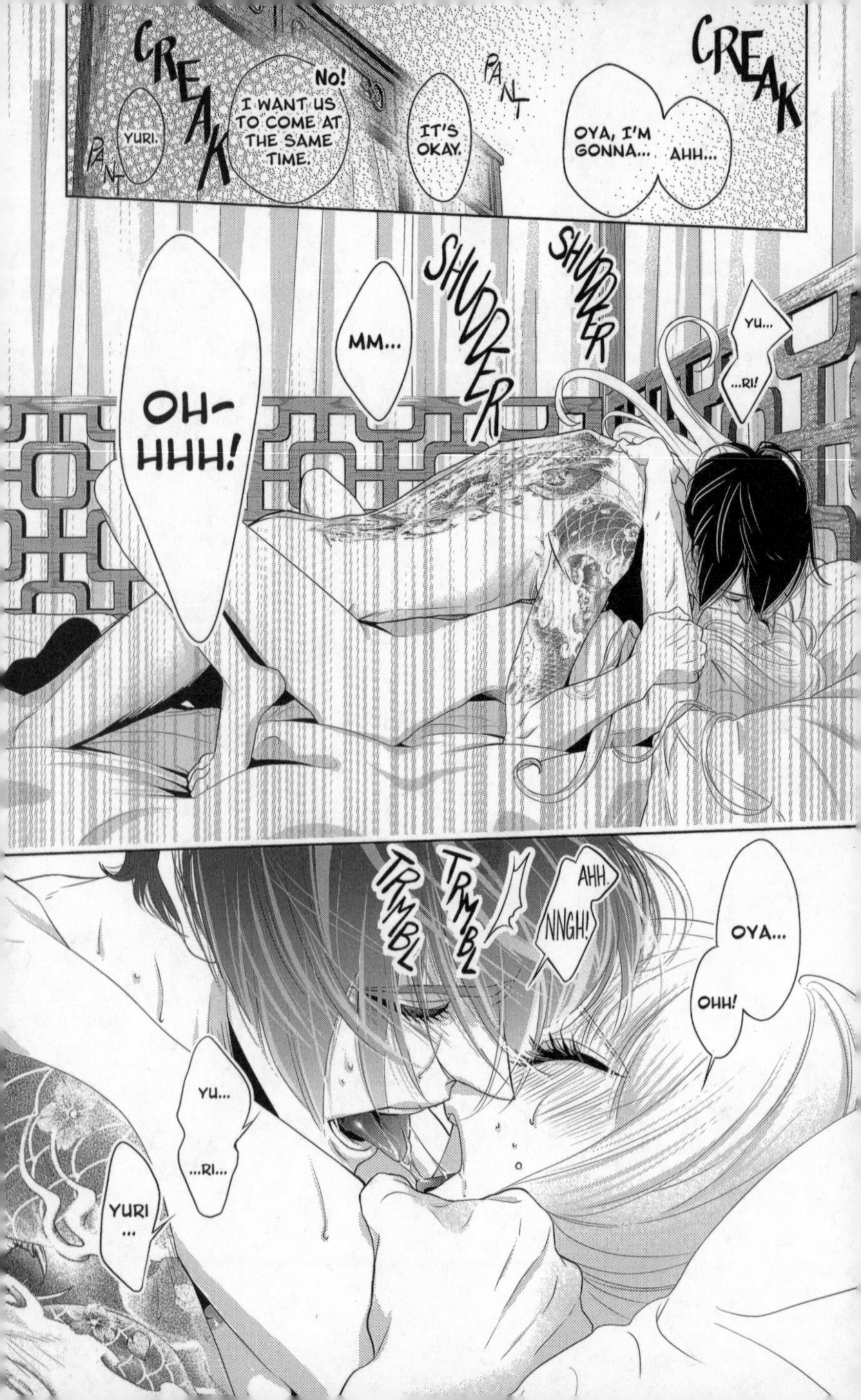
CREAK
OYA, I'M GONNA... AHH...
PANT
IT'S OKAY.
NO! I WANT US TO COME AT THE SAME TIME.
CREAK
YURI.
PANT
YU... ...RI!
SHUDDER
SHUDDER
MM...
OH-HHH!
OYA... OHH!
AHH. NNGH!
TRMBL
TRMBL
YU... ...RI...
YURI...

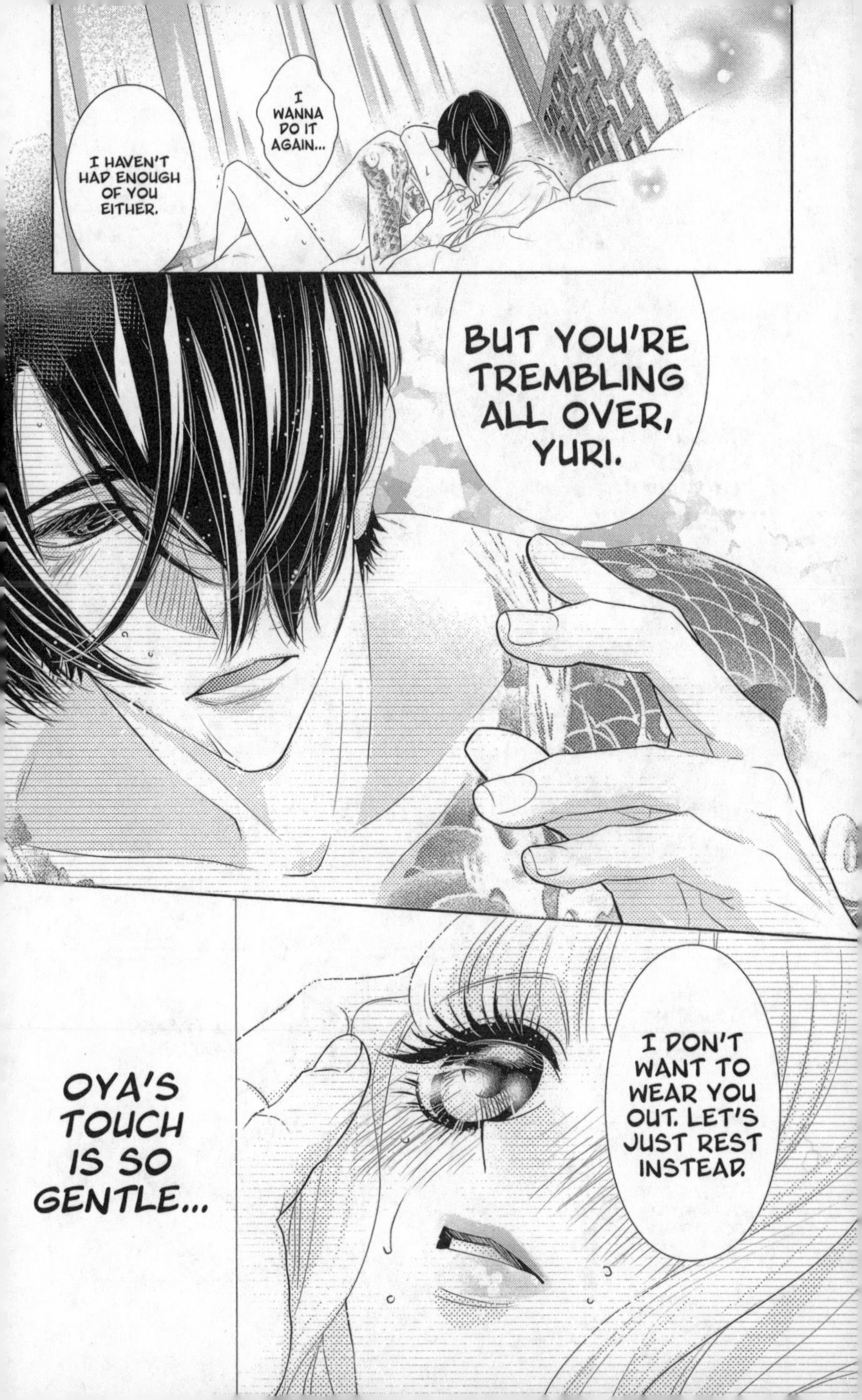
I WANNA DO IT AGAIN...
I HAVEN'T HAD ENOUGH OF YOU EITHER.
BUT YOU'RE TREMBLING ALL OVER, YURI.
I DON'T WANT TO WEAR YOU OUT. LET'S JUST REST INSTEAD.
OYA'S TOUCH IS SO GENTLE...

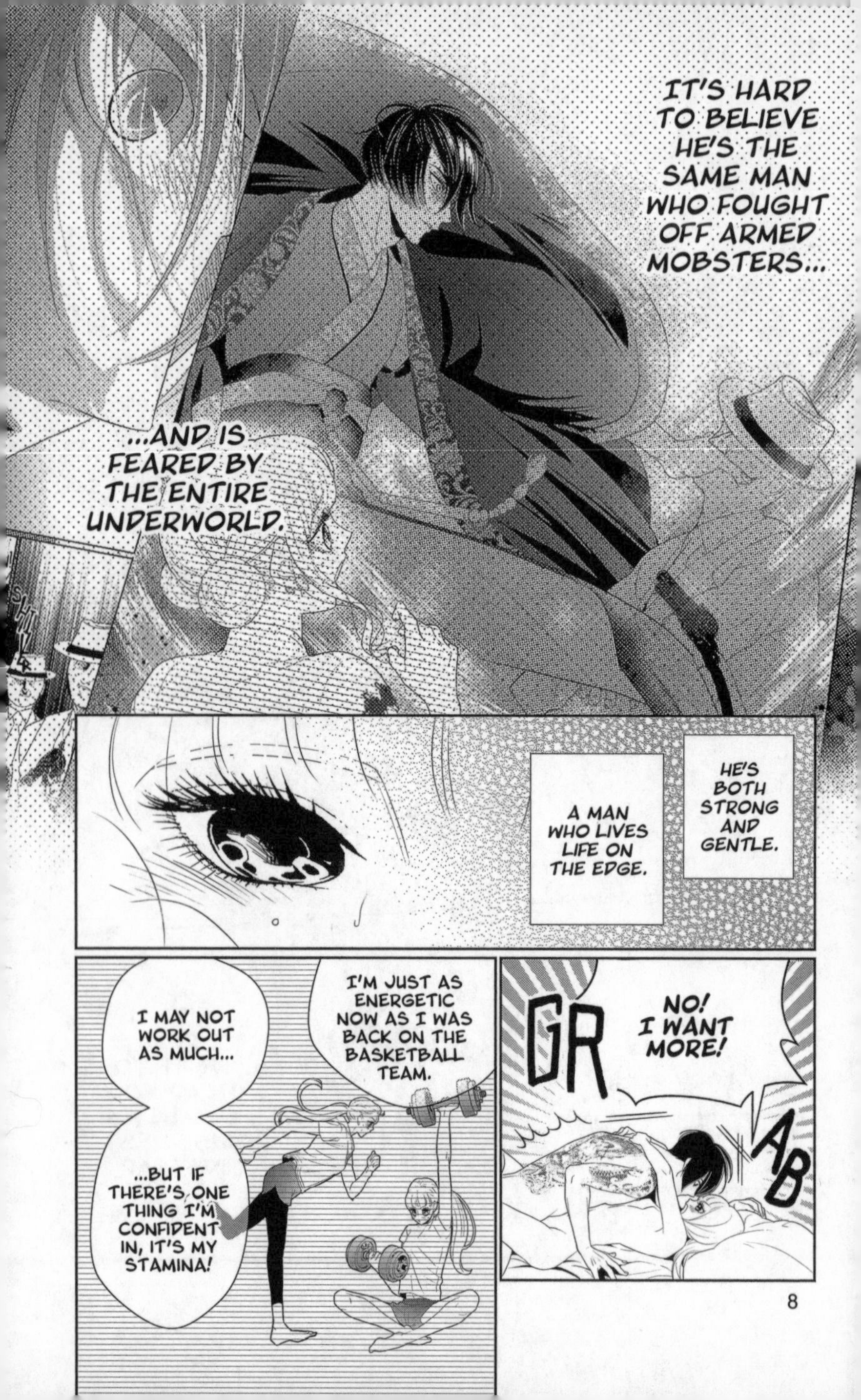
IT'S HARD TO BELIEVE HE'S THE SAME MAN WHO FOUGHT OFF ARMED MOBSTERS...
...AND IS FEARED BY THE ENTIRE UNDERWORLD.
HE'S BOTH STRONG AND GENTLE.
A MAN WHO LIVES LIFE ON THE EDGE.
NO! I WANT MORE!
GR
AB
I'M JUST AS ENERGETIC NOW AS I WAS BACK ON THE BASKETBALL TEAM.
I MAY NOT WORK OUT AS MUCH...
...BUT IF THERE'S ONE THING I'M CONFIDENT IN, IT'S MY STAMINA!

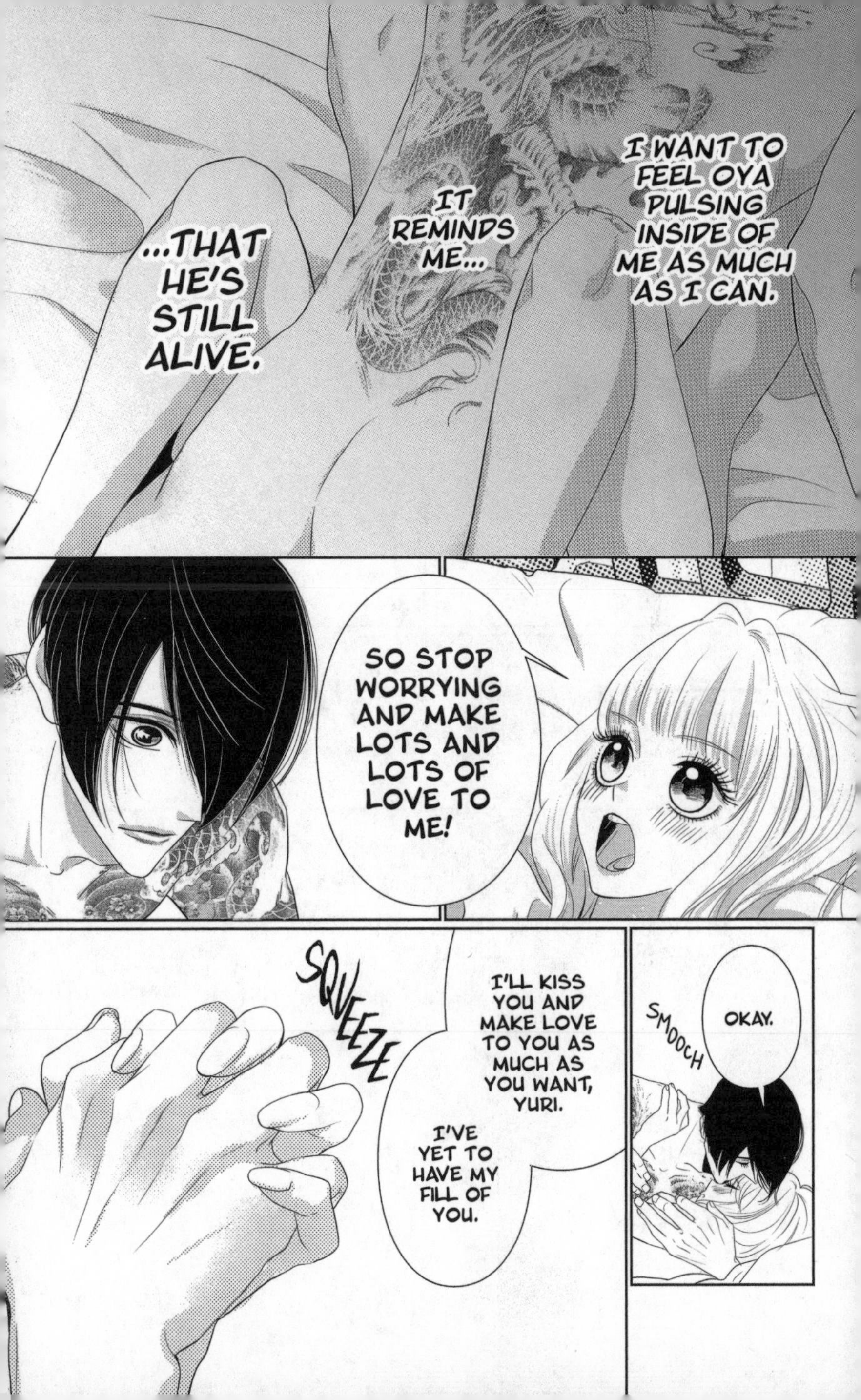
I WANT TO FEEL OYA PULSING INSIDE OF ME AS MUCH AS I CAN.
IT REMINDS ME...
...THAT HE'S STILL ALIVE.
SO STOP WORRYING AND MAKE LOTS AND LOTS OF LOVE TO ME!
OKAY.
SMOOCH
I'LL KISS YOU AND MAKE LOVE TO YOU AS MUCH AS YOU WANT, YURI.
I'VE YET TO HAVE MY FILL OF YOU.
SQUEEZE

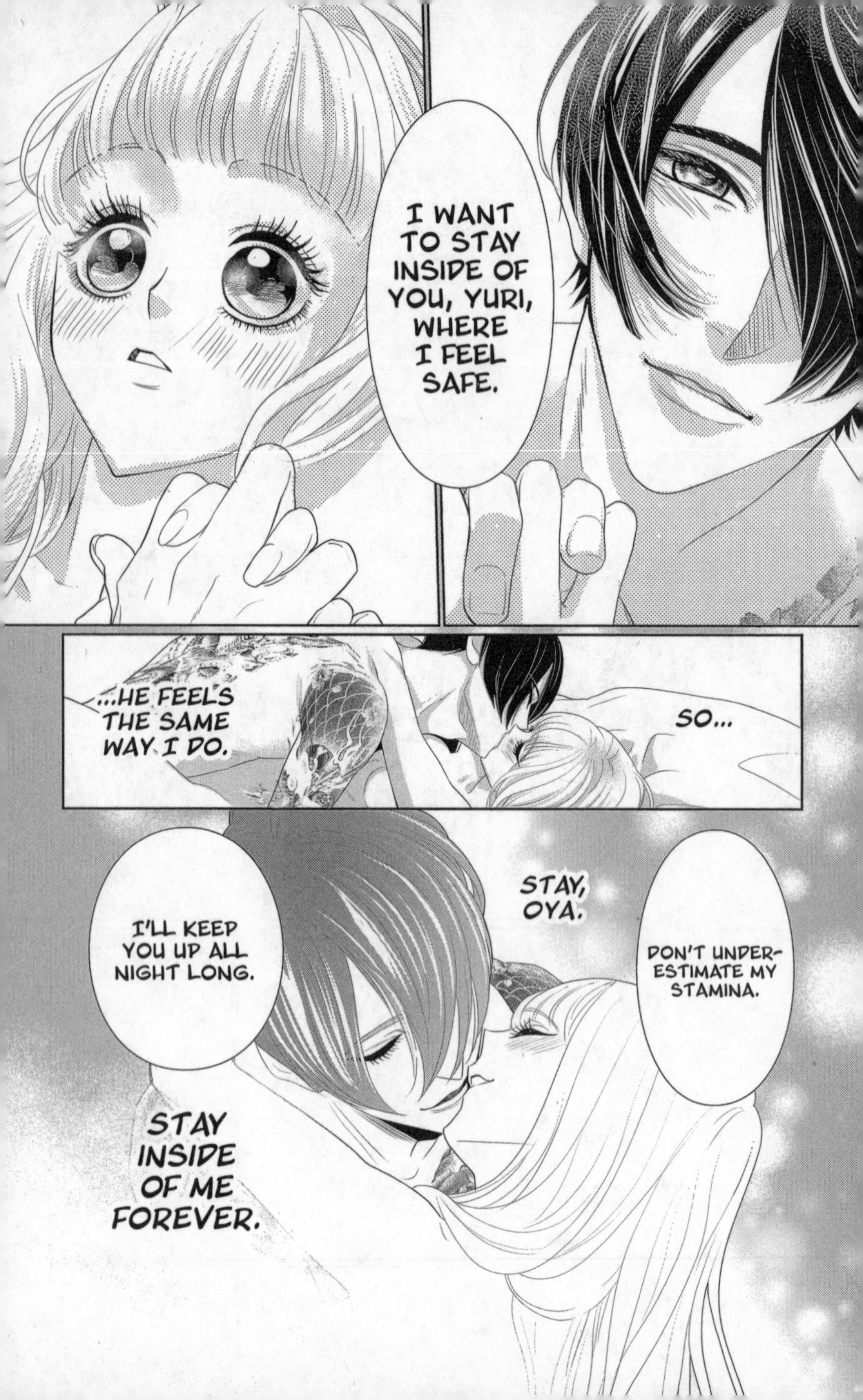
I WANT TO STAY INSIDE OF YOU, YURI, WHERE I FEEL SAFE.
SO...
...HE FEELS THE SAME WAY I DO.
DON'T UNDER-ESTIMATE MY STAMINA.
STAY, OYA.
I'LL KEEP YOU UP ALL NIGHT LONG.
STAY INSIDE OF ME FOREVER.

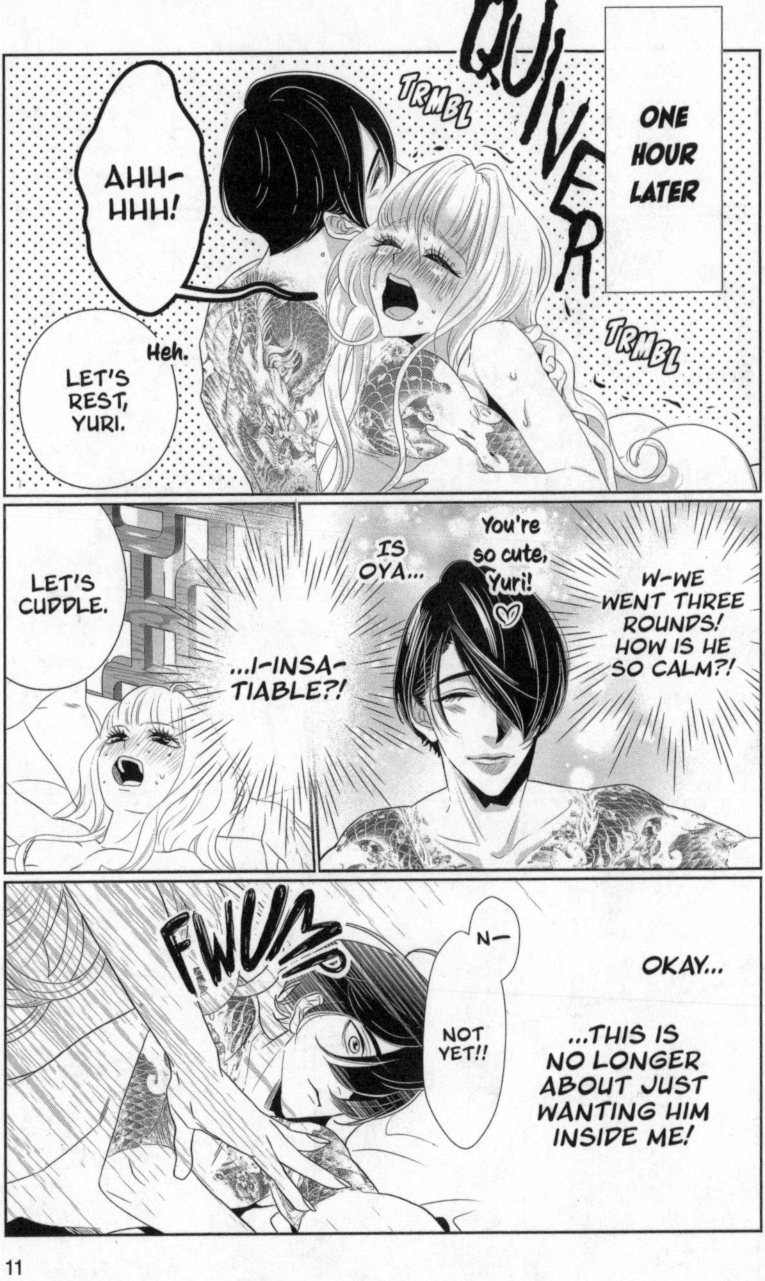
ONE HOUR LATER
QUIVER
TRMBL
AHH-HHH!
TRMBL
Heh.
LET'S REST, YURI.
W-WE WENT THREE ROUNDS! HOW IS HE SO CALM?!
You're so cute, Yuri!
IS OYA...
...I-INSATIABLE?!
LET'S CUDDLE.
OKAY...
...THIS IS NO LONGER ABOUT JUST WANTING HIM INSIDE ME!
N—
NOT YET!!
FWUMP

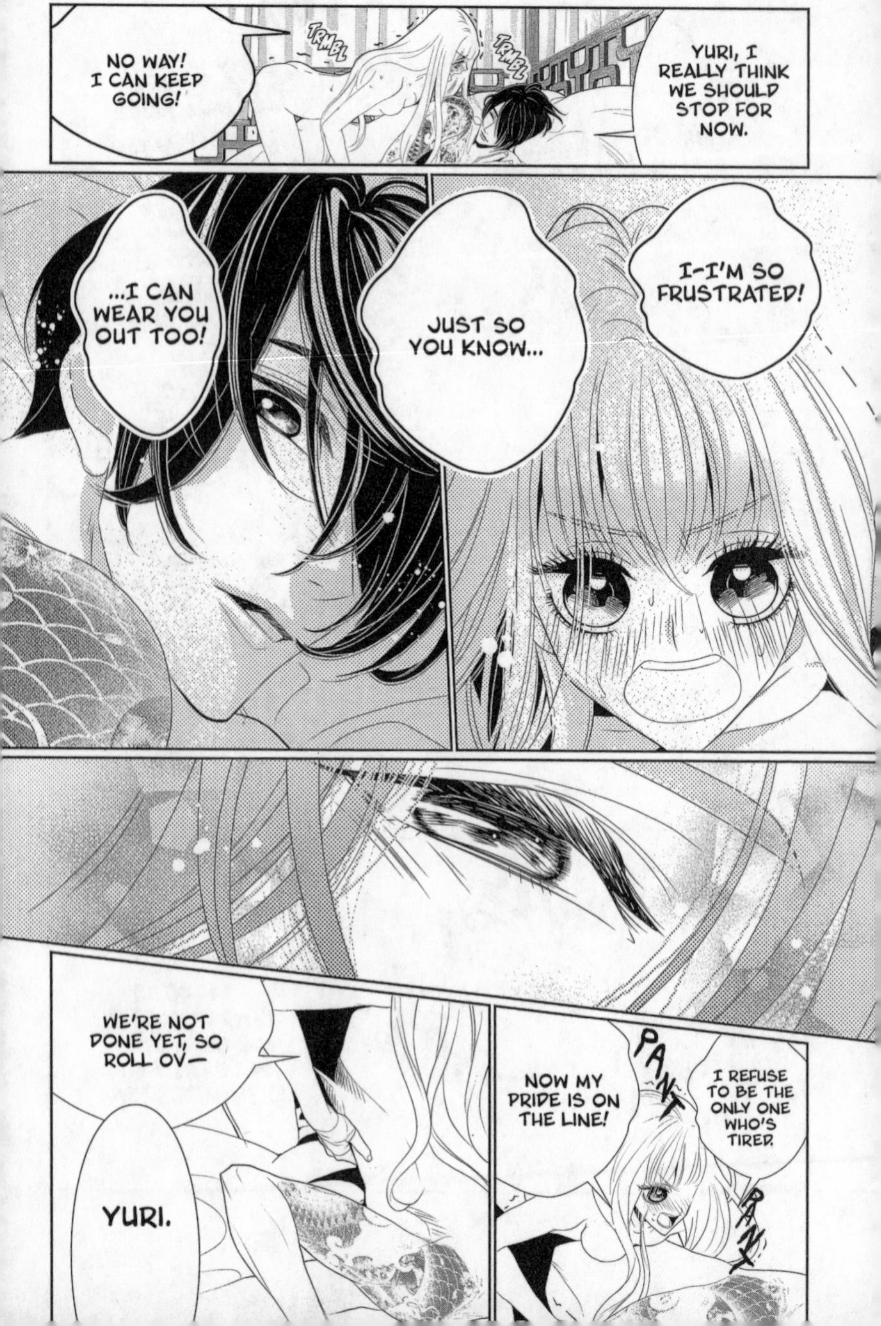
YURI, I REALLY THINK WE SHOULD STOP FOR NOW.
TRMBL
TRMBL
NO WAY! I CAN KEEP GOING!
I-I'M SO FRUSTRATED!
JUST SO YOU KNOW...
...I CAN WEAR YOU OUT TOO!
I REFUSE TO BE THE ONLY ONE WHO'S TIRED.
PANT
NOW MY PRIDE IS ON THE LINE!
PANT
WE'RE NOT DONE YET, SO ROLL OV—
YURI.

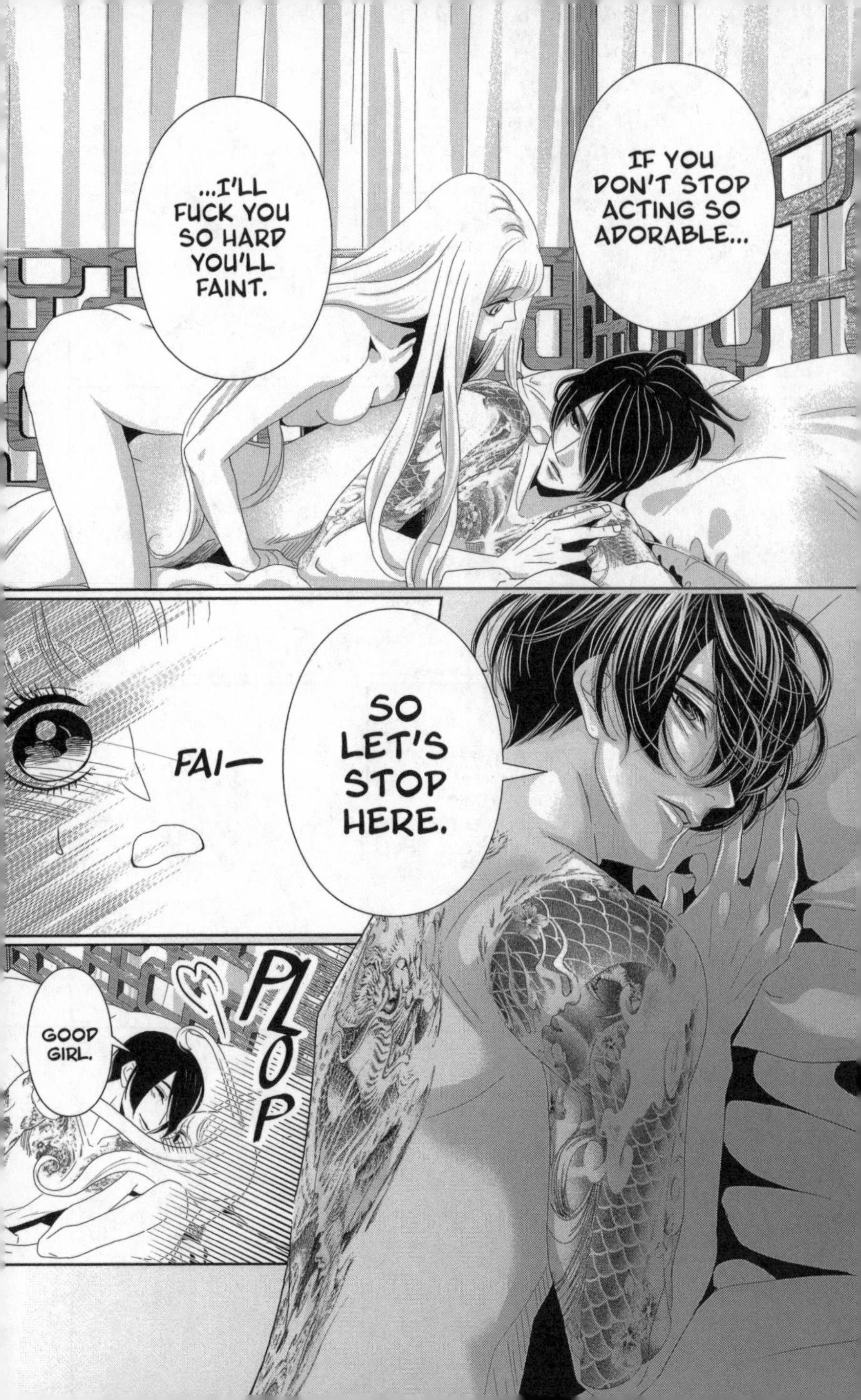
IF YOU DON'T STOP ACTING SO ADORABLE...
...I'LL FUCK YOU SO HARD YOU'LL FAINT.
SO LET'S STOP HERE.
FAI—
PLOP
GOOD GIRL.

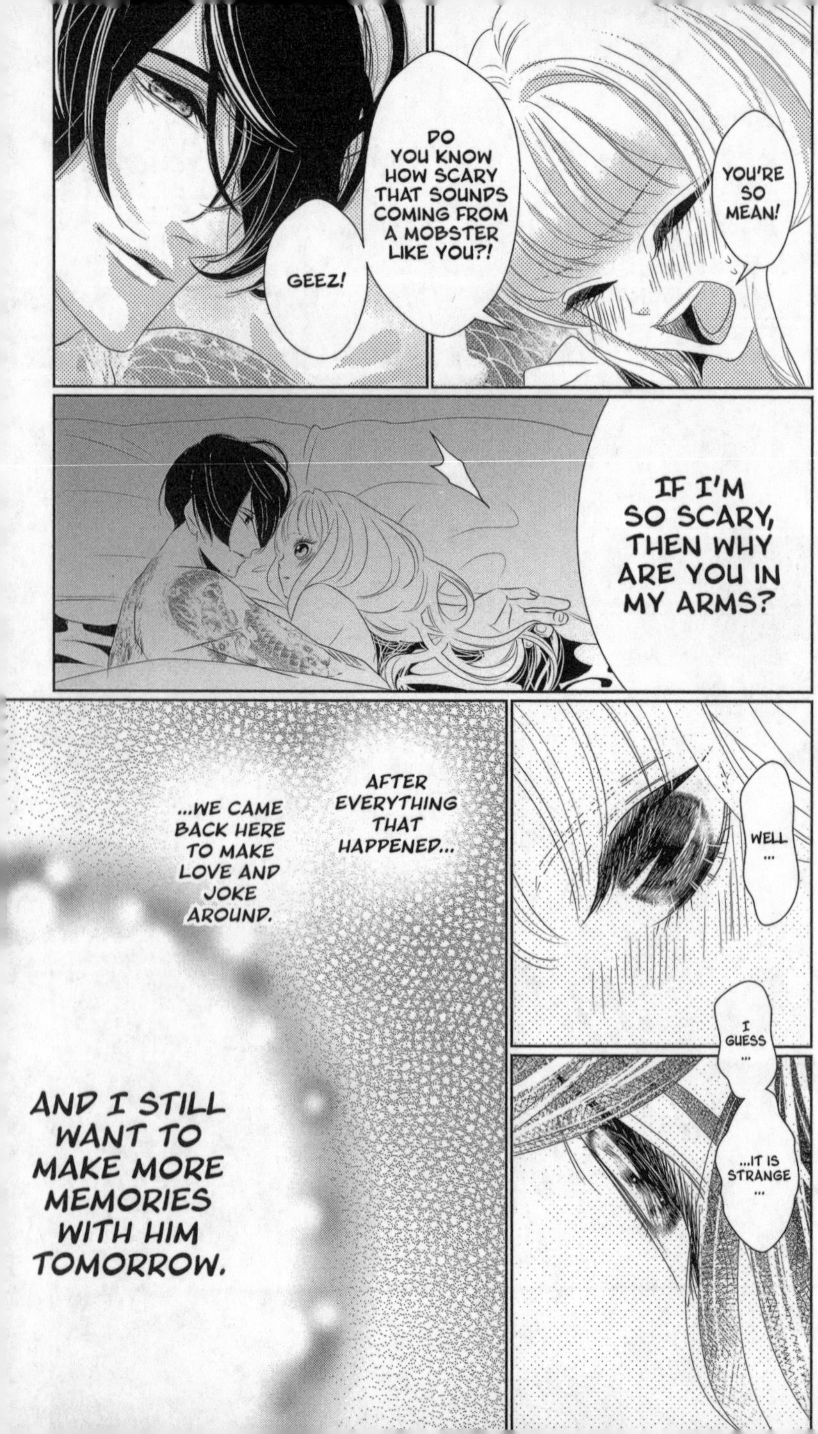
YOU'RE SO MEAN!
DO YOU KNOW HOW SCARY THAT SOUNDS COMING FROM A MOBSTER LIKE YOU?!
GEEZ!
IF I'M SO SCARY, THEN WHY ARE YOU IN MY ARMS?
WELL...
I GUESS...
...IT IS STRANGE...
AFTER EVERYTHING THAT HAPPENED...
...WE CAME BACK HERE TO MAKE LOVE AND JOKE AROUND.
AND I STILL WANT TO MAKE MORE MEMORIES WITH HIM TOMORROW.

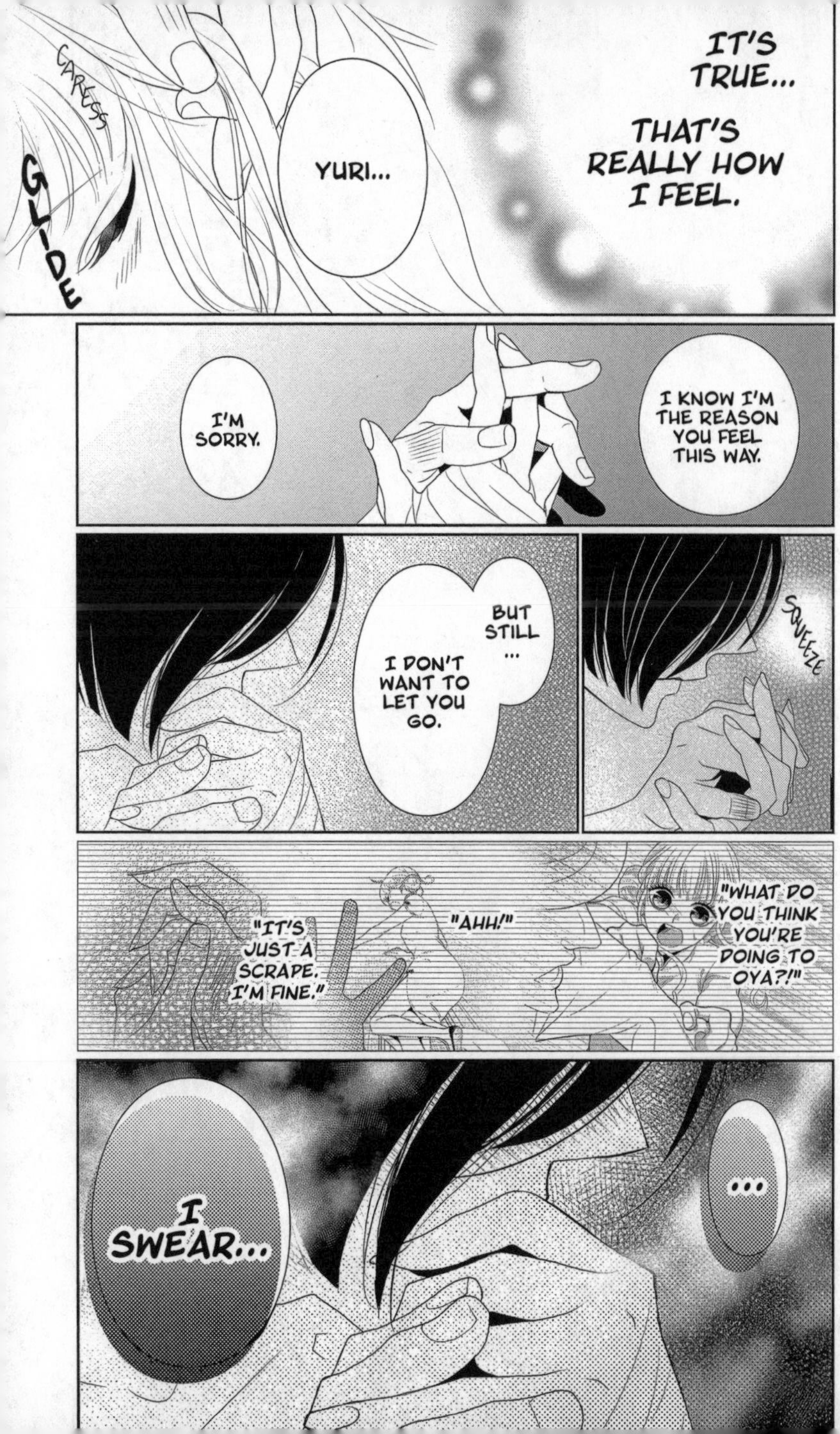
IT'S TRUE...
THAT'S REALLY HOW I FEEL.
YURI...
CARESS
GLIDE
I KNOW I'M THE REASON YOU FEEL THIS WAY.
I'M SORRY.
SQUEEZE
BUT STILL...
I DON'T WANT TO LET YOU GO.
"WHAT DO YOU THINK YOU'RE DOING TO OYA?!"
"AHH!"
"IT'S JUST A SCRAPE. I'M FINE."
...
I SWEAR...

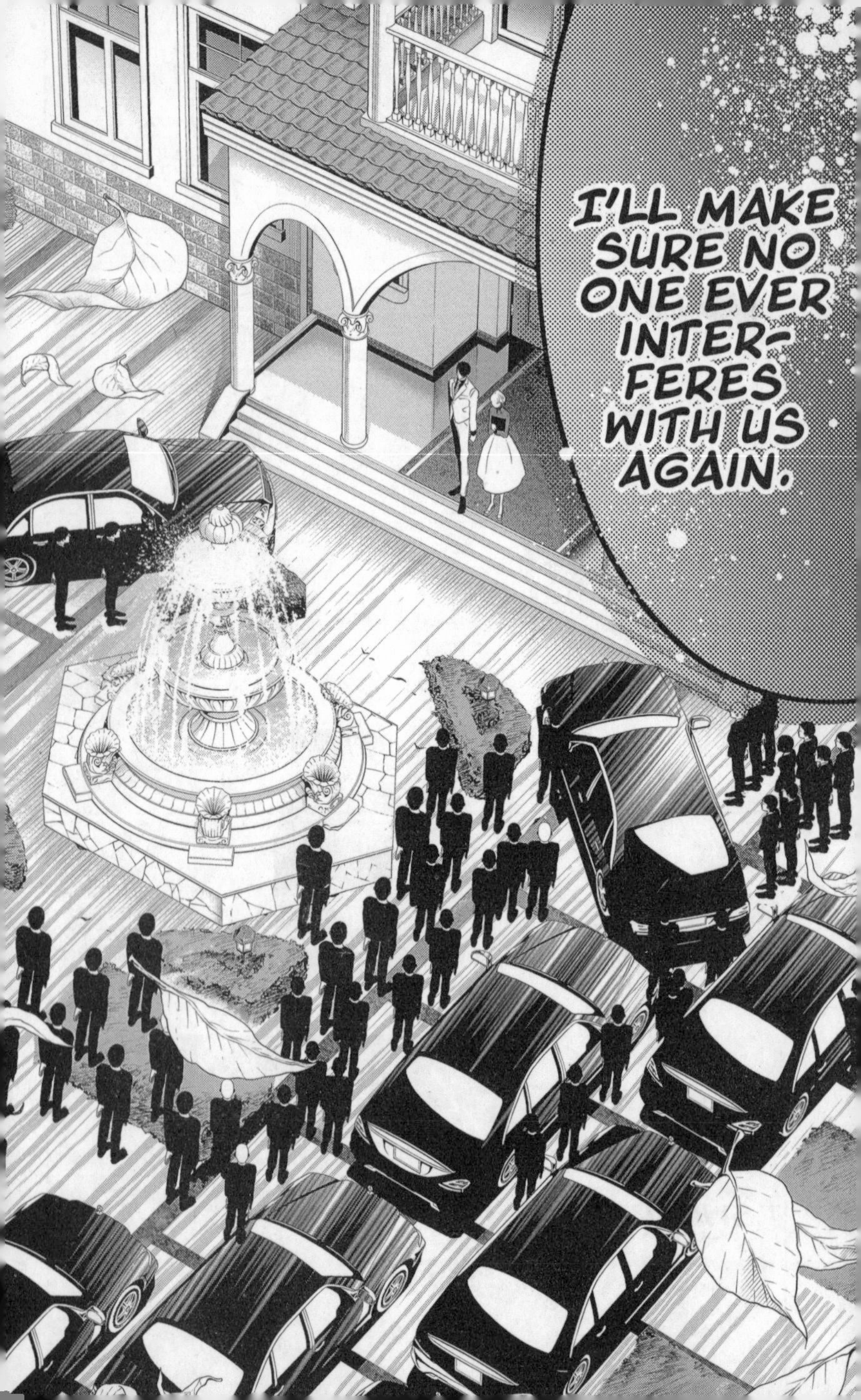
I'LL MAKE SURE NO ONE EVER INTER-FERES WITH US AGAIN.

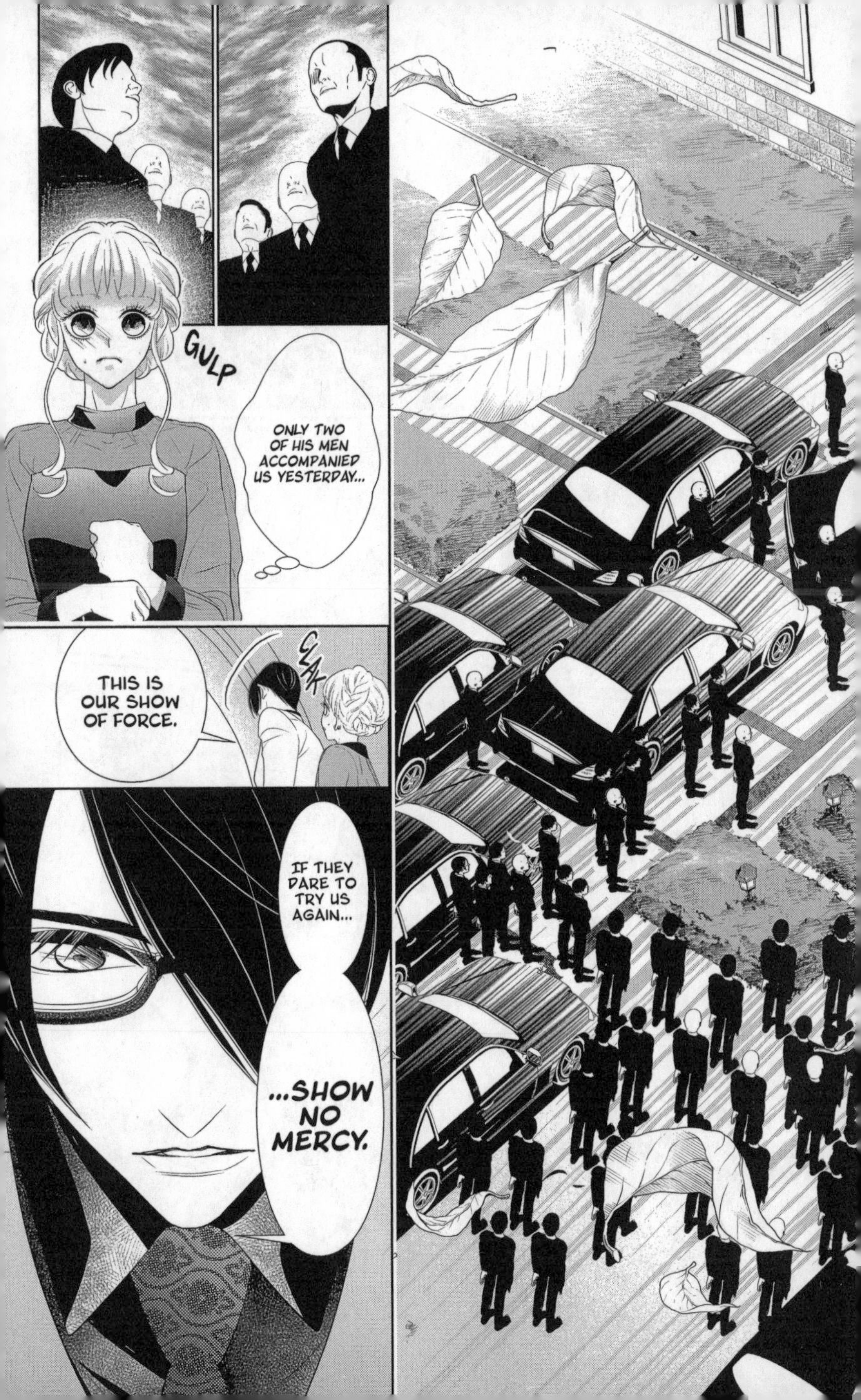
ONLY TWO OF HIS MEN ACCOMPANIED US YESTERDAY...
GULP
CLAK
THIS IS OUR SHOW OF FORCE.
IF THEY DARE TO TRY US AGAIN...
...SHOW NO MERCY.

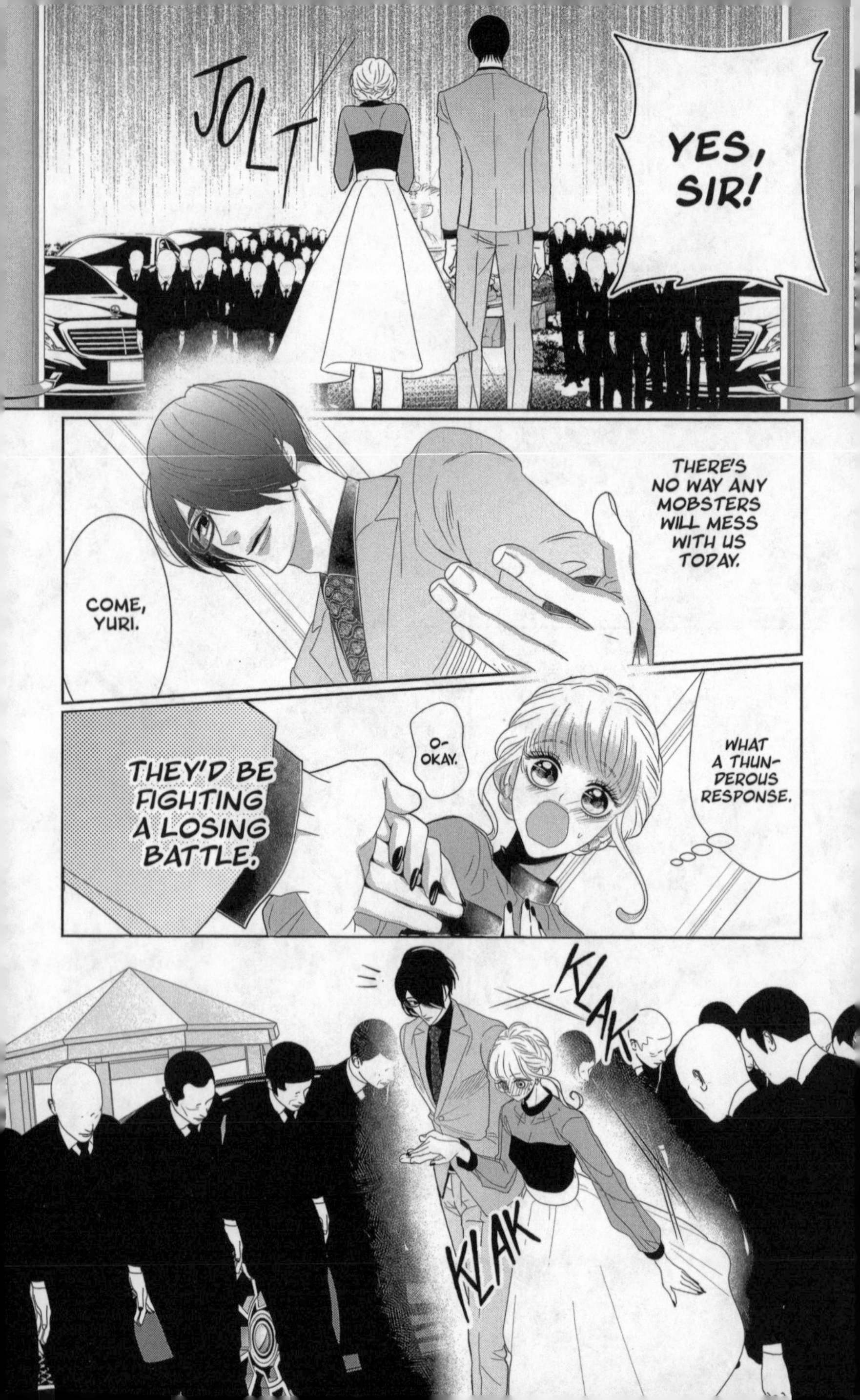
YES, SIR!
JOLT
THERE'S NO WAY ANY MOBSTERS WILL MESS WITH US TODAY.
COME, YURI.
WHAT A THUN-DEROUS RESPONSE.
O-OKAY.
THEY'D BE FIGHTING A LOSING BATTLE.
KLAK
KLAK

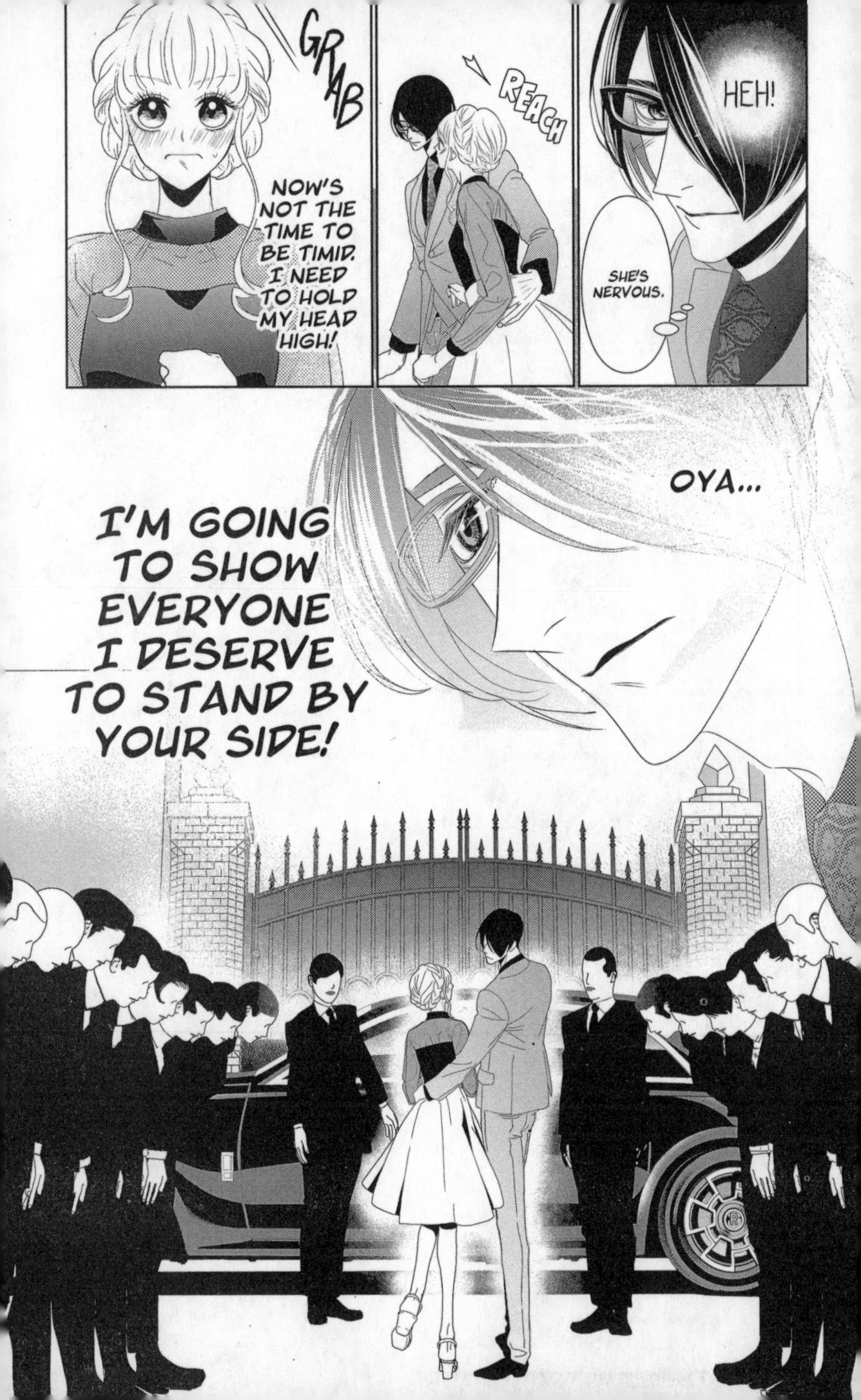
HEH!
SHE'S NERVOUS.
REACH
GRAB
NOW'S NOT THE TIME TO BE TIMID. I NEED TO HOLD MY HEAD HIGH!
OYA...
I'M GOING TO SHOW EVERYONE I DESERVE TO STAND BY YOUR SIDE!

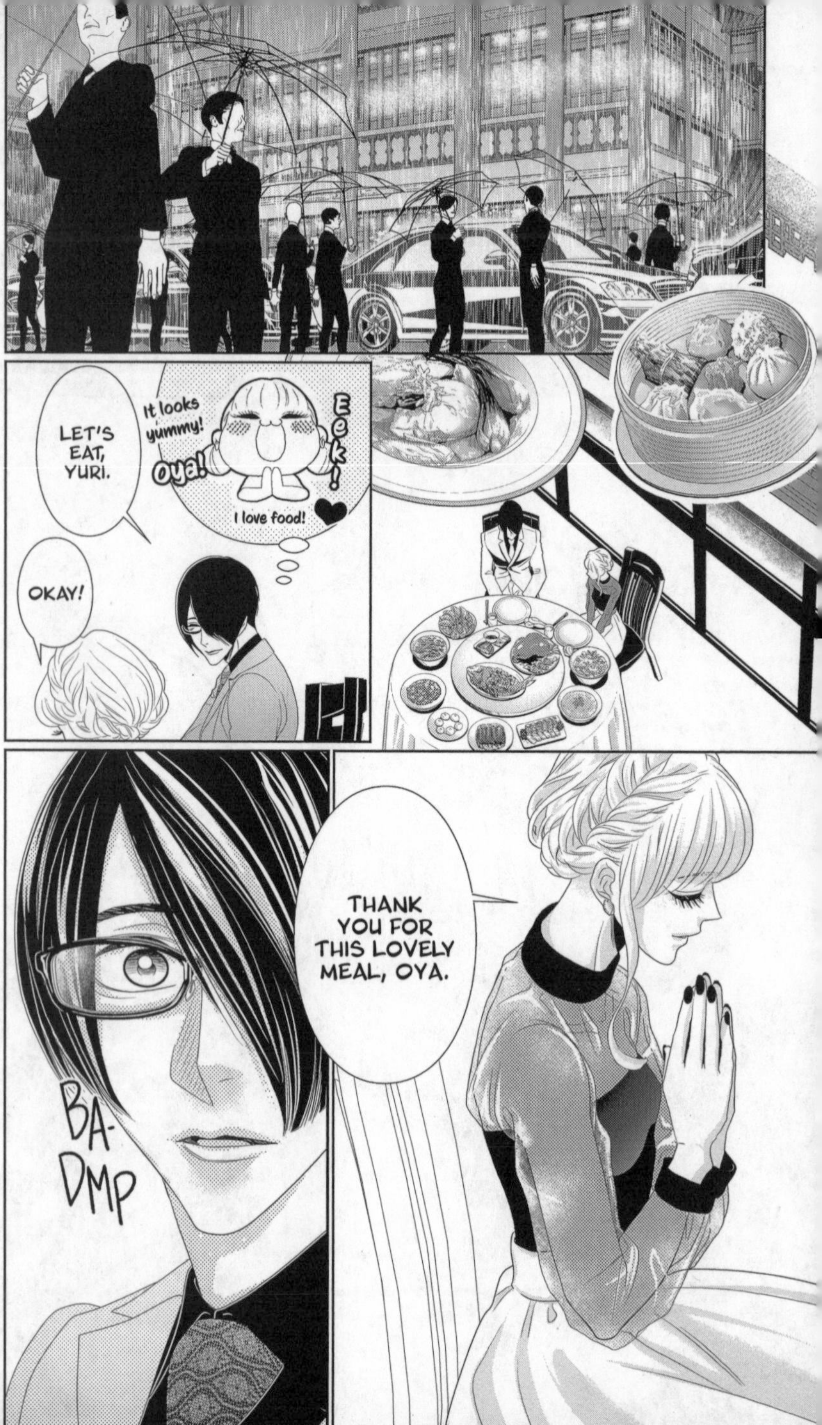

LET'S EAT, YURI.
It looks yummy! Oya! I love food!
Eek!
OKAY!
THANK YOU FOR THIS LOVELY MEAL, OYA.
BA-DMP

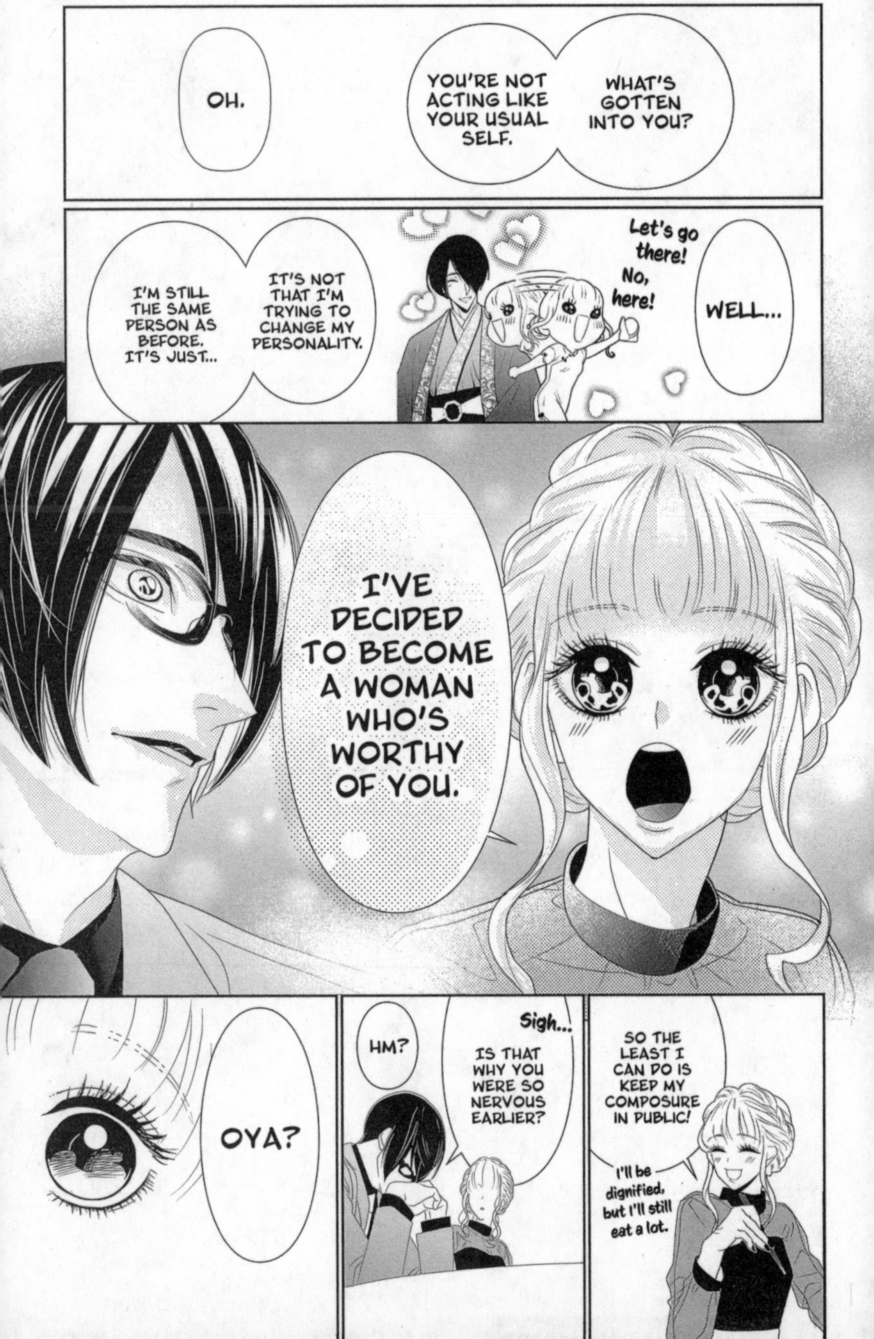
WHAT'S GOTTEN INTO YOU?
YOU'RE NOT ACTING LIKE YOUR USUAL SELF.
OH.
WELL...
Let's go there!
No, here!
IT'S NOT THAT I'M TRYING TO CHANGE MY PERSONALITY.
I'M STILL THE SAME PERSON AS BEFORE. IT'S JUST...
I'VE DECIDED TO BECOME A WOMAN WHO'S WORTHY OF YOU.
SO THE LEAST I CAN DO IS KEEP MY COMPOSURE IN PUBLIC!
I'll be dignified, but I'll still eat a lot.
Sigh...
IS THAT WHY YOU WERE SO NERVOUS EARLIER?
HM?
OYA?

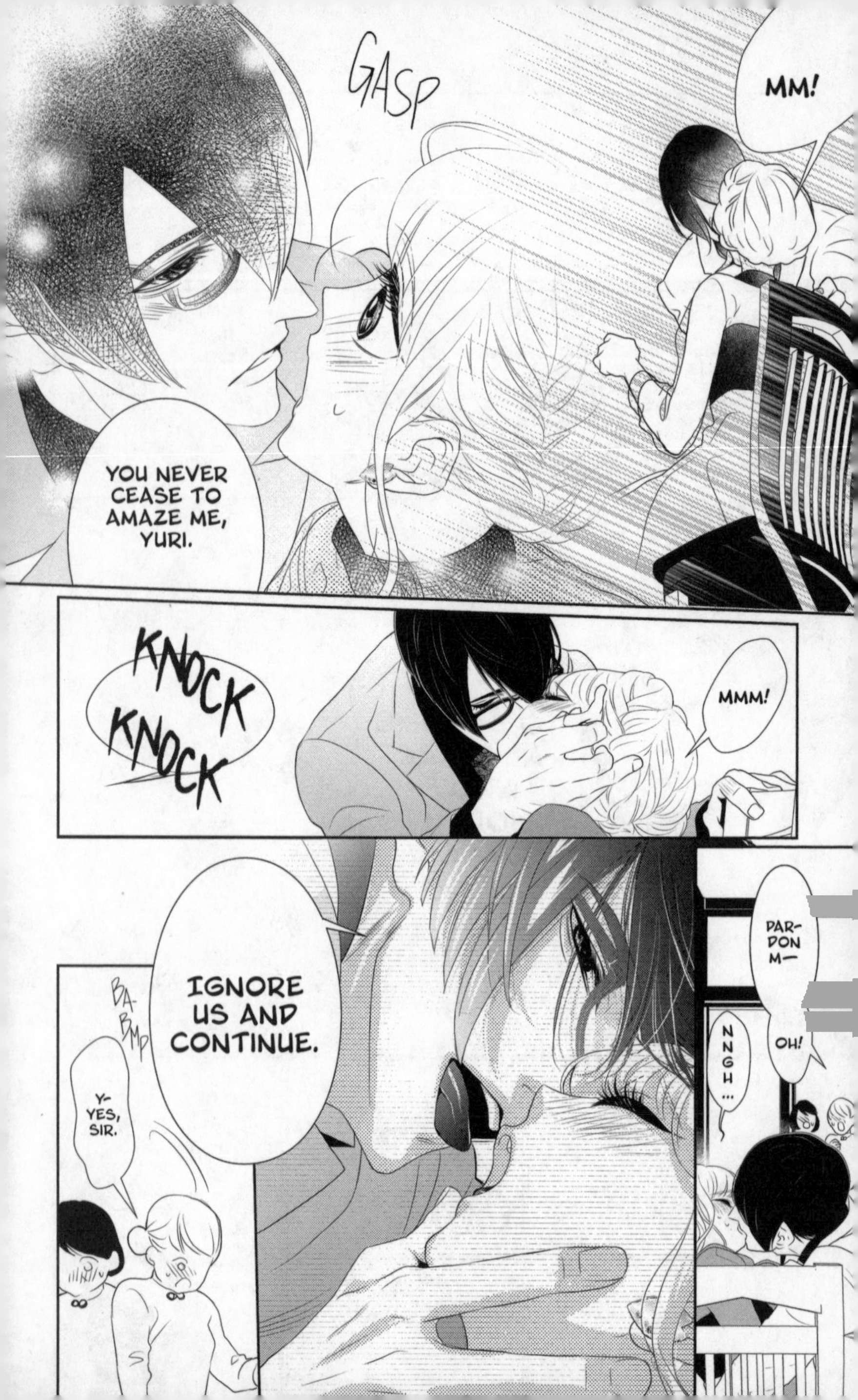
MM!
GASP
YOU NEVER CEASE TO AMAZE ME, YURI.
MMM!
KNOCK KNOCK
PARDON M—
OH!
NNGH...
IGNORE US AND CONTINUE.
BA-BMP
Y-YES, SIR.

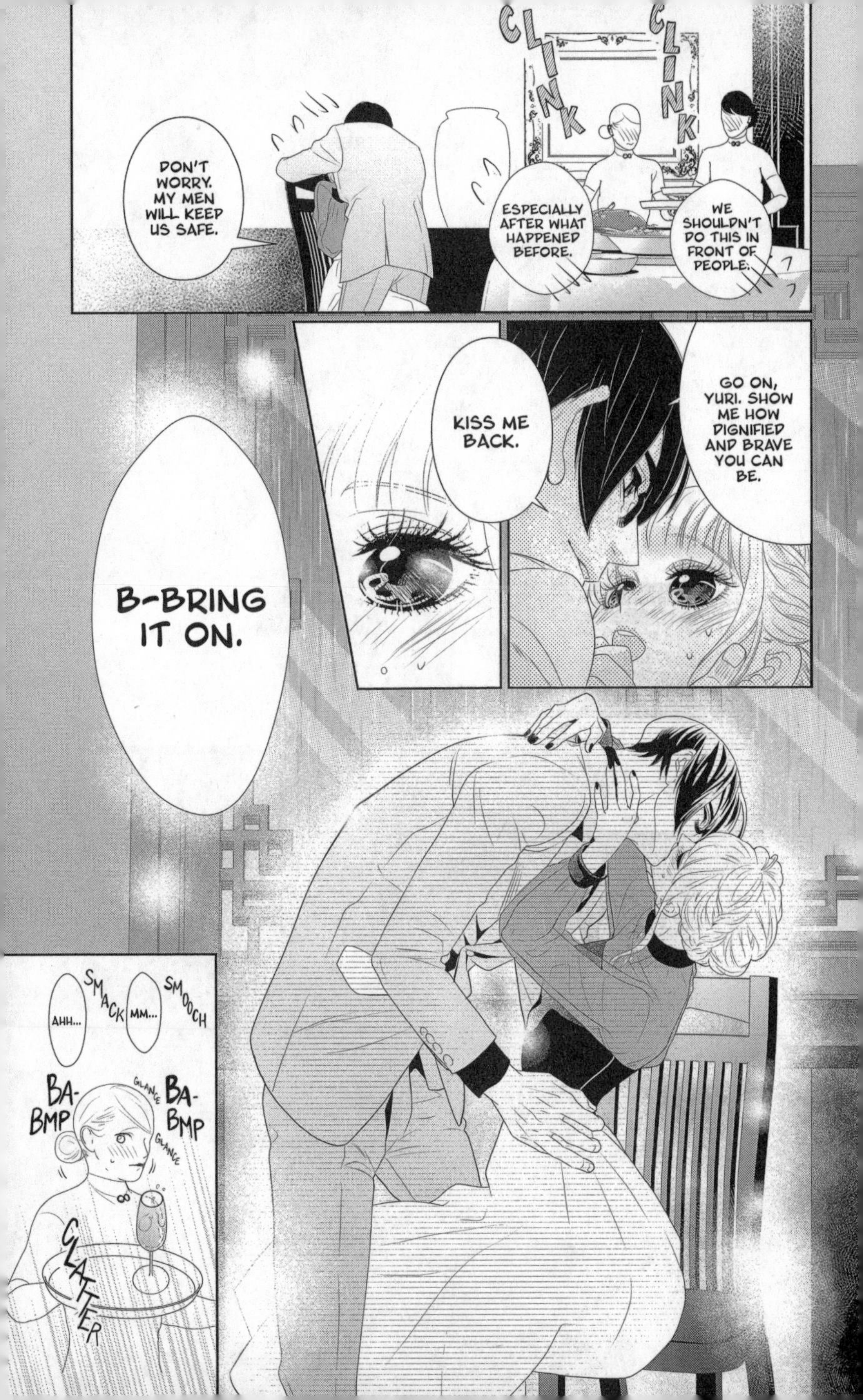
CLINK
CLINK
WE SHOULDN'T DO THIS IN FRONT OF PEOPLE.
ESPECIALLY AFTER WHAT HAPPENED BEFORE.
DON'T WORRY. MY MEN WILL KEEP US SAFE.
GO ON, YURI. SHOW ME HOW DIGNIFIED AND BRAVE YOU CAN BE.
KISS ME BACK.
B-BRING IT ON.
SMOOCH
MM...
SMACK
AHH...
BA-BMP
GLANCE
BA-BMP
GLANCE
CLATTER

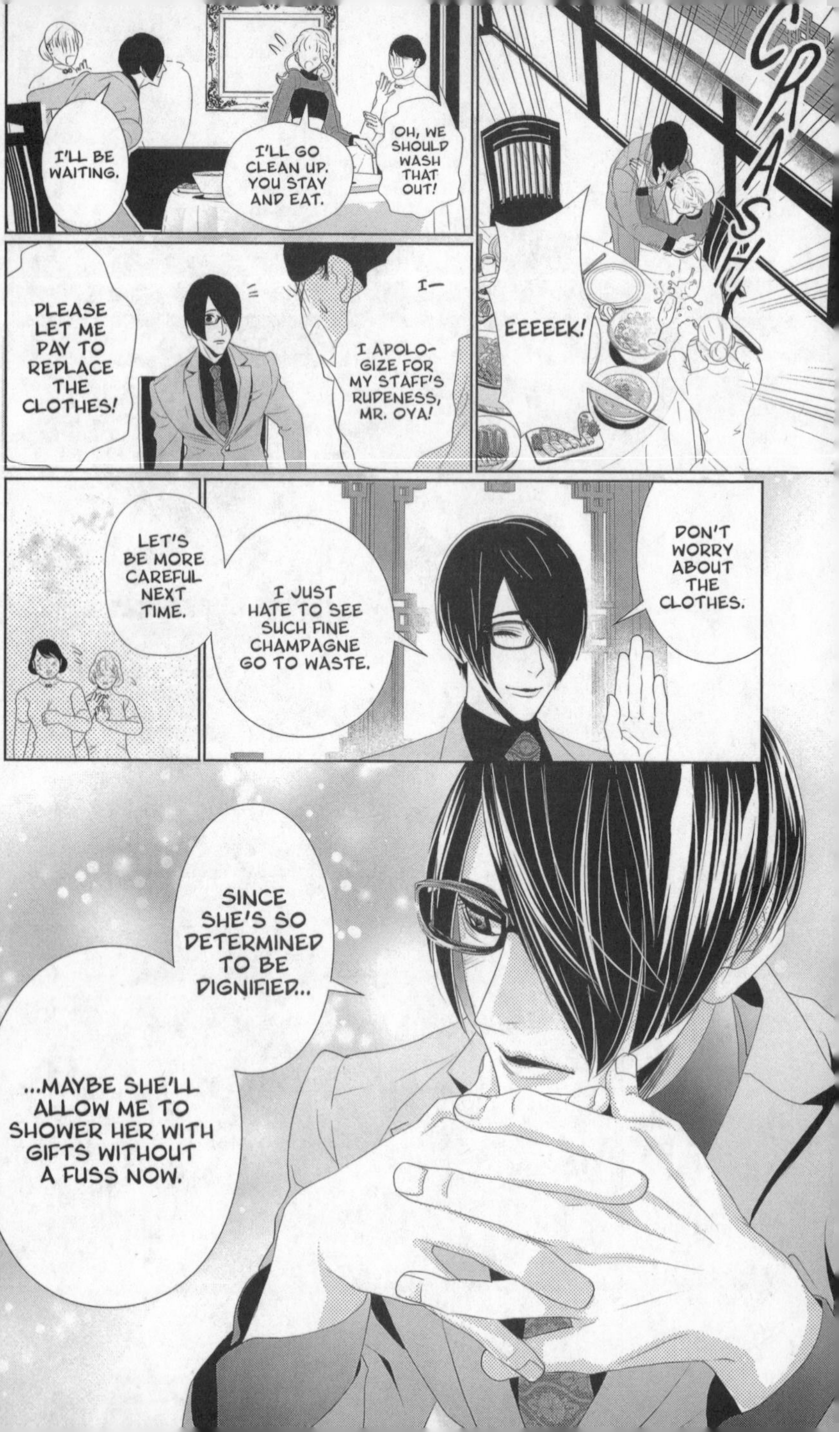
CRASH
EEEEK!
OH, WE SHOULD WASH THAT OUT!
I'LL GO CLEAN UP. YOU STAY AND EAT.
I'LL BE WAITING.
I—
I APOLOGIZE FOR MY STAFF'S RUDENESS, MR. OYA!
PLEASE LET ME PAY TO REPLACE THE CLOTHES!
DON'T WORRY ABOUT THE CLOTHES.
I JUST HATE TO SEE SUCH FINE CHAMPAGNE GO TO WASTE.
LET'S BE MORE CAREFUL NEXT TIME.
SINCE SHE'S SO DETERMINED TO BE DIGNIFIED...
...MAYBE SHE'LL ALLOW ME TO SHOWER HER WITH GIFTS WITHOUT A FUSS NOW.

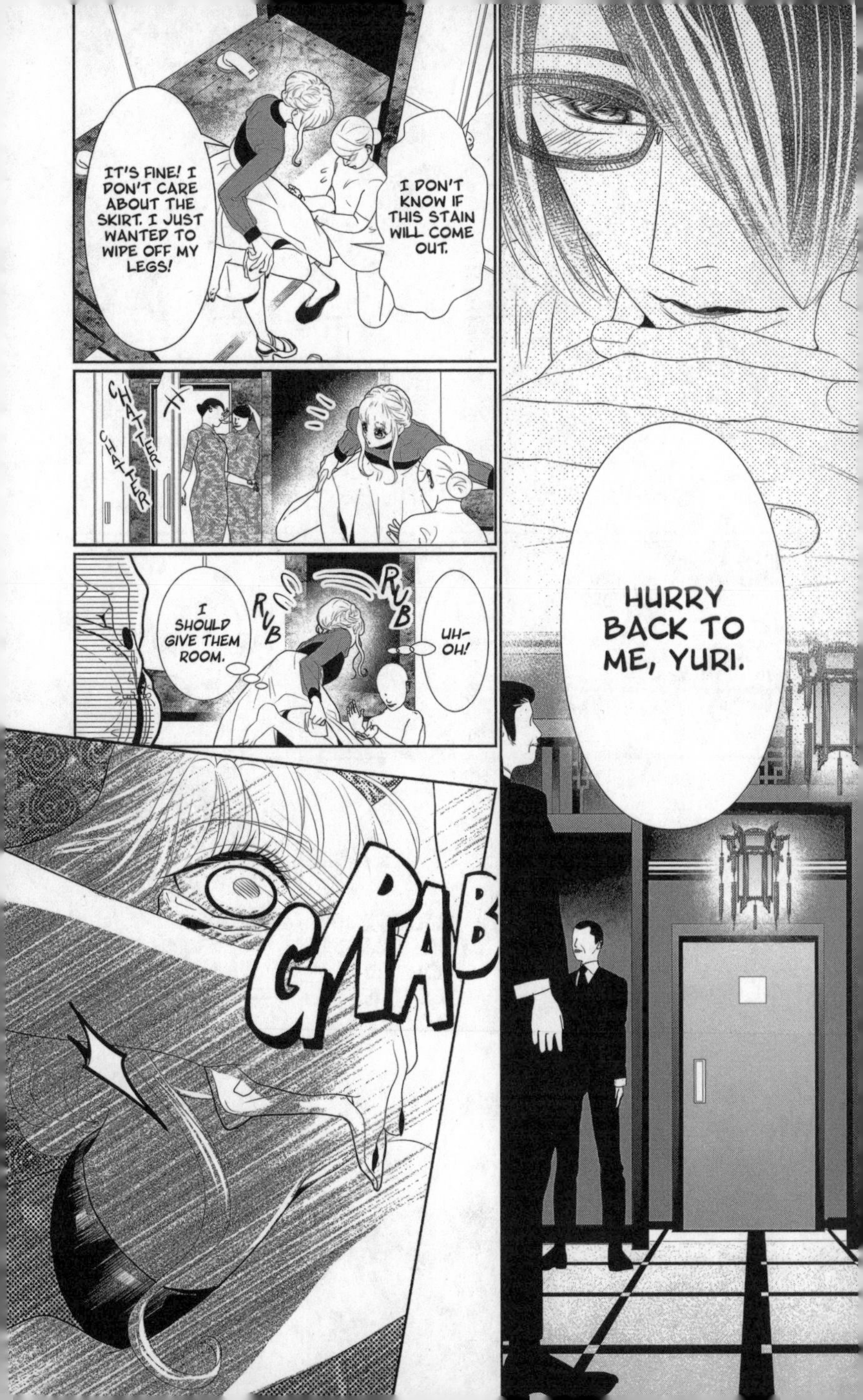
HURRY BACK TO ME, YURI.
I DON'T KNOW IF THIS STAIN WILL COME OUT.
IT'S FINE! I DON'T CARE ABOUT THE SKIRT. I JUST WANTED TO WIPE OFF MY LEGS!
CHATTER
CHATTER
UH-OH!
RUB
RUB
I SHOULD GIVE THEM ROOM.
GRAB

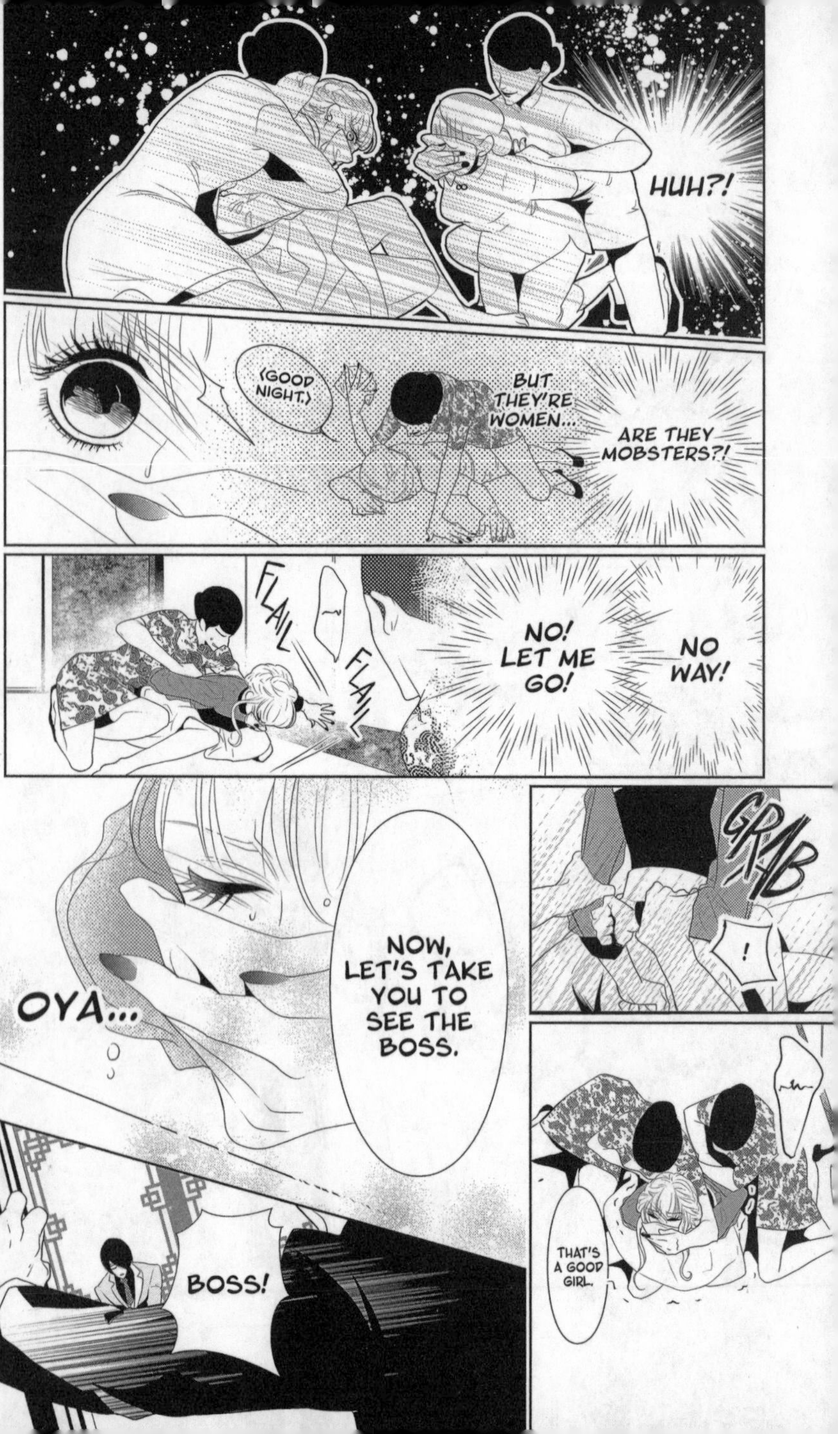
HUH?!
ARE THEY MOBSTERS?!
BUT THEY'RE WOMEN...
⟨GOOD NIGHT.⟩
NO WAY!
NO! LET ME GO!
FLAIL FLAIL
GRAB
!
THAT'S A GOOD GIRL.
NOW, LET'S TAKE YOU TO SEE THE BOSS.
OYA...
BOSS!

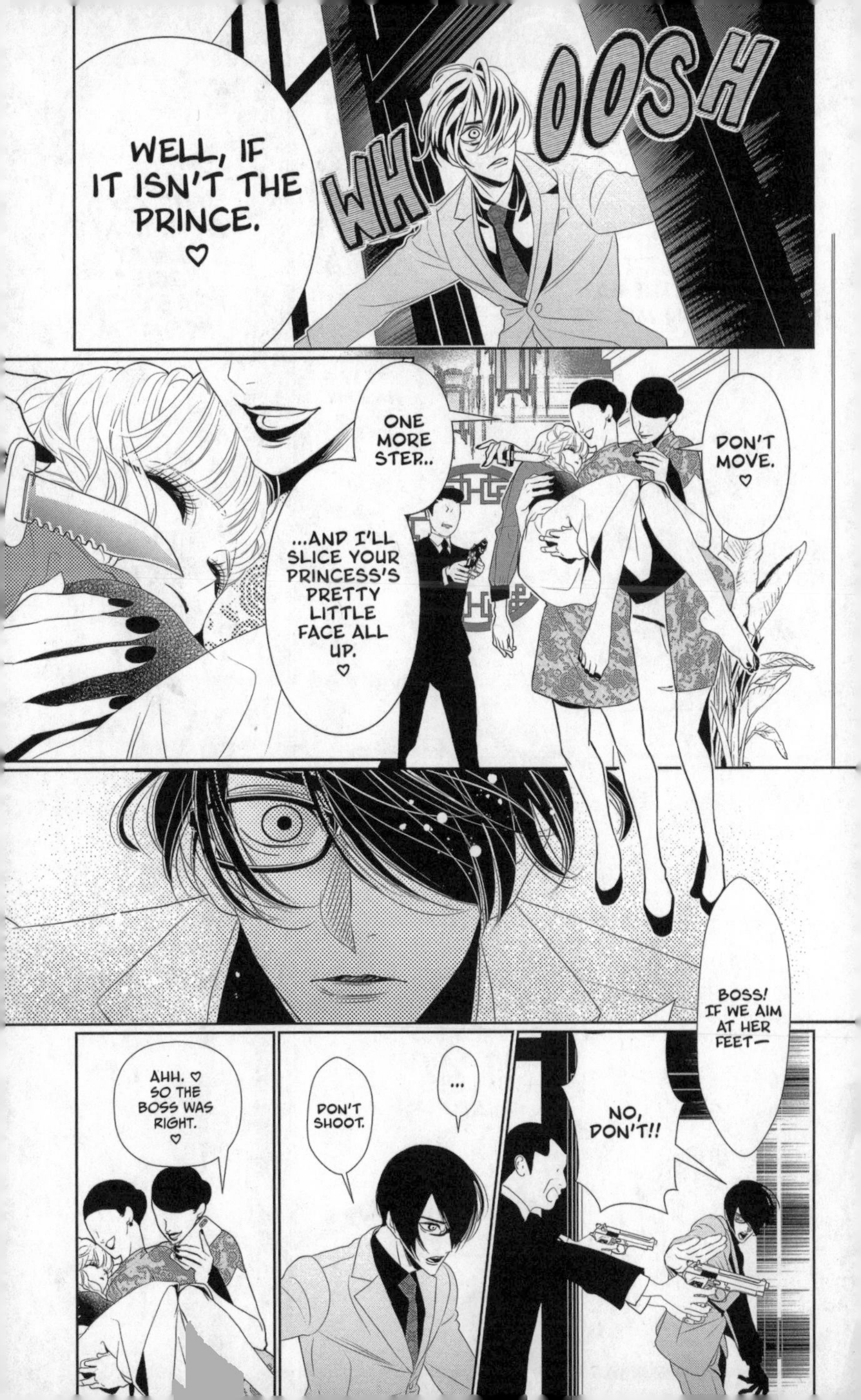
WHOOSH
WELL, IF IT ISN'T THE PRINCE. ♡
DON'T MOVE. ♡
ONE MORE STEP..
...AND I'LL SLICE YOUR PRINCESS'S PRETTY LITTLE FACE ALL UP. ♡
BOSS! IF WE AIM AT HER FEET—
NO, DON'T!!
...
DON'T SHOOT.
AHH. ♡ SO THE BOSS WAS RIGHT. ♡

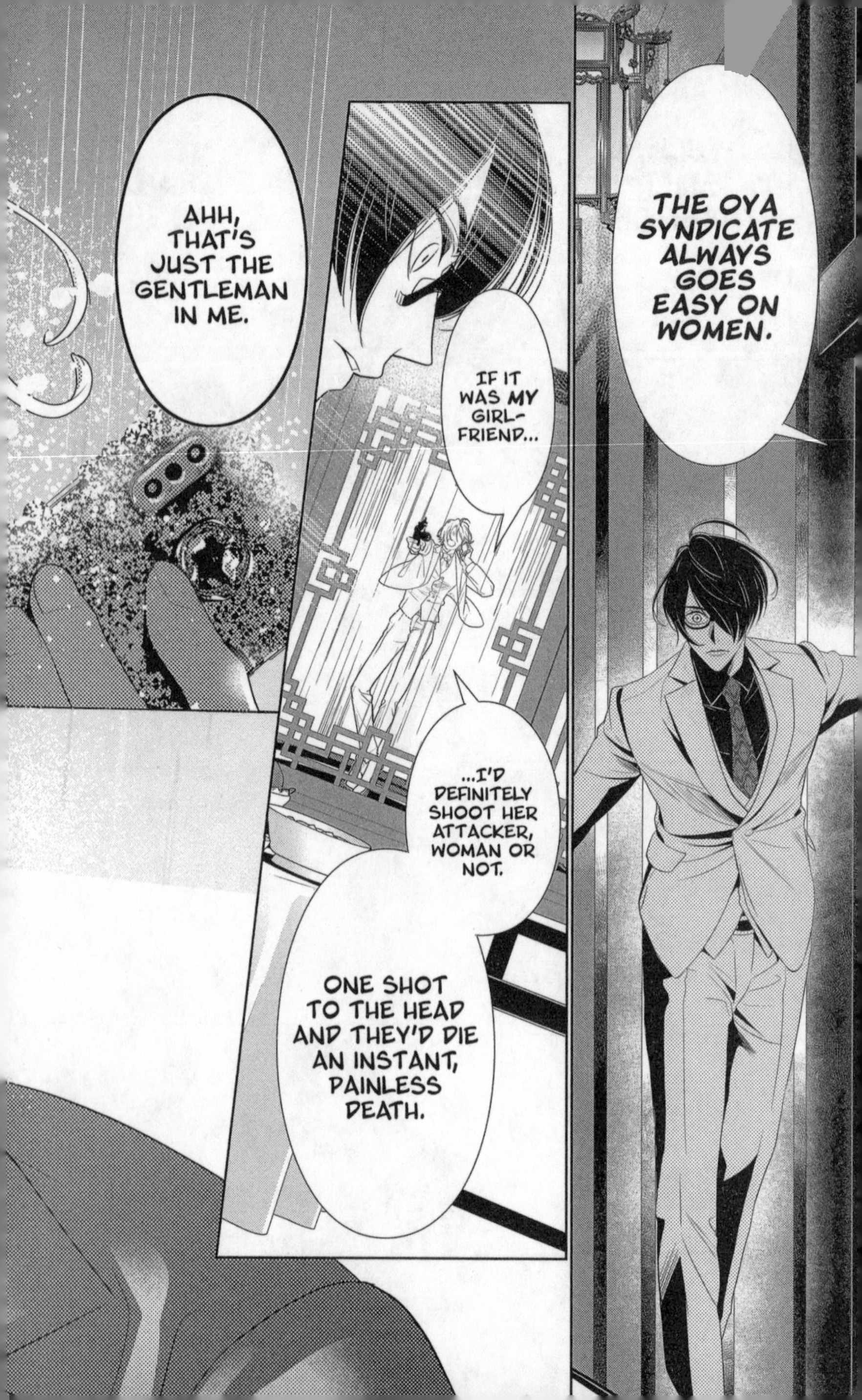
THE OYA SYNDICATE ALWAYS GOES EASY ON WOMEN.
IF IT WAS MY GIRL-FRIEND...
...I'D DEFINITELY SHOOT HER ATTACKER, WOMAN OR NOT.
ONE SHOT TO THE HEAD AND THEY'D DIE AN INSTANT, PAINLESS DEATH.
AHH, THAT'S JUST THE GENTLEMAN IN ME.

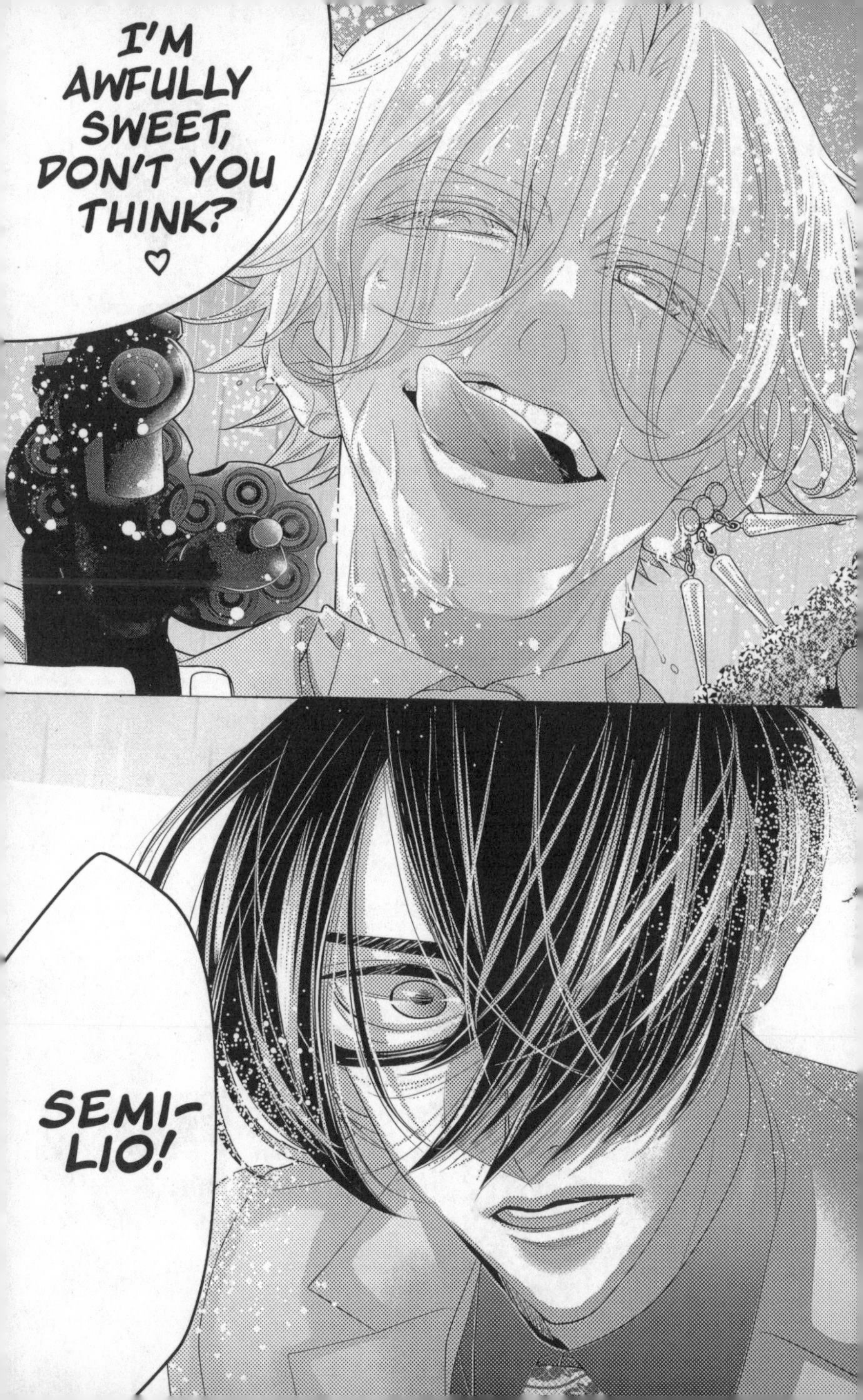
I'M AWFULLY SWEET, DON'T YOU THINK? ♡
SEMI-LIO!

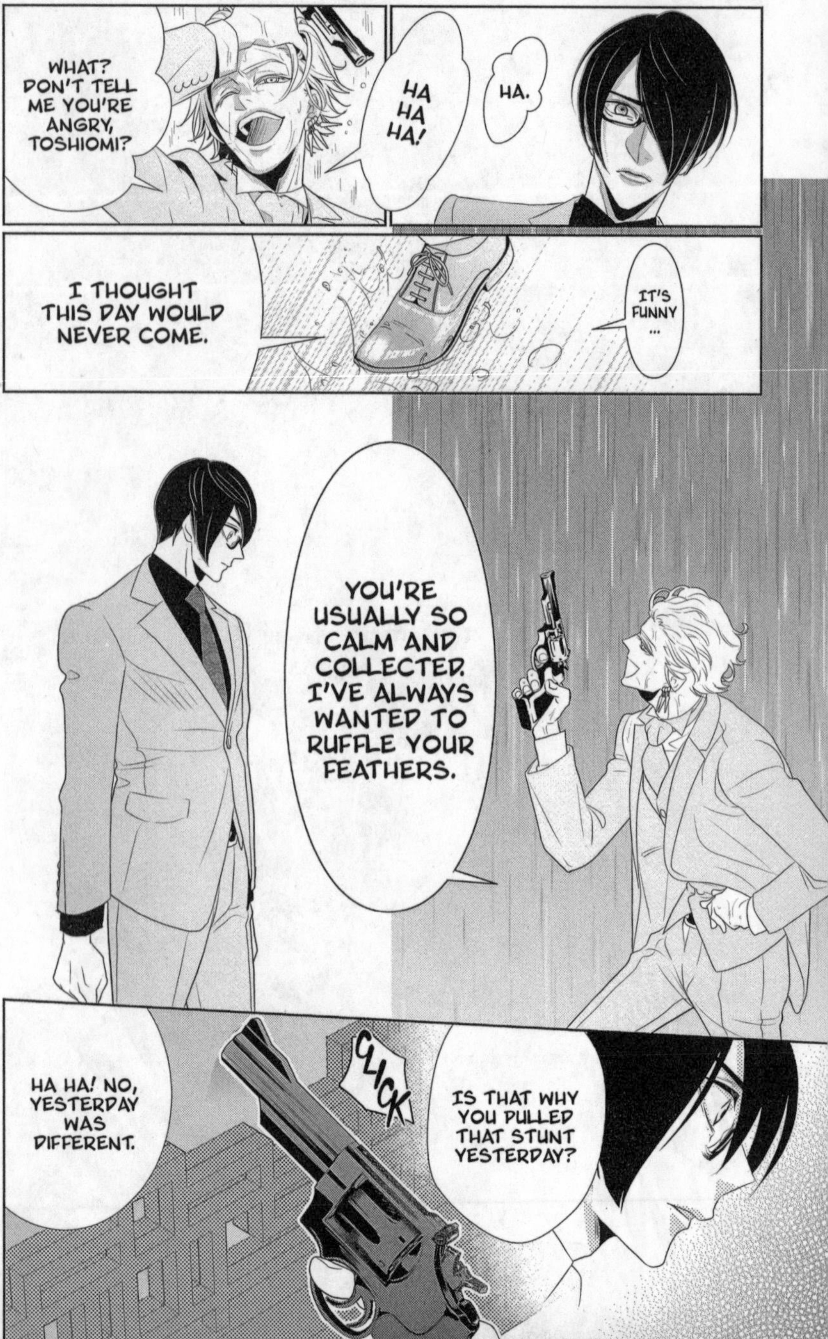
HA.
HA HA HA!
WHAT? DON'T TELL ME YOU'RE ANGRY, TOSHIOMI?
IT'S FUNNY ...
I THOUGHT THIS DAY WOULD NEVER COME.
YOU'RE USUALLY SO CALM AND COLLECTED. I'VE ALWAYS WANTED TO RUFFLE YOUR FEATHERS.
IS THAT WHY YOU PULLED THAT STUNT YESTERDAY?
CLICK
HA HA! NO, YESTERDAY WAS DIFFERENT.

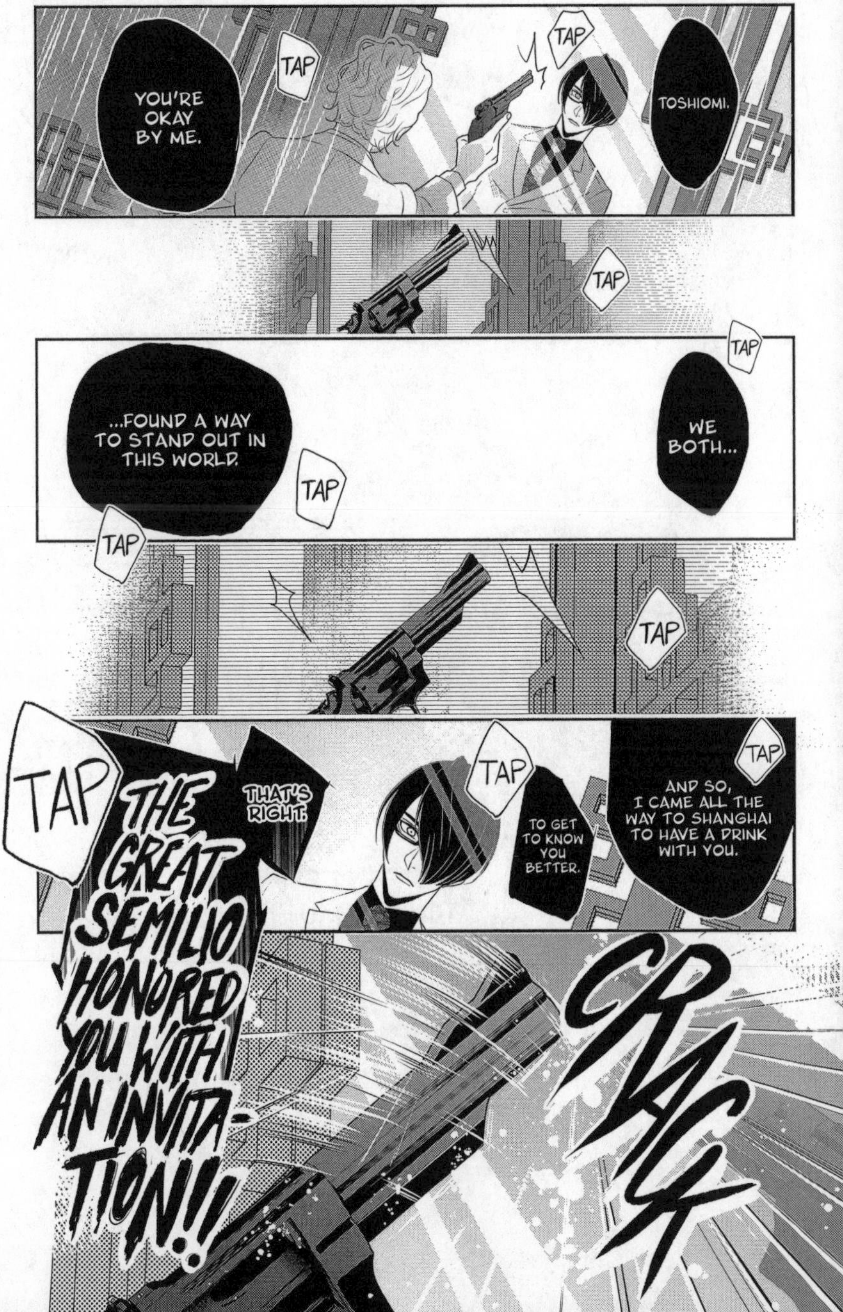
TOSHIOMI.
TAP
TAP
YOU'RE OKAY BY ME.
TAP
TAP
WE BOTH...
TAP
...FOUND A WAY TO STAND OUT IN THIS WORLD.
TAP
TAP
TAP
AND SO, I CAME ALL THE WAY TO SHANGHAI TO HAVE A DRINK WITH YOU.
TO GET TO KNOW YOU BETTER.
TAP
THAT'S RIGHT.
TAP
THE GREAT SEMILIO HONORED YOU WITH AN INVITA-TION!!
CRACK

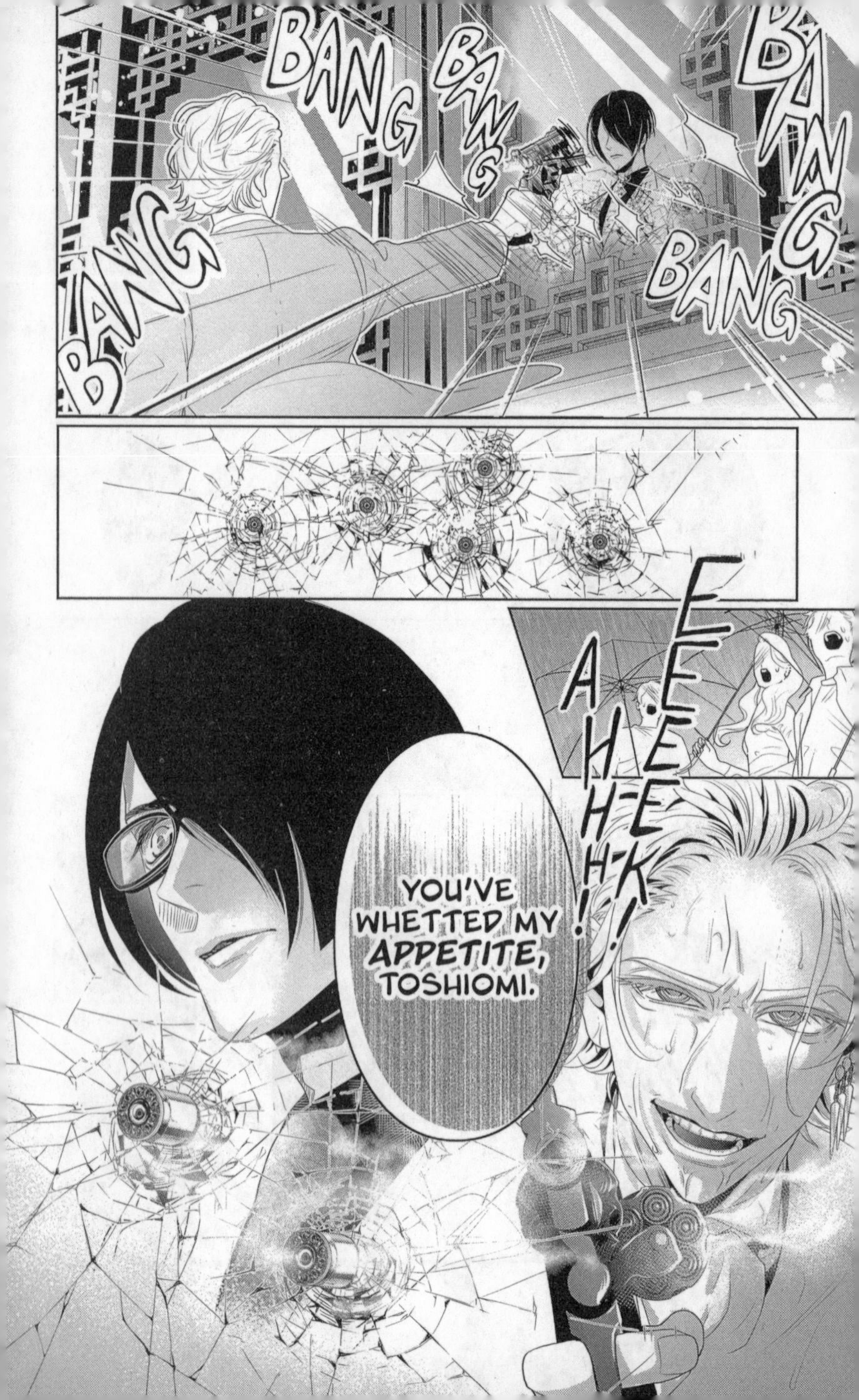
BANG
BANG
BANG
BANG
BANG
EEEEEK!!
AHHHH!!
YOU'VE WHETTED MY APPETITE, TOSHIOMI.

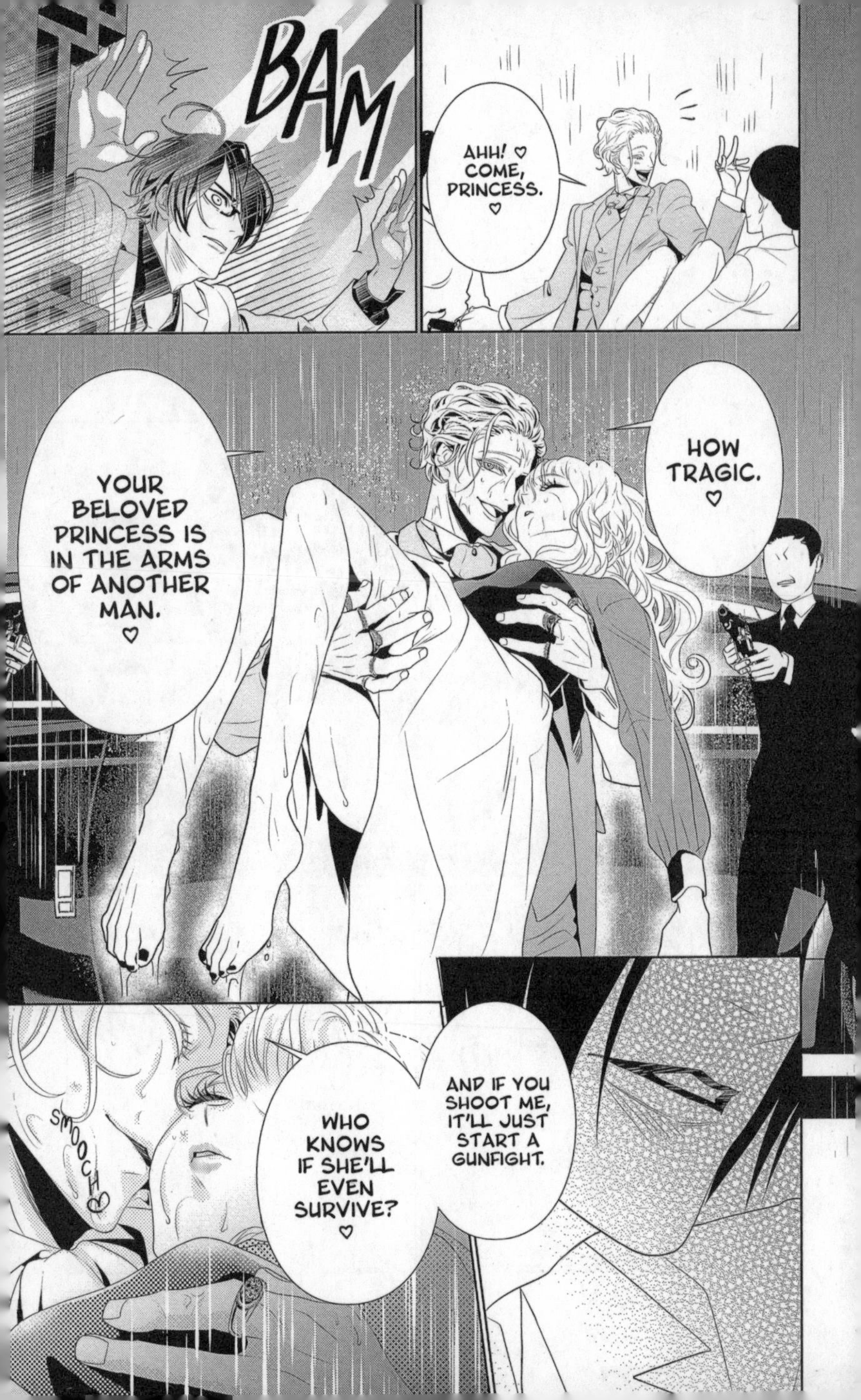
AHH! ♡ COME, PRINCESS. ♡
BAM
HOW TRAGIC. ♡
YOUR BELOVED PRINCESS IS IN THE ARMS OF ANOTHER MAN. ♡
AND IF YOU SHOOT ME, IT'LL JUST START A GUNFIGHT.
WHO KNOWS IF SHE'LL EVEN SURVIVE? ♡
SMOOCH ♡

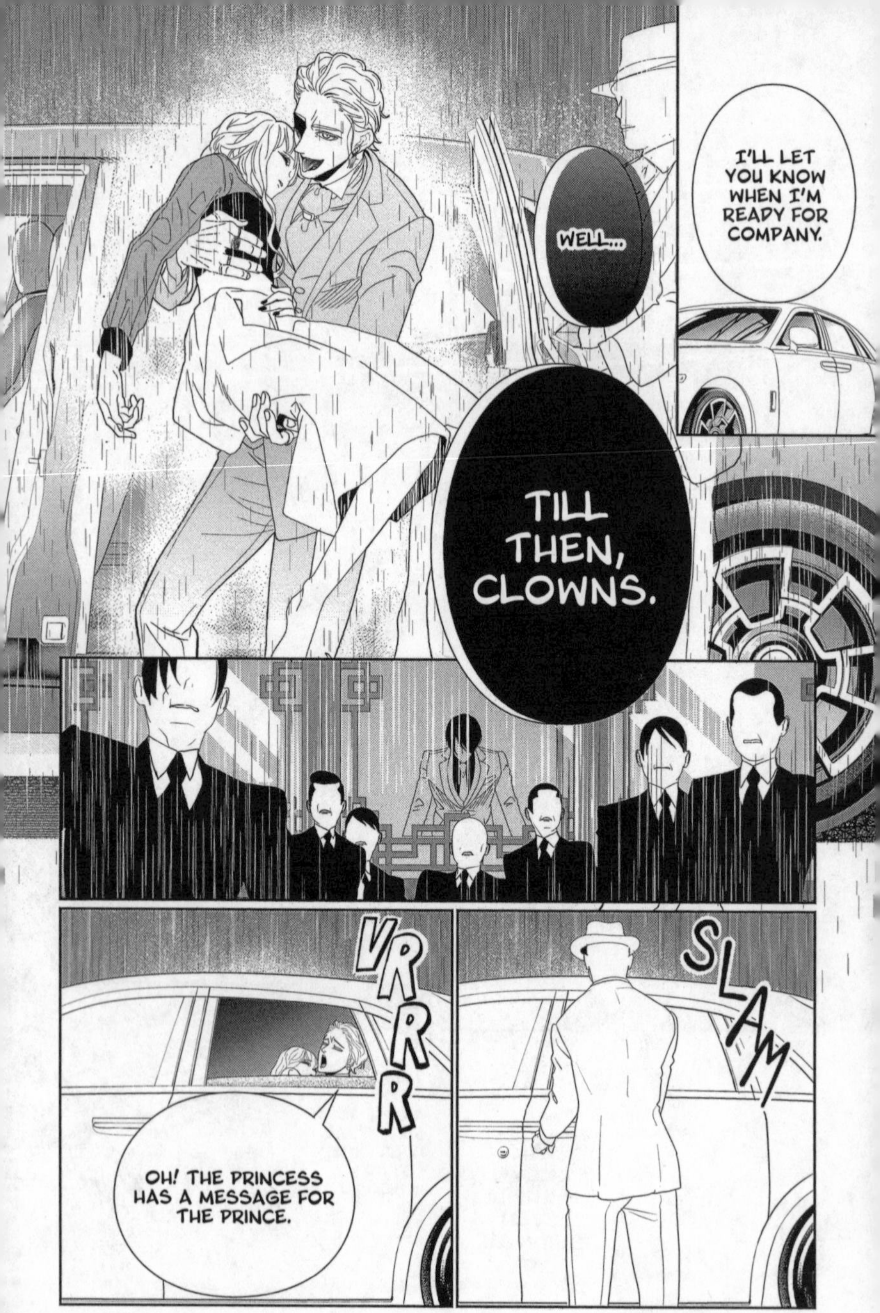
I'LL LET YOU KNOW WHEN I'M READY FOR COMPANY.
WELL...
TILL THEN, CLOWNS.
SLAM
VRRR
OH! THE PRINCESS HAS A MESSAGE FOR THE PRINCE.

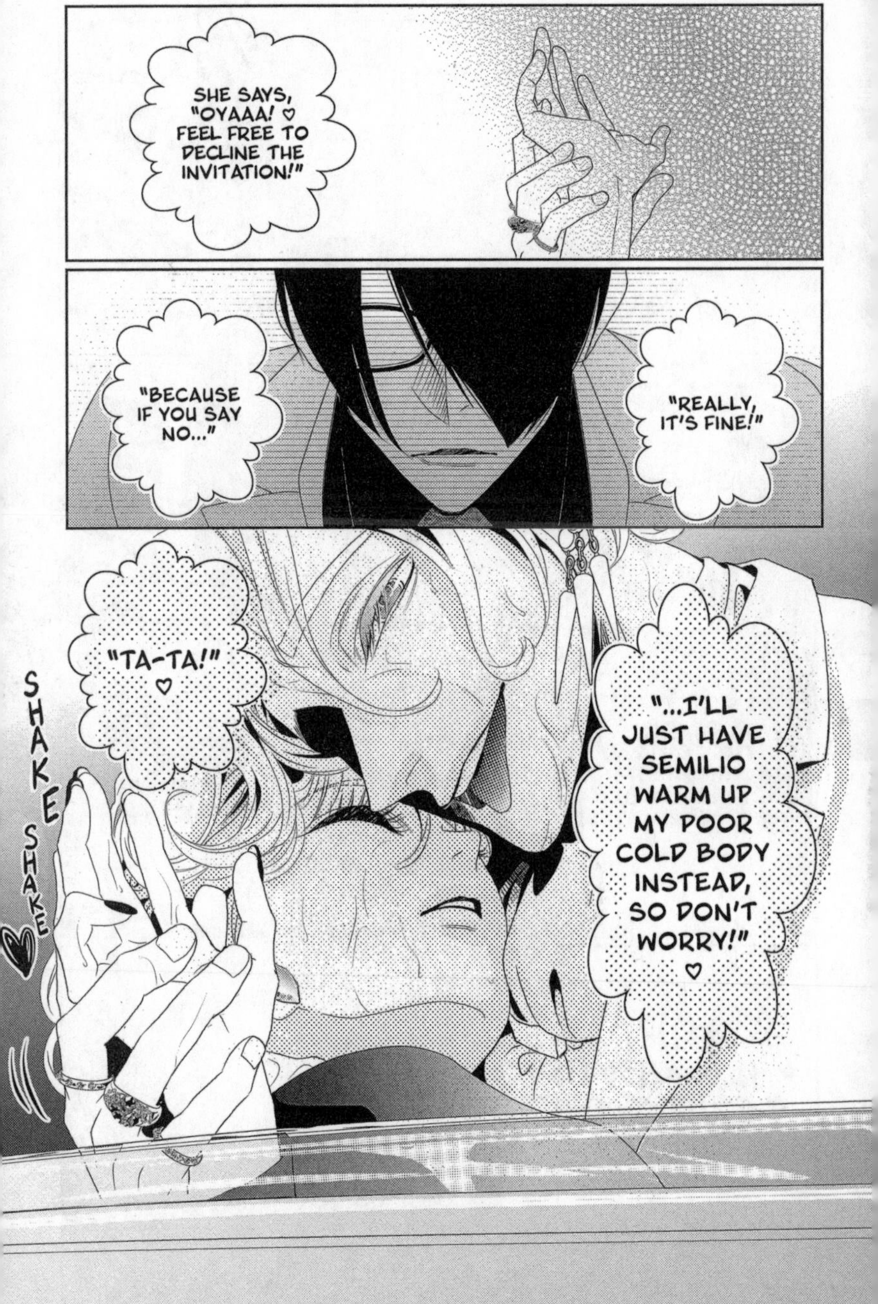
SHE SAYS, "OYAAA! ♡ FEEL FREE TO DECLINE THE INVITATION!"
"REALLY, IT'S FINE!"
"BECAUSE IF YOU SAY NO..."
"...I'LL JUST HAVE SEMILIO WARM UP MY POOR COLD BODY INSTEAD, SO DON'T WORRY!" ♡
"TA-TA!" ♡
SHAKE SHAKE

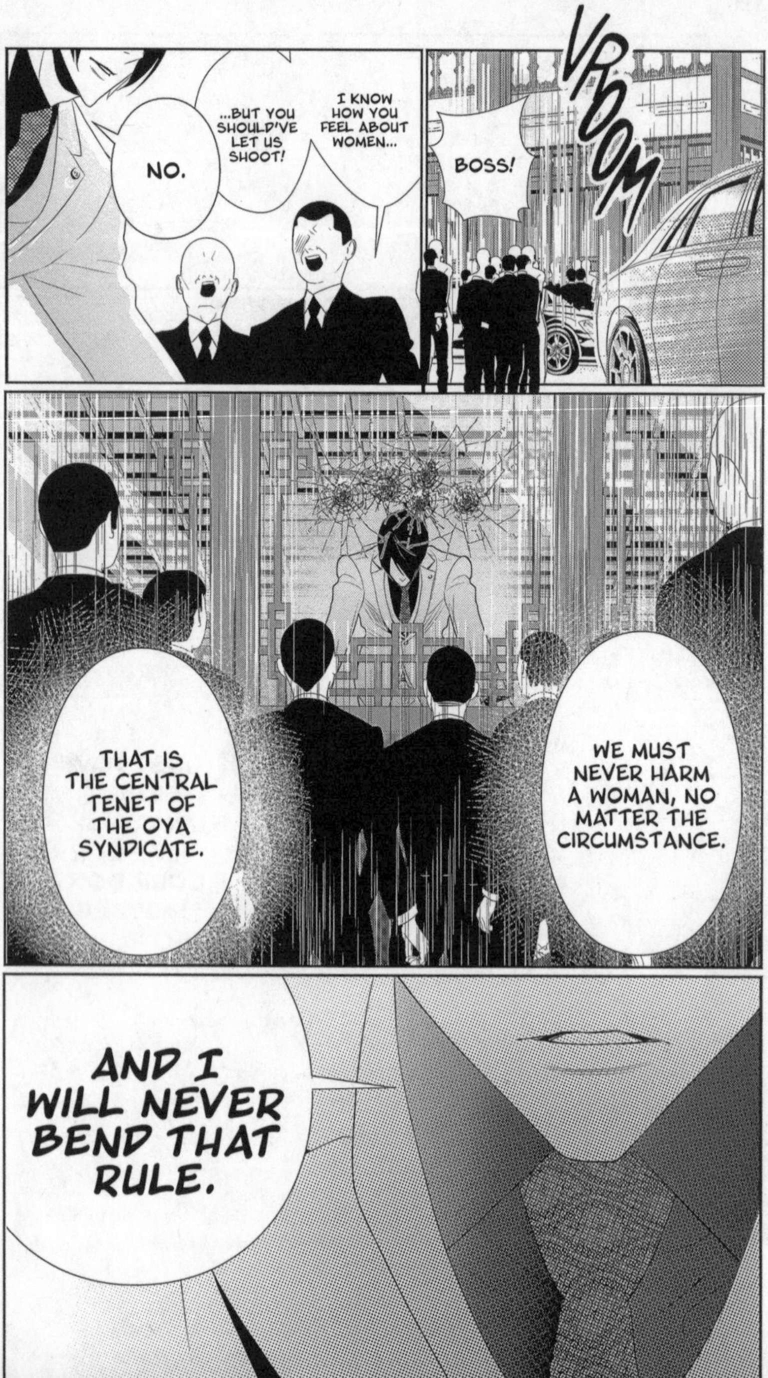
BOSS!
VROOM
I KNOW HOW YOU FEEL ABOUT WOMEN...
...BUT YOU SHOULD'VE LET US SHOOT!
NO.
WE MUST NEVER HARM A WOMAN, NO MATTER THE CIRCUMSTANCE.
THAT IS THE CENTRAL TENET OF THE OYA SYNDICATE.
AND I WILL NEVER BEND THAT RULE.

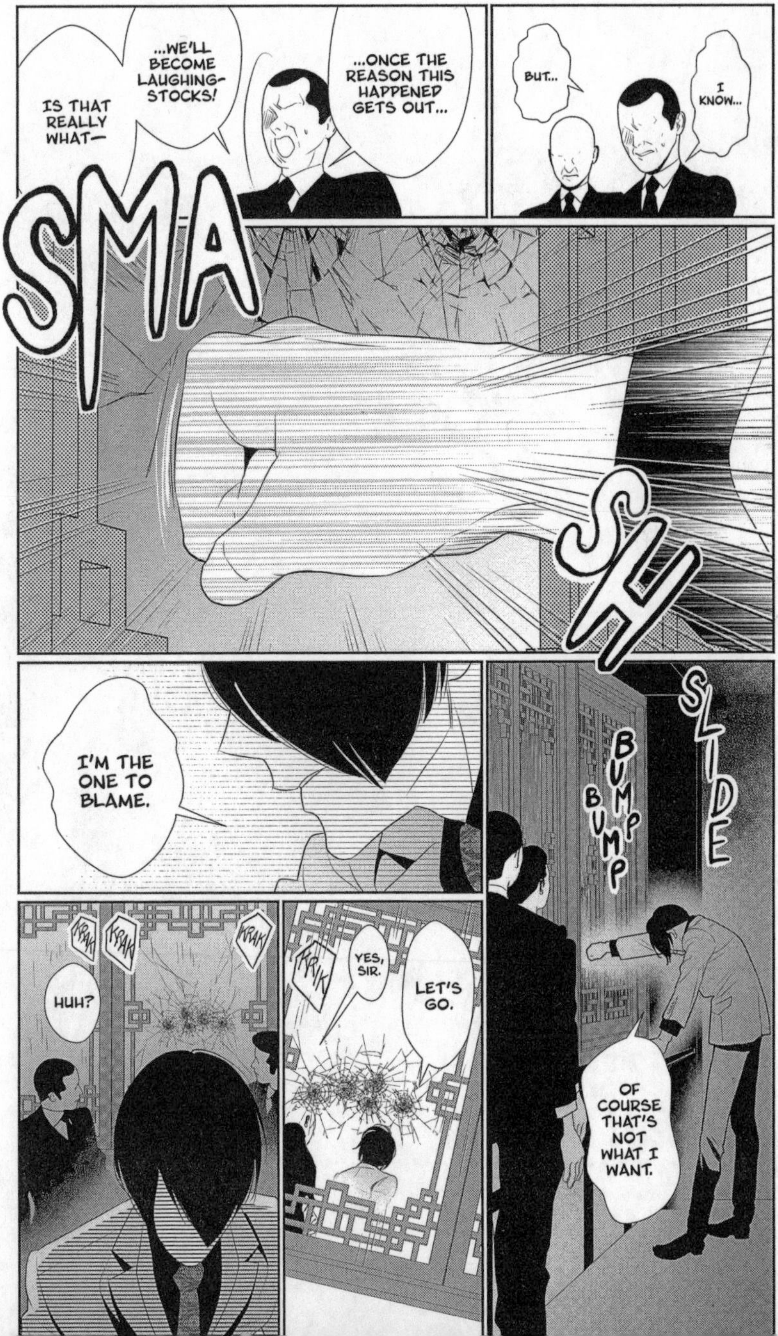
I KNOW...
BUT...
...ONCE THE REASON THIS HAPPENED GETS OUT...
...WE'LL BECOME LAUGHING-STOCKS!
IS THAT REALLY WHAT—
SMA
SH
SLIDE
BUMP
BUMP
OF COURSE THAT'S NOT WHAT I WANT.
I'M THE ONE TO BLAME.
KRIK
YES, SIR.
LET'S GO.
KRAK
KRAK
KRAK
HUH?

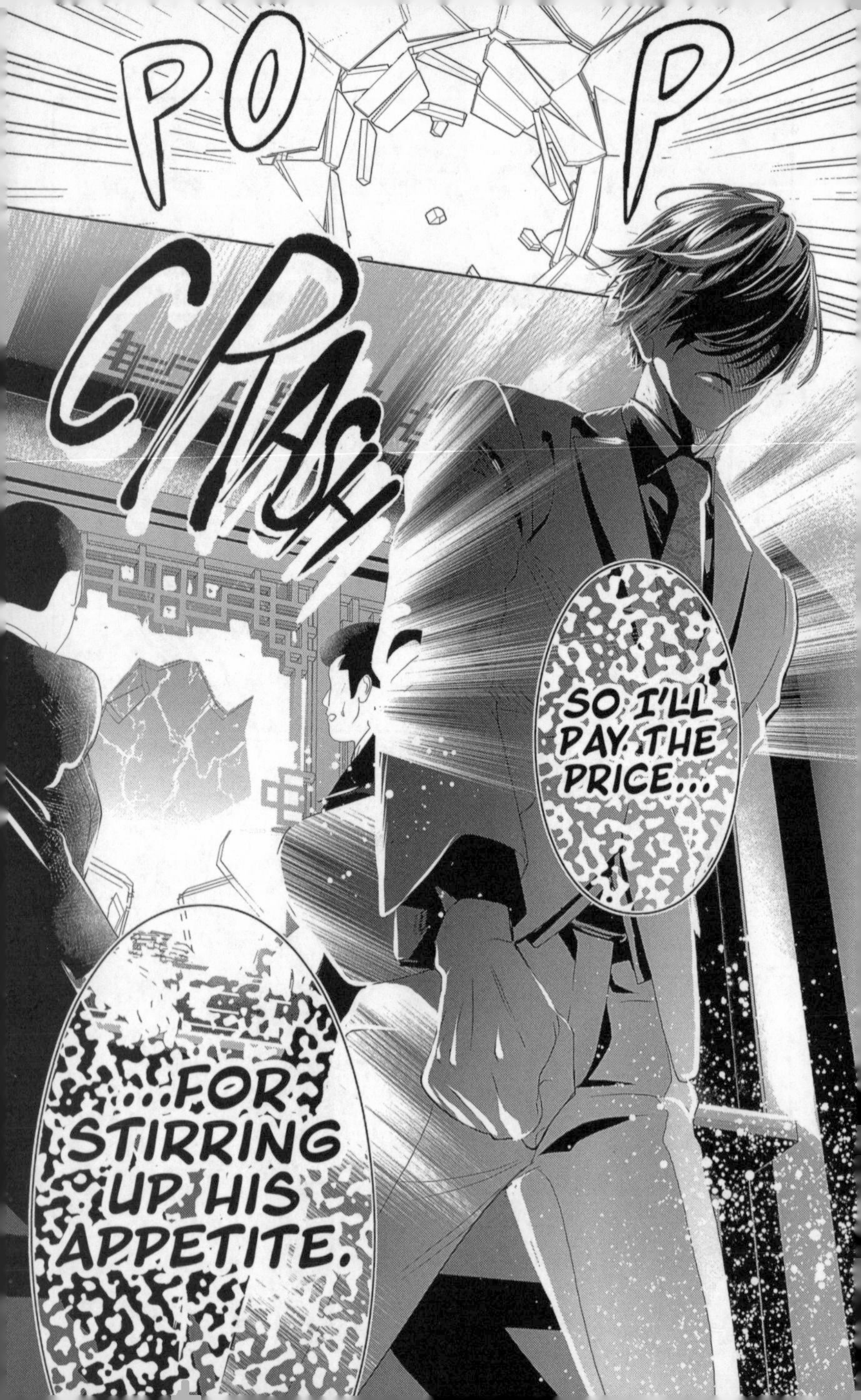
POP
CRASH
SO I'LL PAY THE PRICE...
...FOR STIRRING UP HIS APPETITE.

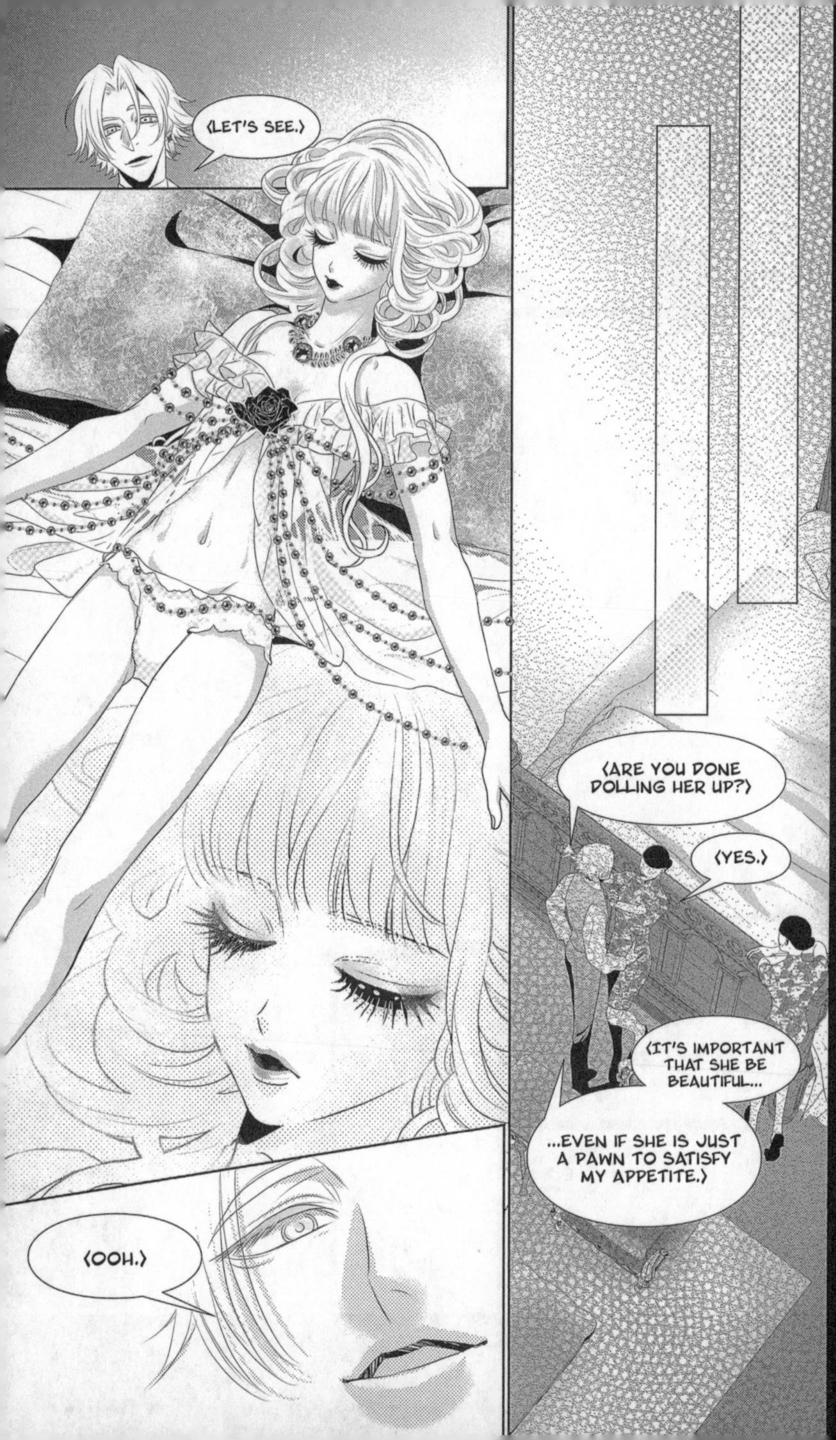
〈ARE YOU DONE DOLLING HER UP?〉
〈YES.〉
〈IT'S IMPORTANT THAT SHE BE BEAUTIFUL...
...EVEN IF SHE IS JUST A PAWN TO SATISFY MY APPETITE.〉
〈LET'S SEE.〉
〈OOH.〉

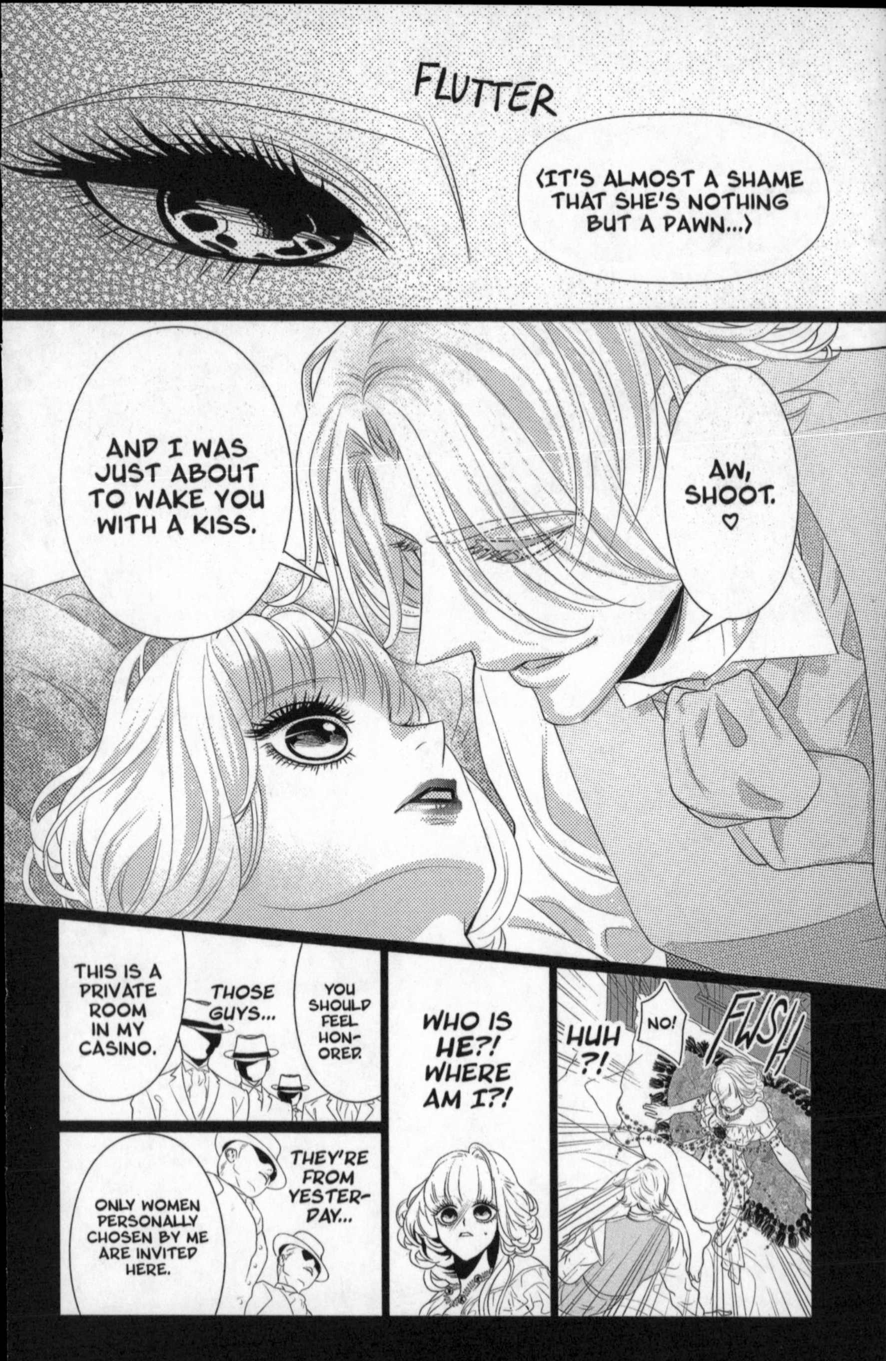
FLUTTER
〈IT'S ALMOST A SHAME THAT SHE'S NOTHING BUT A PAWN...〉
AW, SHOOT. ♡
AND I WAS JUST ABOUT TO WAKE YOU WITH A KISS.
FWSH
NO!
HUH?!
WHO IS HE?! WHERE AM I?!
YOU SHOULD FEEL HONORED.
THOSE GUYS...
THIS IS A PRIVATE ROOM IN MY CASINO.
THEY'RE FROM YESTERDAY...
ONLY WOMEN PERSONALLY CHOSEN BY ME ARE INVITED HERE.

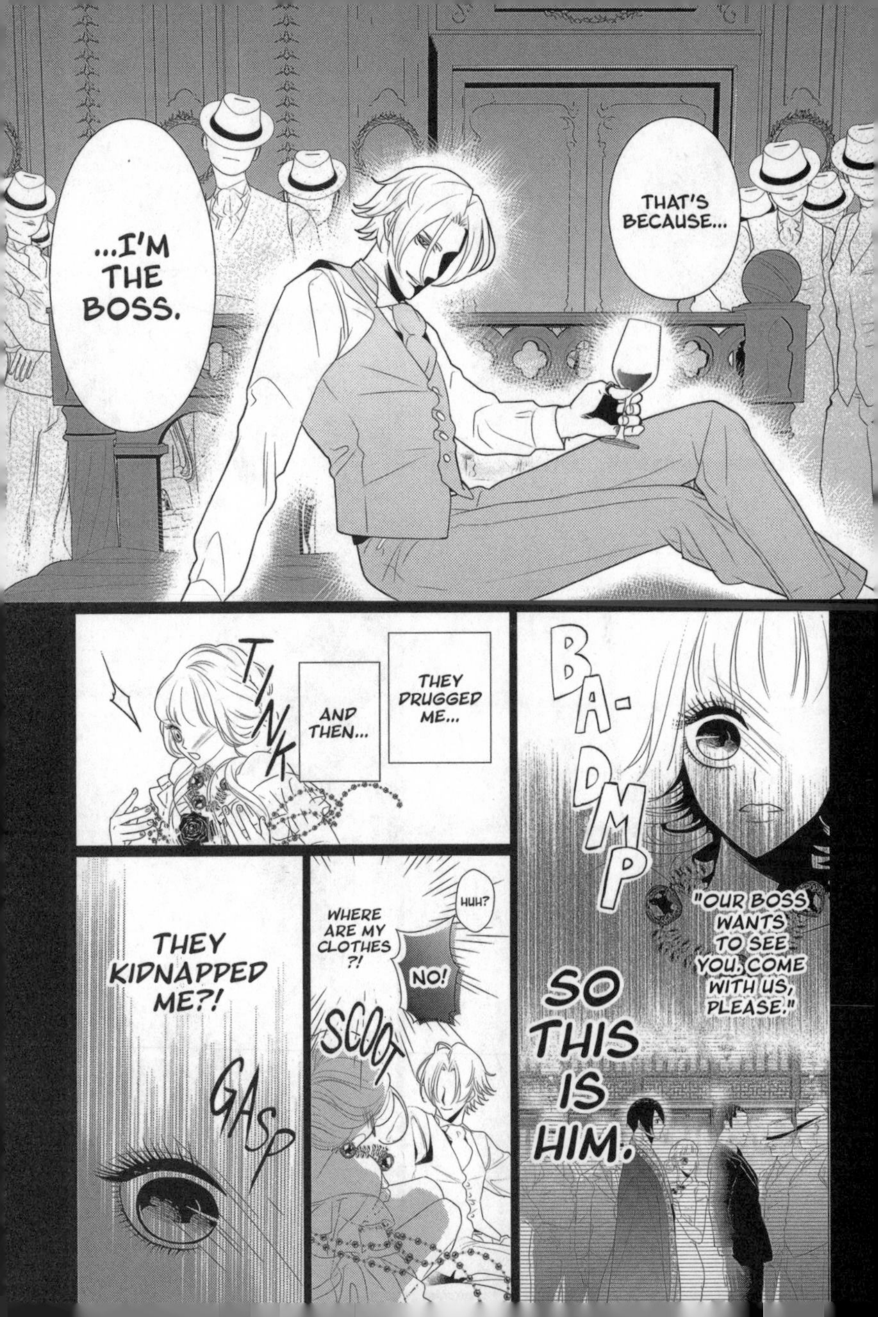
THAT'S BECAUSE...
...I'M THE BOSS.
BA-DMP
"OUR BOSS WANTS TO SEE YOU. COME WITH US, PLEASE."
SO THIS IS HIM.
THEY DRUGGED ME...
AND THEN...
TINK
HUH?
WHERE ARE MY CLOTHES?!
NO!
SCOOT
THEY KIDNAPPED ME?!
GASP

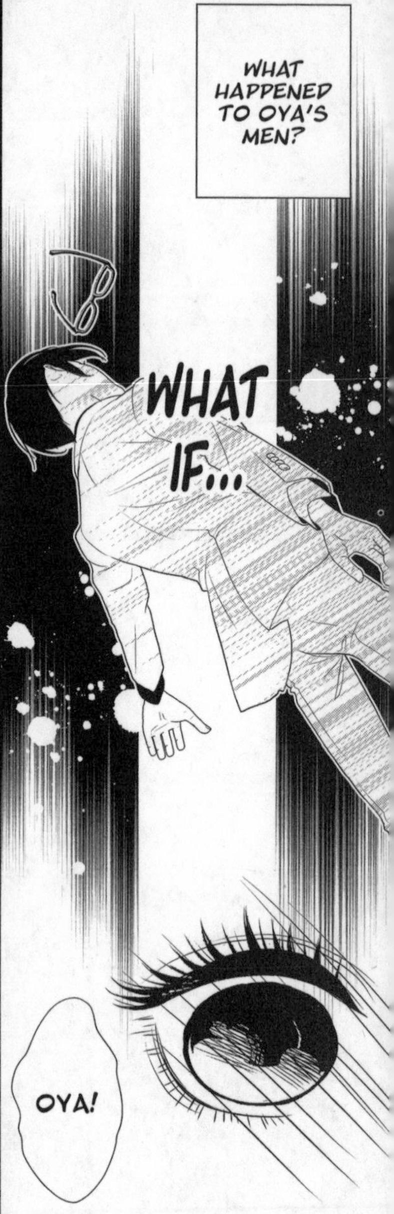
WHAT HAPPENED TO OYA'S MEN?
WHAT IF...
OYA!
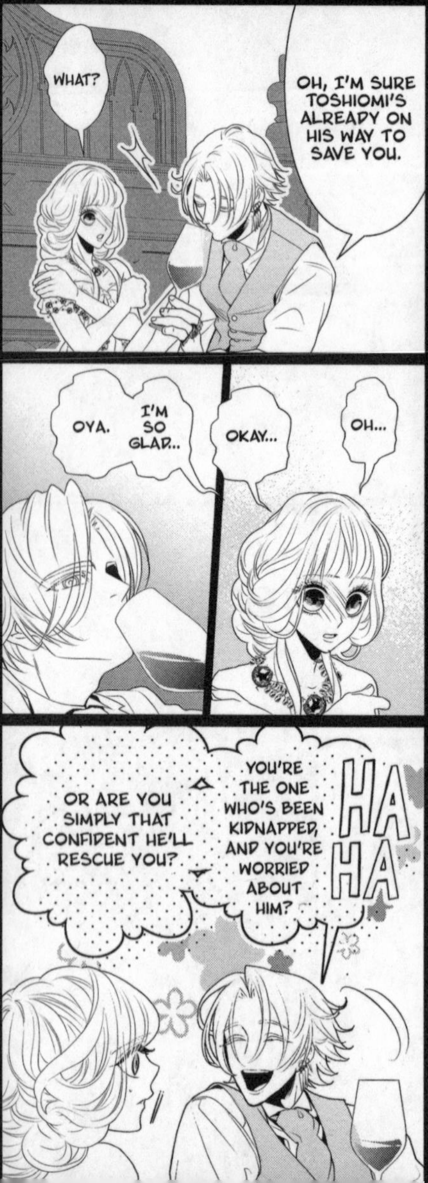
OH, I'M SURE TOSHIOMI'S ALREADY ON HIS WAY TO SAVE YOU.
WHAT?
OH...
OKAY...
I'M SO GLAD...
OYA.
HA HA
YOU'RE THE ONE WHO'S BEEN KIDNAPPED, AND YOU'RE WORRIED ABOUT HIM?
OR ARE YOU SIMPLY THAT CONFIDENT HE'LL RESCUE YOU?

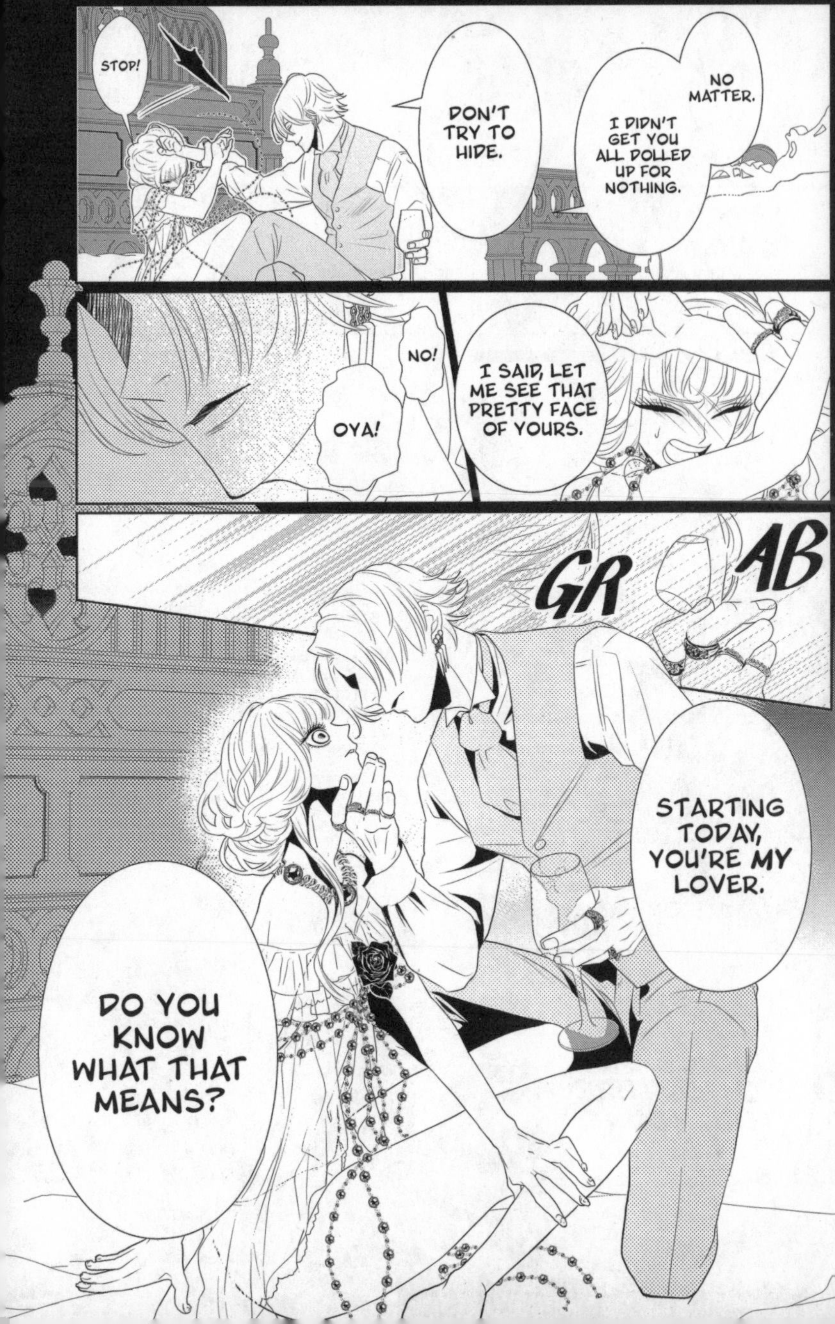
NO MATTER. I DIDN'T GET YOU ALL DOLLED UP FOR NOTHING.
DON'T TRY TO HIDE.
STOP!
I SAID, LET ME SEE THAT PRETTY FACE OF YOURS.
NO!
OYA!
GRAB
STARTING TODAY, YOU'RE MY LOVER.
DO YOU KNOW WHAT THAT MEANS?

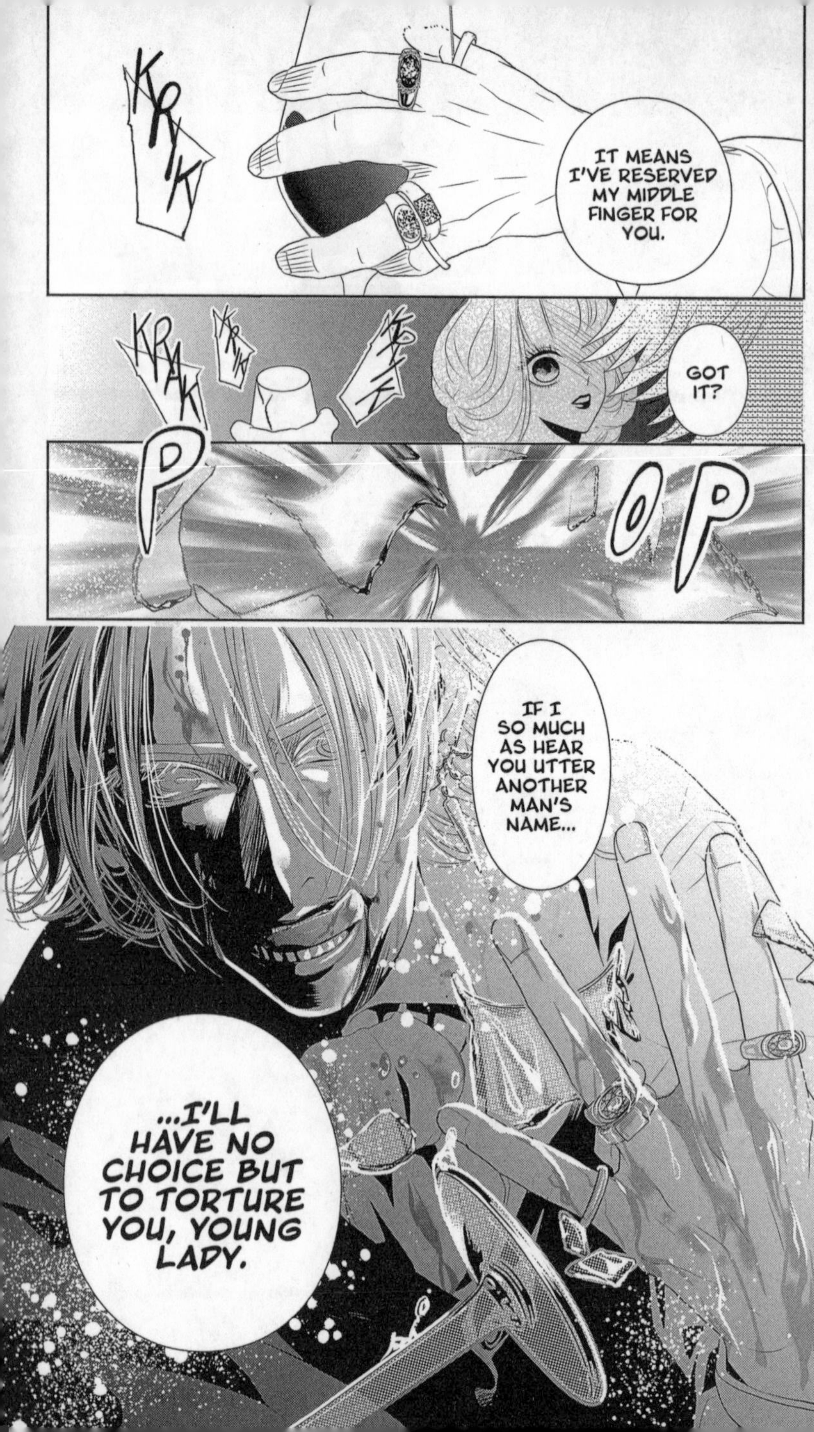
IT MEANS I'VE RESERVED MY MIDDLE FINGER FOR YOU.
KRIK
GOT IT?
KRIK
KRIK
KRAK
POP
IF I SO MUCH AS HEAR YOU UTTER ANOTHER MAN'S NAME...
...I'LL HAVE NO CHOICE BUT TO TORTURE YOU, YOUNG LADY.

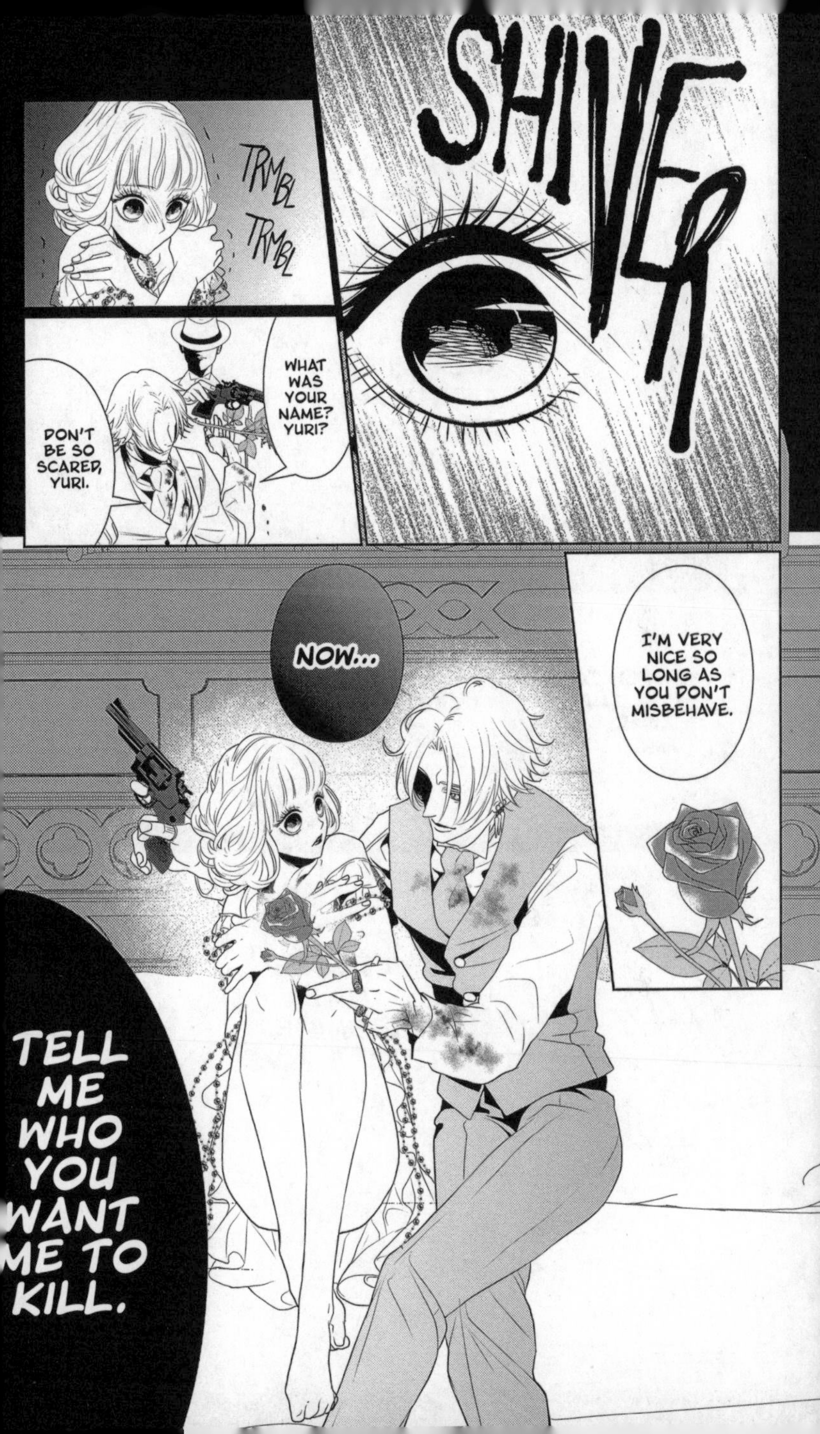
SHIVER
TRMBL TRMBL
WHAT WAS YOUR NAME? YURI?
DON'T BE SO SCARED, YURI.
I'M VERY NICE SO LONG AS YOU DON'T MISBEHAVE.
NOW...
TELL ME WHO YOU WANT ME TO KILL.

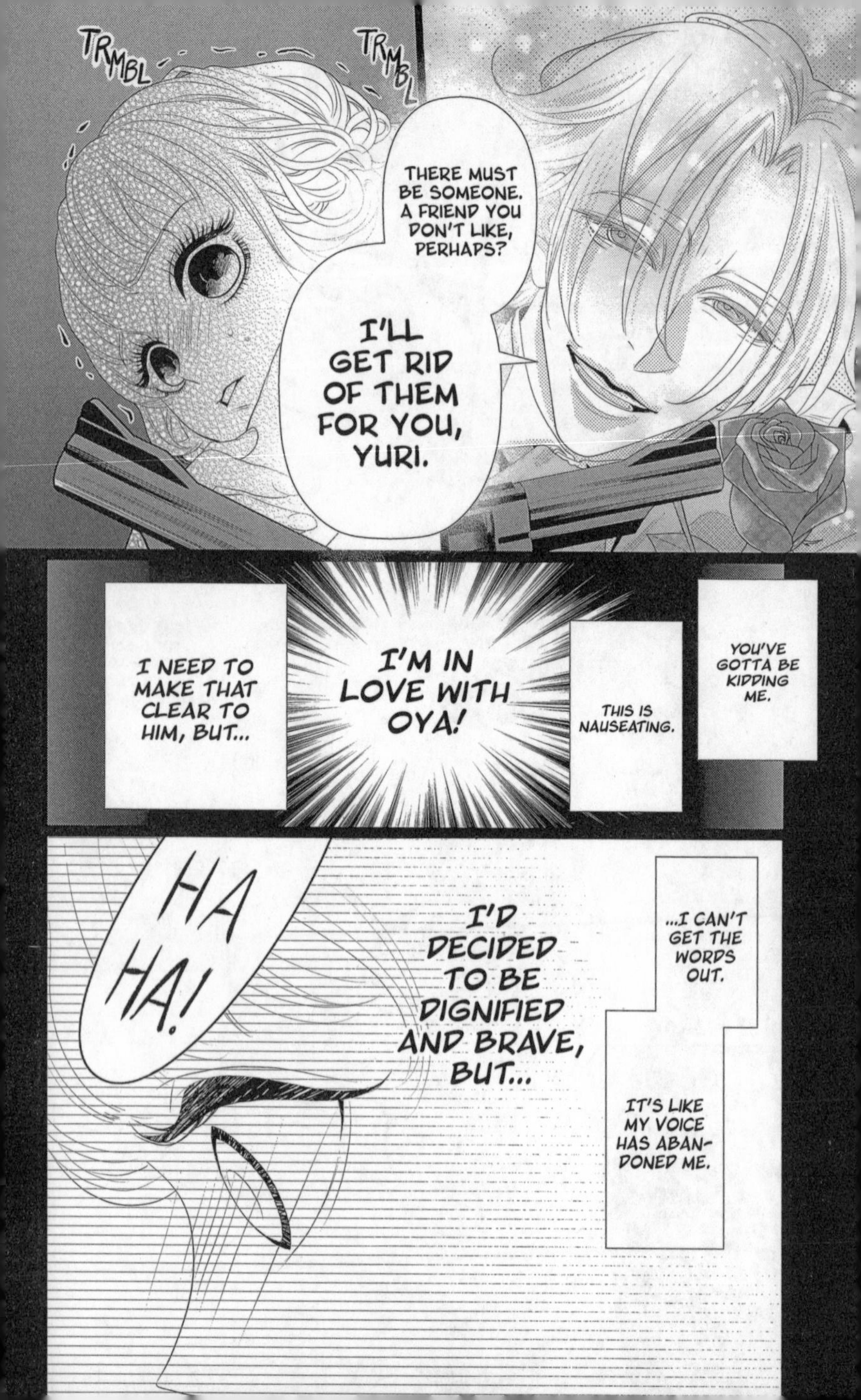
TRMBL
TRMBL
THERE MUST BE SOMEONE. A FRIEND YOU DON'T LIKE, PERHAPS?
I'LL GET RID OF THEM FOR YOU, YURI.
YOU'VE GOTTA BE KIDDING ME.
THIS IS NAUSEATING.
I'M IN LOVE WITH OYA!
I NEED TO MAKE THAT CLEAR TO HIM, BUT...
I'D DECIDED TO BE DIGNIFIED AND BRAVE, BUT...
...I CAN'T GET THE WORDS OUT.
IT'S LIKE MY VOICE HAS ABANDONED ME.
HA HA!

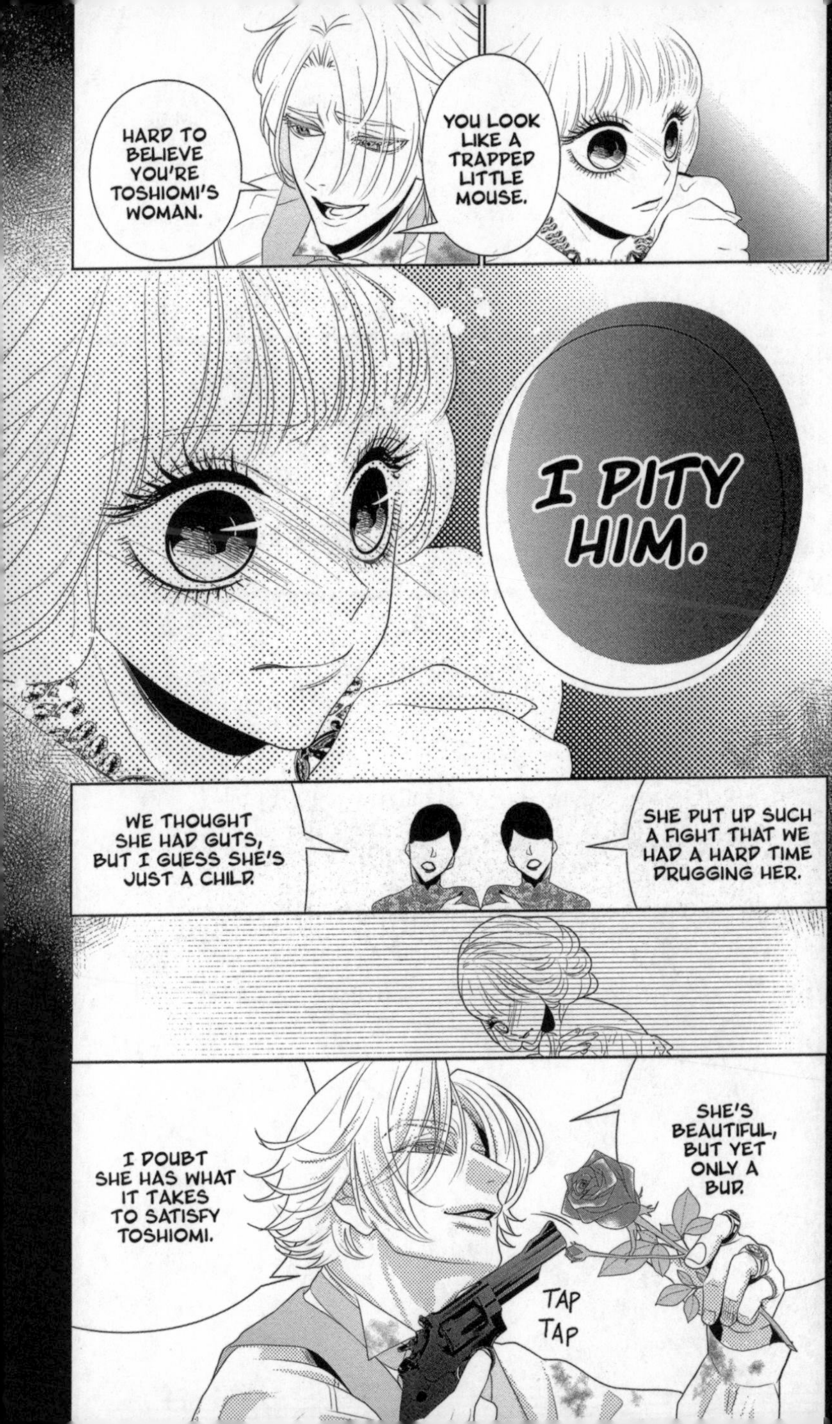
YOU LOOK LIKE A TRAPPED LITTLE MOUSE.
HARD TO BELIEVE YOU'RE TOSHIOMI'S WOMAN.
I PITY HIM.
SHE PUT UP SUCH A FIGHT THAT WE HAD A HARD TIME DRUGGING HER.
WE THOUGHT SHE HAD GUTS, BUT I GUESS SHE'S JUST A CHILD.
SHE'S BEAUTIFUL, BUT YET ONLY A BUD.
I DOUBT SHE HAS WHAT IT TAKES TO SATISFY TOSHIOMI.
TAP TAP

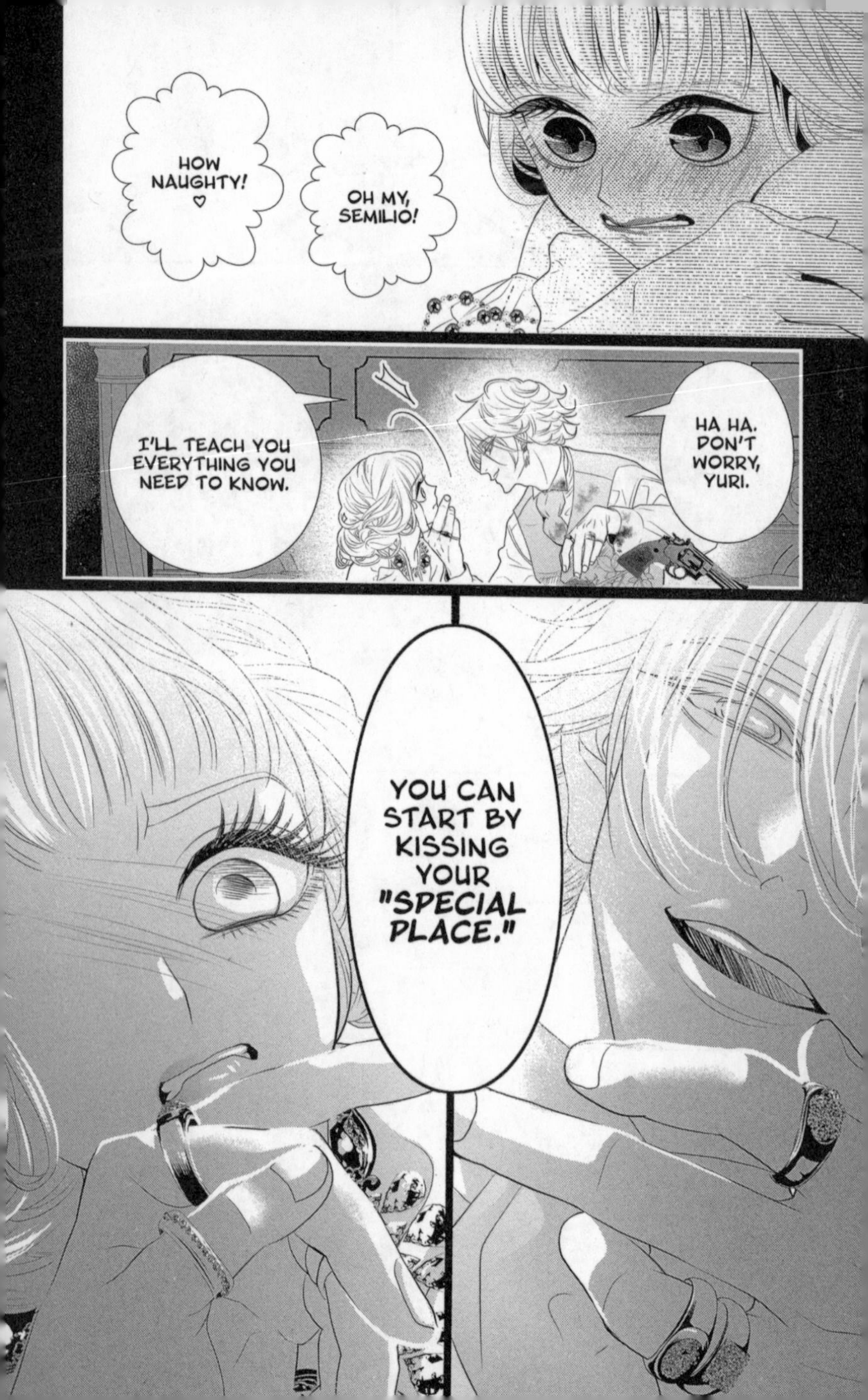
OH MY, SEMILIO!
HOW NAUGHTY! ♡
HA HA. DON'T WORRY, YURI.
I'LL TEACH YOU EVERYTHING YOU NEED TO KNOW.
YOU CAN START BY KISSING YOUR "SPECIAL PLACE."

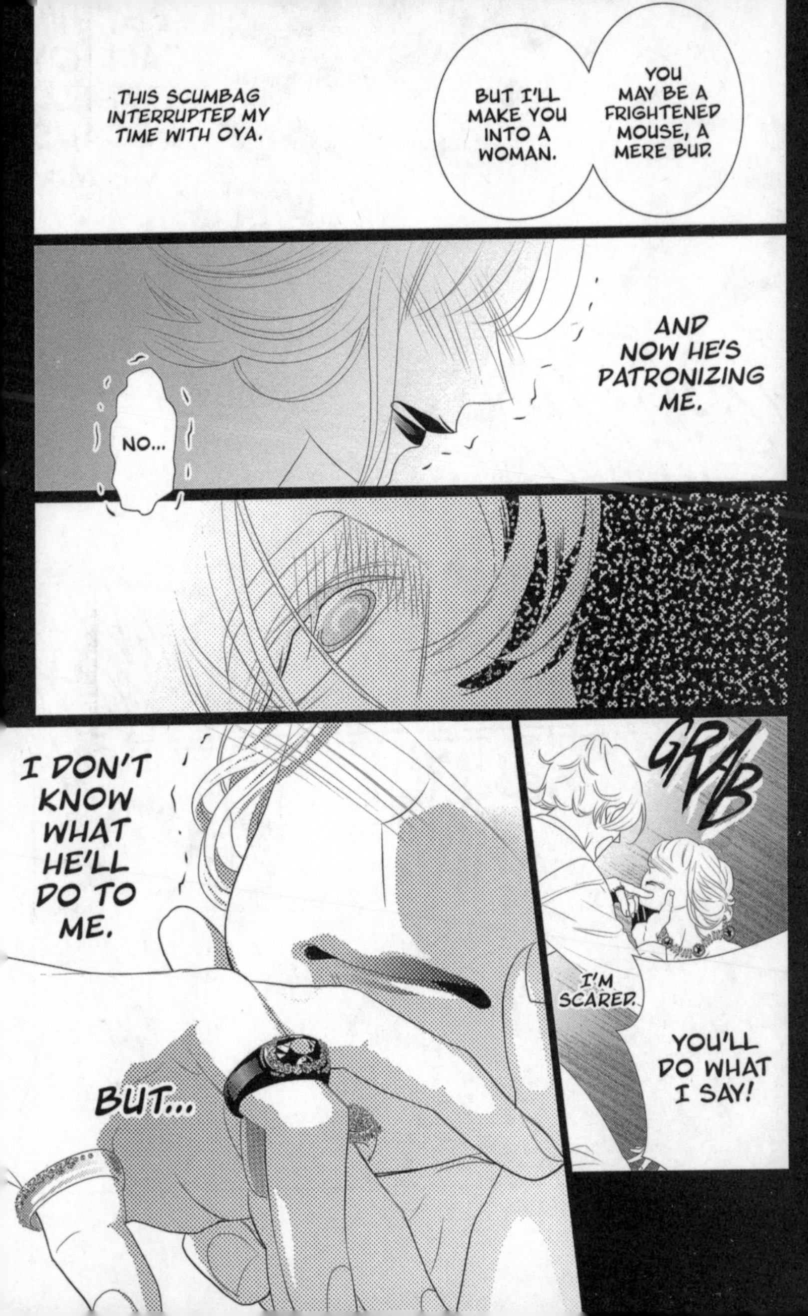
YOU MAY BE A FRIGHTENED MOUSE, A MERE BUD.
BUT I'LL MAKE YOU INTO A WOMAN.
THIS SCUMBAG INTERRUPTED MY TIME WITH OYA.
AND NOW HE'S PATRONIZING ME.
NO...
GRAB
I'M SCARED.
YOU'LL DO WHAT I SAY!
I DON'T KNOW WHAT HE'LL DO TO ME.
BUT...

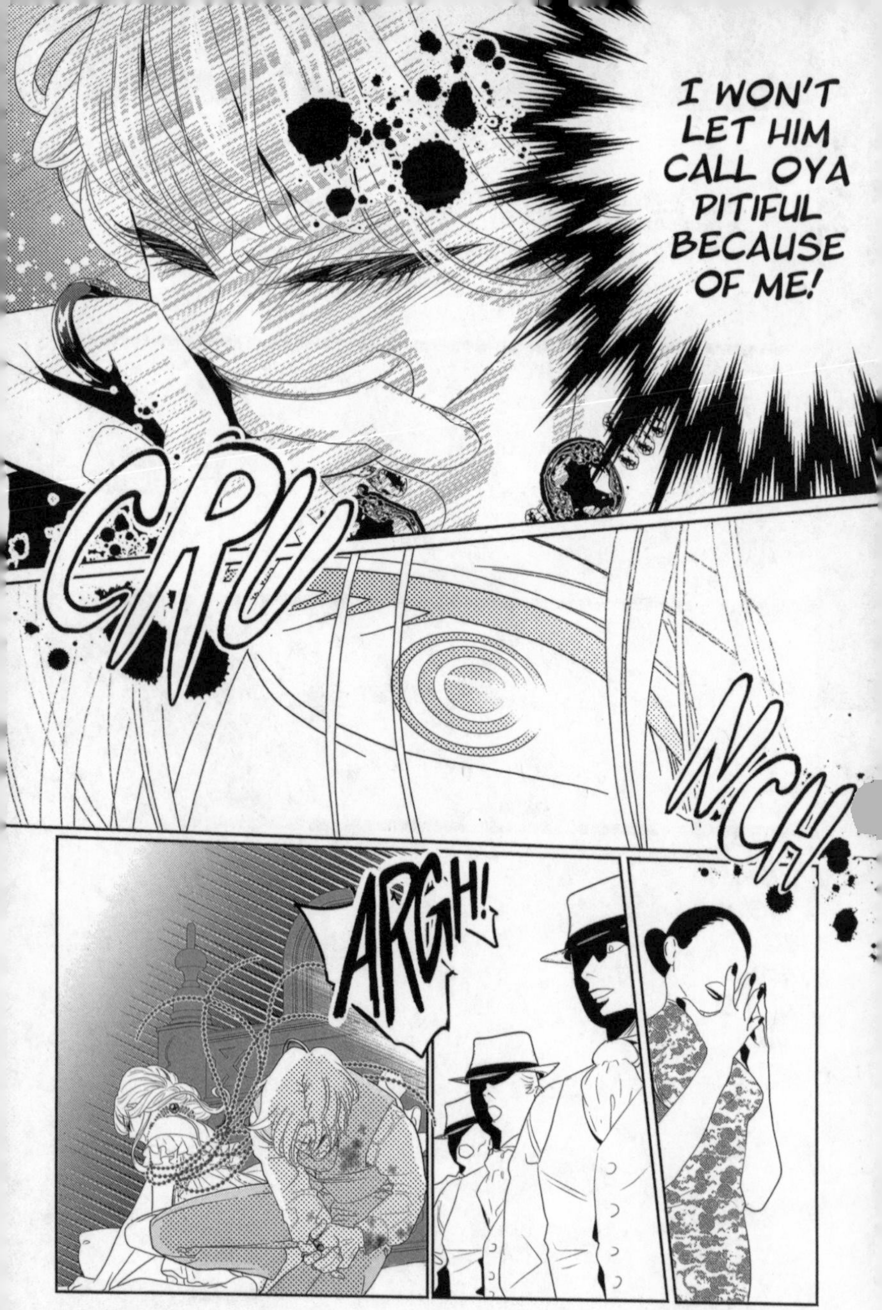
I WON'T LET HIM CALL OYA PITIFUL BECAUSE OF ME!
CRUNCH
ARGH!

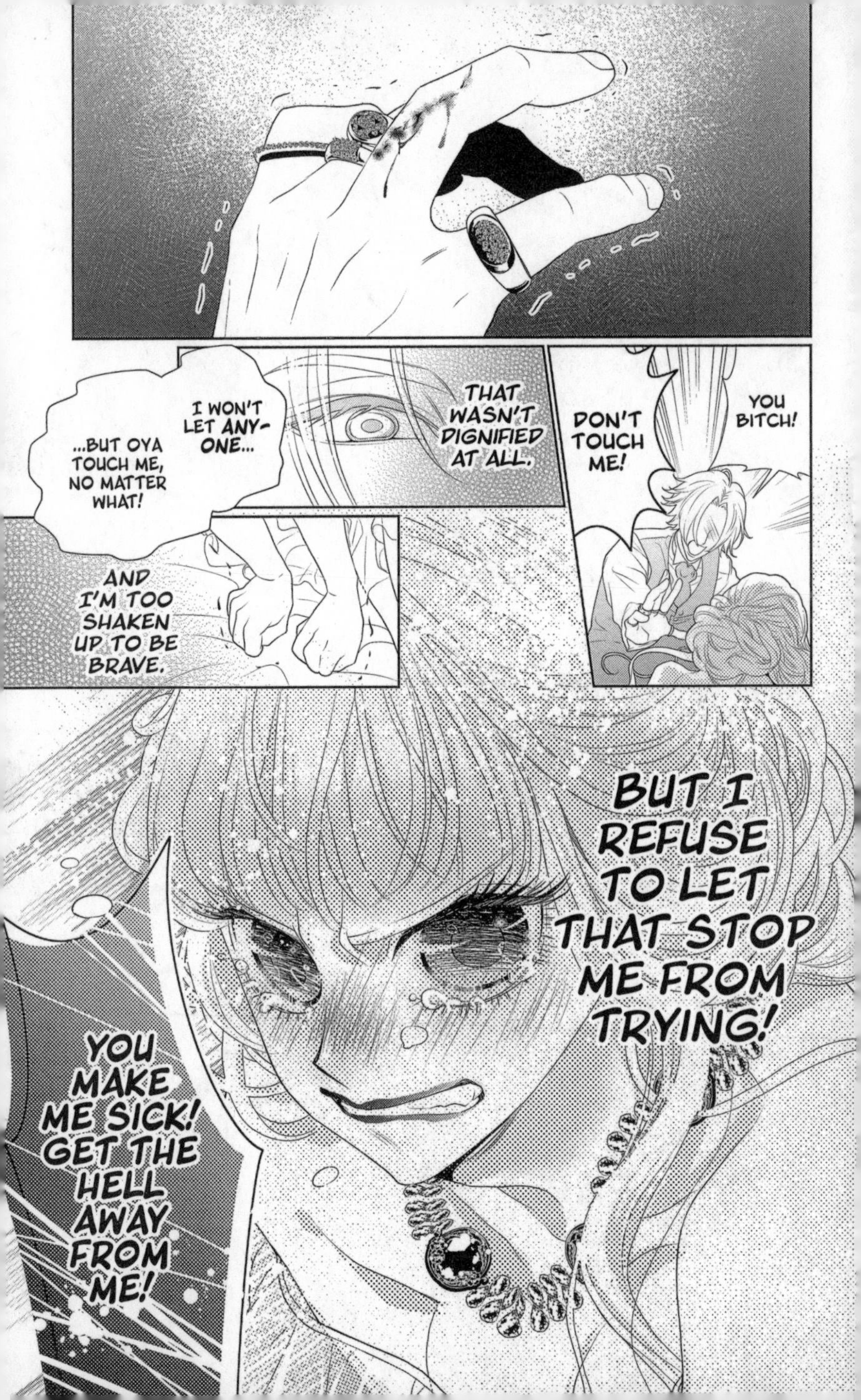
YOU BITCH!
DON'T TOUCH ME!
THAT WASN'T DIGNIFIED AT ALL.
I WON'T LET ANY-ONE...
...BUT OYA TOUCH ME, NO MATTER WHAT!
AND I'M TOO SHAKEN UP TO BE BRAVE.
BUT I REFUSE TO LET THAT STOP ME FROM TRYING!
YOU MAKE ME SICK! GET THE HELL AWAY FROM ME!

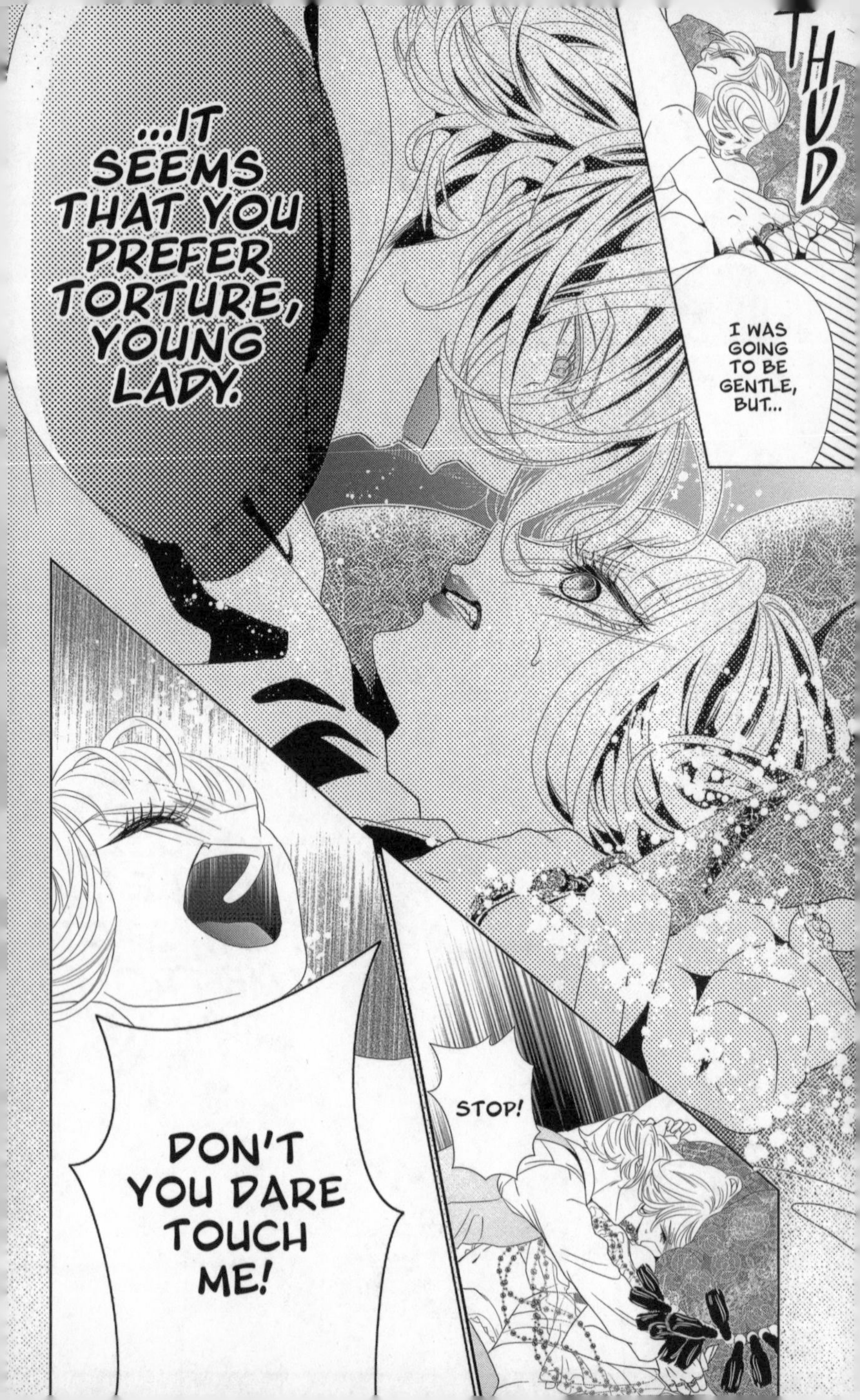
THUD
I WAS GOING TO BE GENTLE, BUT...
...IT SEEMS THAT YOU PREFER TORTURE, YOUNG LADY.
STOP!
DON'T YOU DARE TOUCH ME!

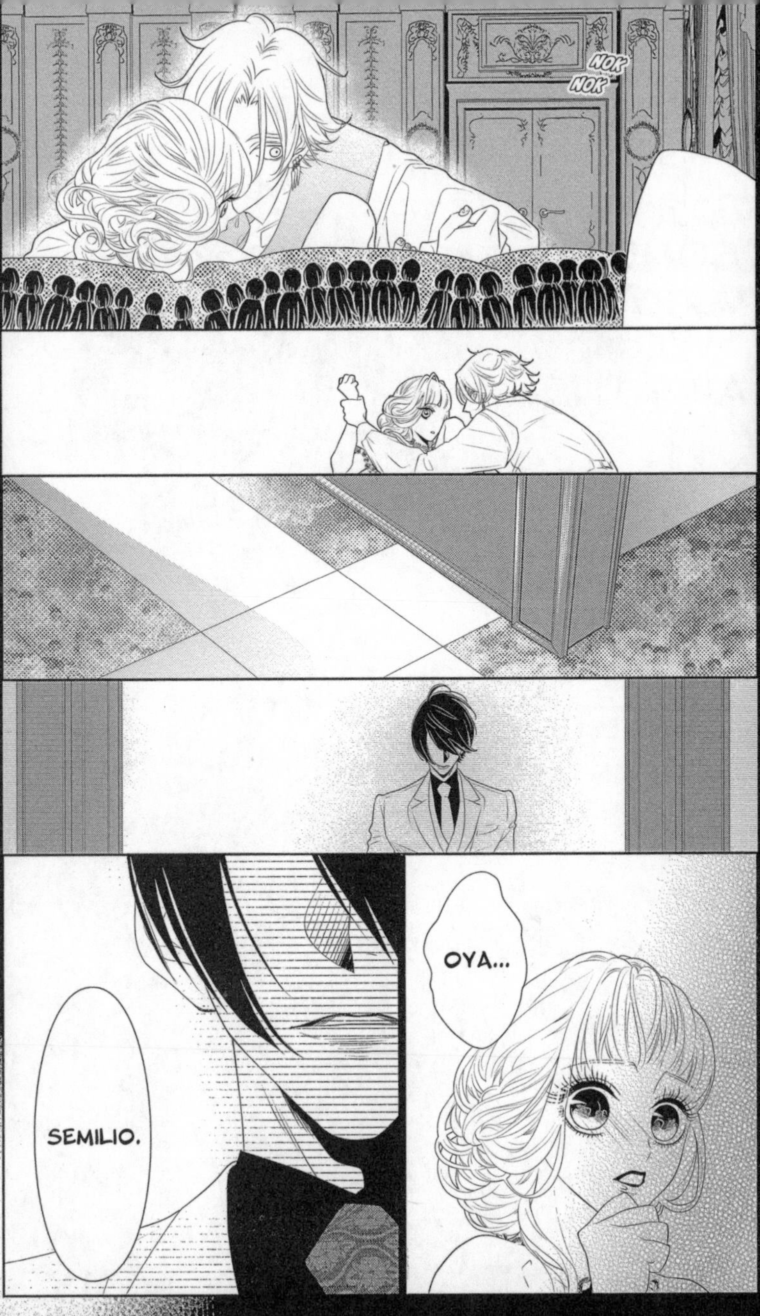
NOK
NOK
OYA...
SEMILIO.

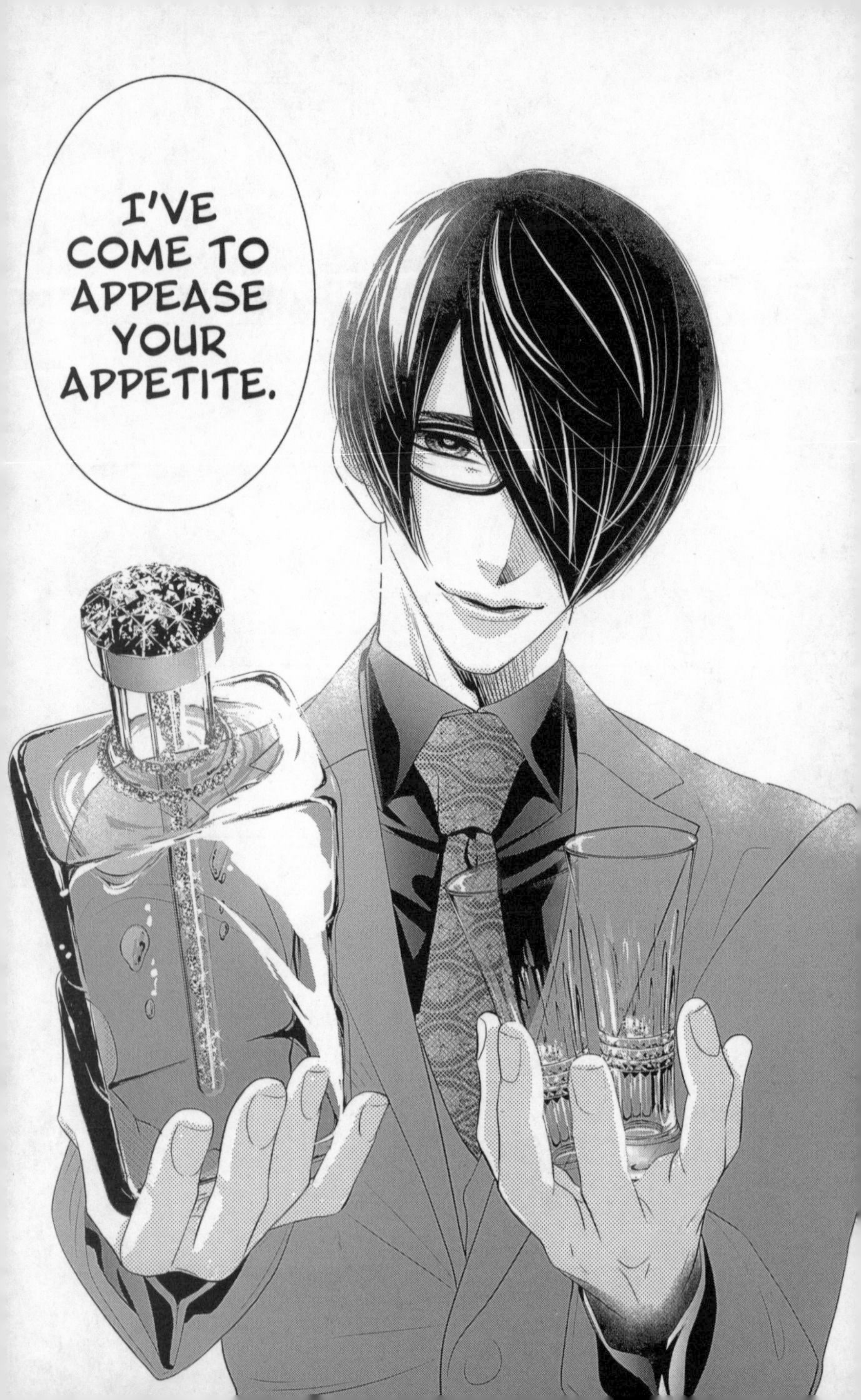
I'VE COME TO APPEASE YOUR APPETITE.

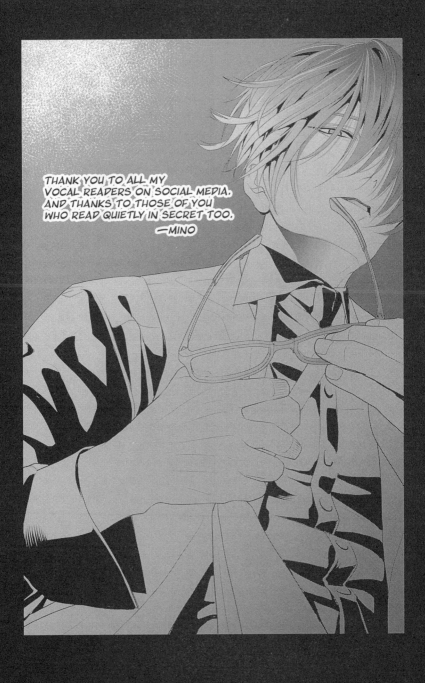

THANK YOU TO ALL MY
VOCAL READERS ON SOCIAL MEDIA,
AND THANKS TO THOSE OF YOU
WHO READ QUIETLY IN SECRET TOO.
—MINO

bonus bullet 05 secret scene

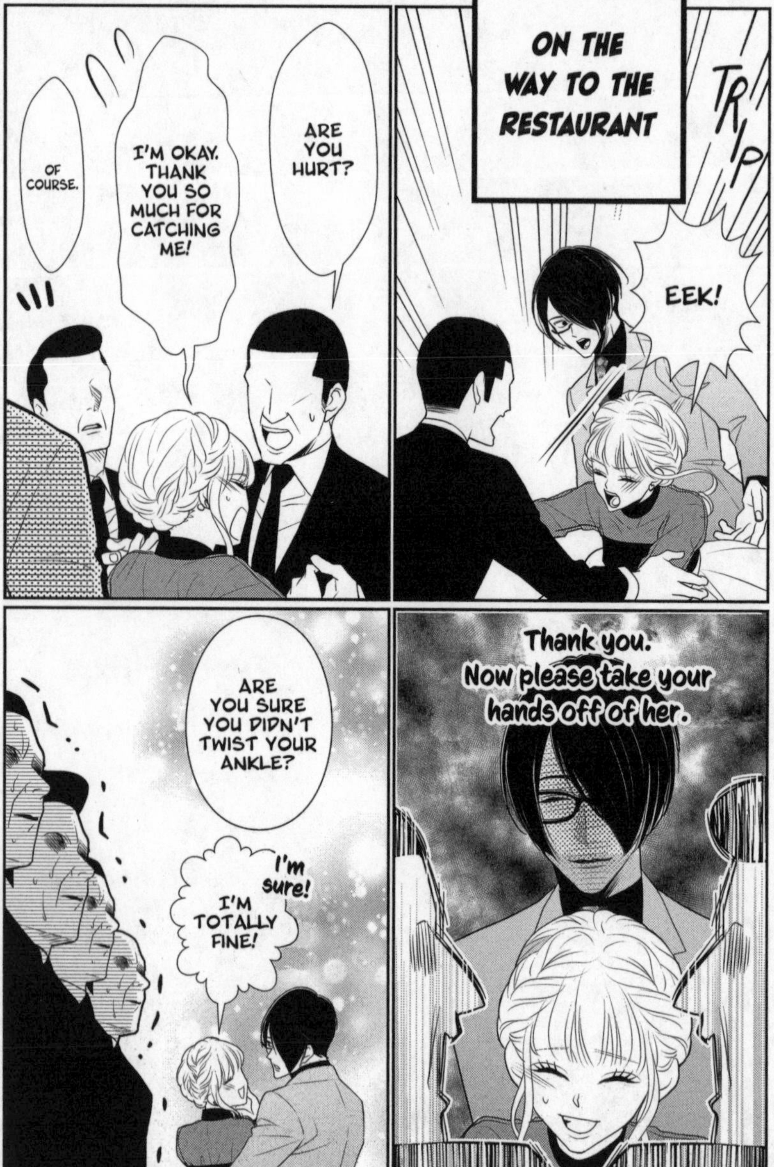
ON THE WAY TO THE RESTAURANT
TRIP
EEK!
ARE YOU HURT?
I'M OKAY. THANK YOU SO MUCH FOR CATCHING ME!
OF COURSE.
Thank you. Now please take your hands off of her.
ARE YOU SURE YOU DIDN'T TWIST YOUR ANKLE?
I'm sure!
I'M TOTALLY FINE!

bullet 06

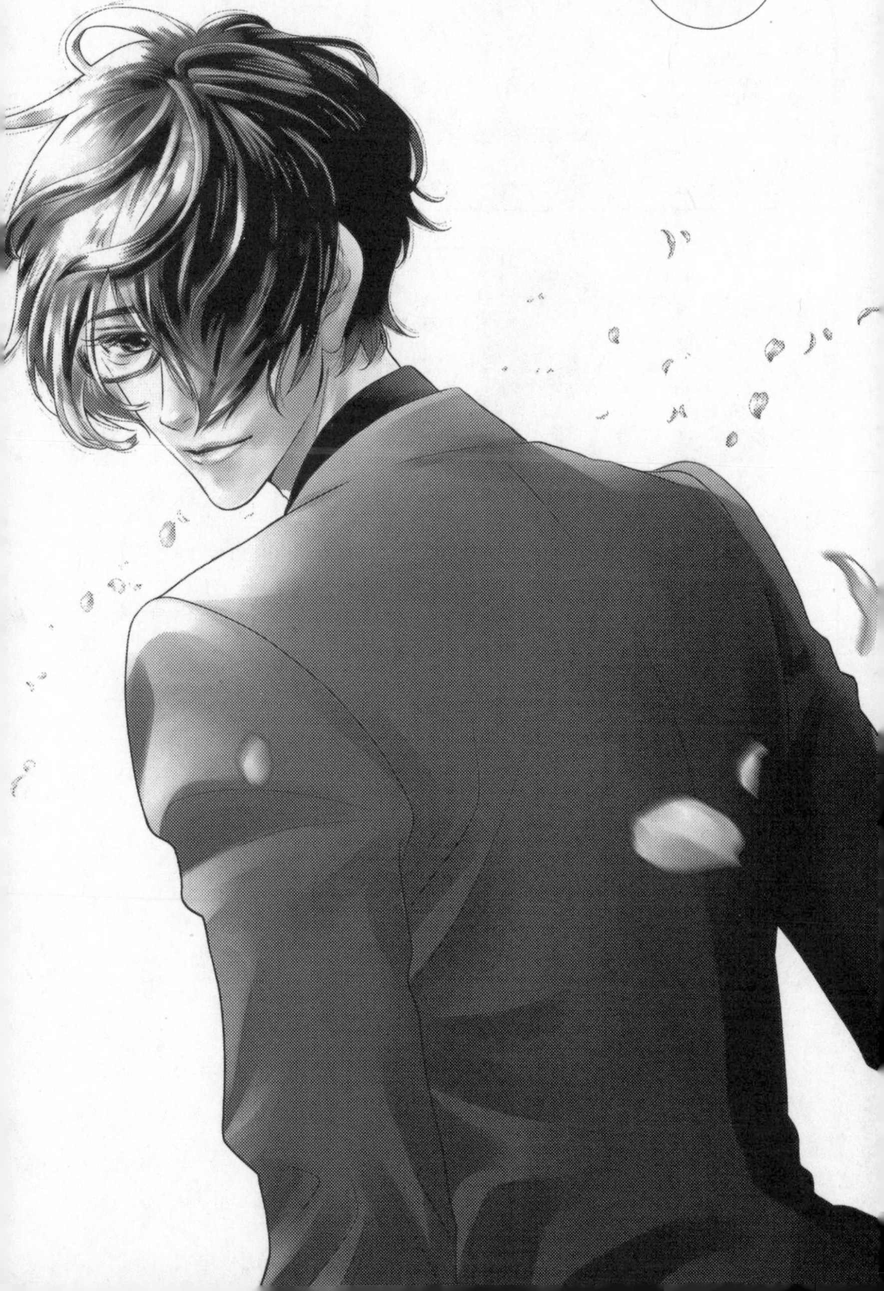

bonus secret scene: She's Mine, Semilio

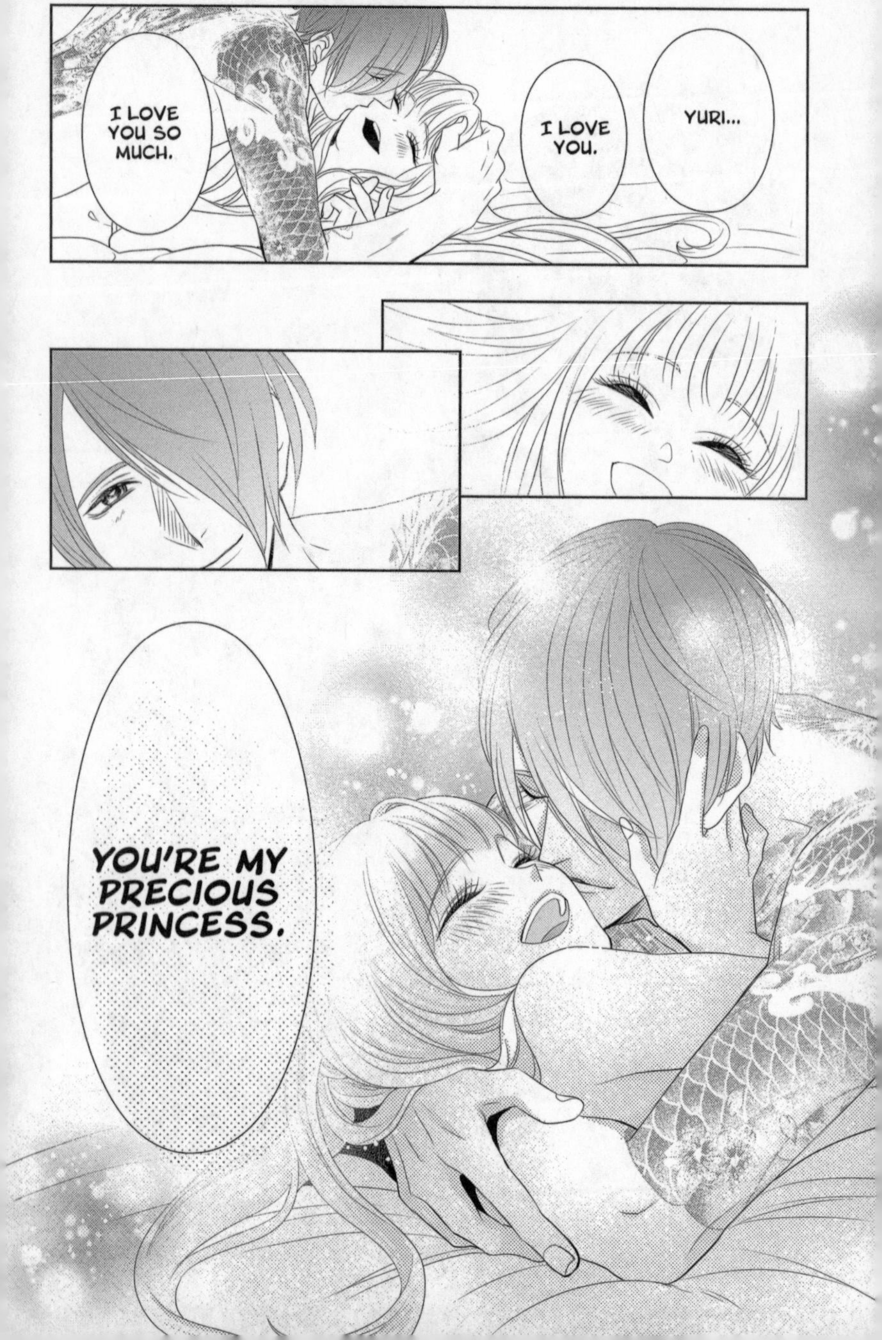
YURI...
I LOVE YOU.
I LOVE YOU SO MUCH.
YOU'RE MY PRECIOUS PRINCESS.

"I'VE COME TO APPEASE YOUR APPETITE!"
HA!
THAT'S NOT THE APPROACH I'D EXPECT...
...FROM A MAN WHOSE GIRLFRIEND WAS JUST KIDNAPPED!

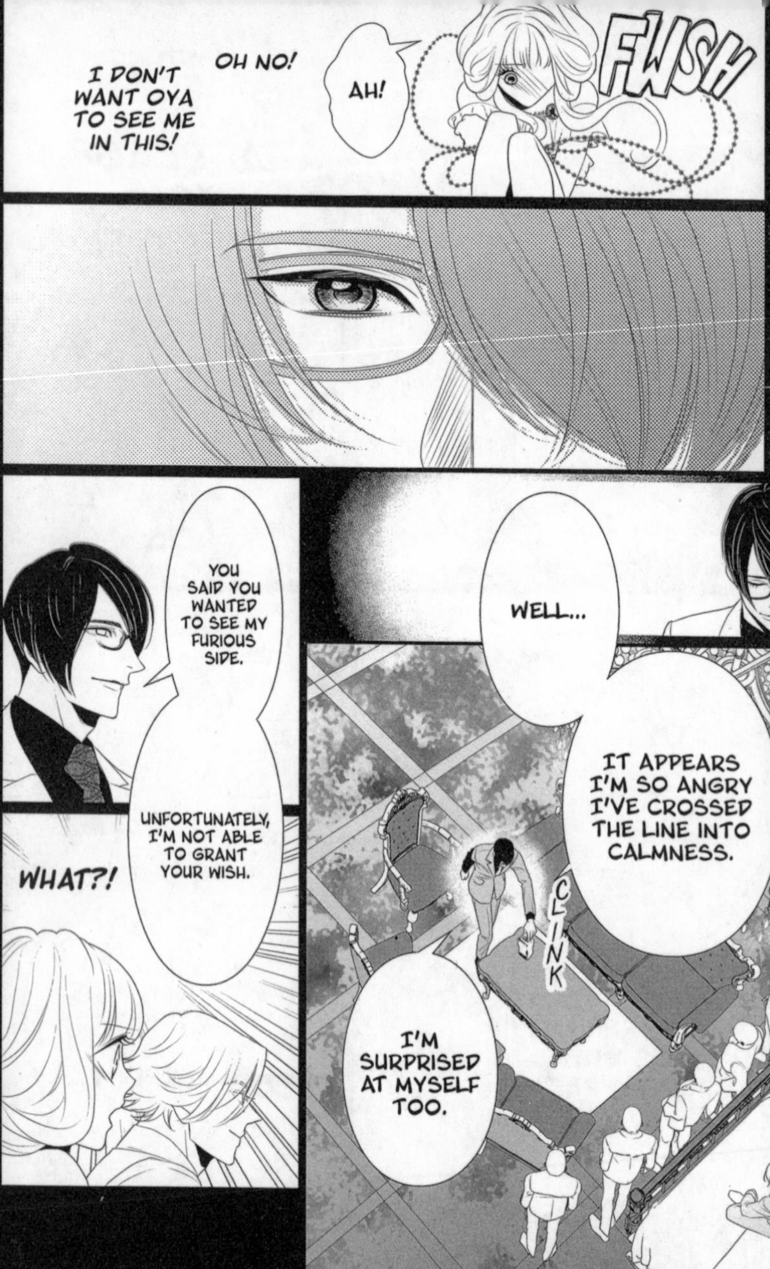
FWSH
AH!
OH NO!
I DON'T WANT OYA TO SEE ME IN THIS!
WELL...
IT APPEARS I'M SO ANGRY I'VE CROSSED THE LINE INTO CALMNESS.
CLINK
I'M SURPRISED AT MYSELF TOO.
YOU SAID YOU WANTED TO SEE MY FURIOUS SIDE.
UNFORTUNATELY, I'M NOT ABLE TO GRANT YOUR WISH.
WHAT?!

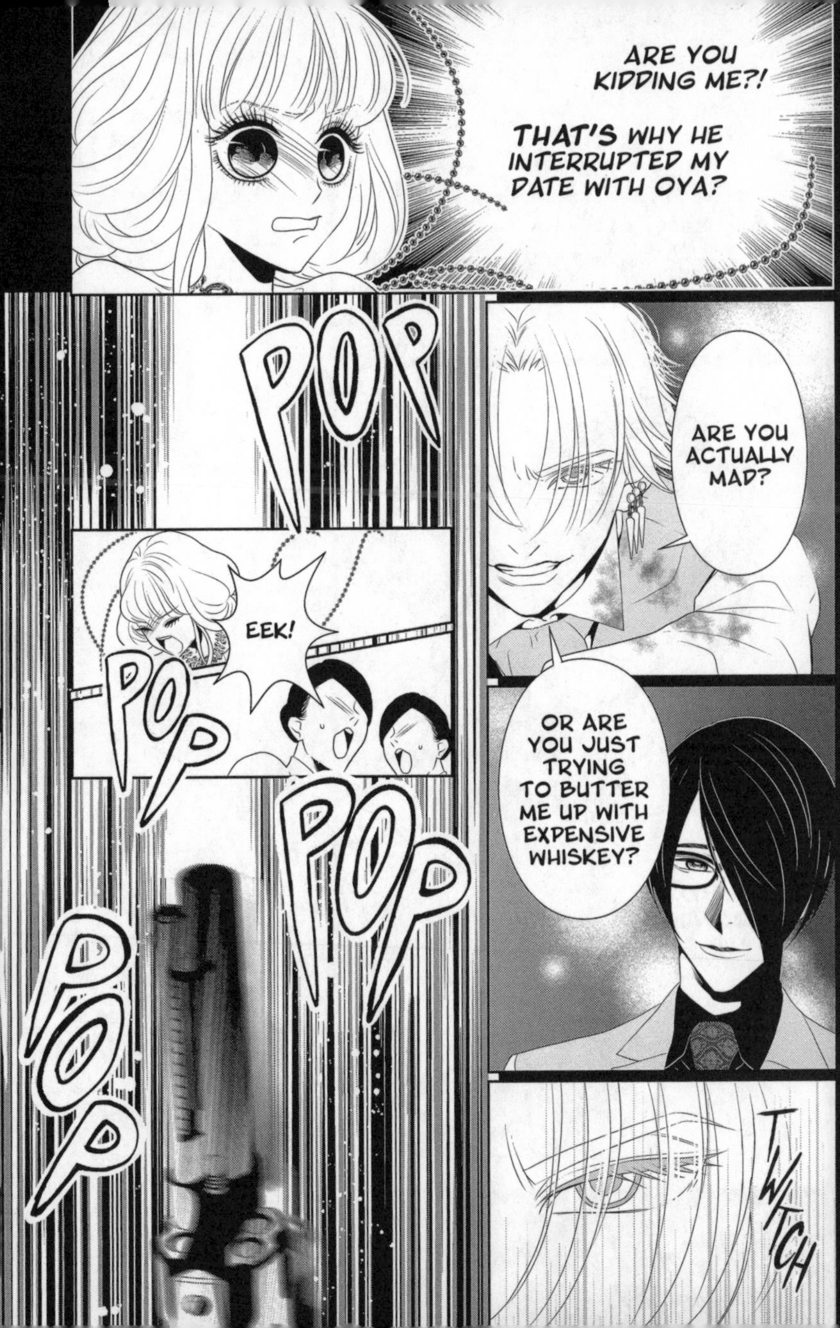
ARE YOU KIDDING ME?!
THAT'S WHY HE INTERRUPTED MY DATE WITH OYA?
ARE YOU ACTUALLY MAD?
OR ARE YOU JUST TRYING TO BUTTER ME UP WITH EXPENSIVE WHISKEY?
TWITCH
POP
EEK!
POP
POP
POP

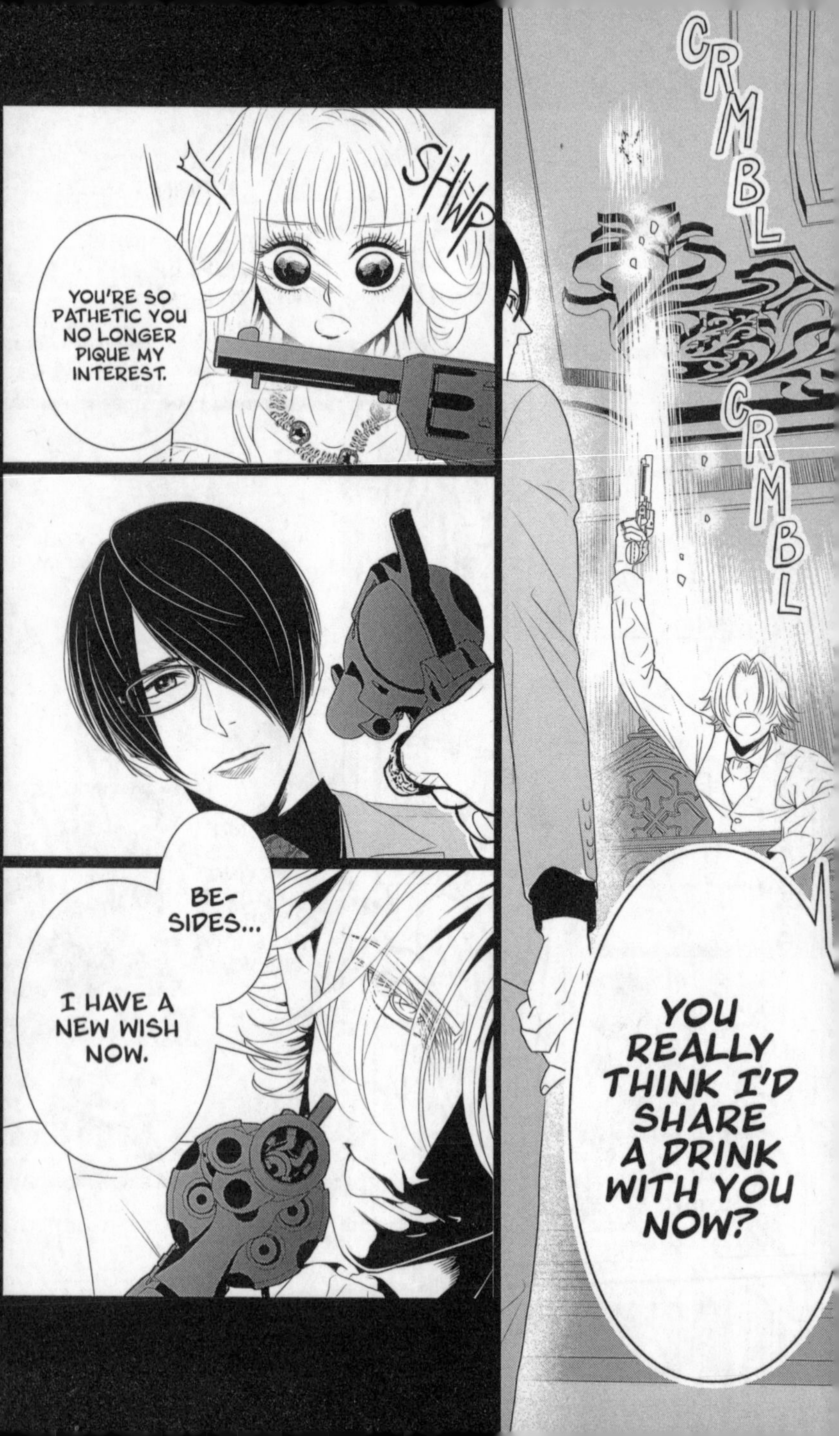
CRMBL
CRMBL
YOU REALLY THINK I'D SHARE A DRINK WITH YOU NOW?
SHWP
YOU'RE SO PATHETIC YOU NO LONGER PIQUE MY INTEREST.
BE-SIDES...
I HAVE A NEW WISH NOW.

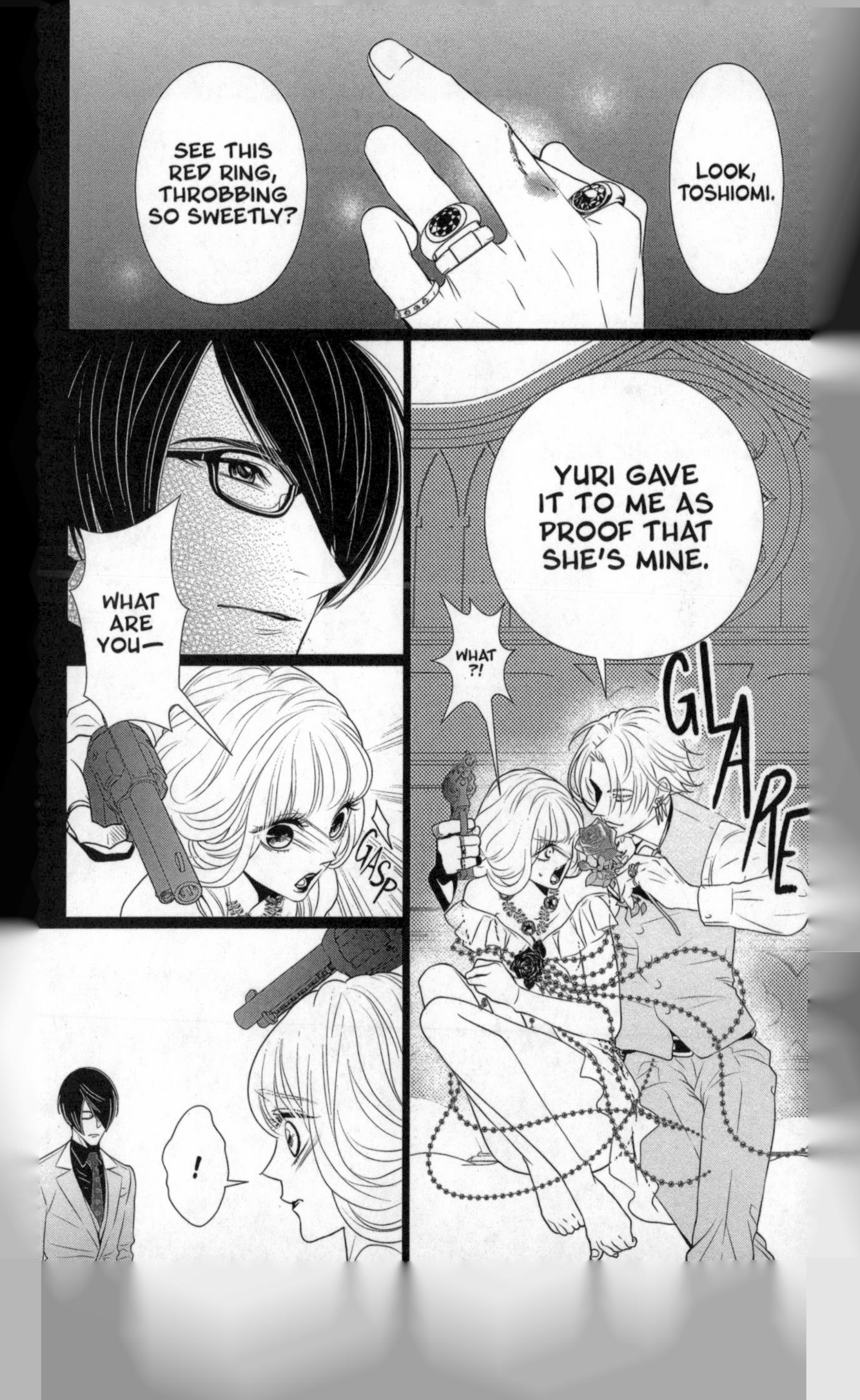
LOOK, TOSHIOMI.
SEE THIS RED RING, THROBBING SO SWEETLY?
YURI GAVE IT TO ME AS PROOF THAT SHE'S MINE.
WHAT?!
GLARE
WHAT ARE YOU—
GASP
!

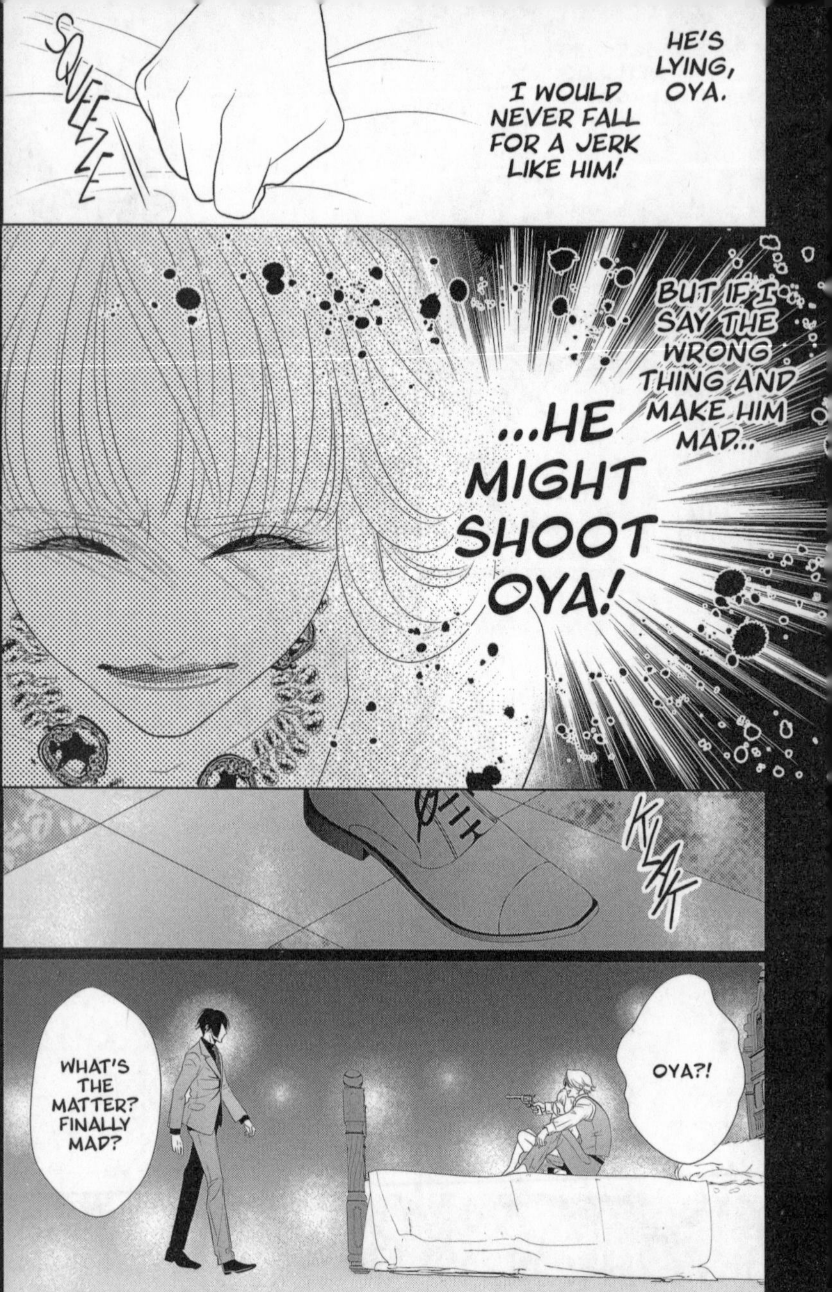
HE'S LYING, OYA.
I WOULD NEVER FALL FOR A JERK LIKE HIM!
SQUEEZE
BUT IF I SAY THE WRONG THING AND MAKE HIM MAD...
...HE MIGHT SHOOT OYA!
KLAK
OYA?!
WHAT'S THE MATTER? FINALLY MAD?

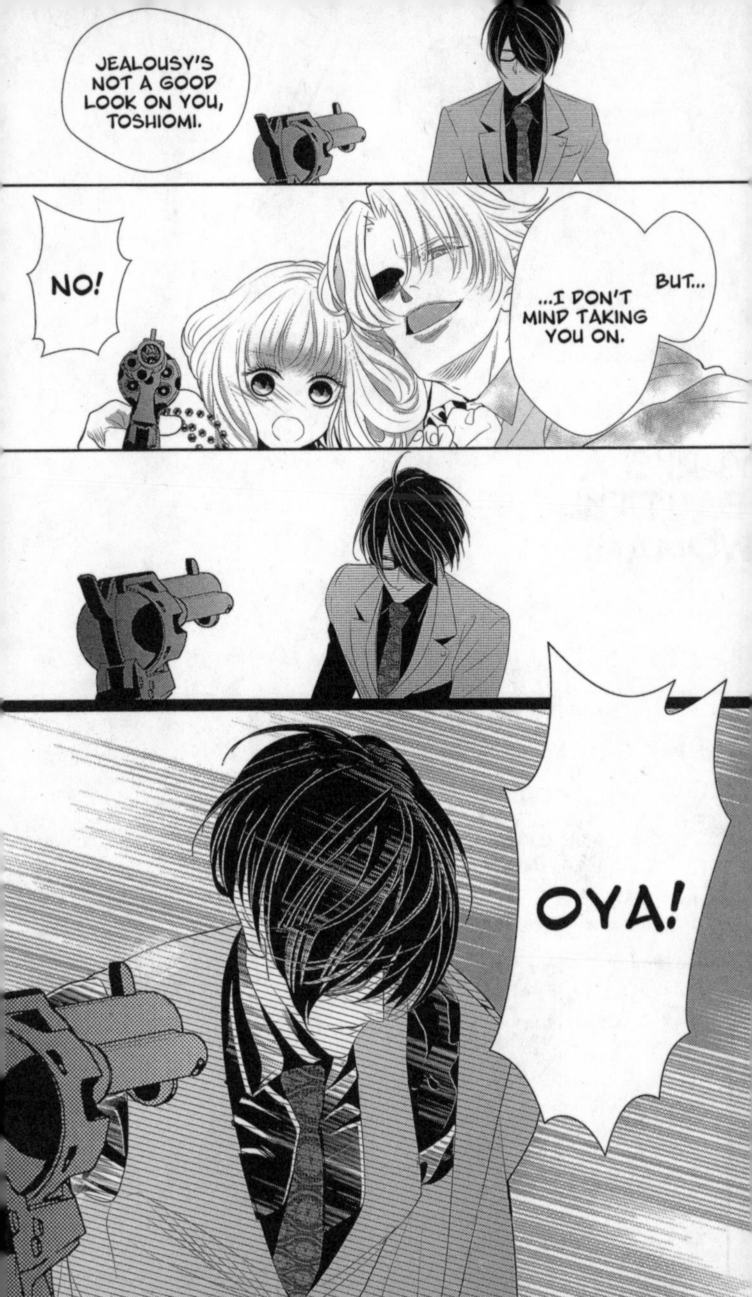
JEALOUSY'S NOT A GOOD LOOK ON YOU, TOSHIOMI.
BUT...
...I DON'T MIND TAKING YOU ON.
NO!
OYA!

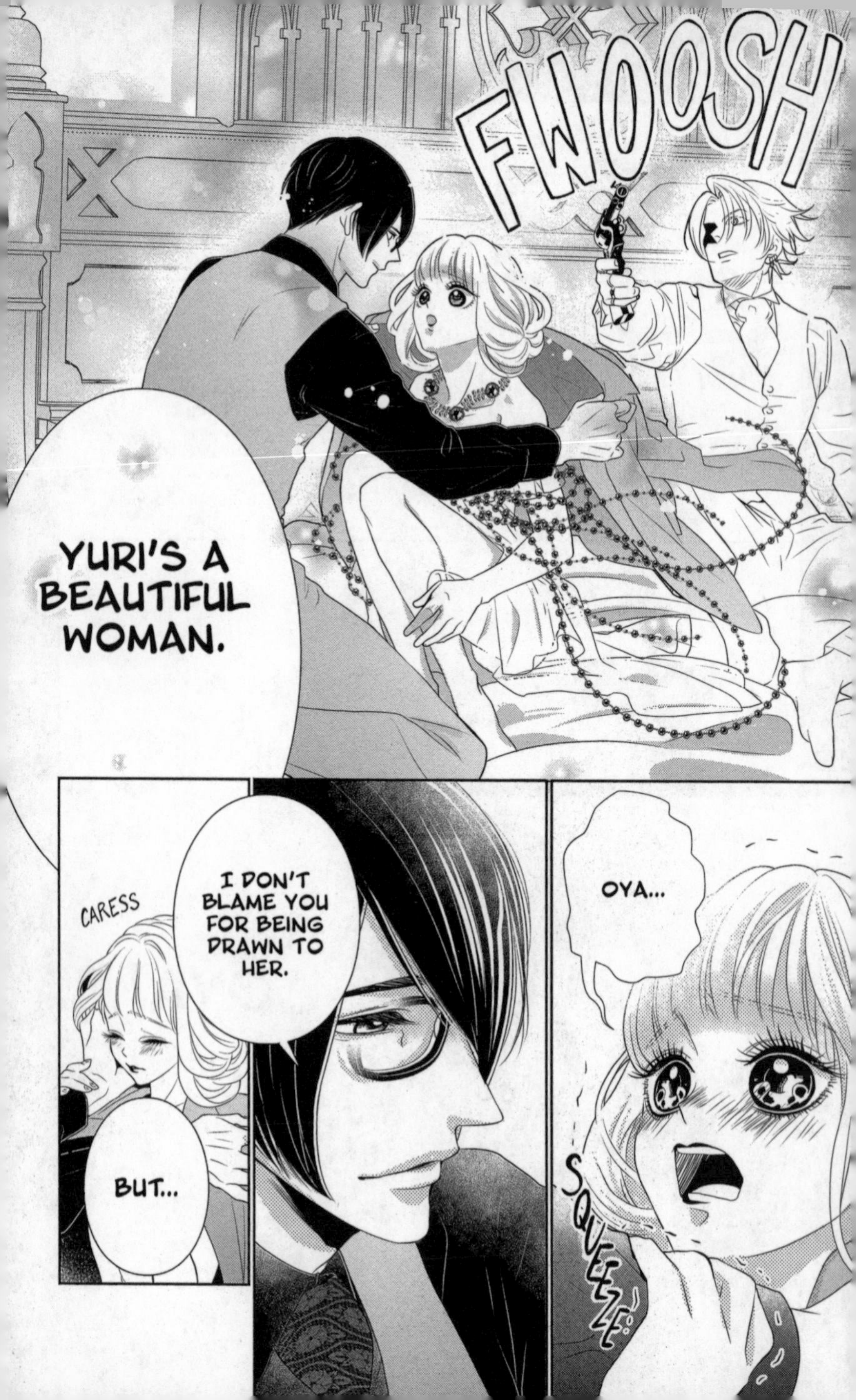
FWOOSH
YURI'S A BEAUTIFUL WOMAN.
OYA...
SQUEEZE
I DON'T BLAME YOU FOR BEING DRAWN TO HER.
CARESS
BUT...

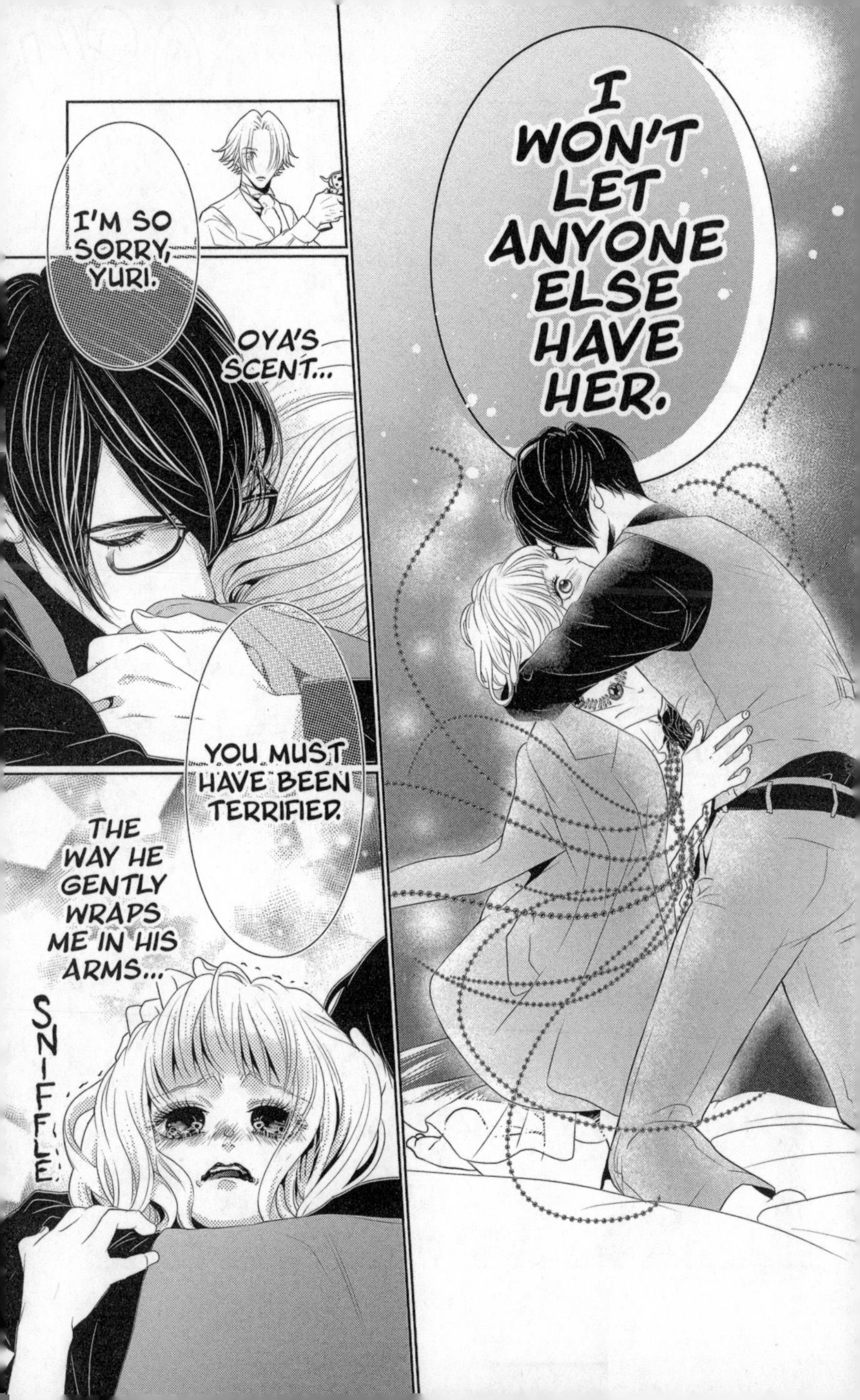
I WON'T LET ANYONE ELSE HAVE HER.
I'M SO SORRY, YURI.
OYA'S SCENT...
YOU MUST HAVE BEEN TERRIFIED.
THE WAY HE GENTLY WRAPS ME IN HIS ARMS...
SNIFFLE

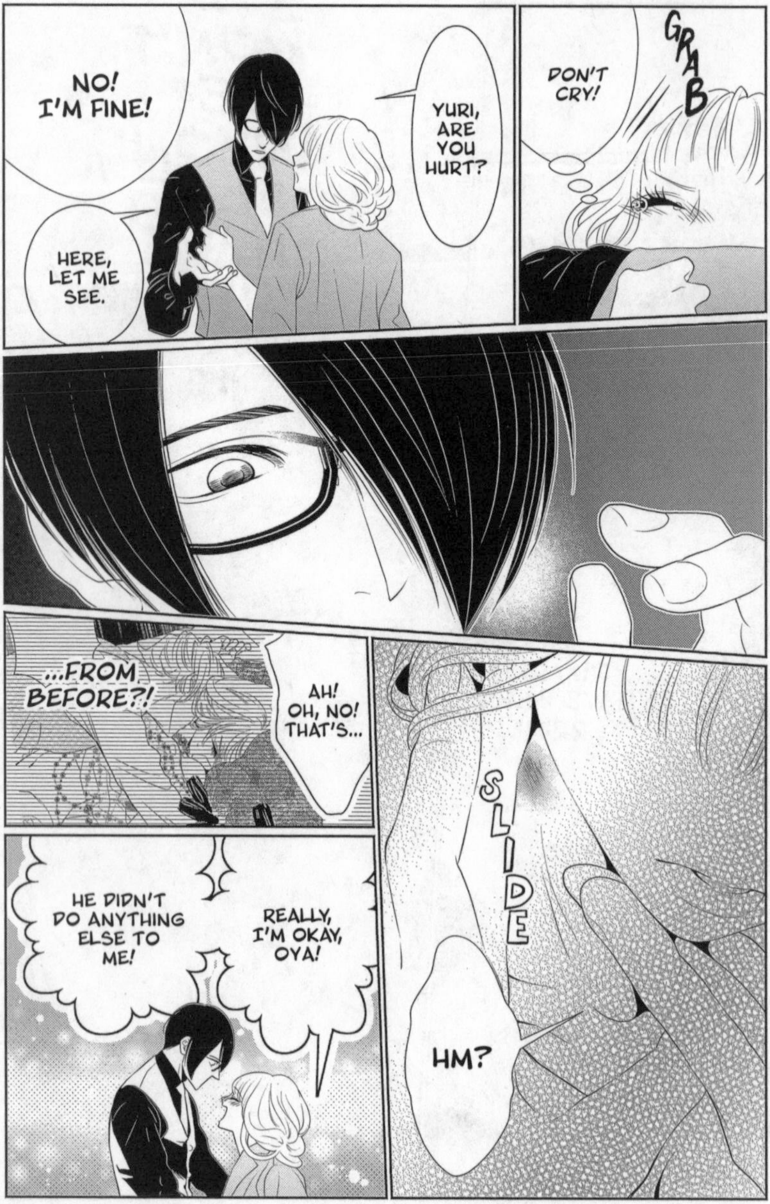
GRAB
DON'T CRY!
YURI, ARE YOU HURT?
NO! I'M FINE!
HERE, LET ME SEE.
SLIDE
HM?
AH! OH, NO! THAT'S...
...FROM BEFORE?!
REALLY, I'M OKAY, OYA!
HE DIDN'T DO ANYTHING ELSE TO ME!

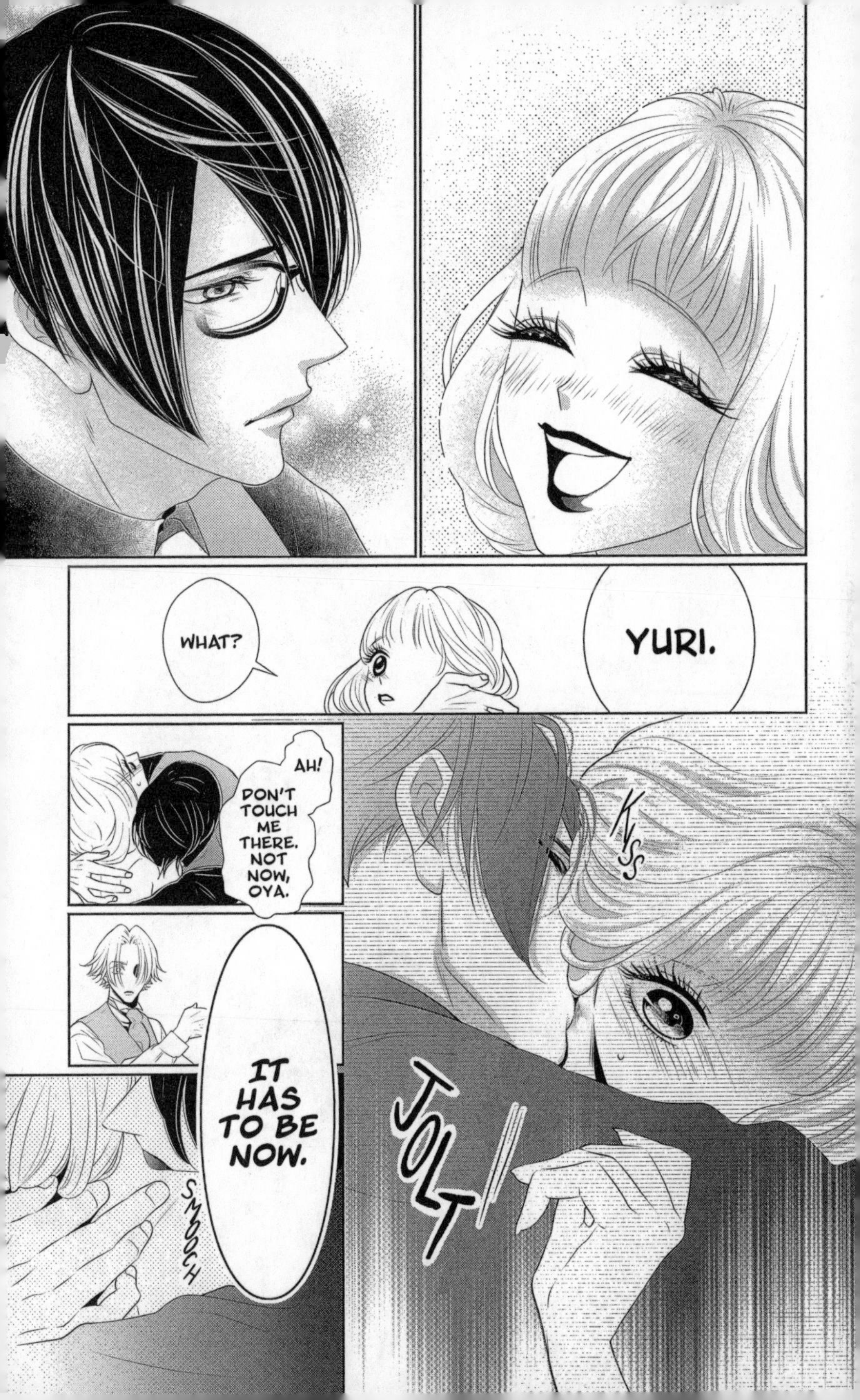
YURI.
WHAT?
KISS
JOLT
AH! DON'T TOUCH ME THERE. NOT NOW, OYA.
IT HAS TO BE NOW.
SMOOCH

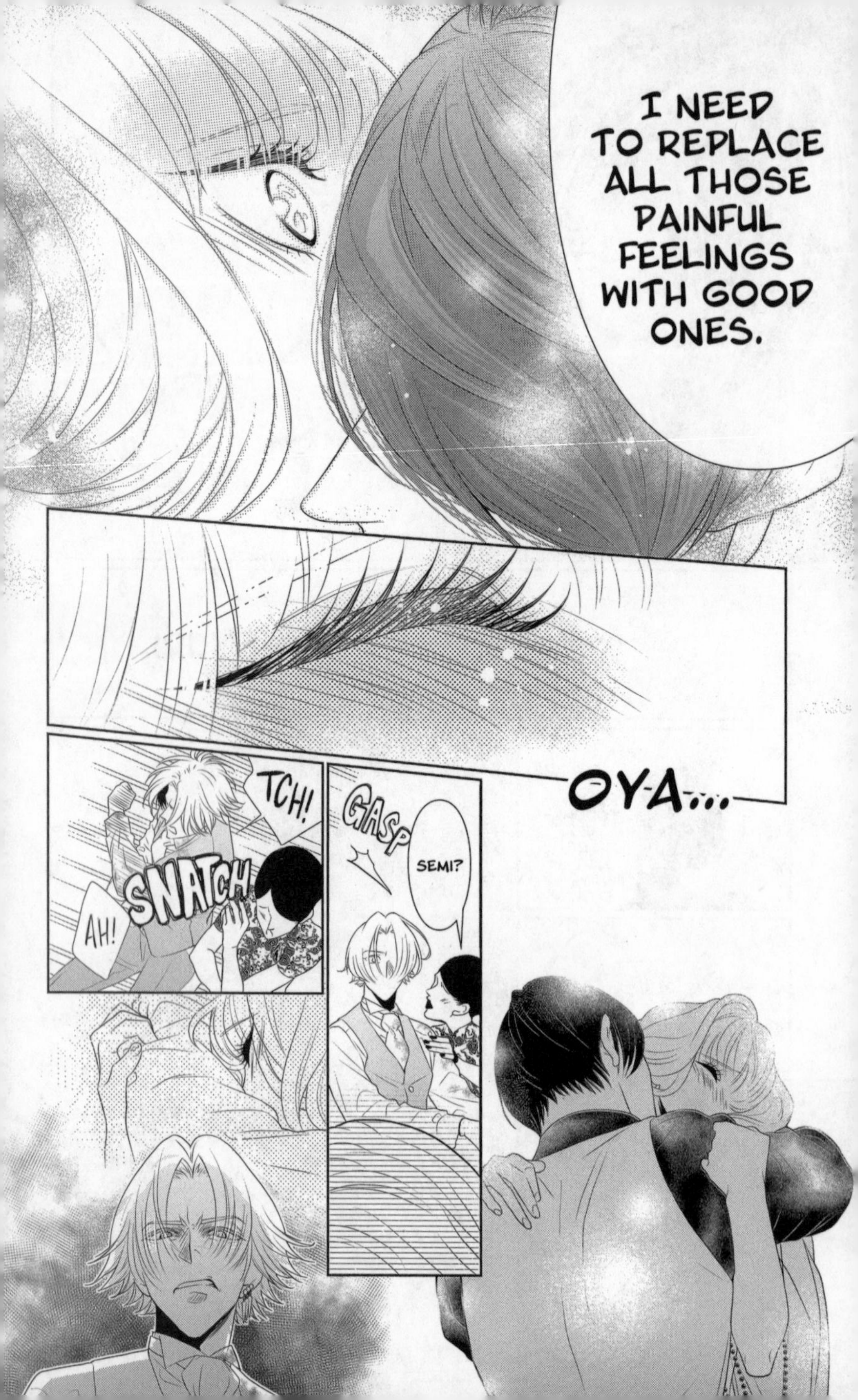
I NEED TO REPLACE ALL THOSE PAINFUL FEELINGS WITH GOOD ONES.
OYA...
GASP
SEMI?
TCH!
SNATCH
AH!

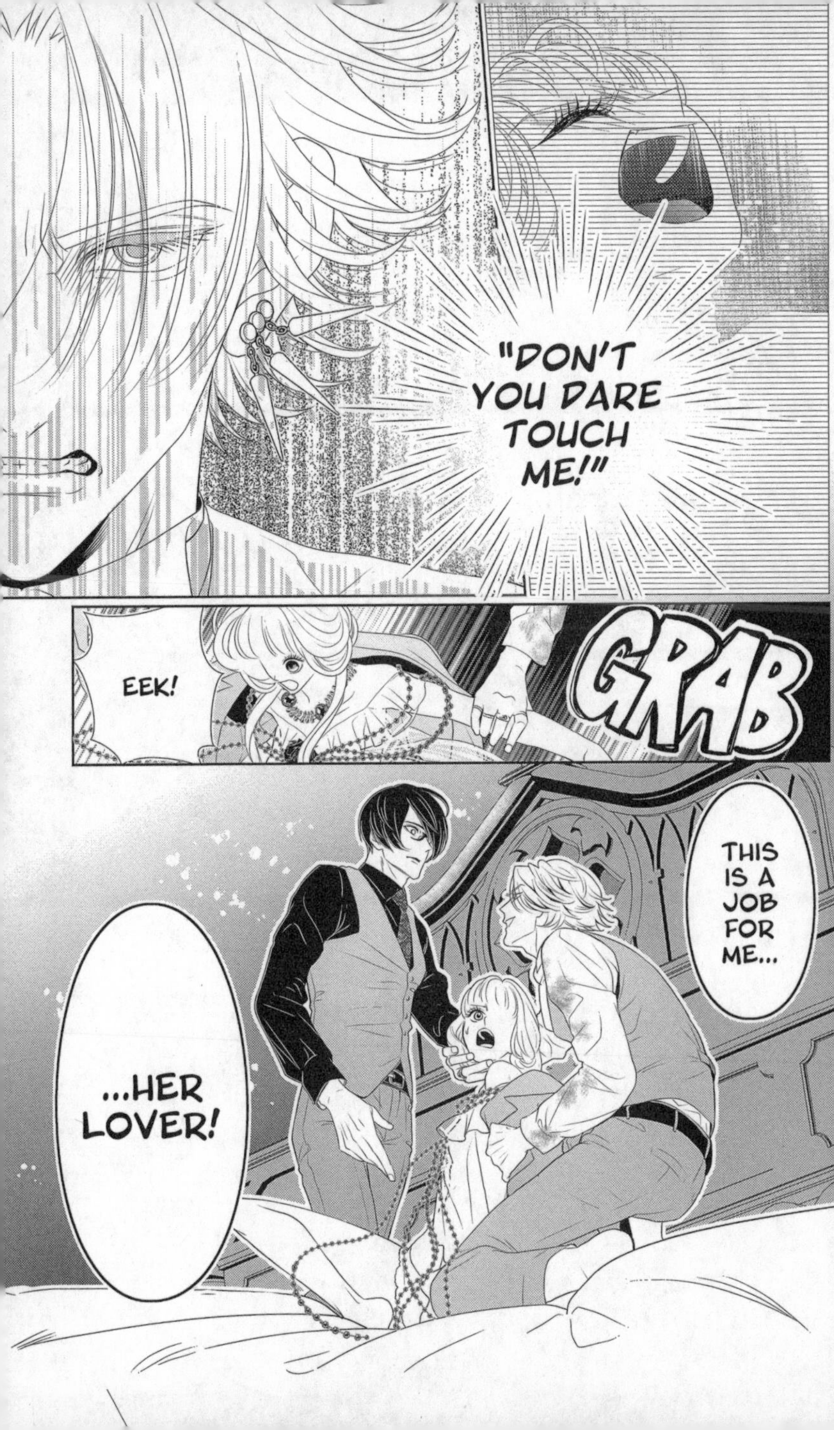
"DON'T YOU DARE TOUCH ME!"
GRAB
EEK!
THIS IS A JOB FOR ME...
...HER LOVER!

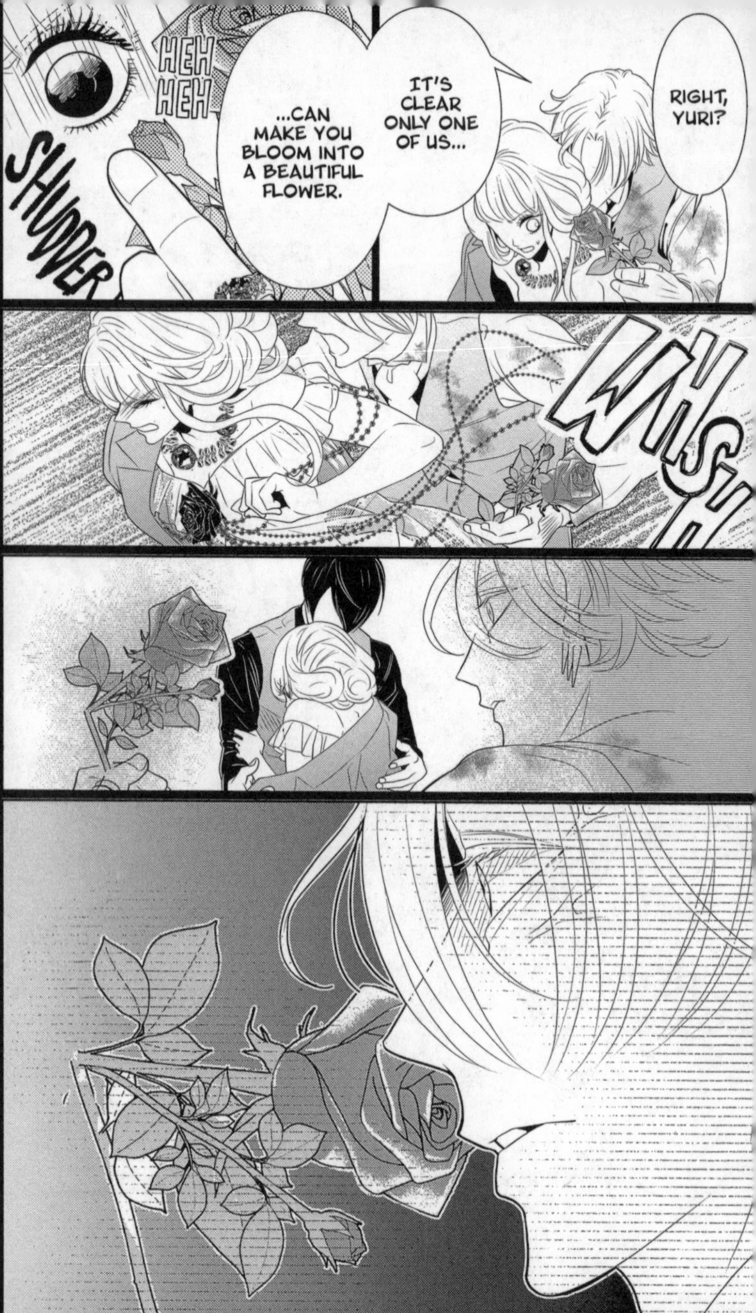
RIGHT, YURI?
IT'S CLEAR ONLY ONE OF US...
...CAN MAKE YOU BLOOM INTO A BEAUTIFUL FLOWER.
HEH HEH
SHUDDER
WHSH

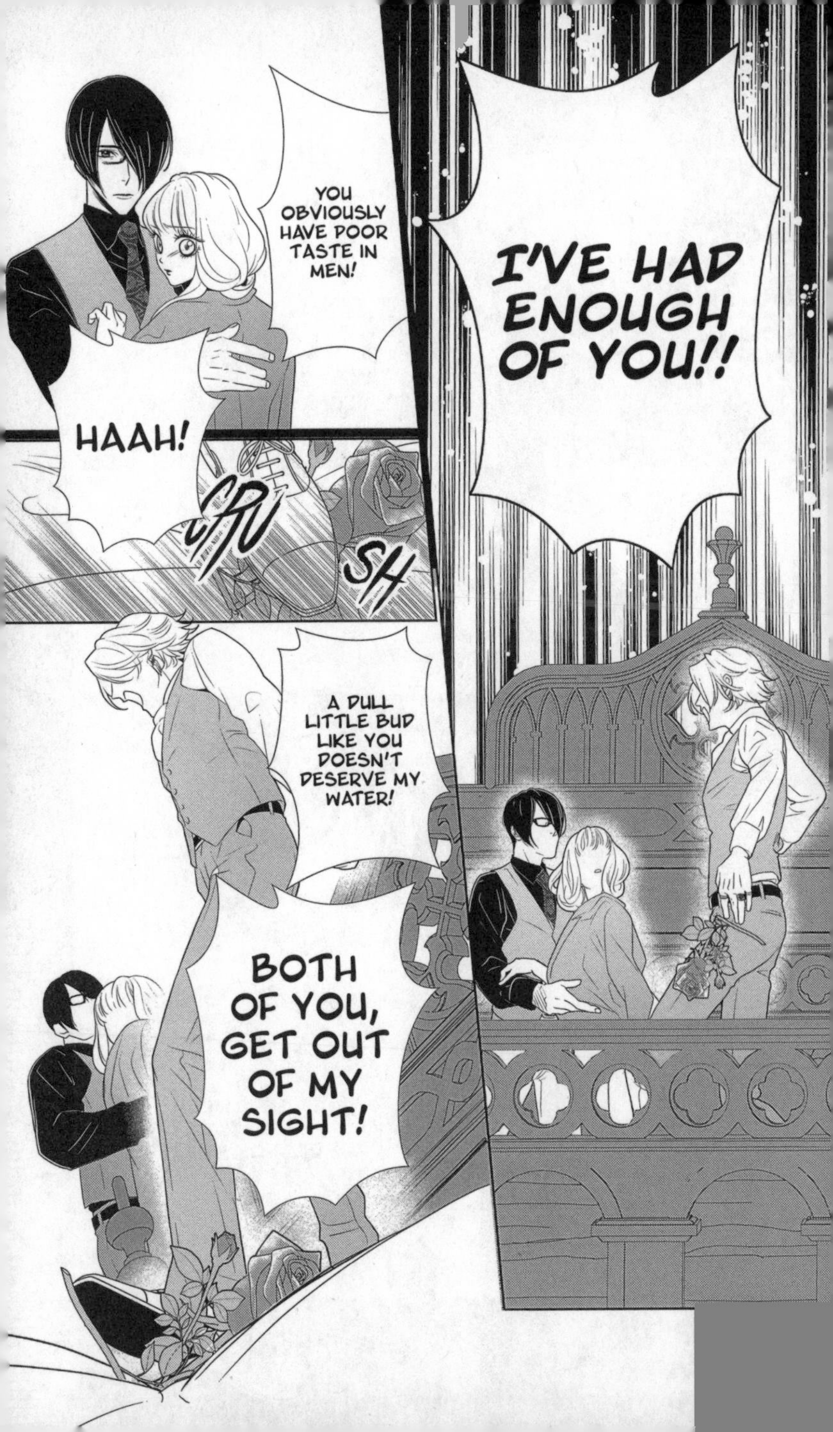
I'VE HAD ENOUGH OF YOU!!
YOU OBVIOUSLY HAVE POOR TASTE IN MEN!
HAAH!
CRUSH
A DULL LITTLE BUD LIKE YOU DOESN'T DESERVE MY WATER!
BOTH OF YOU, GET OUT OF MY SIGHT!

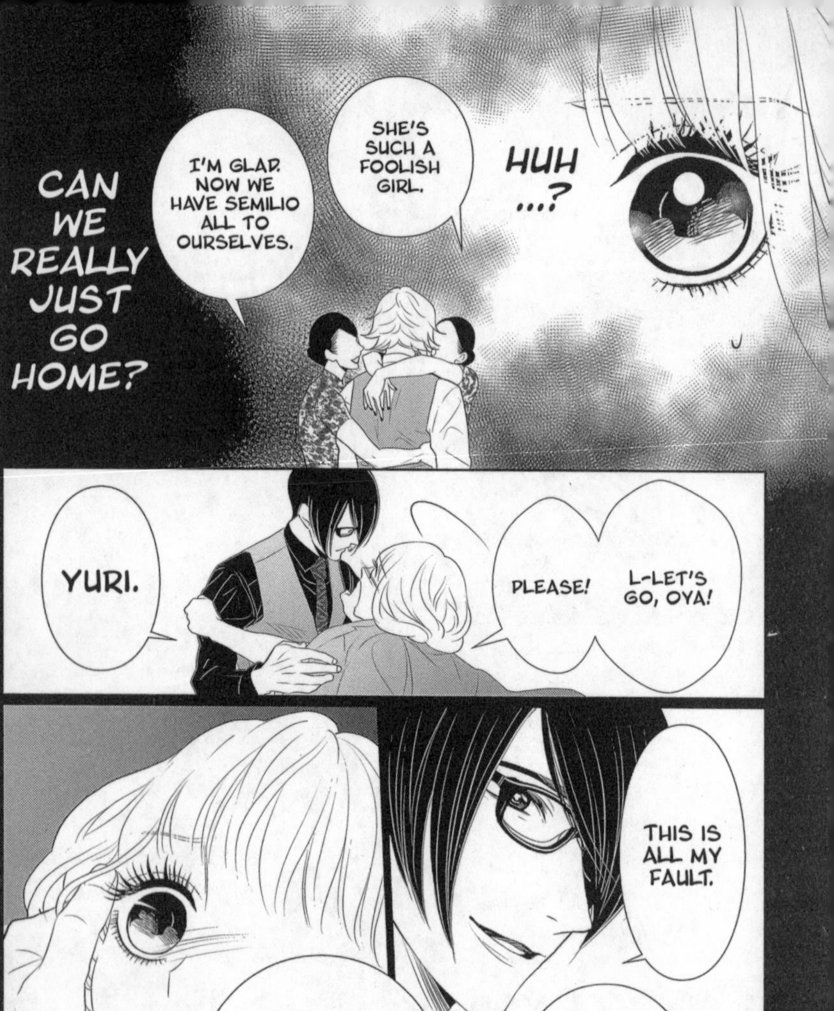
HUH ...?
SHE'S SUCH A FOOLISH GIRL.
I'M GLAD. NOW WE HAVE SEMILIO ALL TO OURSELVES.
CAN WE REALLY JUST GO HOME?
L-LET'S GO, OYA!
PLEASE!
YURI.
THIS IS ALL MY FAULT.
SO I NEED TO TAKE RESPONSIBILITY.
I WANT YOU TO RETURN TO THE VILLA ON YOUR OWN.
WHAT ...?

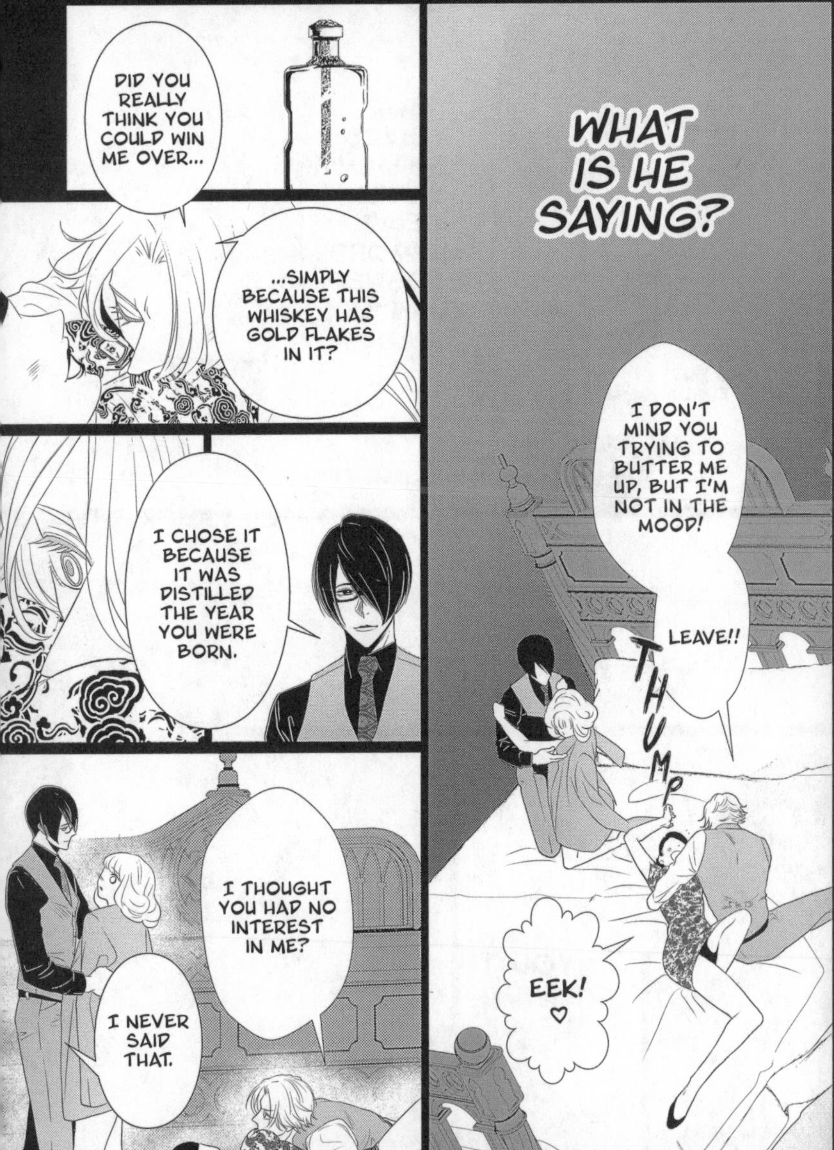
WHAT IS HE SAYING?
I DON'T MIND YOU TRYING TO BUTTER ME UP, BUT I'M NOT IN THE MOOD!
LEAVE!!
THUMP
EEK! ♡
DID YOU REALLY THINK YOU COULD WIN ME OVER...
...SIMPLY BECAUSE THIS WHISKEY HAS GOLD FLAKES IN IT?
I CHOSE IT BECAUSE IT WAS DISTILLED THE YEAR YOU WERE BORN.
I THOUGHT YOU HAD NO INTEREST IN ME?
I NEVER SAID THAT.

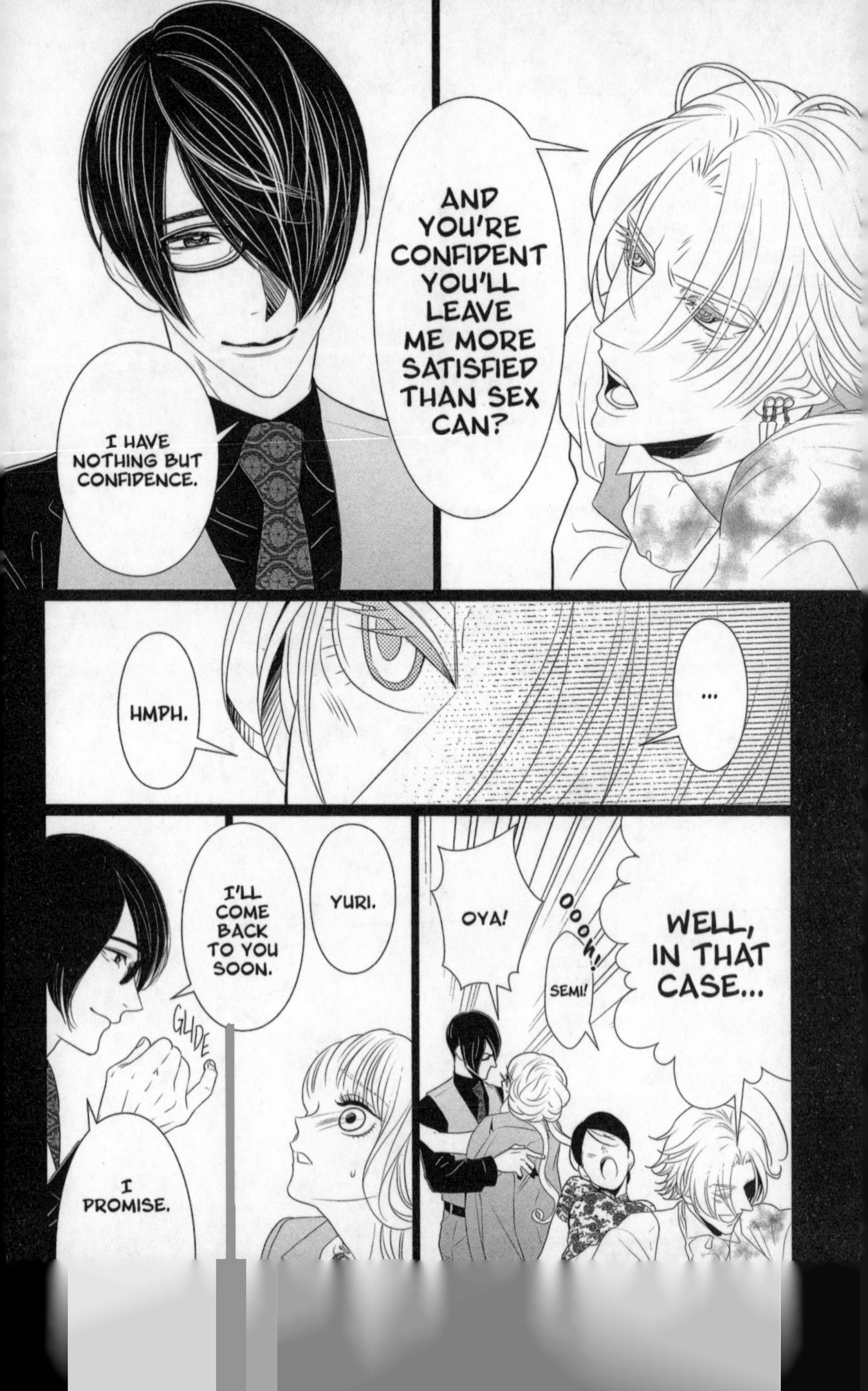
AND YOU'RE CONFIDENT YOU'LL LEAVE ME MORE SATISFIED THAN SEX CAN?
I HAVE NOTHING BUT CONFIDENCE.
...
HMPH.
WELL, IN THAT CASE...
OOOH!
OYA!
SEMI!
YURI.
I'LL COME BACK TO YOU SOON.
GLIDE
I PROMISE.

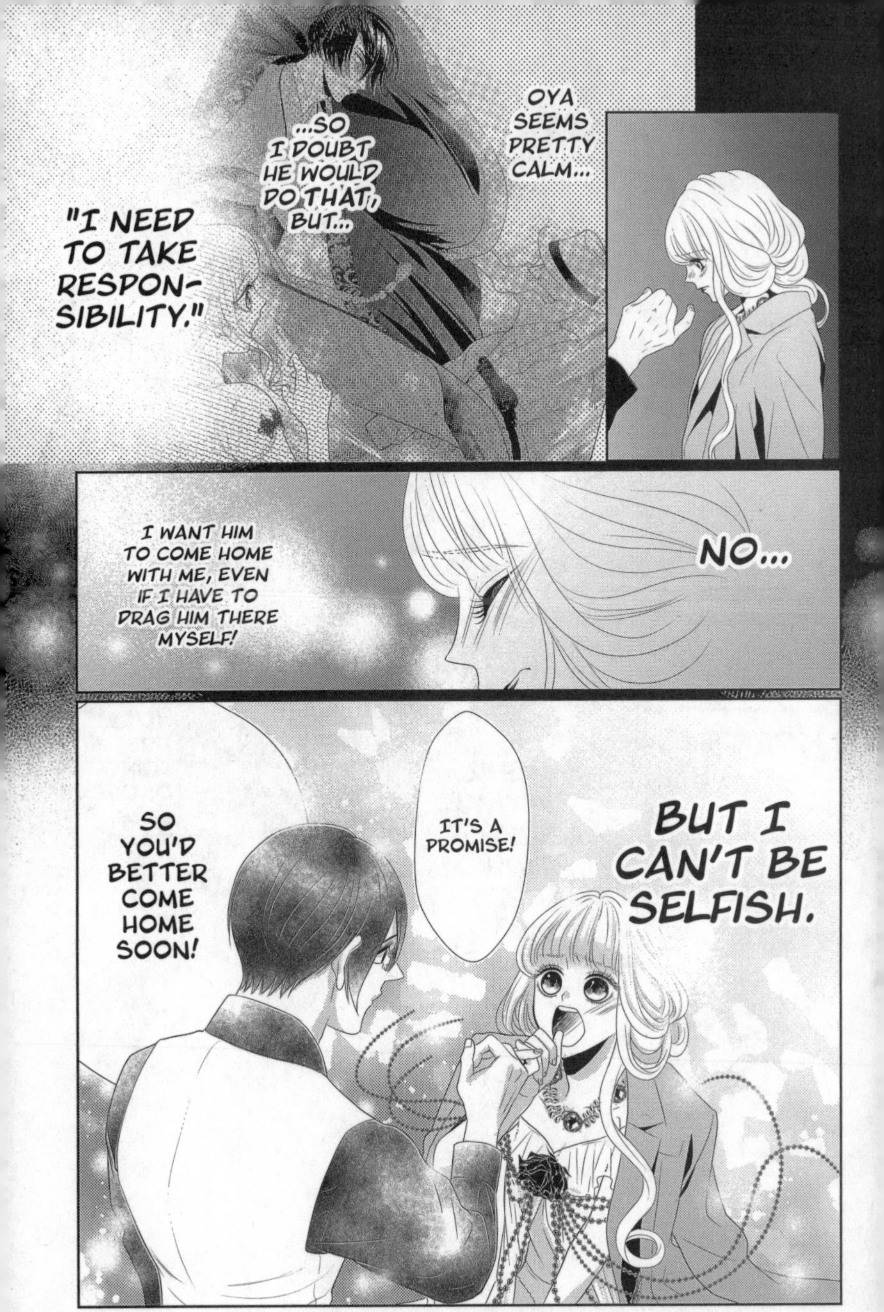
OYA SEEMS PRETTY CALM...
...SO I DOUBT HE WOULD DO THAT, BUT...
"I NEED TO TAKE RESPON-SIBILITY."
NO...
I WANT HIM TO COME HOME WITH ME, EVEN IF I HAVE TO DRAG HIM THERE MYSELF!
BUT I CAN'T BE SELFISH.
IT'S A PROMISE!
SO YOU'D BETTER COME HOME SOON!

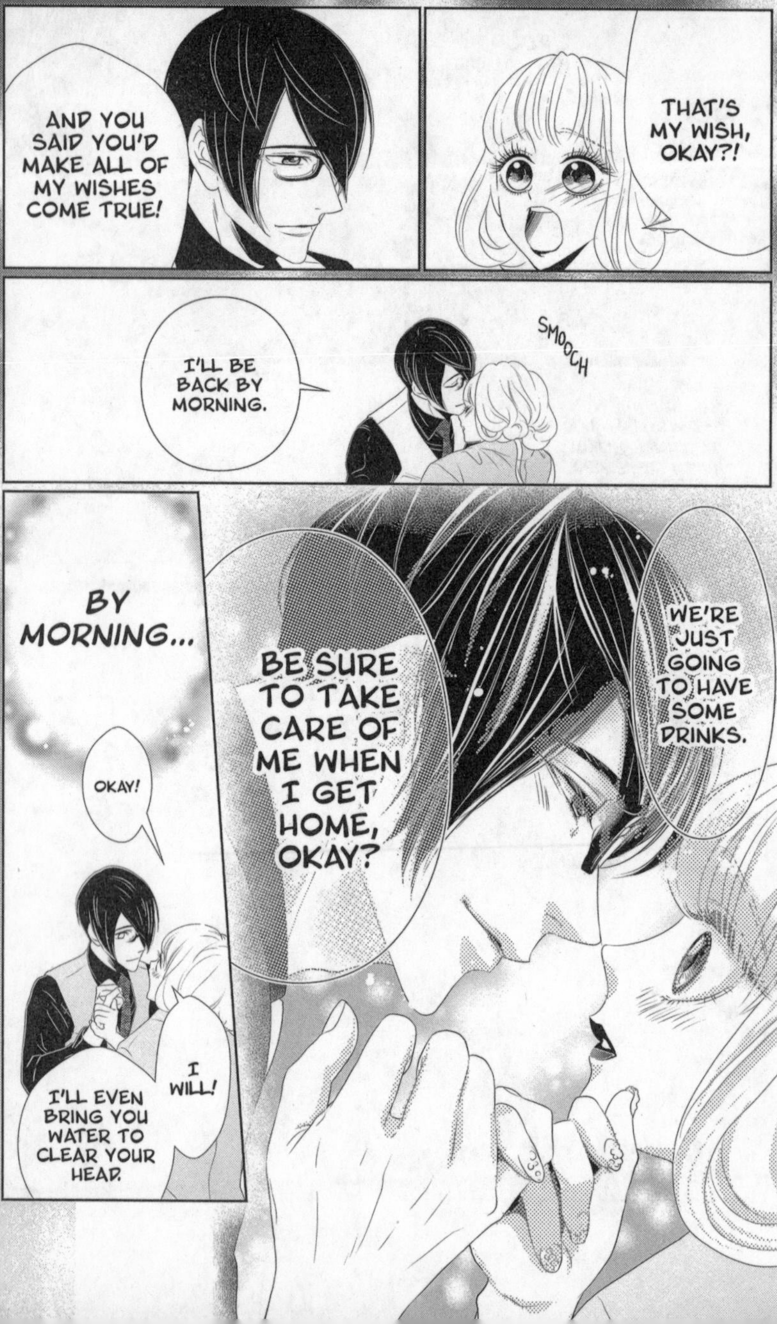

THAT'S MY WISH, OKAY?!
AND YOU SAID YOU'D MAKE ALL OF MY WISHES COME TRUE!
SMOOCH
I'LL BE BACK BY MORNING.
WE'RE JUST GOING TO HAVE SOME DRINKS.
BE SURE TO TAKE CARE OF ME WHEN I GET HOME, OKAY?
BY MORNING...
OKAY!
I WILL!
I'LL EVEN BRING YOU WATER TO CLEAR YOUR HEAD.

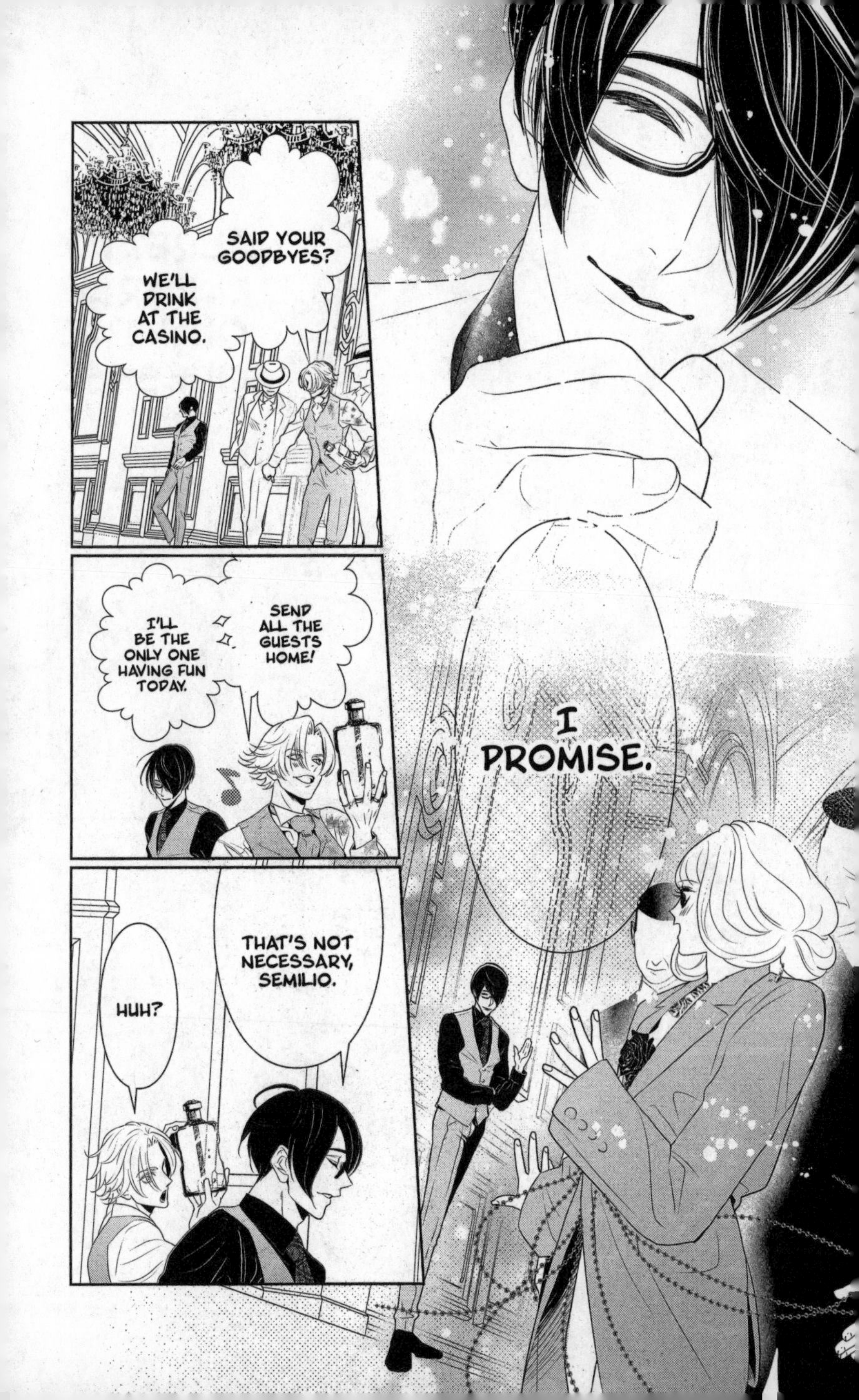
I PROMISE.
SAID YOUR GOODBYES?
WE'LL DRINK AT THE CASINO.
SEND ALL THE GUESTS HOME!
I'LL BE THE ONLY ONE HAVING FUN TODAY.
THAT'S NOT NECESSARY, SEMILIO.
HUH?

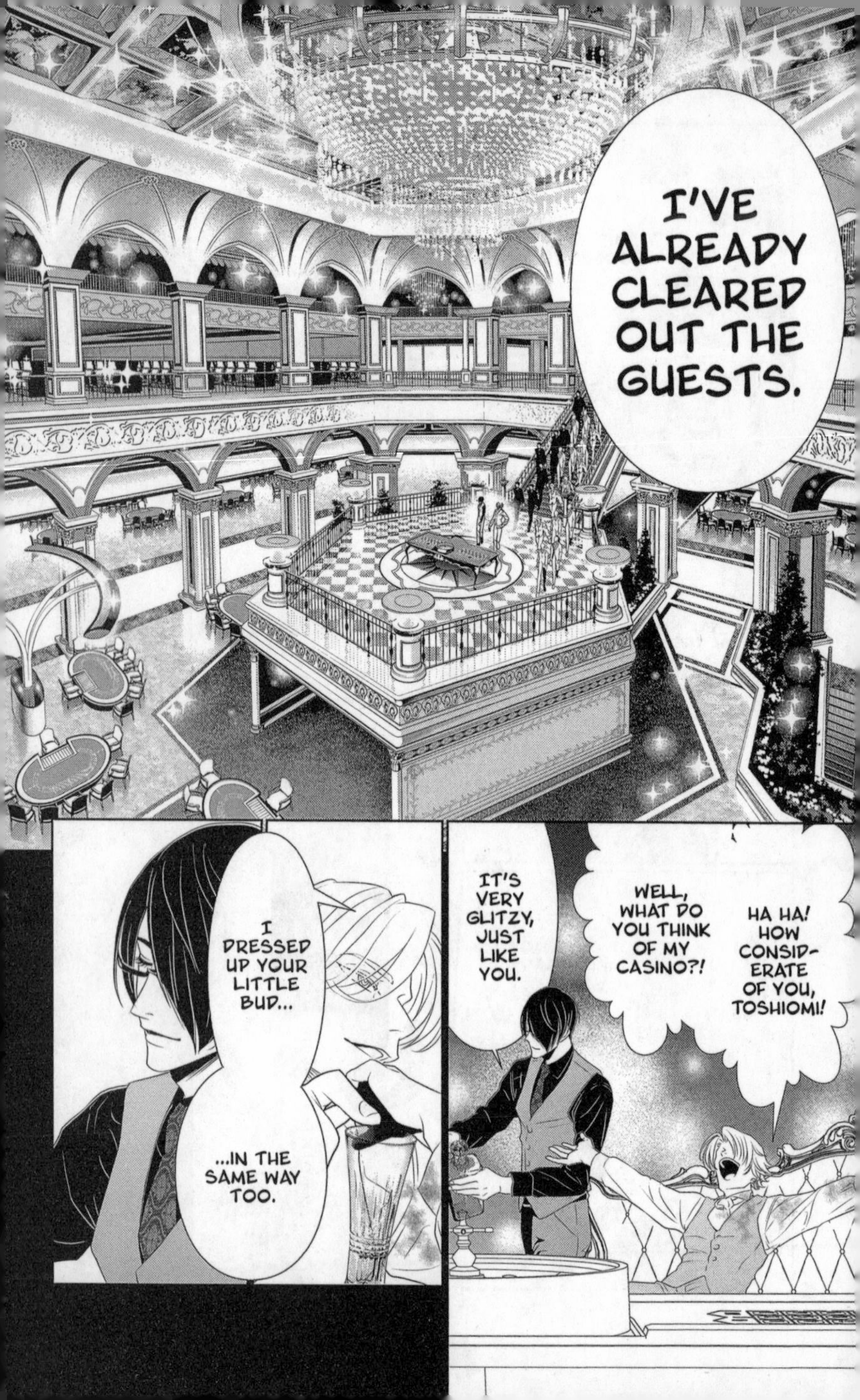
I'VE ALREADY CLEARED OUT THE GUESTS.
HA HA! HOW CONSID-ERATE OF YOU, TOSHIOMI!
WELL, WHAT DO YOU THINK OF MY CASINO?!
IT'S VERY GLITZY, JUST LIKE YOU.
I DRESSED UP YOUR LITTLE BUD...
...IN THE SAME WAY TOO.

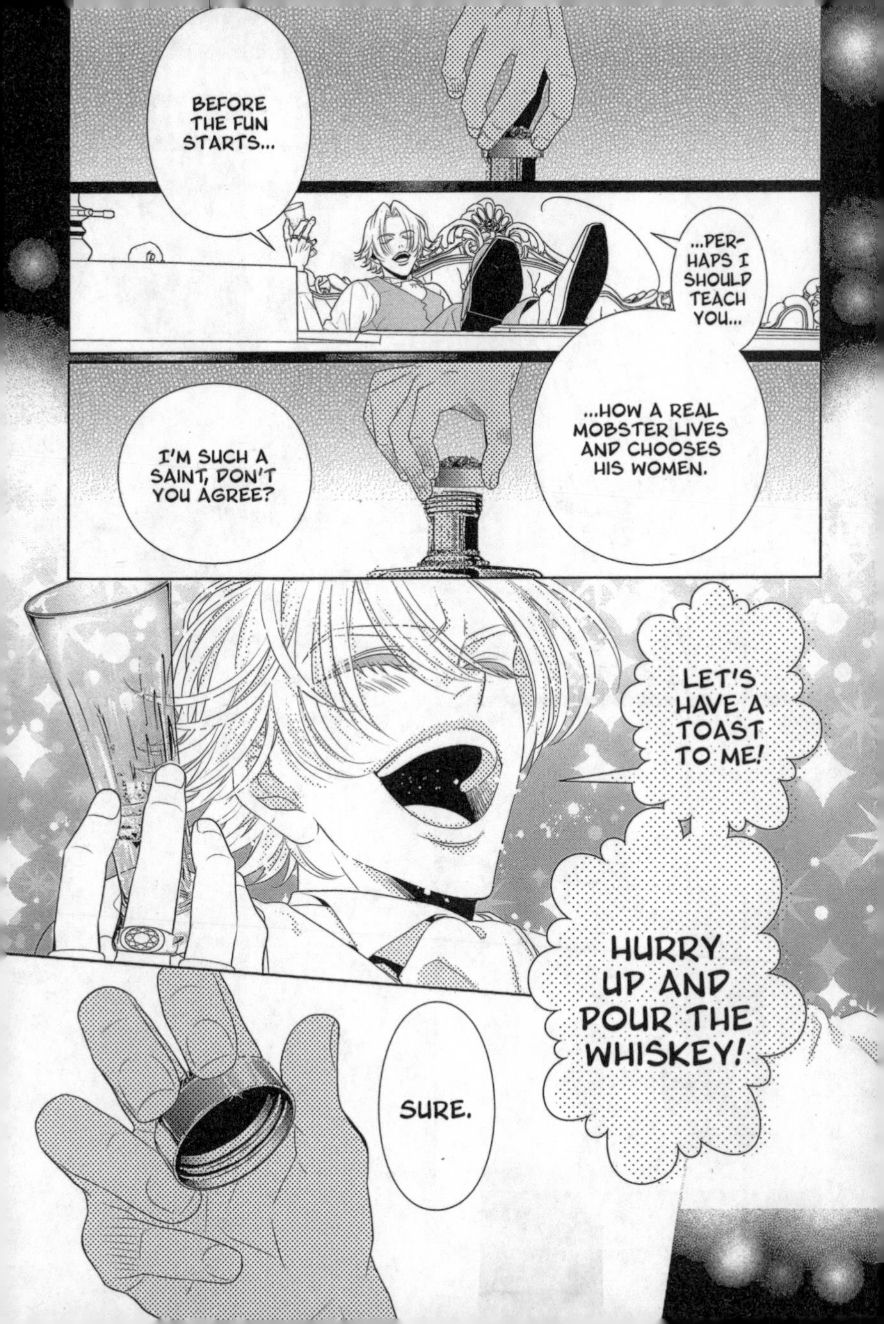
BEFORE THE FUN STARTS...
...PER-HAPS I SHOULD TEACH YOU...
...HOW A REAL MOBSTER LIVES AND CHOOSES HIS WOMEN.
I'M SUCH A SAINT, DON'T YOU AGREE?
LET'S HAVE A TOAST TO ME!
HURRY UP AND POUR THE WHISKEY!
SURE.

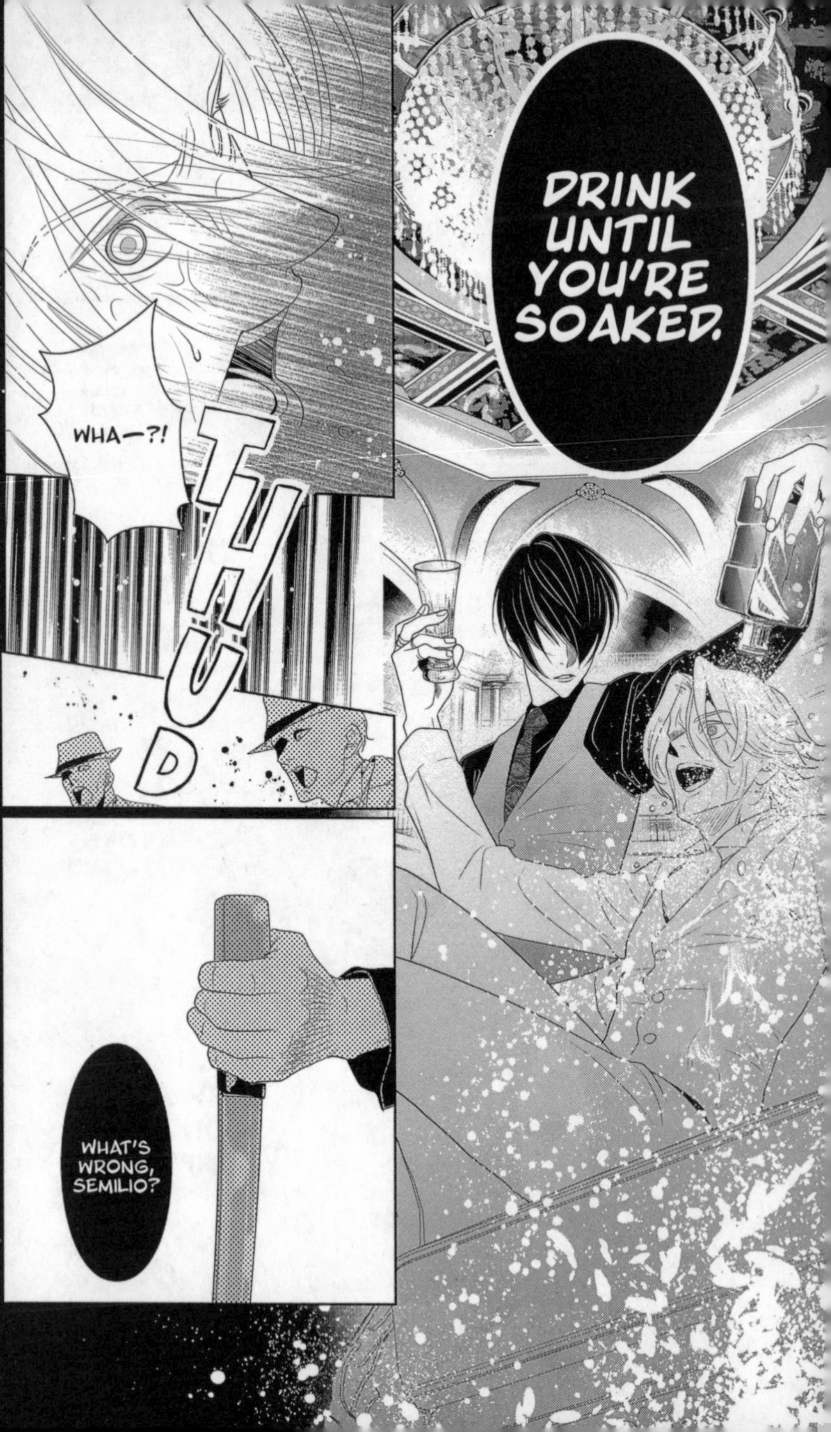
DRINK UNTIL YOU'RE SOAKED.
WHA—?!
THUD
WHAT'S WRONG, SEMILIO?

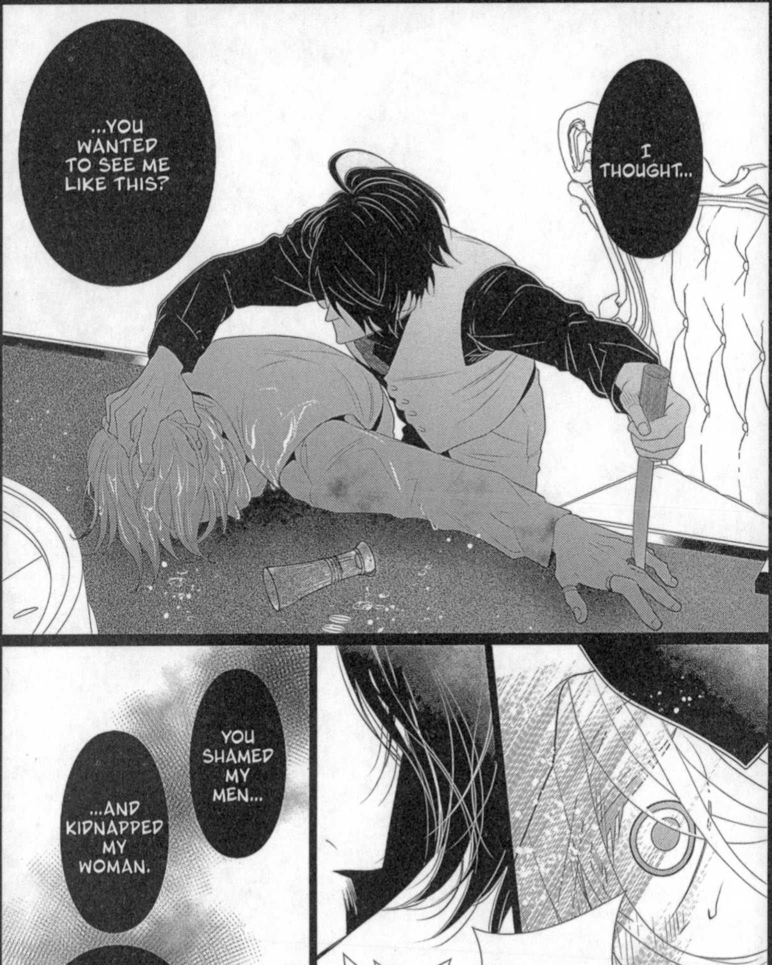
I THOUGHT...
...YOU WANTED TO SEE ME LIKE THIS?
IS THAT WHY...
...YOU SENT YURI HOME WITH A SMILE?
AND HAD MY GUESTS LEAVE TOO?
YOU SHAMED MY MEN...
...AND KIDNAPPED MY WOMAN.
YOU REALLY THOUGHT I'D REACT WITH A SMILE?

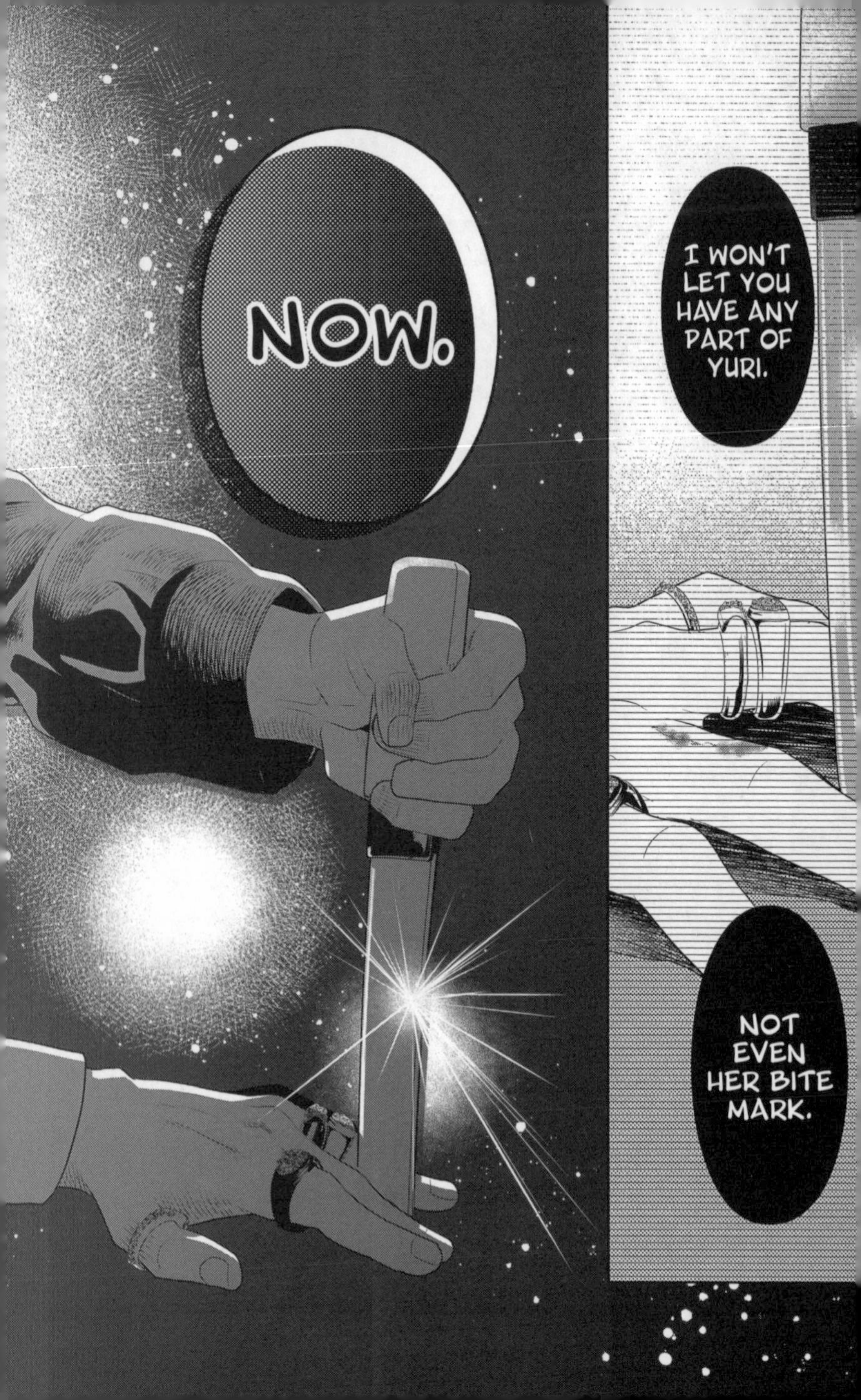
I WON'T LET YOU HAVE ANY PART OF YURI.
NOT EVEN HER BITE MARK.
NOW.

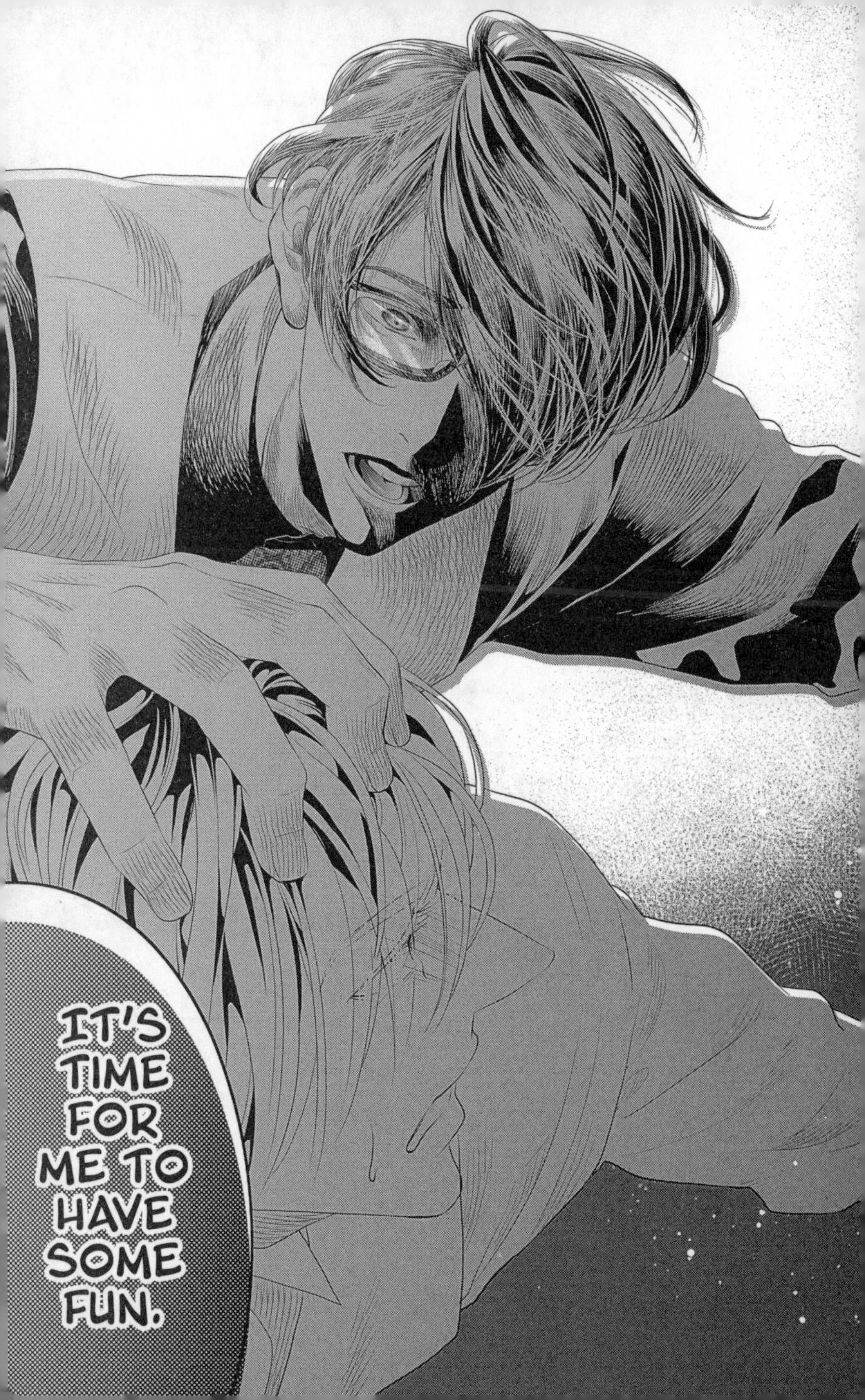
IT'S TIME FOR ME TO HAVE SOME FUN.

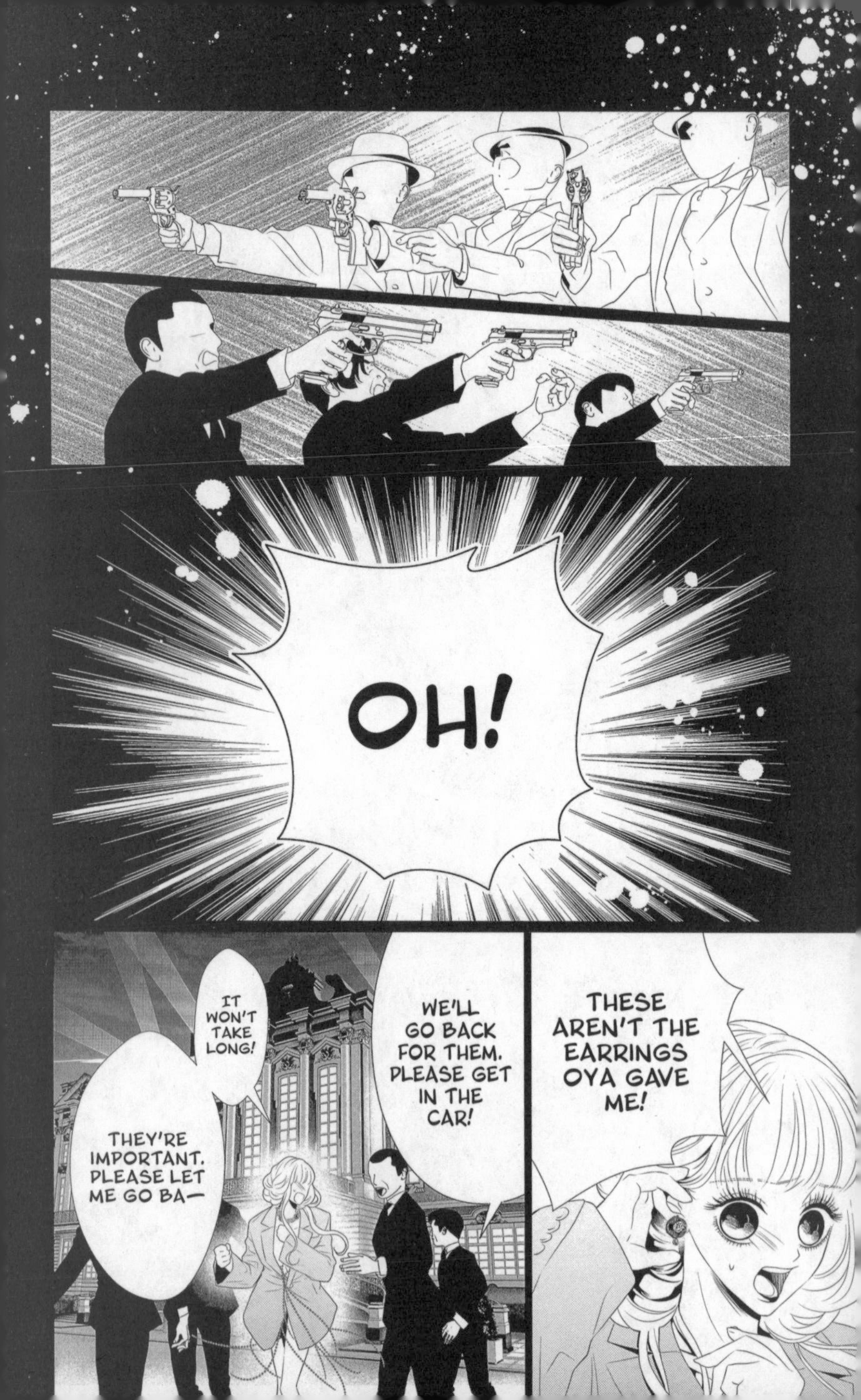
OH!
THESE AREN'T THE EARRINGS OYA GAVE ME!
WE'LL GO BACK FOR THEM. PLEASE GET IN THE CAR!
IT WON'T TAKE LONG!
THEY'RE IMPORTANT. PLEASE LET ME GO BA—

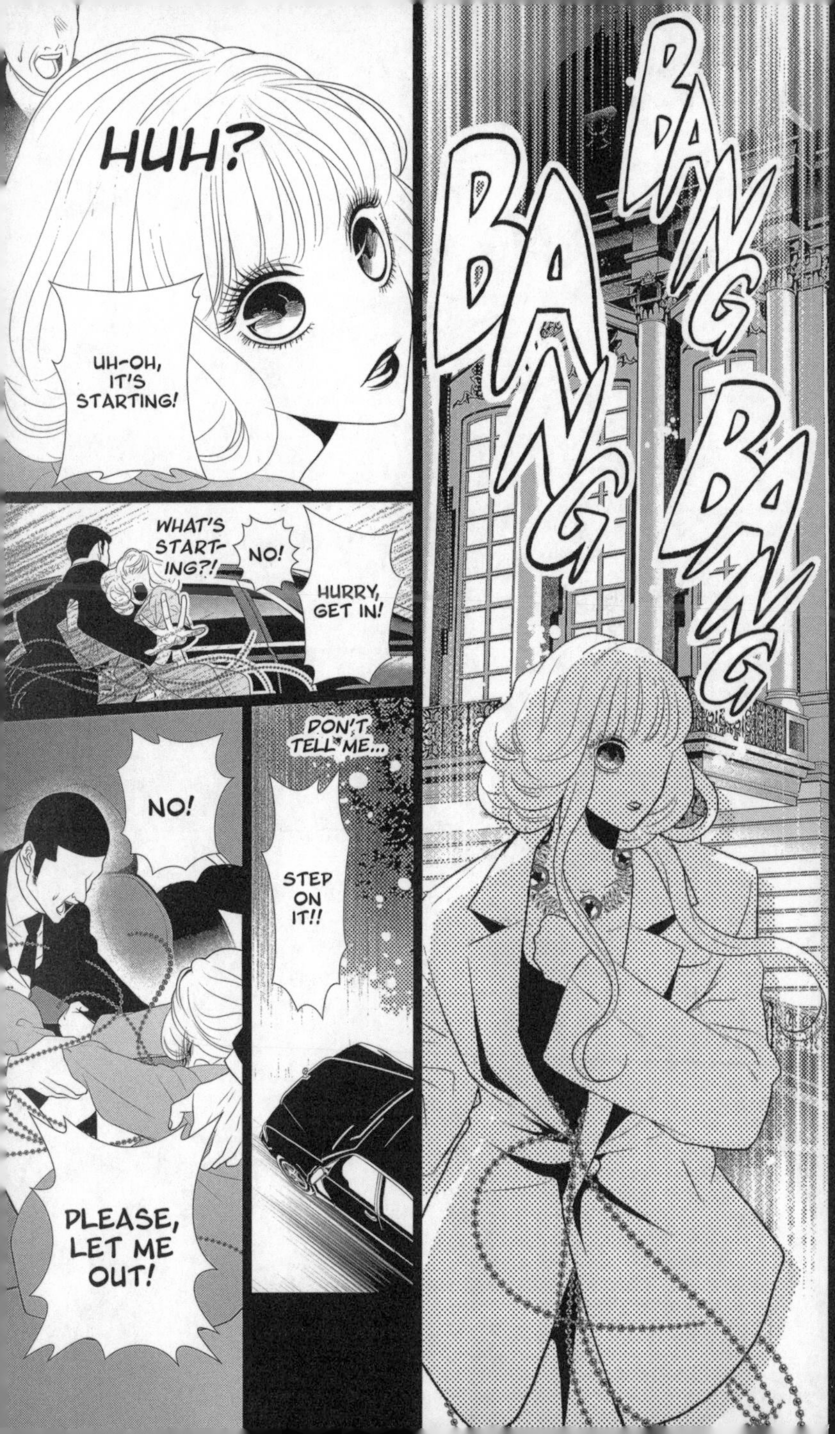
BANG
BANG
BANG
BANG
HUH?
UH-OH, IT'S STARTING!
HURRY, GET IN!
NO!
WHAT'S STARTING?!
DON'T TELL ME...
STEP ON IT!!
NO!
PLEASE, LET ME OUT!

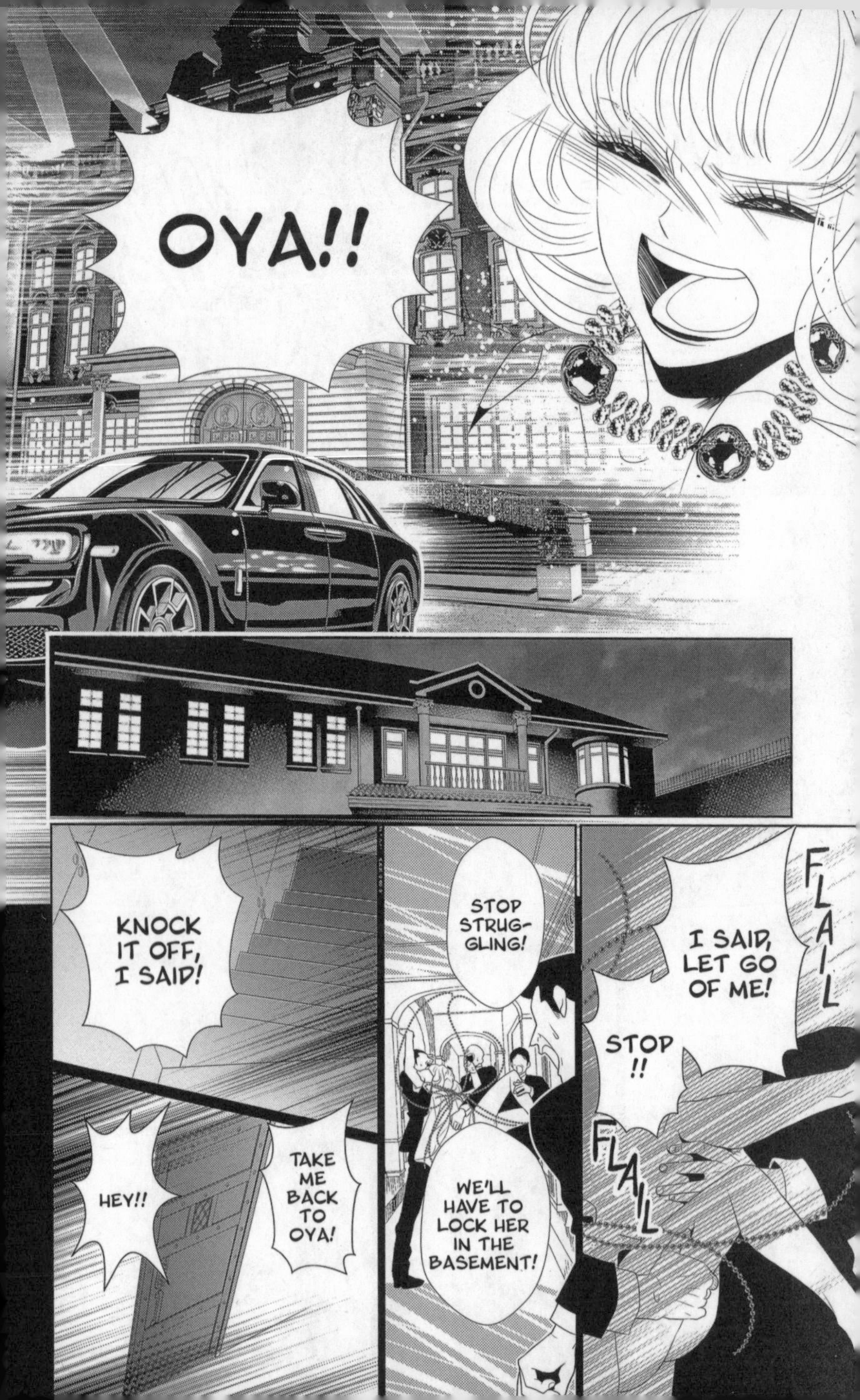
OYA!!
I SAID, LET GO OF ME!
FLAIL
STOP !!
FLAIL
STOP STRUG-GLING!
WE'LL HAVE TO LOCK HER IN THE BASEMENT!
KNOCK IT OFF, I SAID!
TAKE ME BACK TO OYA!
HEY!!

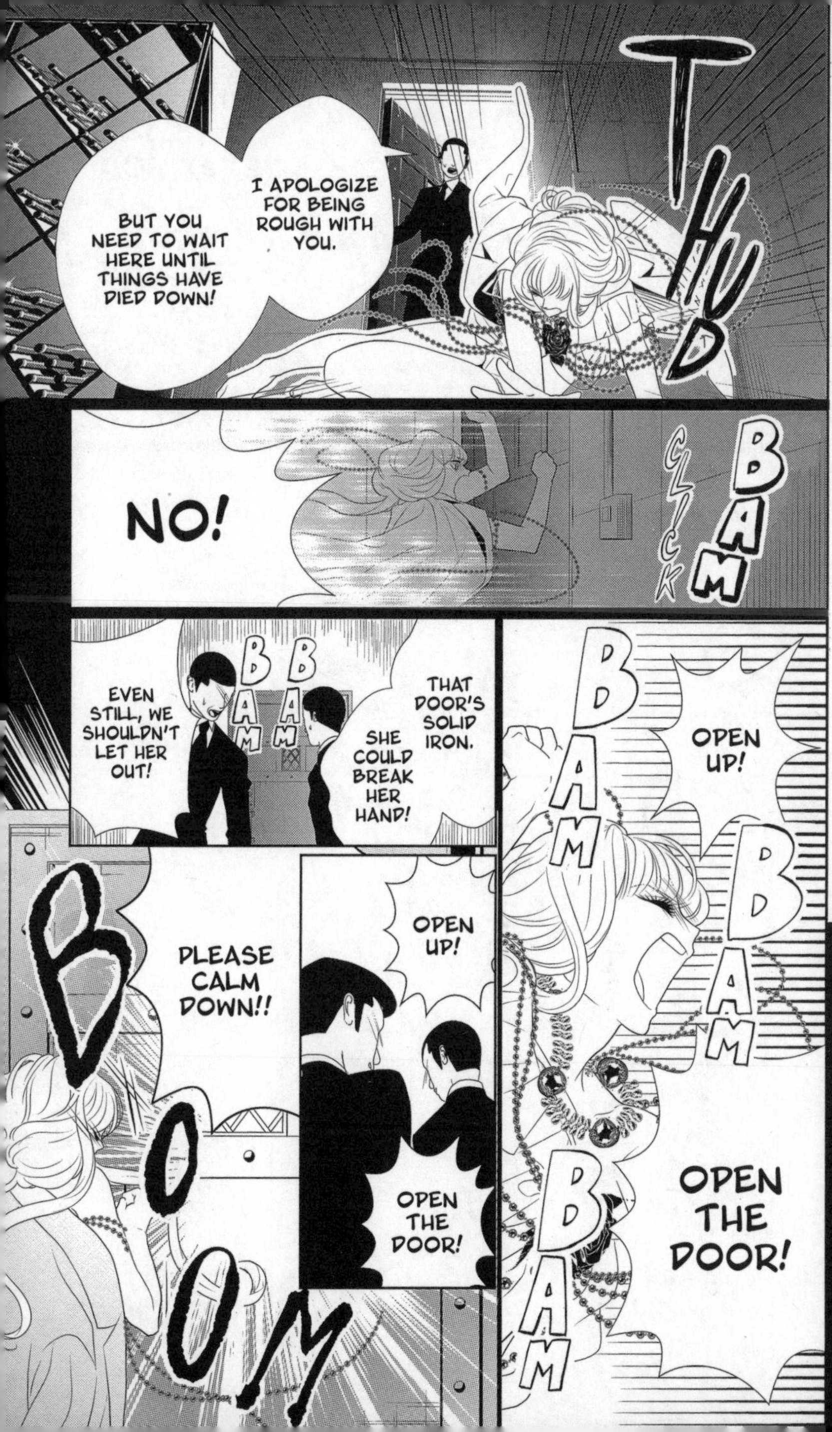
THUD
I APOLOGIZE FOR BEING ROUGH WITH YOU.
BUT YOU NEED TO WAIT HERE UNTIL THINGS HAVE DIED DOWN!
BAM
CLICK
NO!
BAM
OPEN UP!
BAM
BAM
OPEN THE DOOR!
BAM
BAM
THAT DOOR'S SOLID IRON.
SHE COULD BREAK HER HAND!
EVEN STILL, WE SHOULDN'T LET HER OUT!
OPEN UP!
OPEN THE DOOR!
BOOM
PLEASE CALM DOWN!!

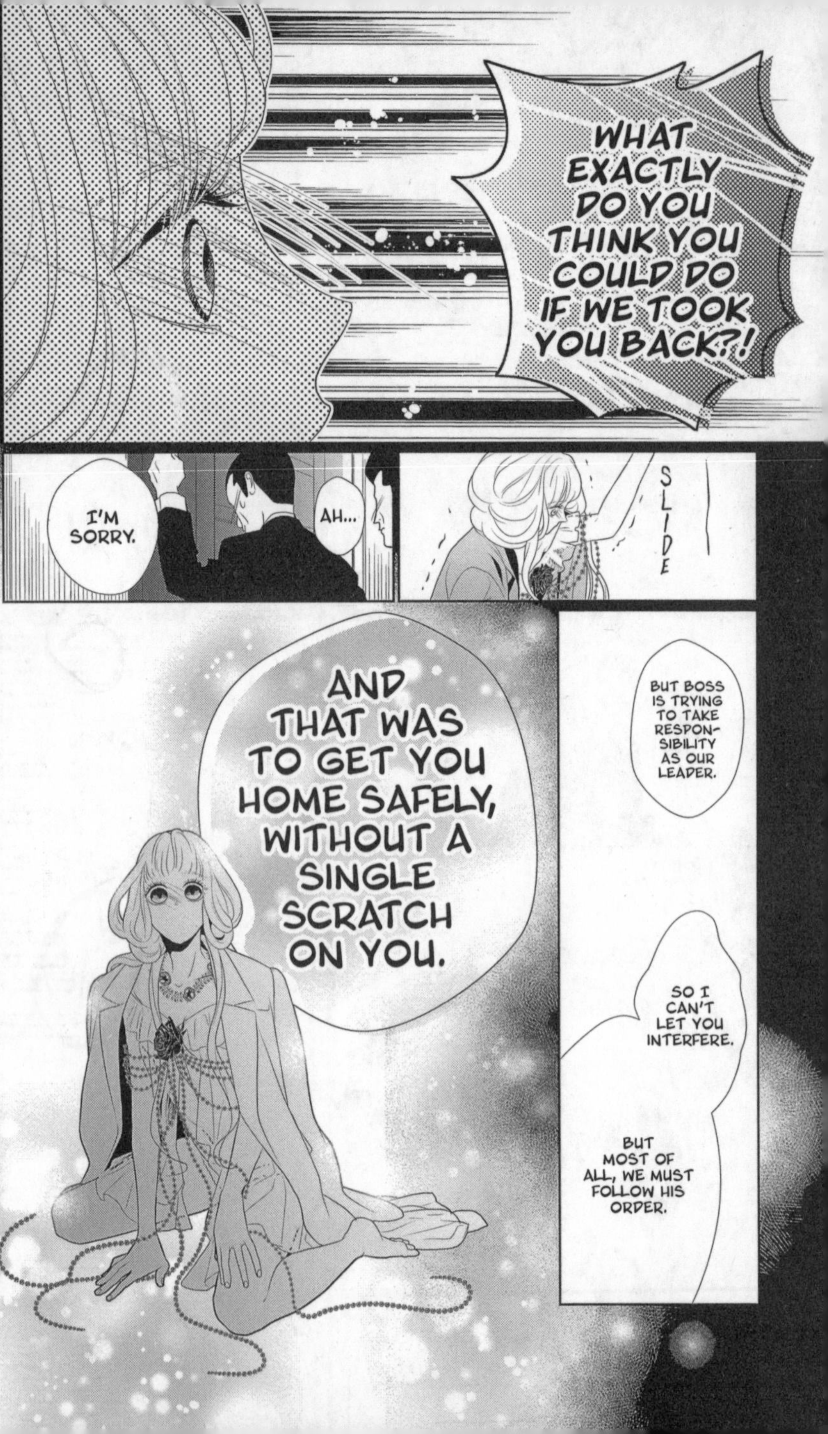
WHAT EXACTLY DO YOU THINK YOU COULD DO IF WE TOOK YOU BACK?!
SLIDE
AH...
I'M SORRY.
BUT BOSS IS TRYING TO TAKE RESPONSIBILITY AS OUR LEADER.
SO I CAN'T LET YOU INTERFERE.
BUT MOST OF ALL, WE MUST FOLLOW HIS ORDER.
AND THAT WAS TO GET YOU HOME SAFELY, WITHOUT A SINGLE SCRATCH ON YOU.

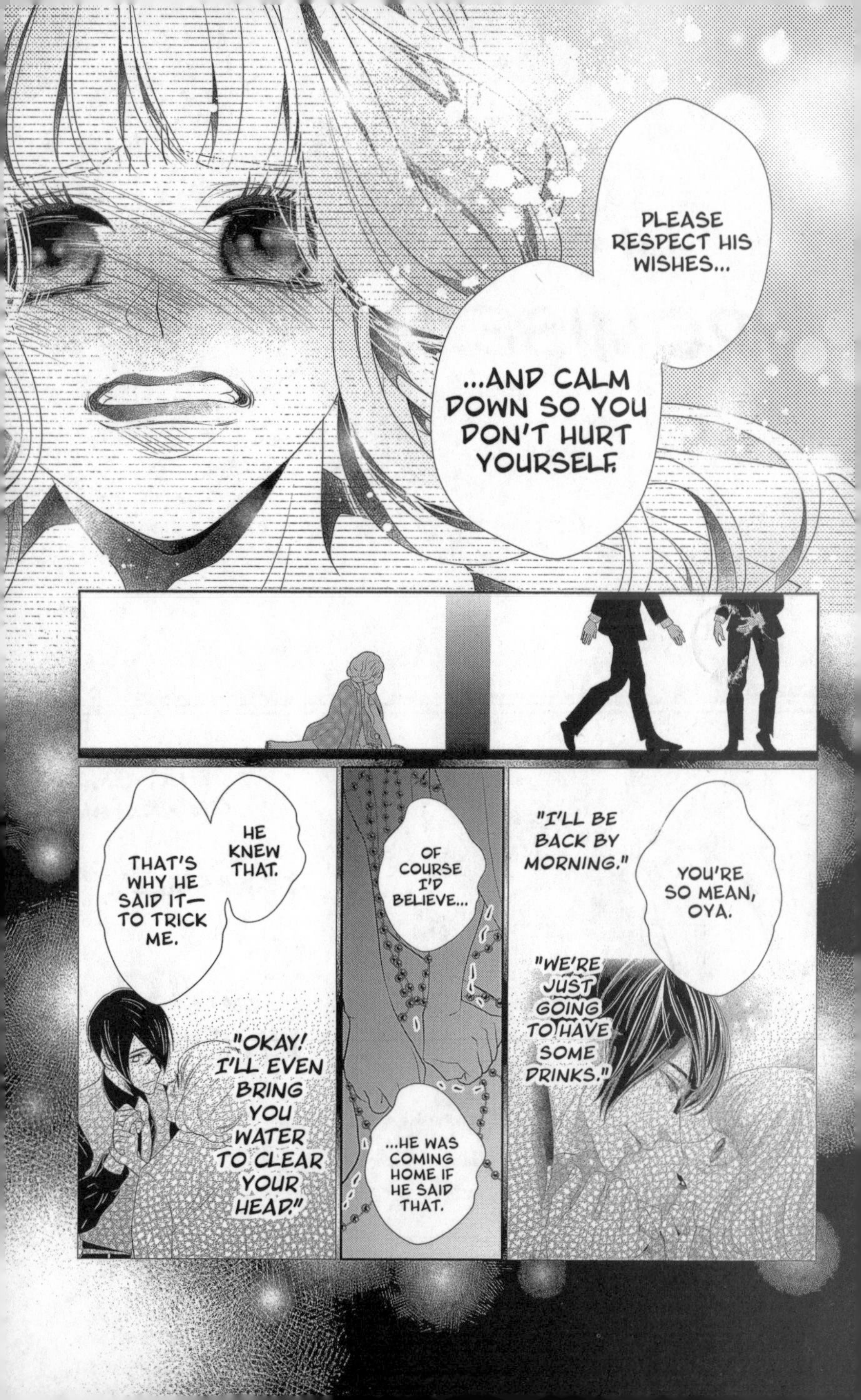
PLEASE RESPECT HIS WISHES...
...AND CALM DOWN SO YOU DON'T HURT YOURSELF.
YOU'RE SO MEAN, OYA.
"I'LL BE BACK BY MORNING."
"WE'RE JUST GOING TO HAVE SOME DRINKS."
OF COURSE I'D BELIEVE...
...HE WAS COMING HOME IF HE SAID THAT.
HE KNEW THAT.
THAT'S WHY HE SAID IT—TO TRICK ME.
"OKAY! I'LL EVEN BRING YOU WATER TO CLEAR YOUR HEAD!"

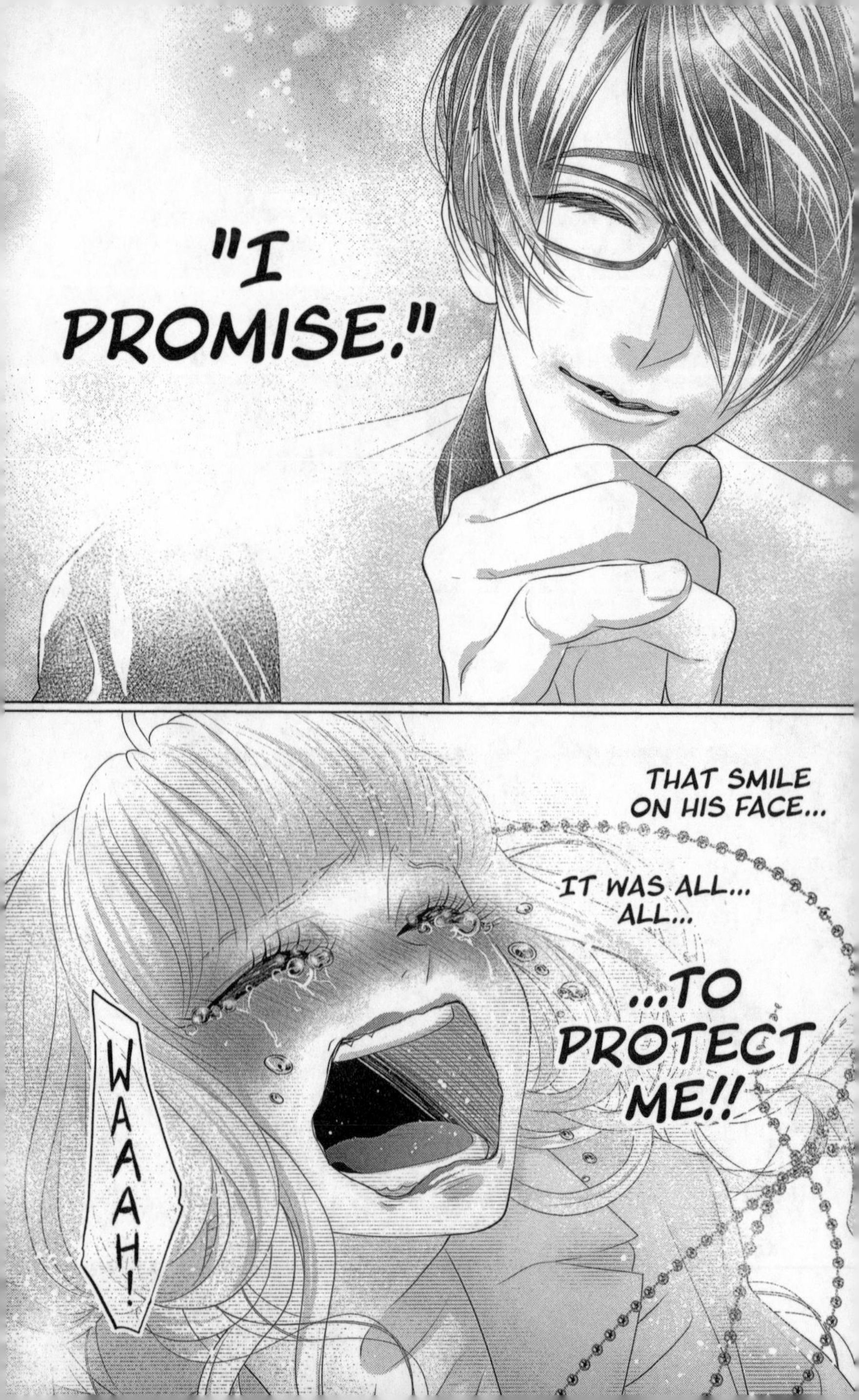
"I PROMISE."
THAT SMILE ON HIS FACE...
IT WAS ALL... ALL...
...TO PROTECT ME!!
WAAAH!

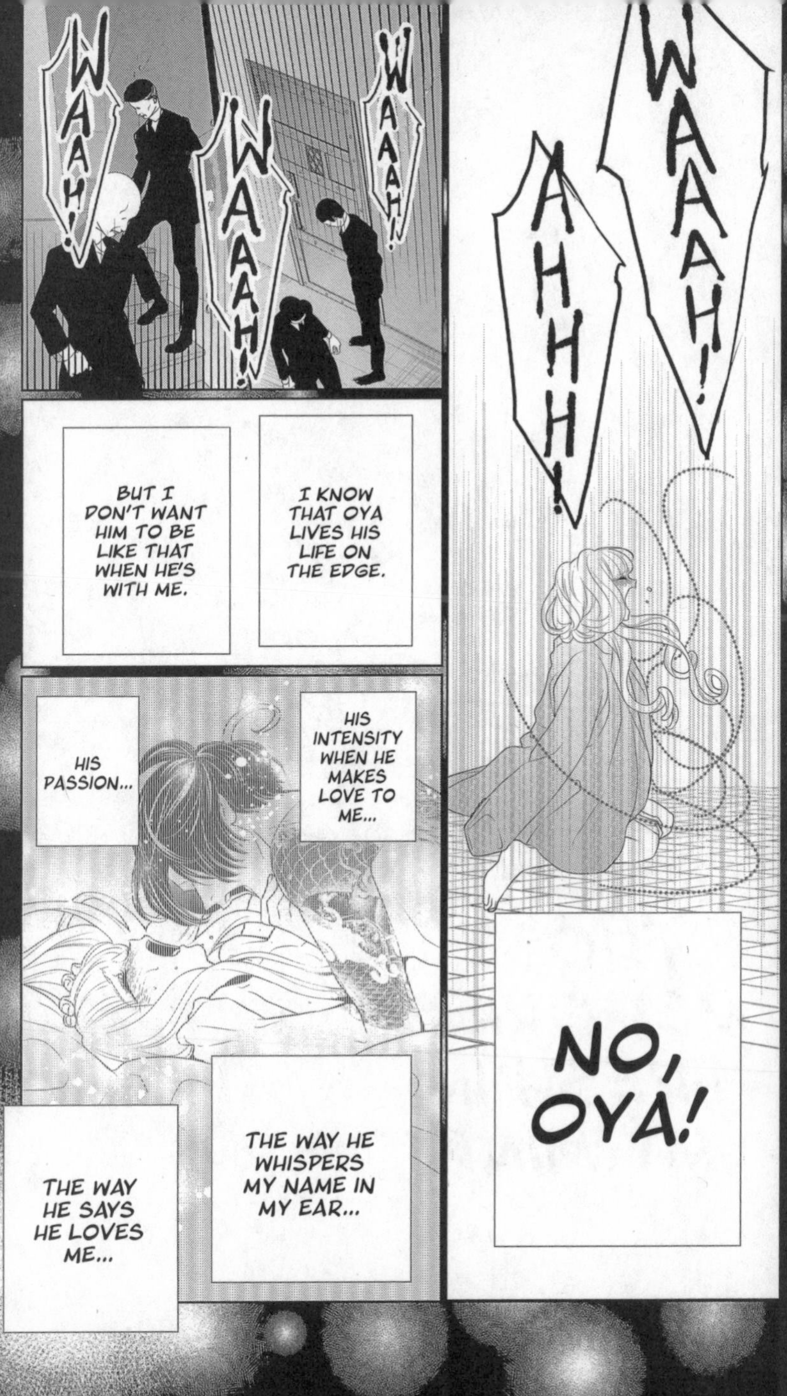
WAAAH!
AHHH!
NO, OYA!
WAAAH!
WAAAH!
WAAH!
I KNOW THAT OYA LIVES HIS LIFE ON THE EDGE.
BUT I DON'T WANT HIM TO BE LIKE THAT WHEN HE'S WITH ME.
HIS INTENSITY WHEN HE MAKES LOVE TO ME...
HIS PASSION...
THE WAY HE WHISPERS MY NAME IN MY EAR...
THE WAY HE SAYS HE LOVES ME...

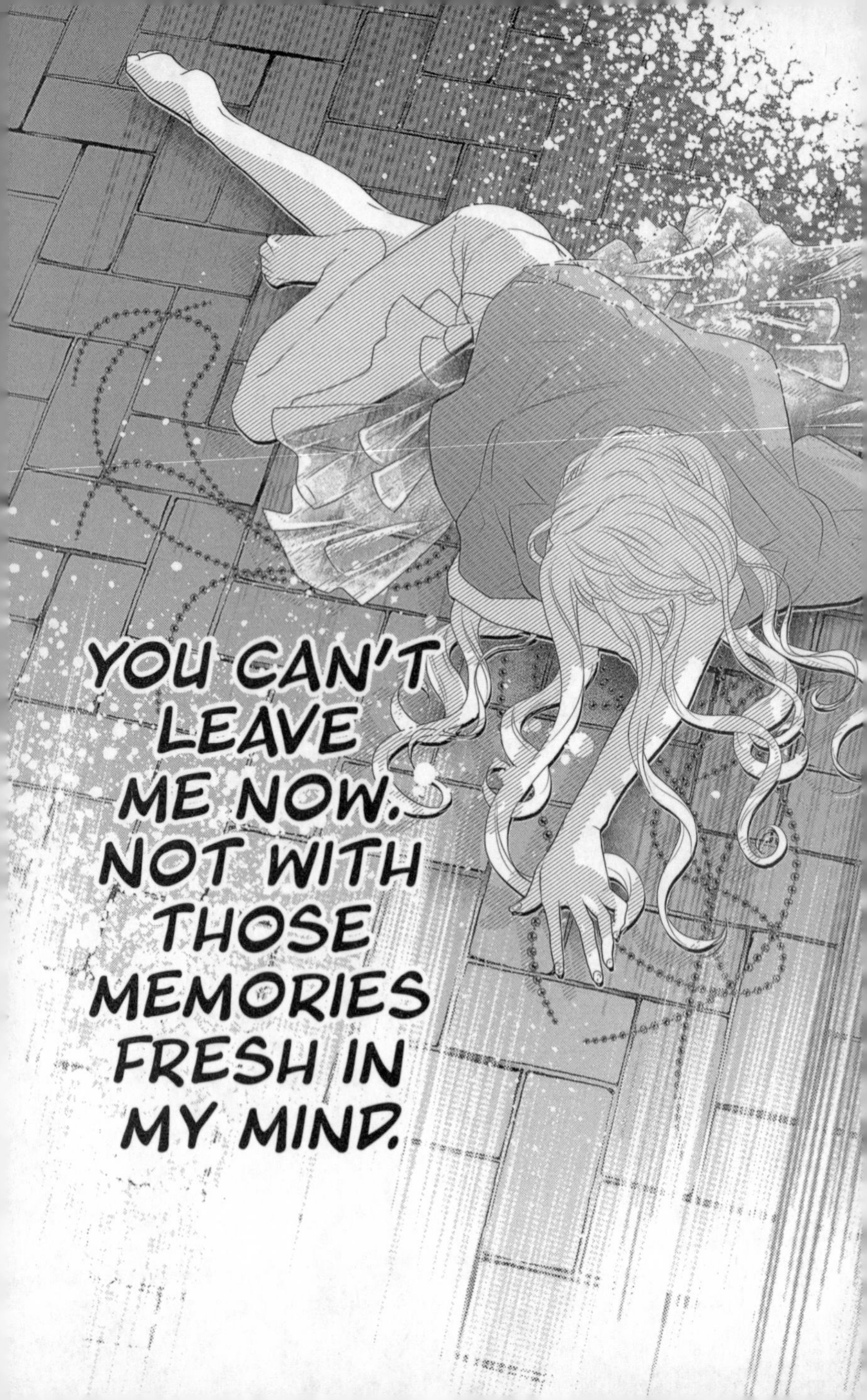
YOU CAN'T LEAVE ME NOW. NOT WITH THOSE MEMORIES FRESH IN MY MIND.

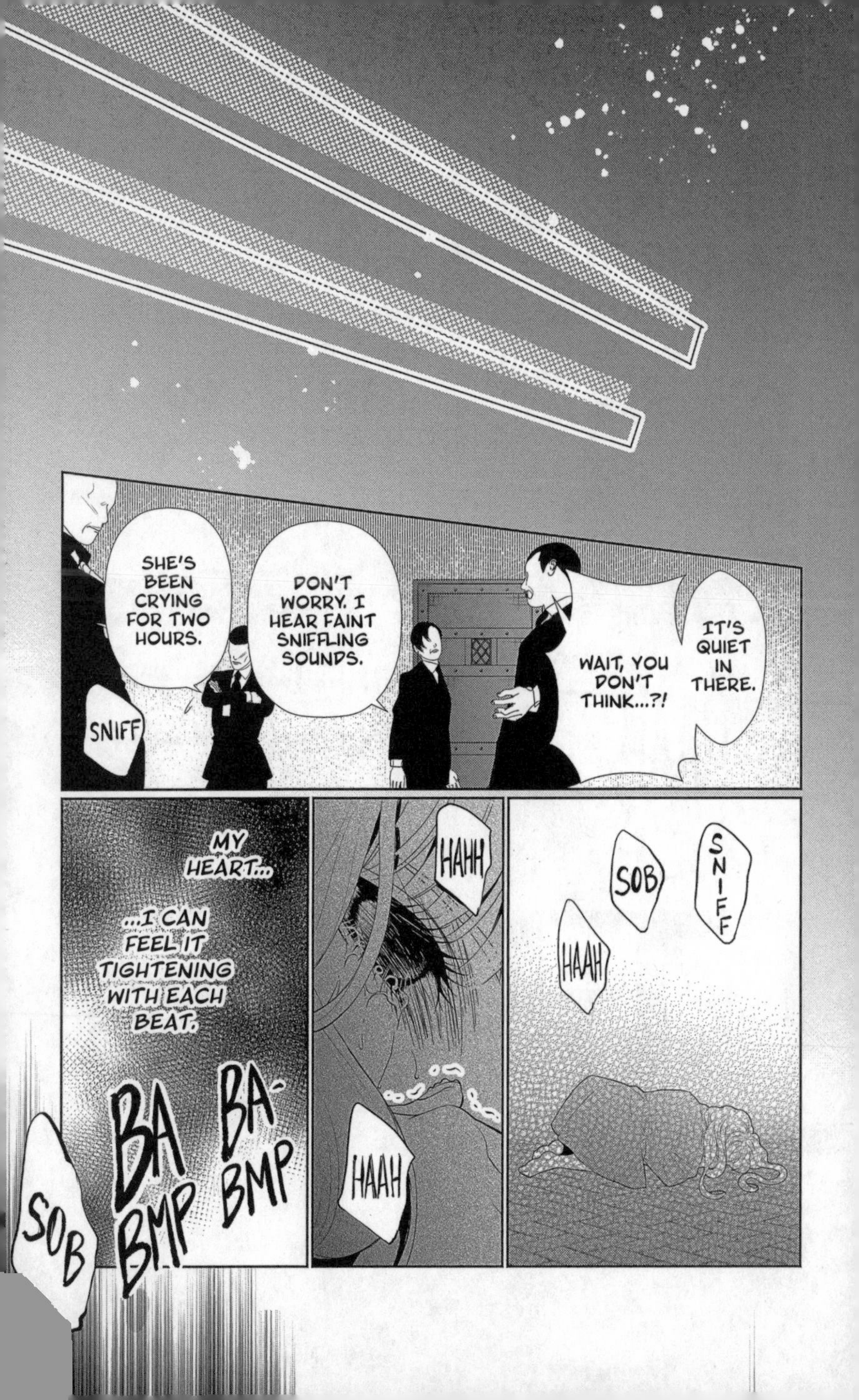
IT'S QUIET IN THERE.
WAIT, YOU DON'T THINK...?!
DON'T WORRY. I HEAR FAINT SNIFFLING SOUNDS.
SHE'S BEEN CRYING FOR TWO HOURS.
SNIFF
SNIFF
SOB
HAAH
HAHH
HAAH
MY HEART...
...I CAN FEEL IT TIGHTENING WITH EACH BEAT.
BA-BMP
BA-BMP
SOB

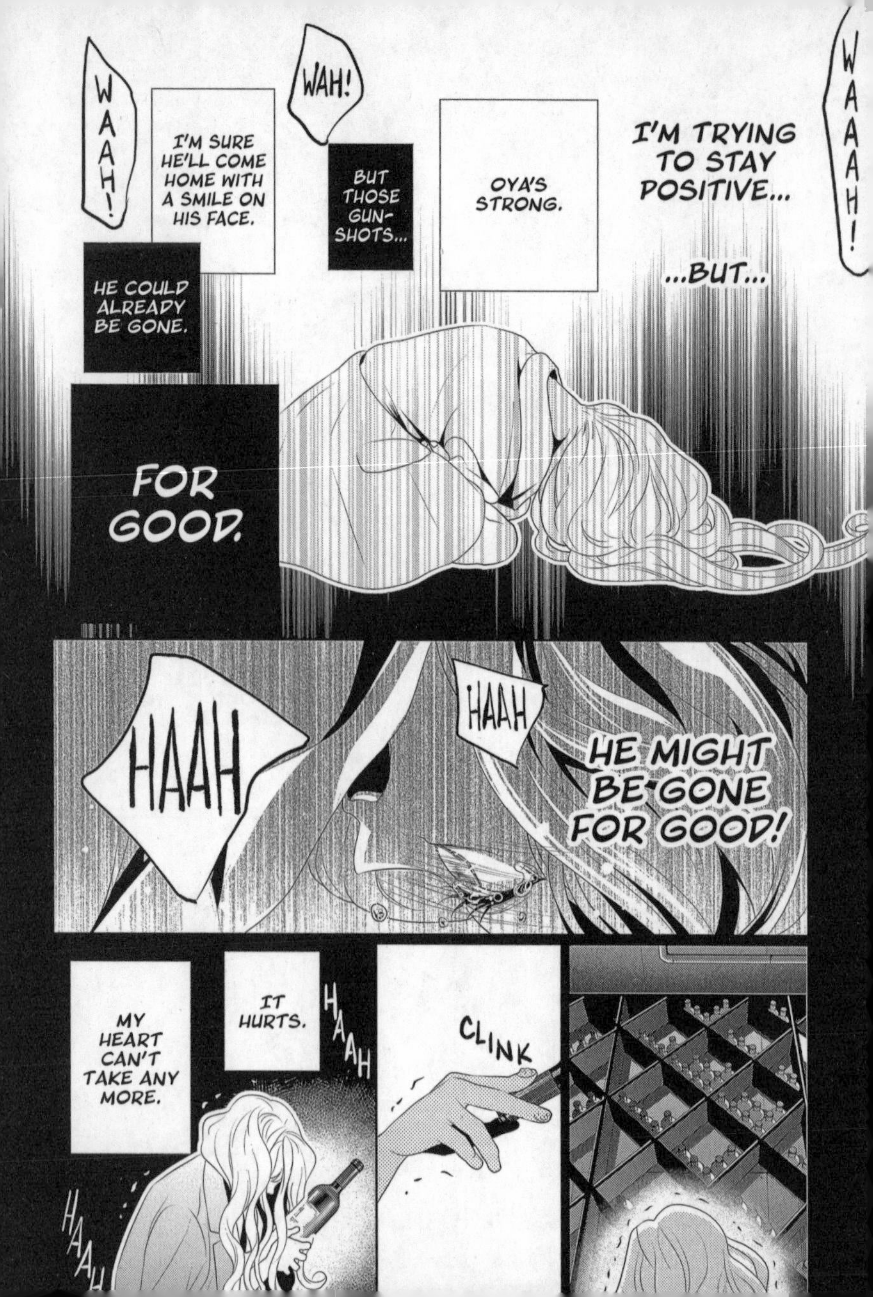
WAAAAH!
I'M TRYING TO STAY POSITIVE...
...BUT...
OYA'S STRONG.
WAH!
BUT THOSE GUN-SHOTS...
I'M SURE HE'LL COME HOME WITH A SMILE ON HIS FACE.
WAAAH!
HE COULD ALREADY BE GONE.
FOR GOOD.
HAAH
HE MIGHT BE GONE FOR GOOD!
HAAH
CLINK
IT HURTS.
HAAAH
MY HEART CAN'T TAKE ANY MORE.
HAAAH

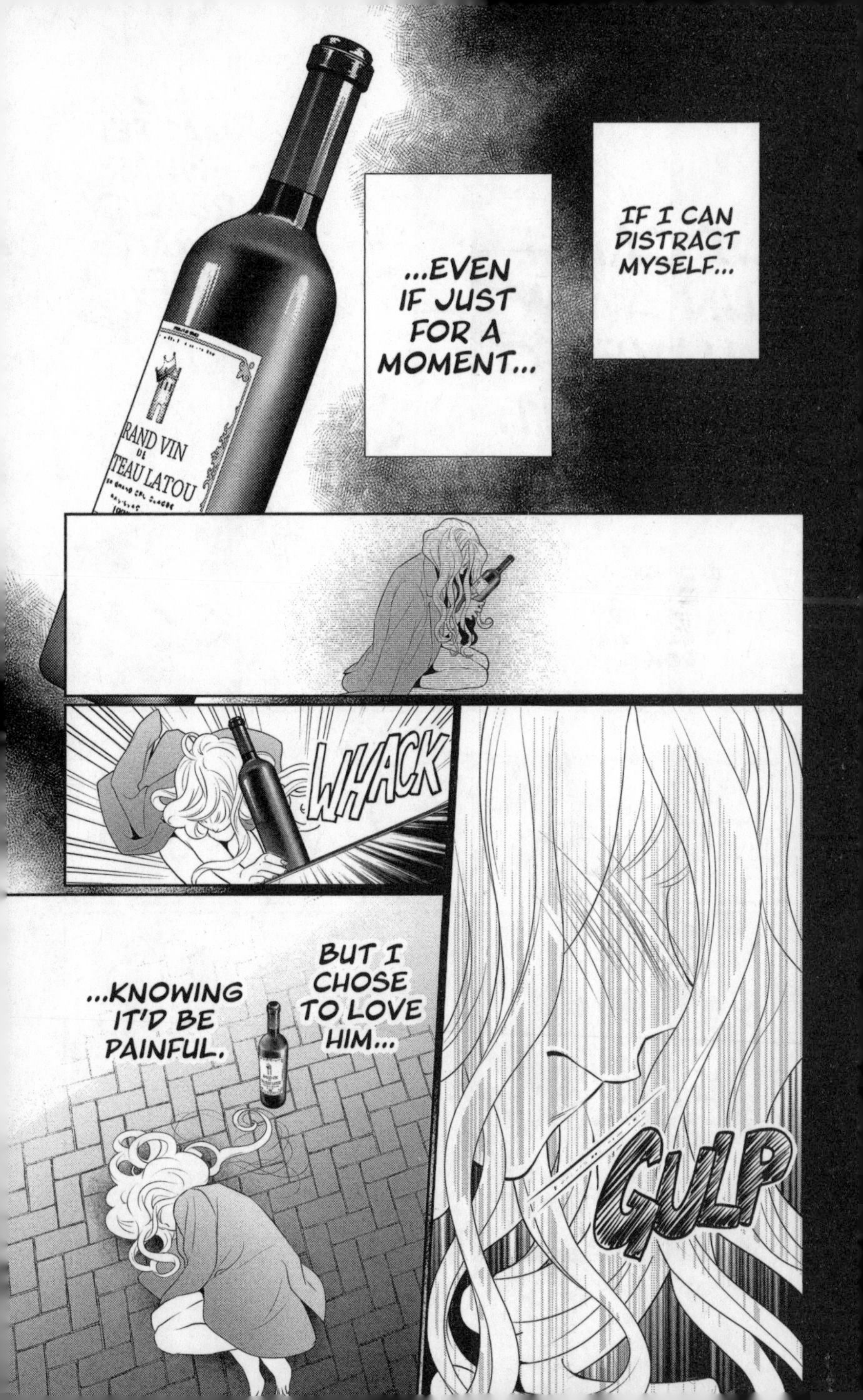
IF I CAN DISTRACT MYSELF...
...EVEN IF JUST FOR A MOMENT...
RAND VIN
TEAU LATOU
GULP
WHACK
BUT I CHOSE TO LOVE HIM...
...KNOWING IT'D BE PAINFUL.

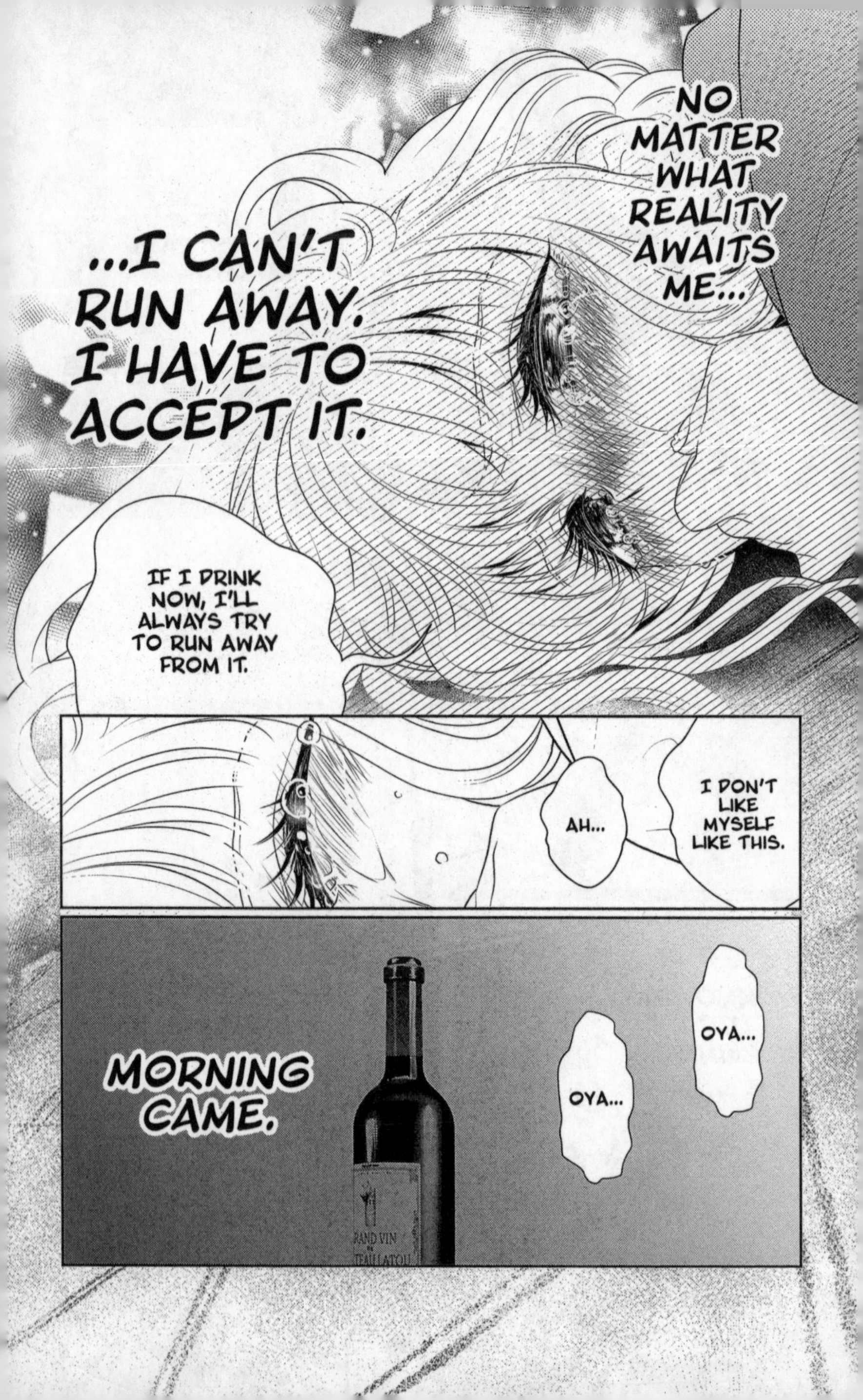
NO MATTER WHAT REALITY AWAITS ME...
...I CAN'T RUN AWAY. I HAVE TO ACCEPT IT.
IF I DRINK NOW, I'LL ALWAYS TRY TO RUN AWAY FROM IT.
I DON'T LIKE MYSELF LIKE THIS.
AH...
OYA...
OYA...
MORNING CAME.

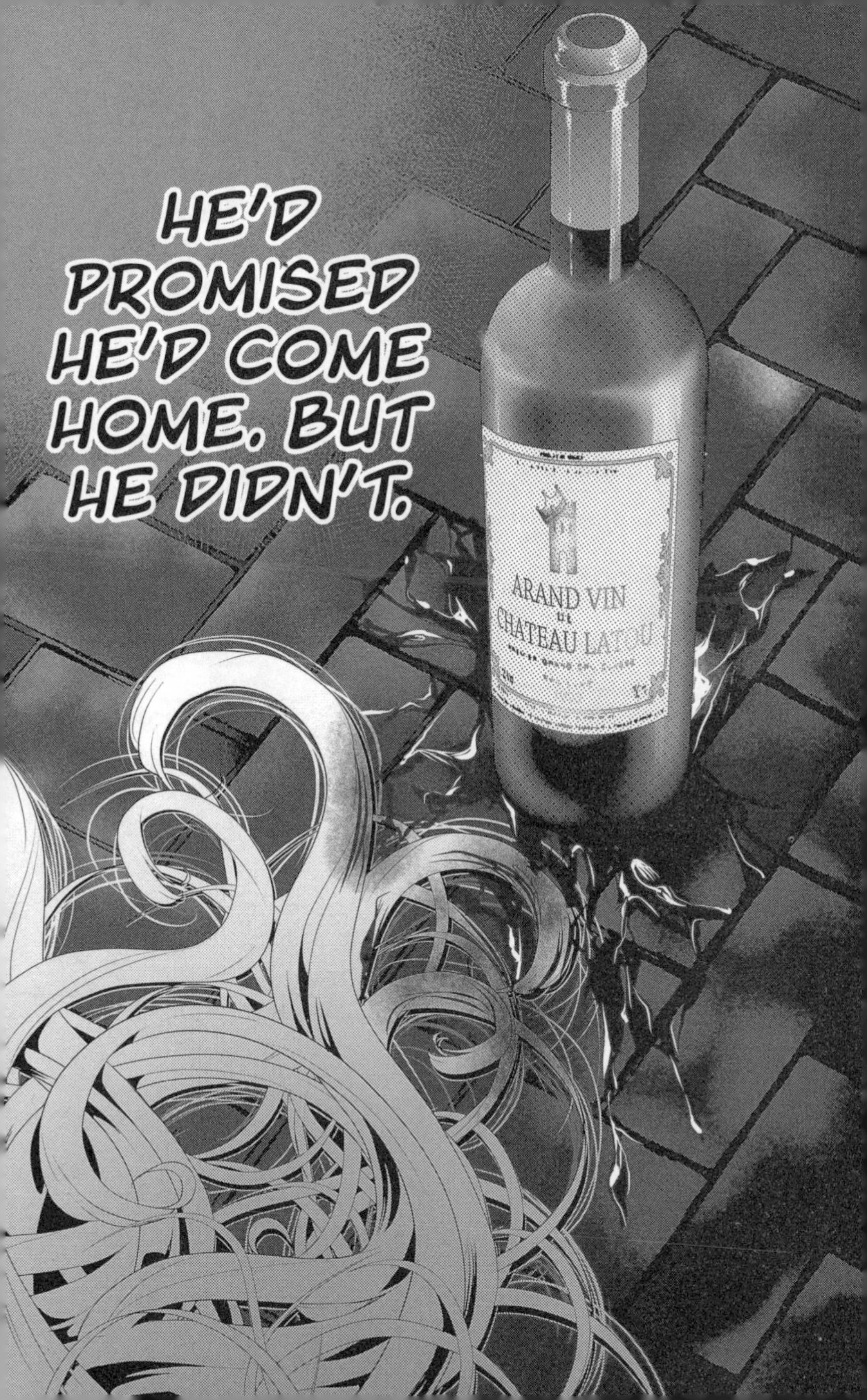
HE'D PROMISED HE'D COME HOME. BUT HE DIDN'T.

bonus illustration: Thinking of You

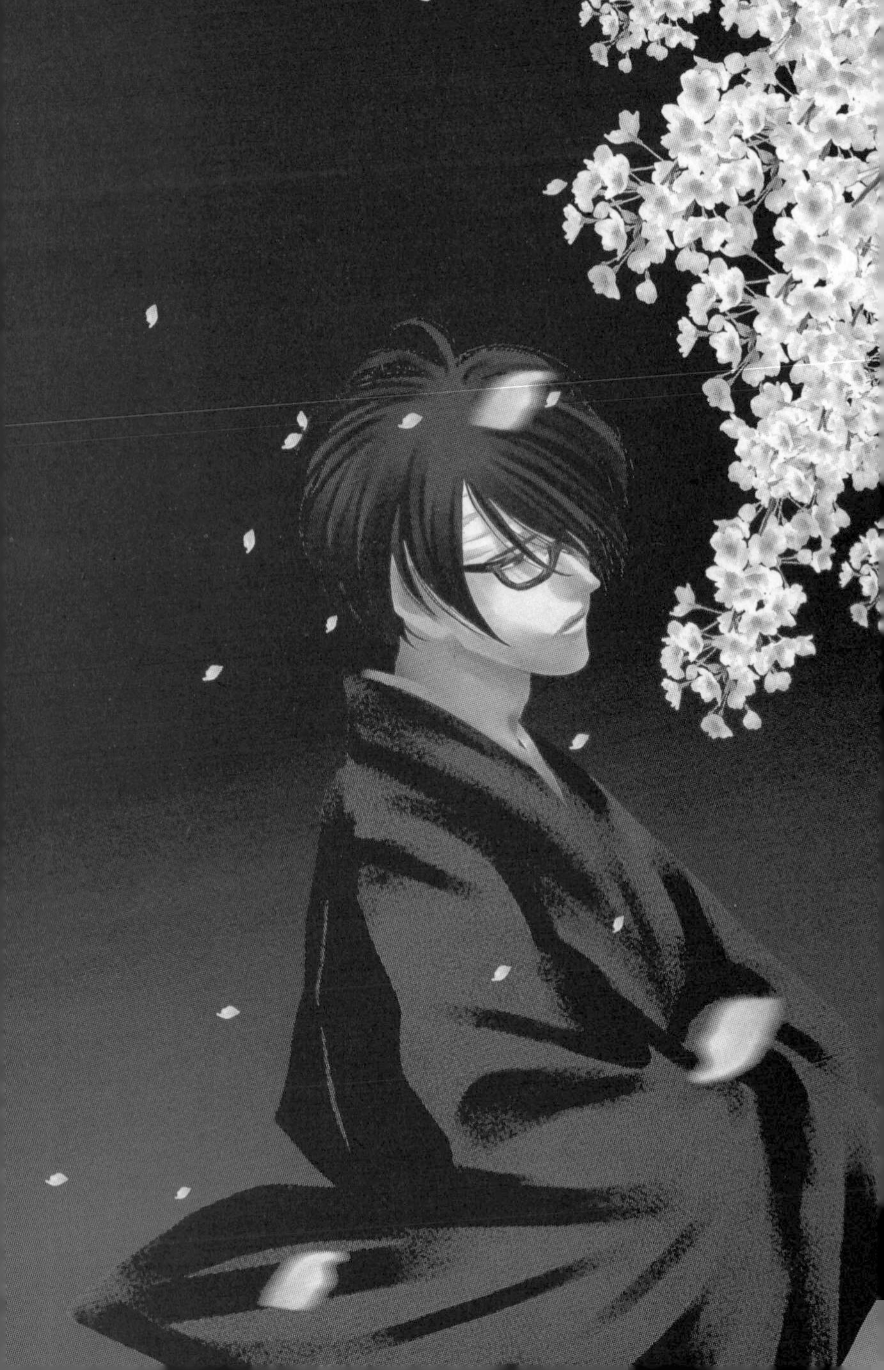

bullet 07

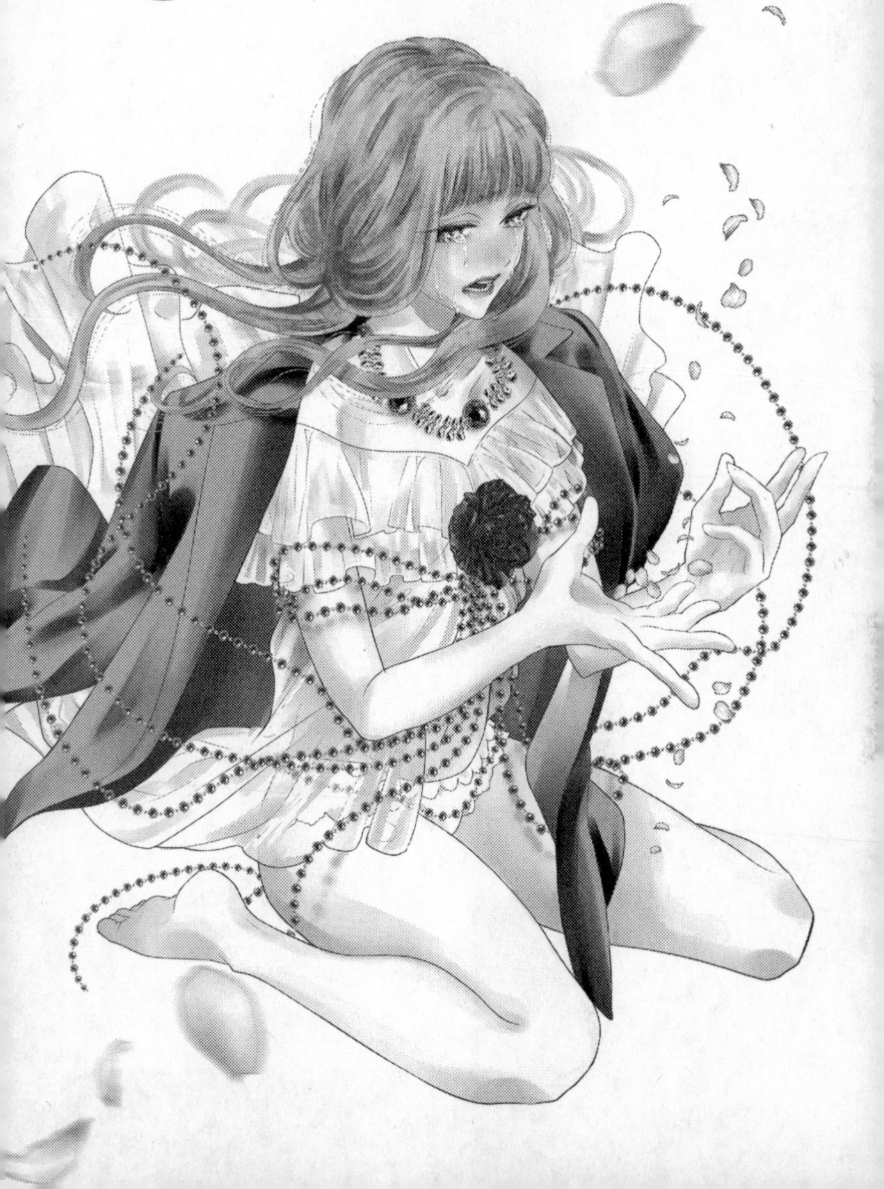

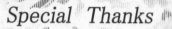

Special Thanks

- MY READERS

- CHEESE! EDITORIAL
  DEPARTMENT

- EDITOR:
  MORIHARA

- DESIGNER:
  ITOU
  (BAYBRIDGE STUDIO)

- EVERYONE AT THE
  PRINT SHOP

- ASSISTANTS:
  ISHIDA, ISHIKURA,
  SAITO, TOYONAGA

- MY FAMILY, FRIENDS
  AND CAT
  ROCK MUSIC AND
  CIGARETTES

- EVERYONE INVOLVED
  IN PUBLISHING THIS
  MANGA

THANK YOU.

—MINO

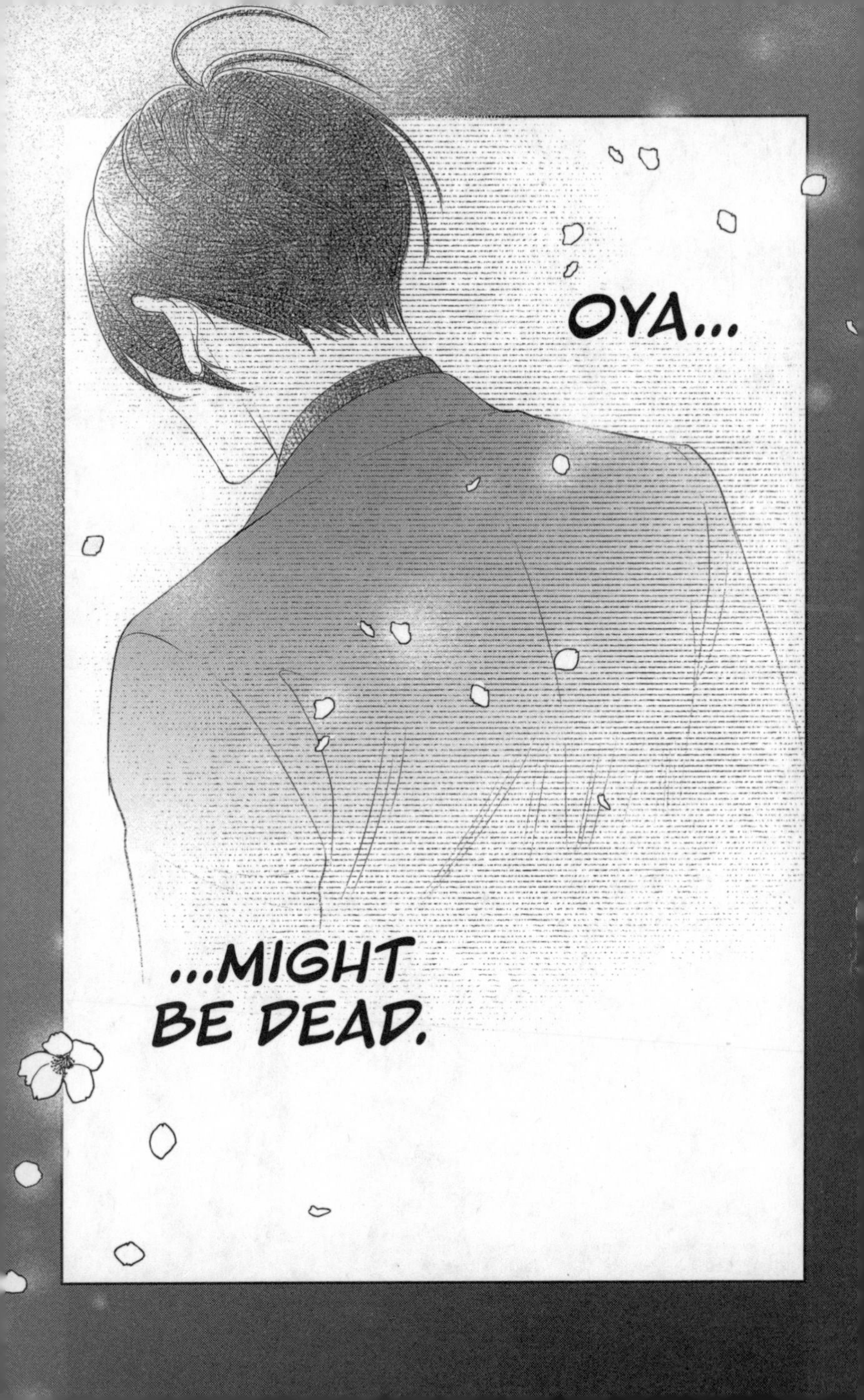
OYA...
...MIGHT BE DEAD.

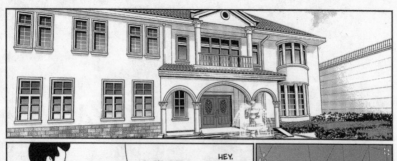

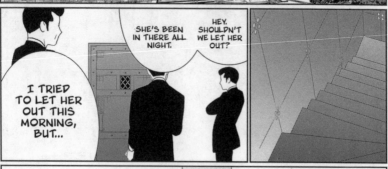

HEY. SHOULDN'T WE LET HER OUT?
SHE'S BEEN IN THERE ALL NIGHT.
I TRIED TO LET HER OUT THIS MORNING, BUT...
"I WANT TO STAY HERE FOR A LITTLE LONGER..."
"I'LL TELL YOU WHEN I'M READY TO COME OUT."

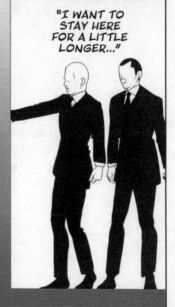

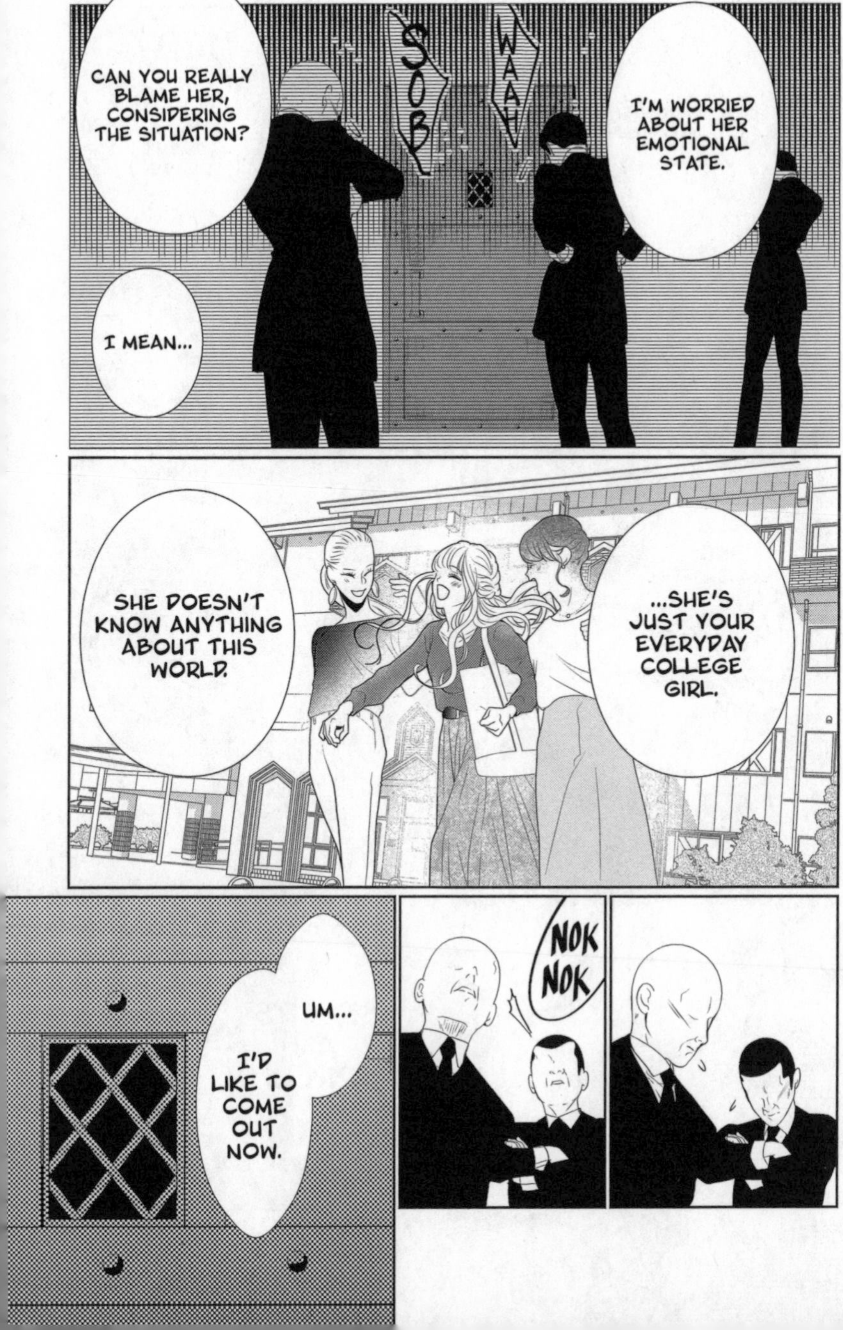
I'M WORRIED ABOUT HER EMOTIONAL STATE.
WAAH
SOB
CAN YOU REALLY BLAME HER, CONSIDERING THE SITUATION?
I MEAN...
...SHE'S JUST YOUR EVERYDAY COLLEGE GIRL.
SHE DOESN'T KNOW ANYTHING ABOUT THIS WORLD.
NOK NOK
UM...
I'D LIKE TO COME OUT NOW.

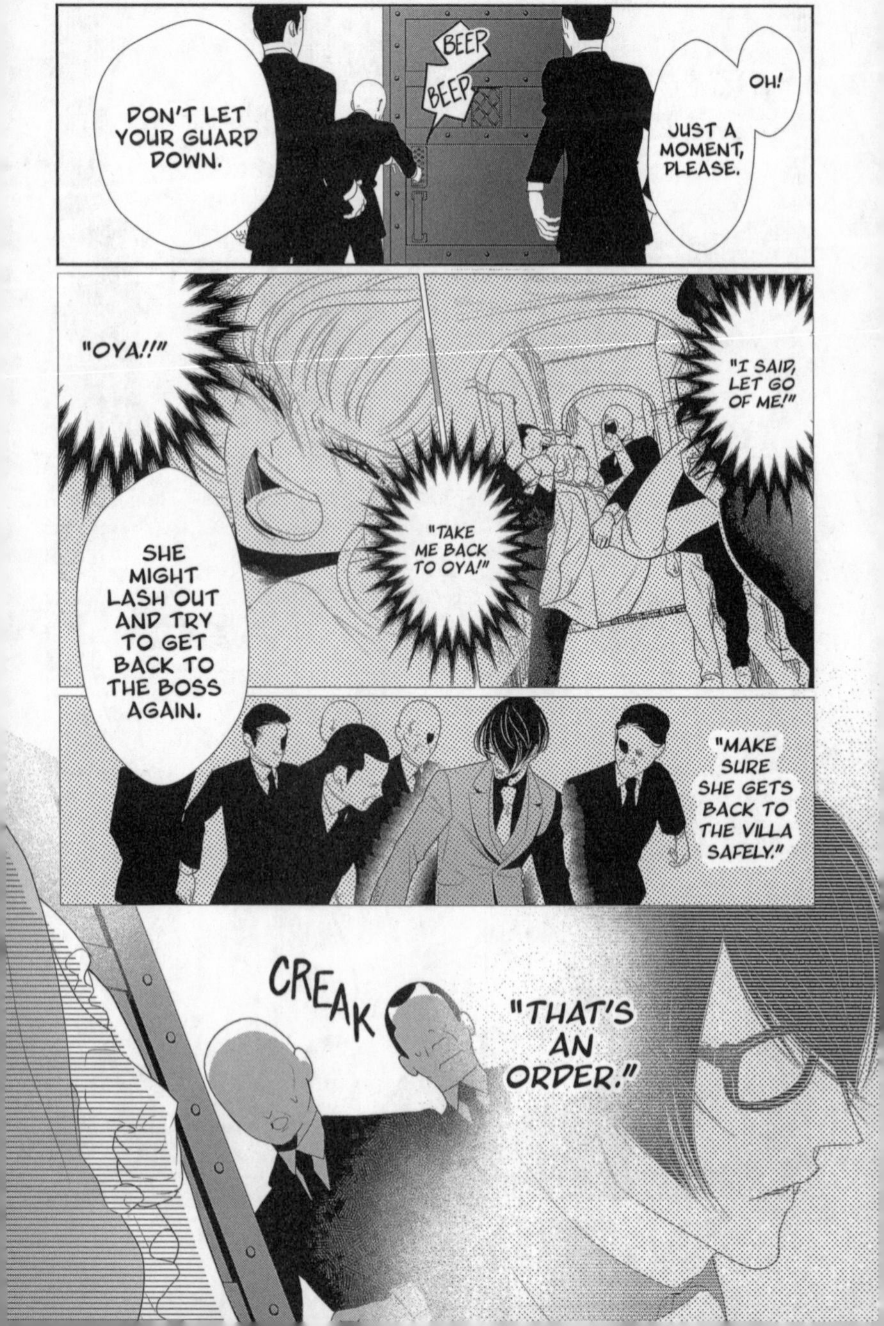
OH!
JUST A MOMENT, PLEASE.
BEEP
BEEP
DON'T LET YOUR GUARD DOWN.
"I SAID, LET GO OF ME!"
"TAKE ME BACK TO OYA!"
"OYA!!"
SHE MIGHT LASH OUT AND TRY TO GET BACK TO THE BOSS AGAIN.
"MAKE SURE SHE GETS BACK TO THE VILLA SAFELY."
"THAT'S AN ORDER."
CREAK

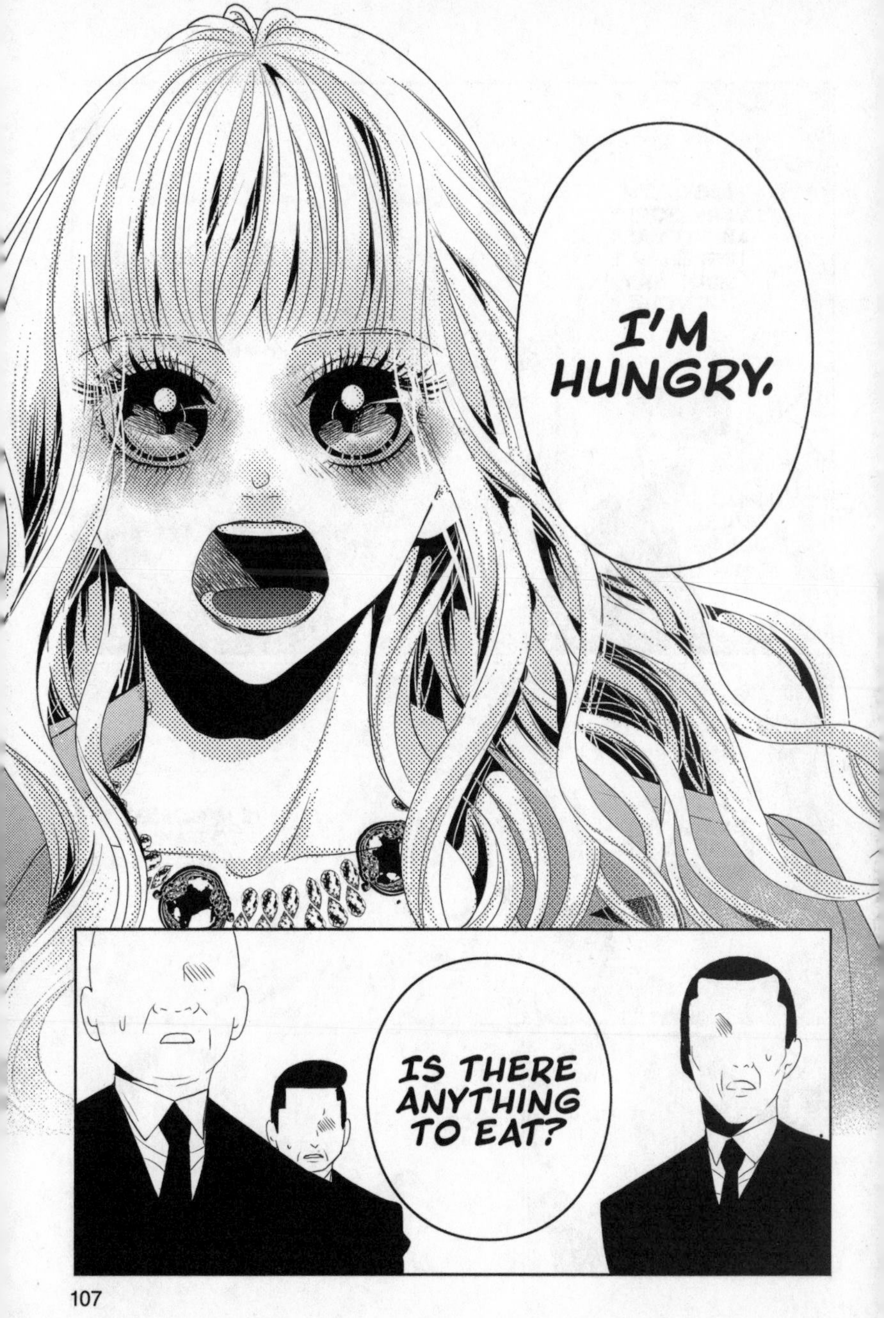
I'M HUNGRY.
IS THERE ANYTHING TO EAT?

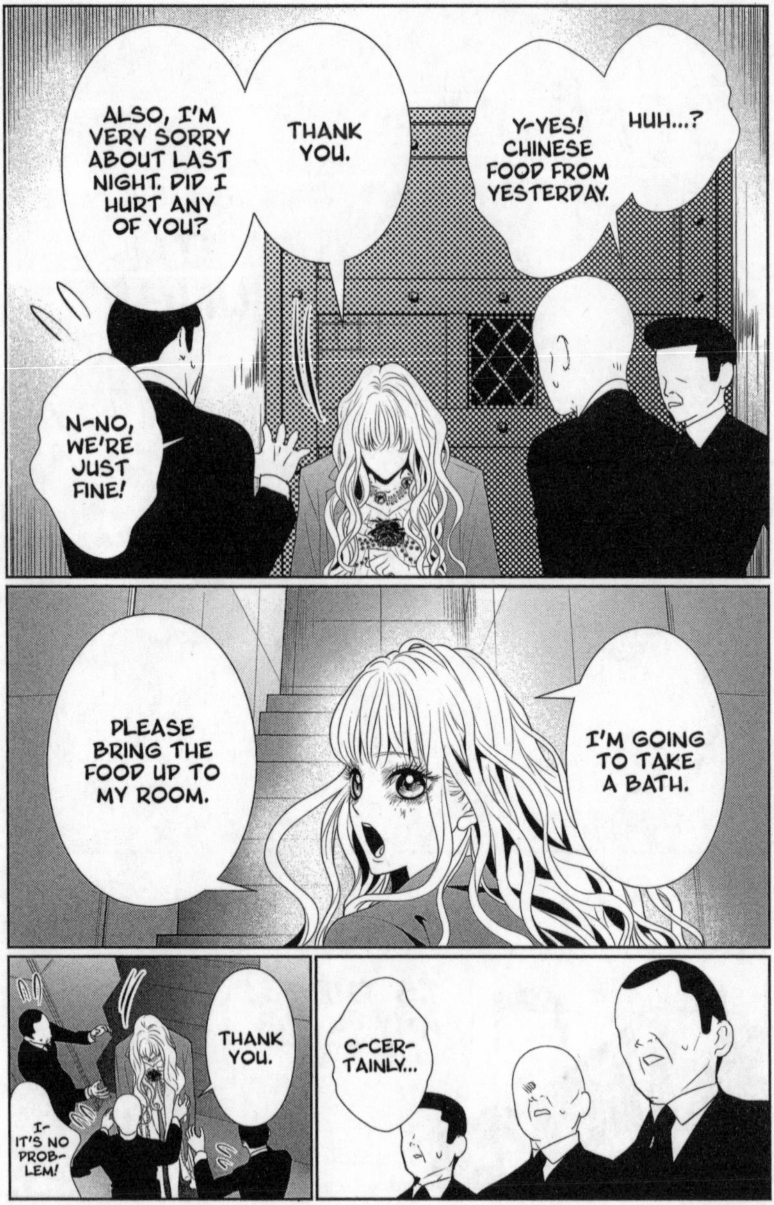
HUH...?
Y-YES! CHINESE FOOD FROM YESTERDAY.
THANK YOU.
ALSO, I'M VERY SORRY ABOUT LAST NIGHT. DID I HURT ANY OF YOU?
N-NO, WE'RE JUST FINE!
I'M GOING TO TAKE A BATH.
PLEASE BRING THE FOOD UP TO MY ROOM.
C-CER-TAINLY...
THANK YOU.
I- IT'S NO PROB-LEM!

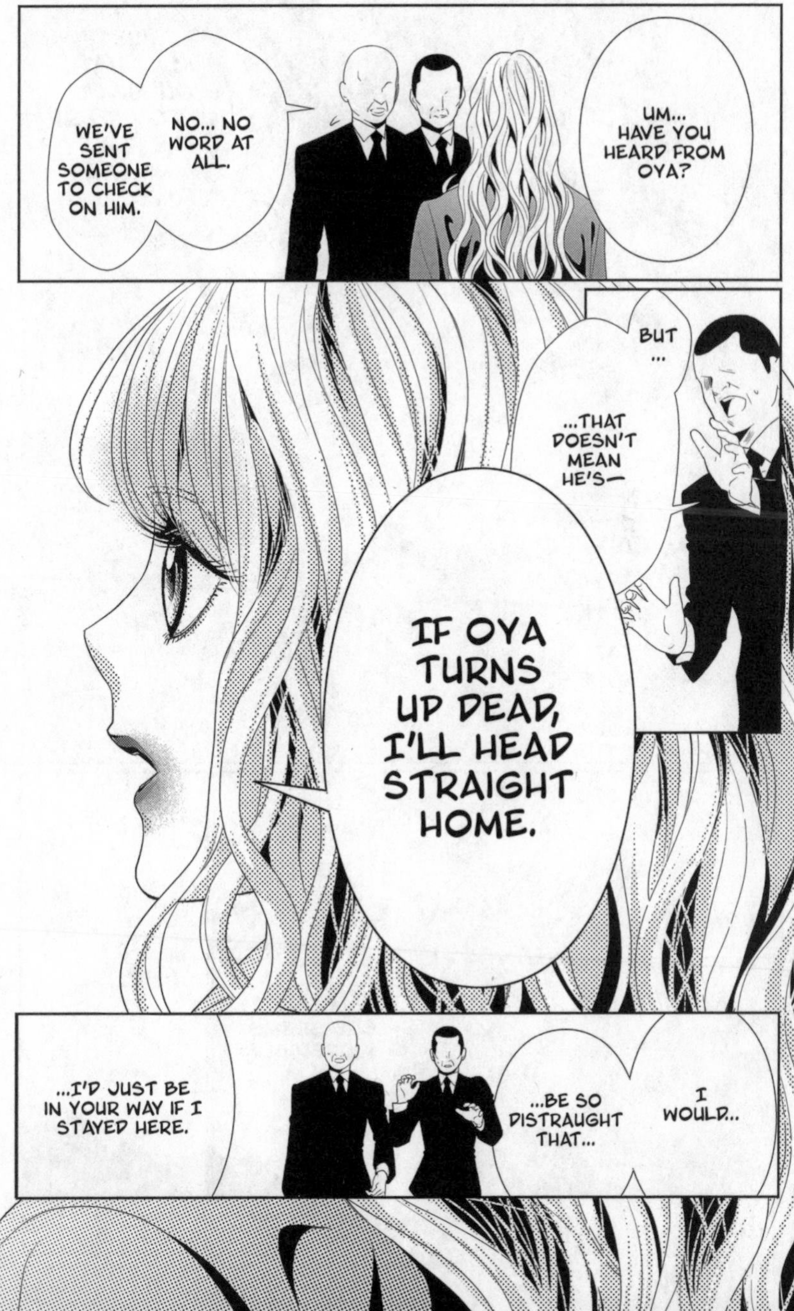
UM... HAVE YOU HEARD FROM OYA?
NO... NO WORD AT ALL.
WE'VE SENT SOMEONE TO CHECK ON HIM.
BUT ...
...THAT DOESN'T MEAN HE'S—
IF OYA TURNS UP DEAD, I'LL HEAD STRAIGHT HOME.
I WOULD...
...BE SO DISTRAUGHT THAT...
...I'D JUST BE IN YOUR WAY IF I STAYED HERE.

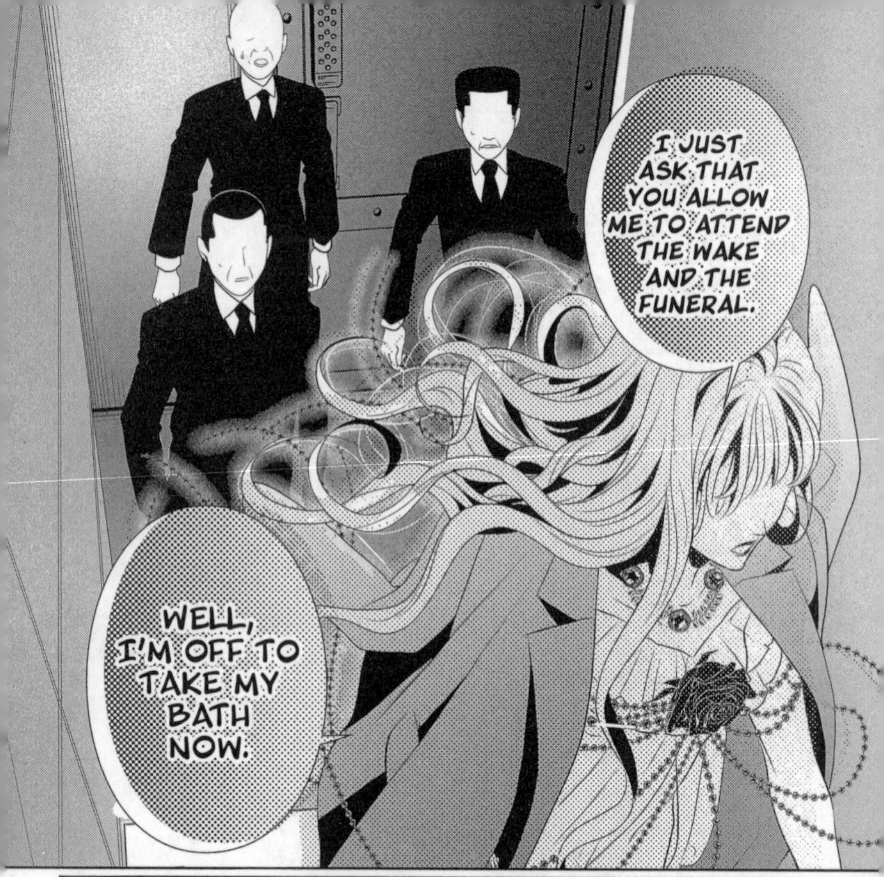
I JUST ASK THAT YOU ALLOW ME TO ATTEND THE WAKE AND THE FUNERAL.
WELL, I'M OFF TO TAKE MY BATH NOW.
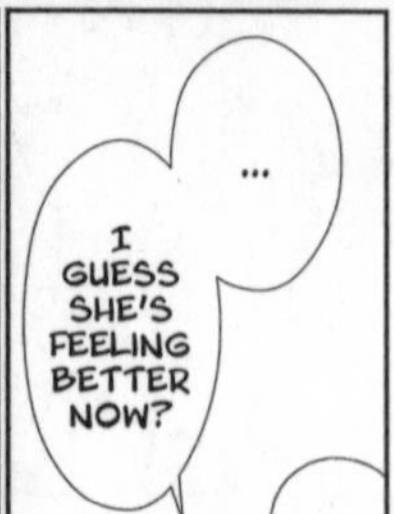
...
I GUESS SHE'S FEELING BETTER NOW?
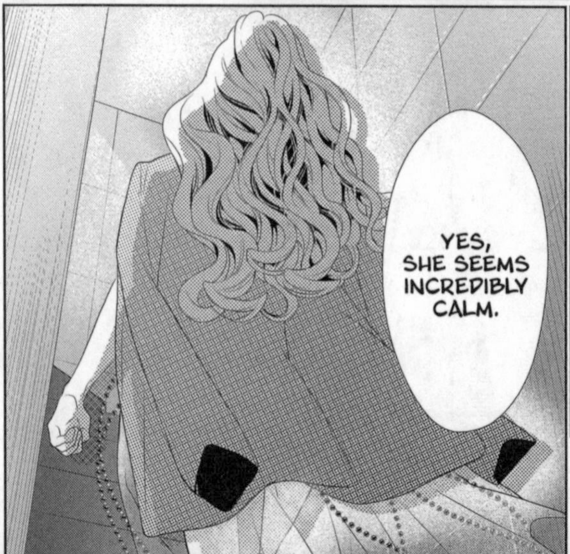
YES, SHE SEEMS INCREDIBLY CALM.

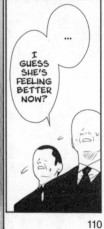

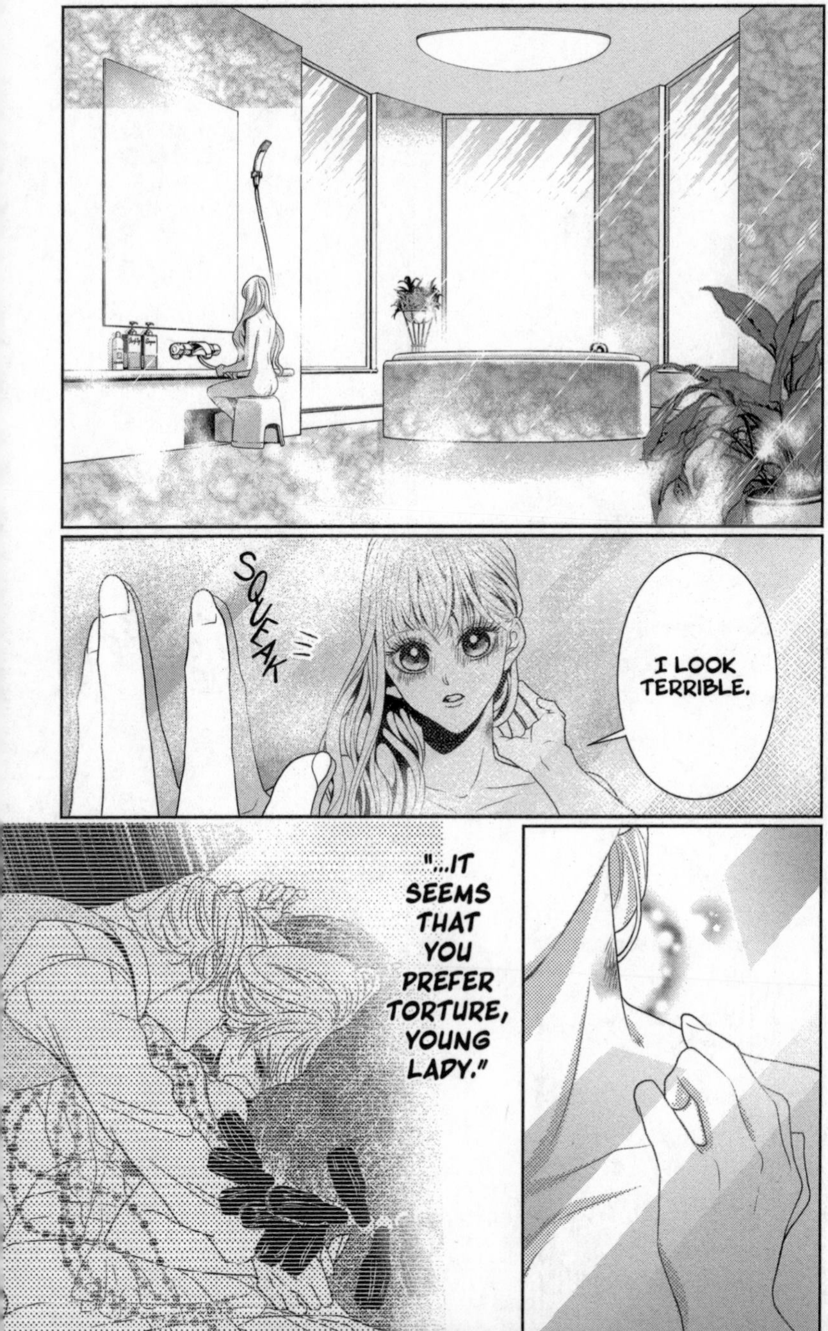
I LOOK TERRIBLE.
SQUEAK
"...IT SEEMS THAT YOU PREFER TORTURE, YOUNG LADY."

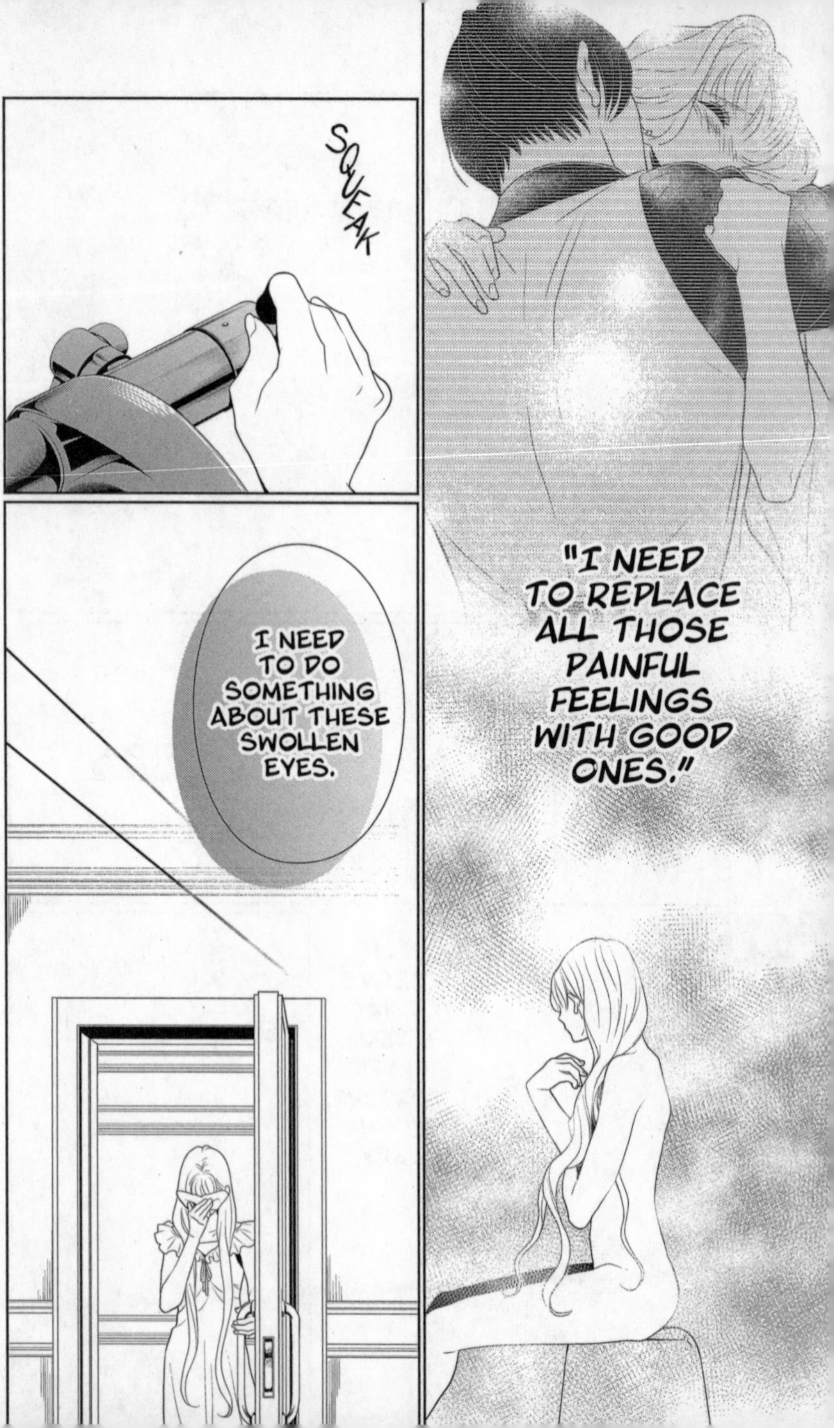
"I NEED TO REPLACE ALL THOSE PAINFUL FEELINGS WITH GOOD ONES."
SQUEAK
I NEED TO DO SOMETHING ABOUT THESE SWOLLEN EYES.

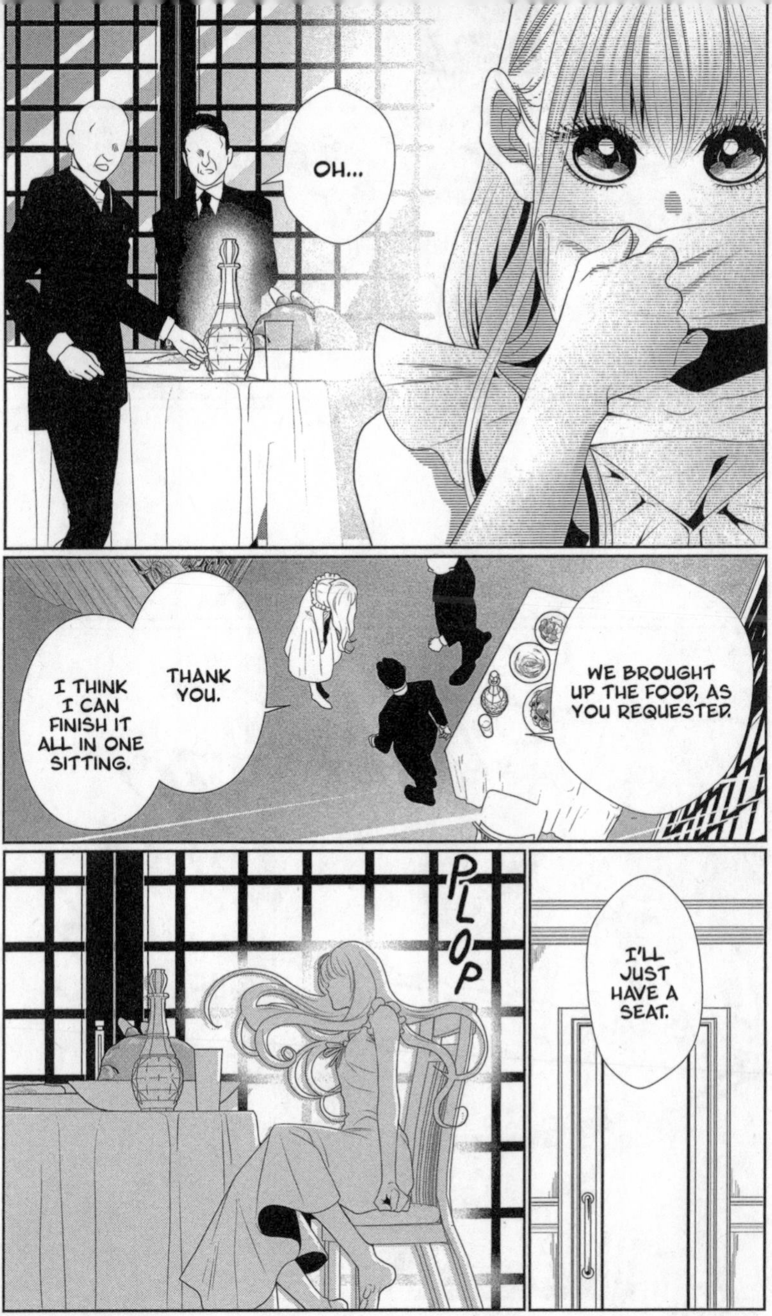
OH...
WE BROUGHT UP THE FOOD, AS YOU REQUESTED.
THANK YOU.
I THINK I CAN FINISH IT ALL IN ONE SITTING.
I'LL JUST HAVE A SEAT.
PLOP

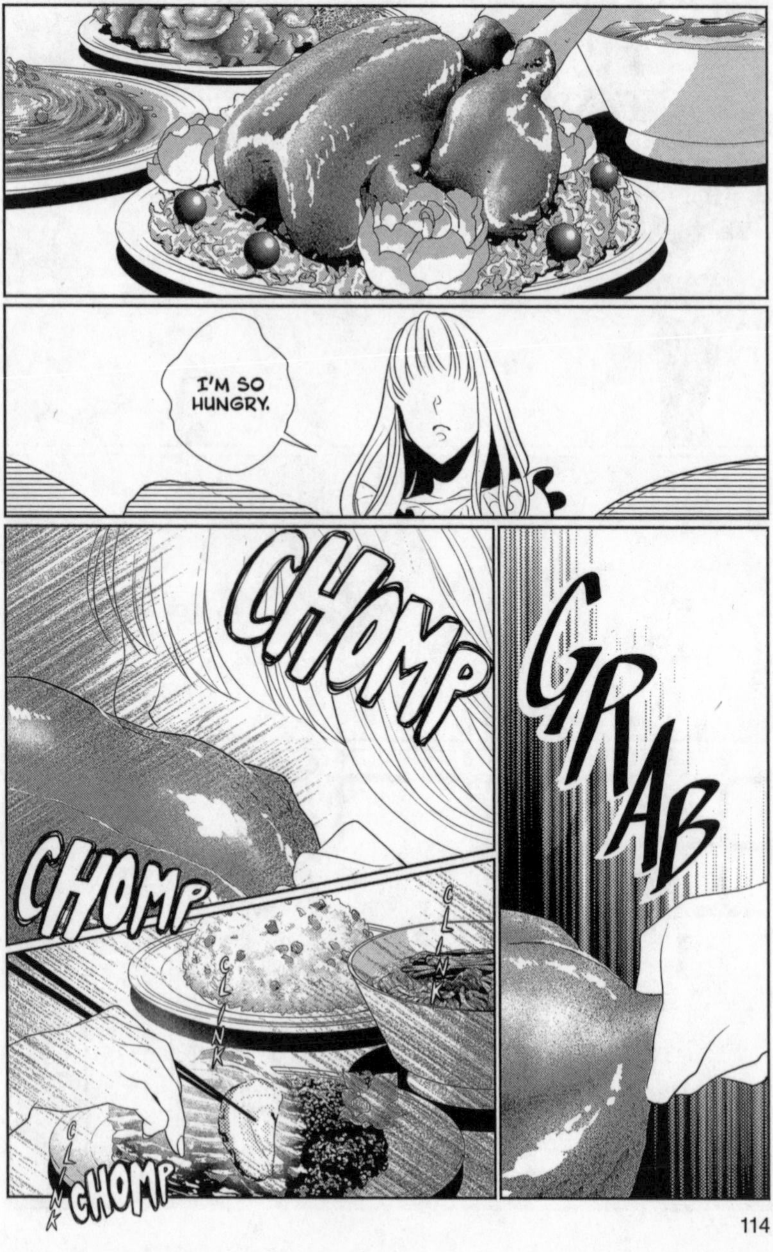
I'M SO HUNGRY.
GRAB
CHOMP
CHOMP
CLINK
CLINK
CLINK
CHOMP

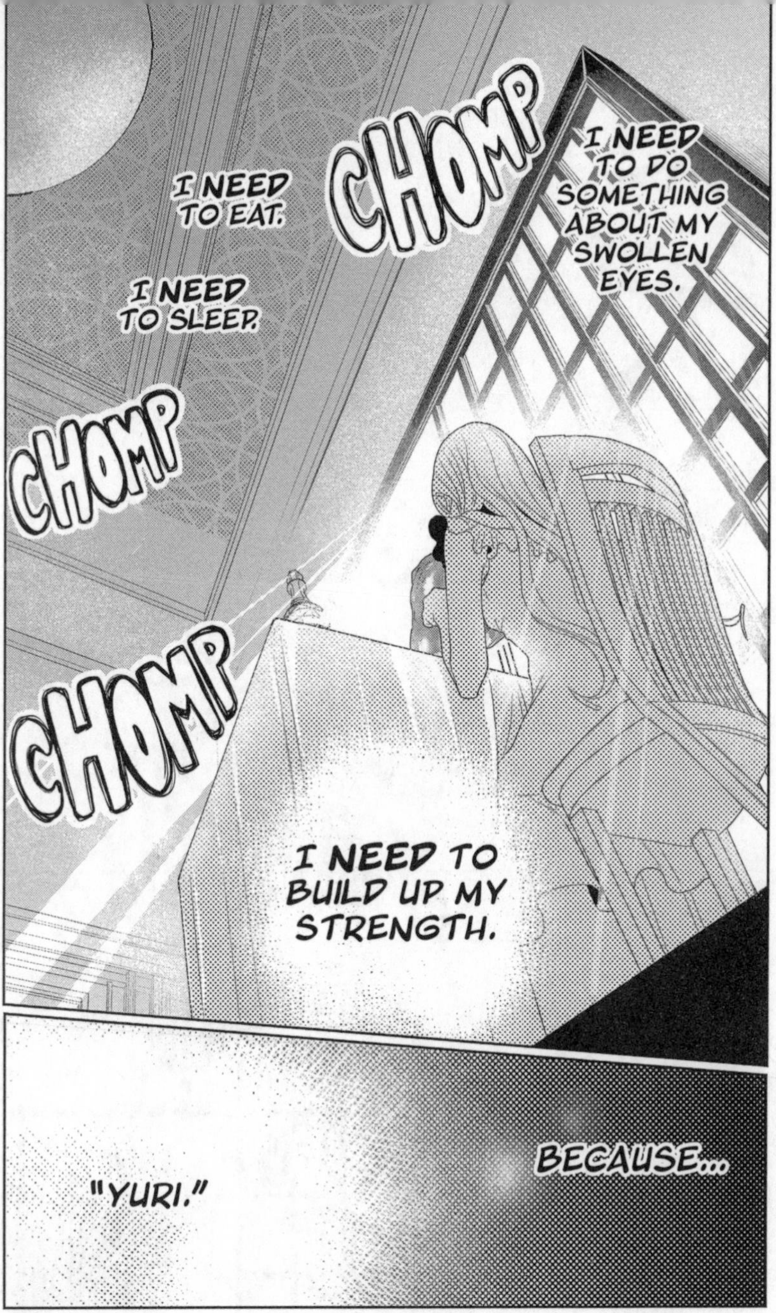
I NEED TO DO SOMETHING ABOUT MY SWOLLEN EYES.
CHOMP
I NEED TO EAT.
I NEED TO SLEEP.
CHOMP
CHOMP
I NEED TO BUILD UP MY STRENGTH.
BECAUSE...
"YURI."

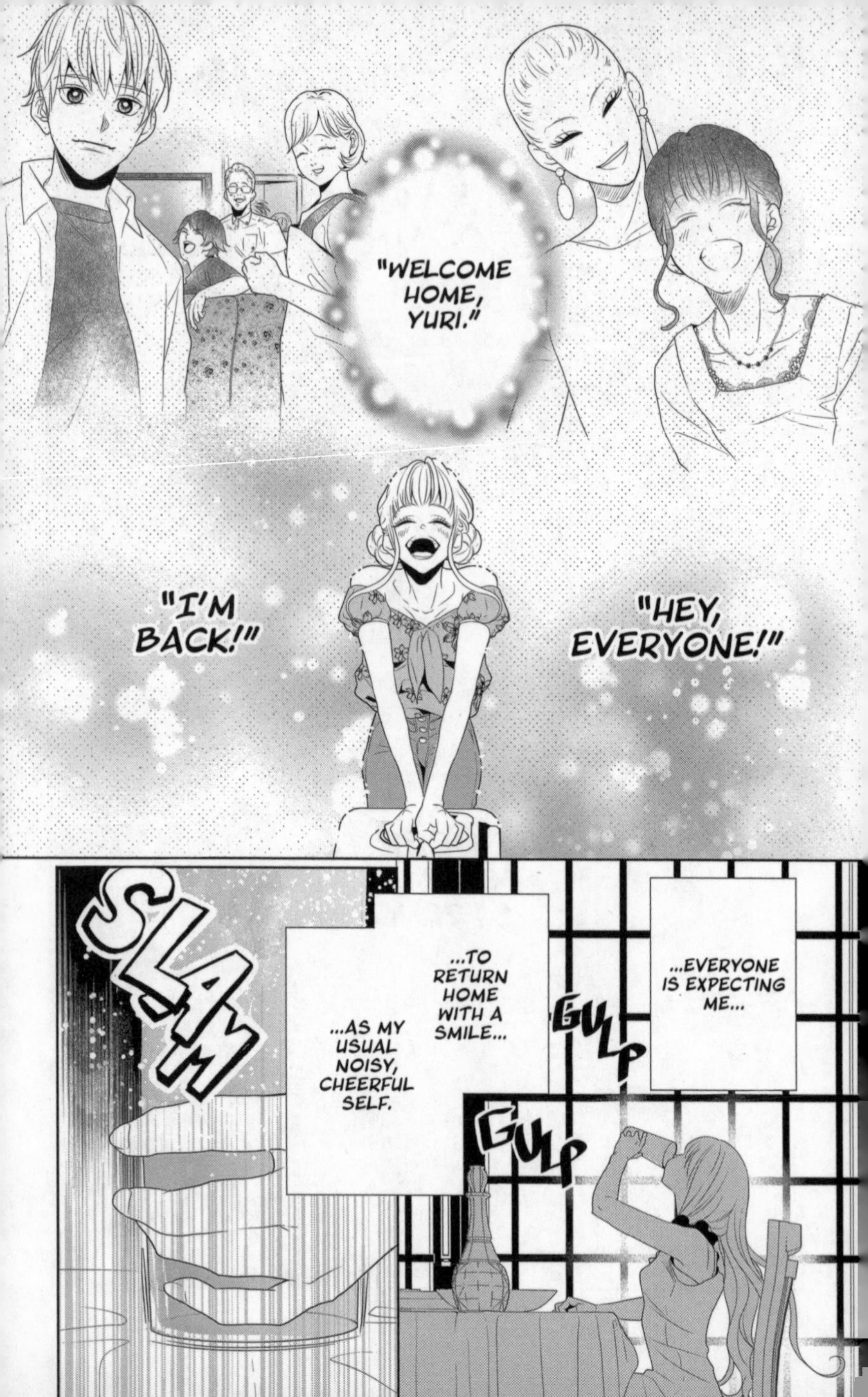
"WELCOME HOME, YURI."
"HEY, EVERYONE!"
"I'M BACK!"
...EVERYONE IS EXPECTING ME...
...TO RETURN HOME WITH A SMILE...
...AS MY USUAL NOISY, CHEERFUL SELF.
GULP
GULP
SLAM

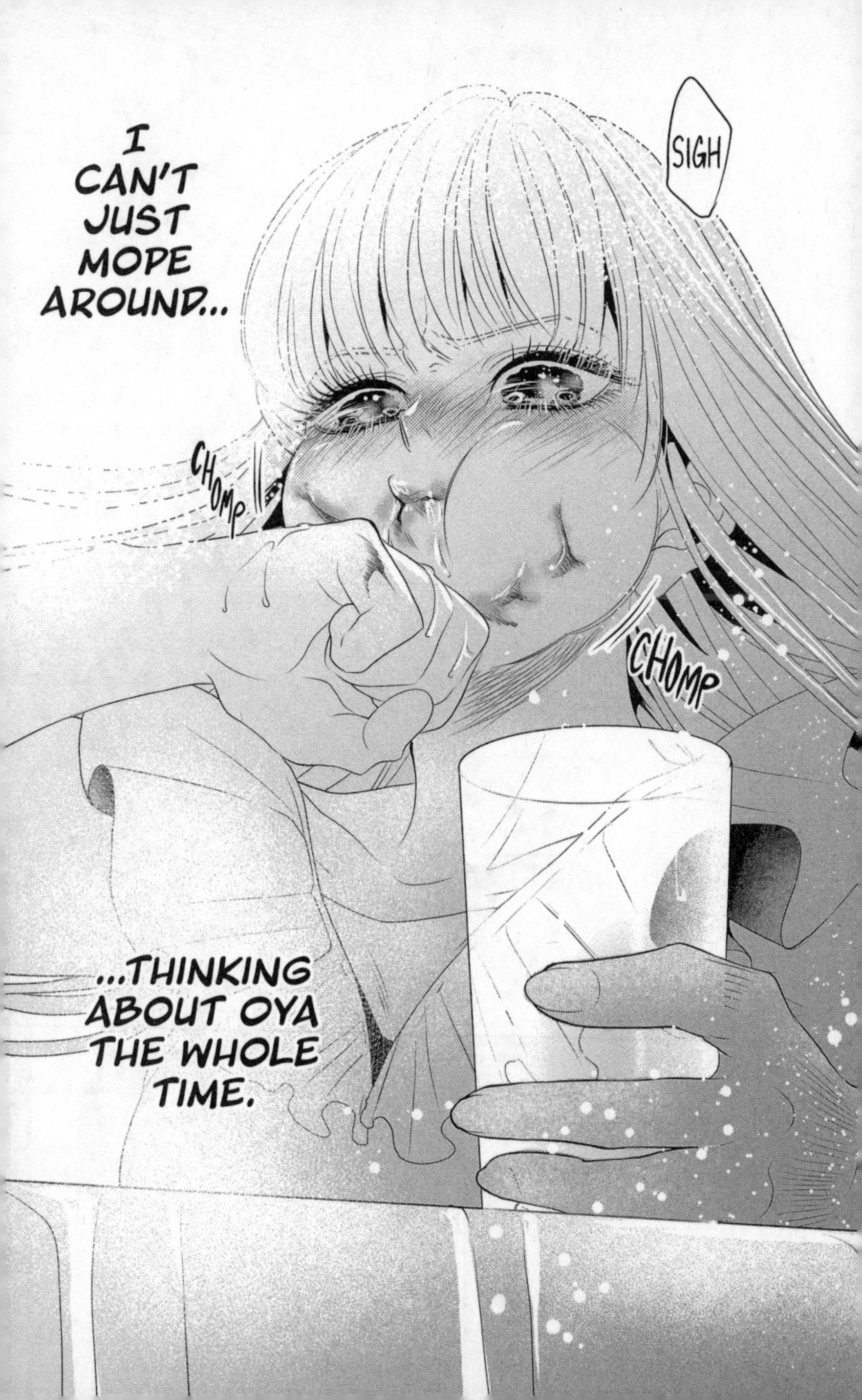
SIGH
I CAN'T JUST MOPE AROUND...
CHOMP
CHOMP
...THINKING ABOUT OYA THE WHOLE TIME.

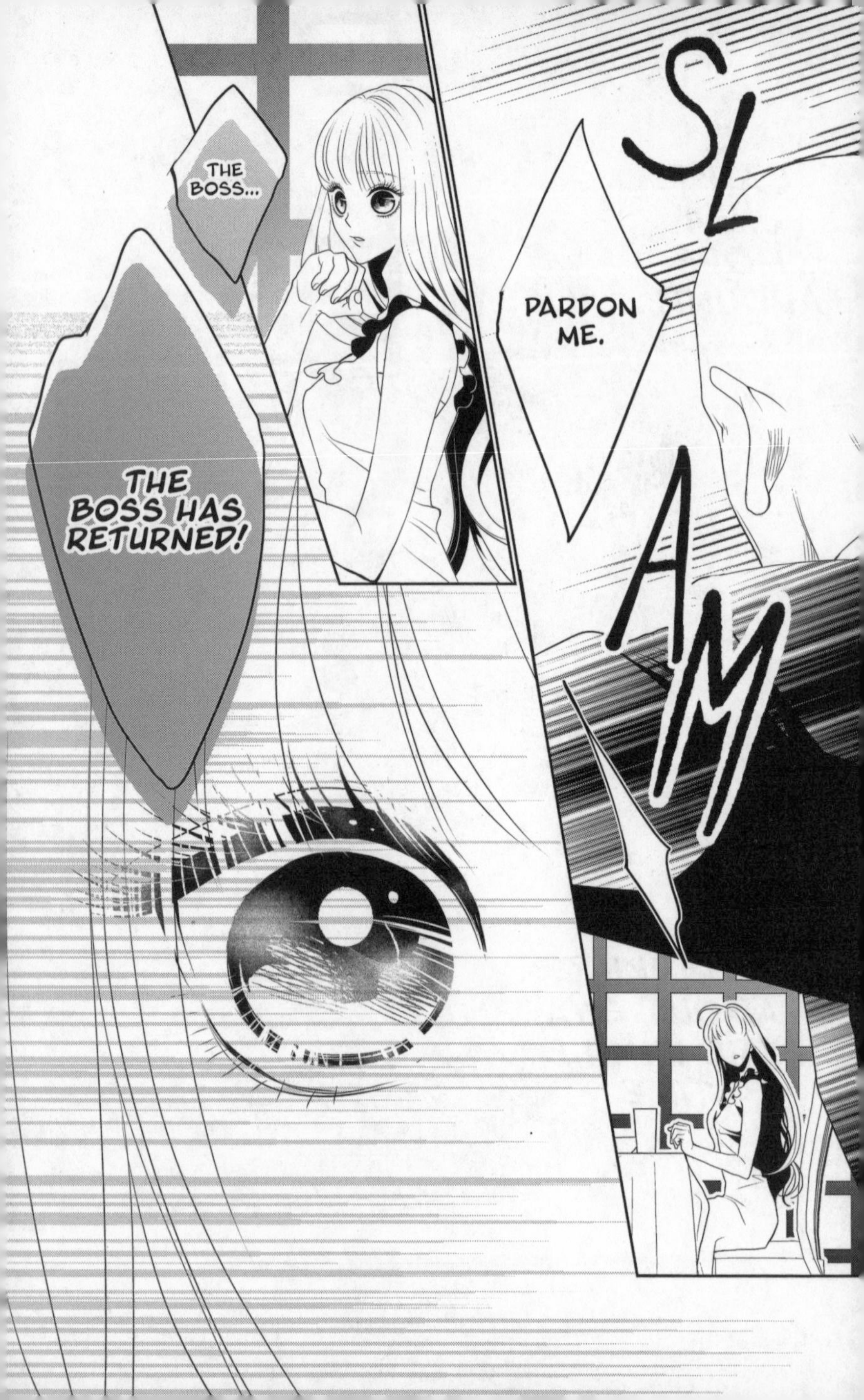
PARDON ME.
SLAM
THE BOSS...
THE BOSS HAS RETURNED!

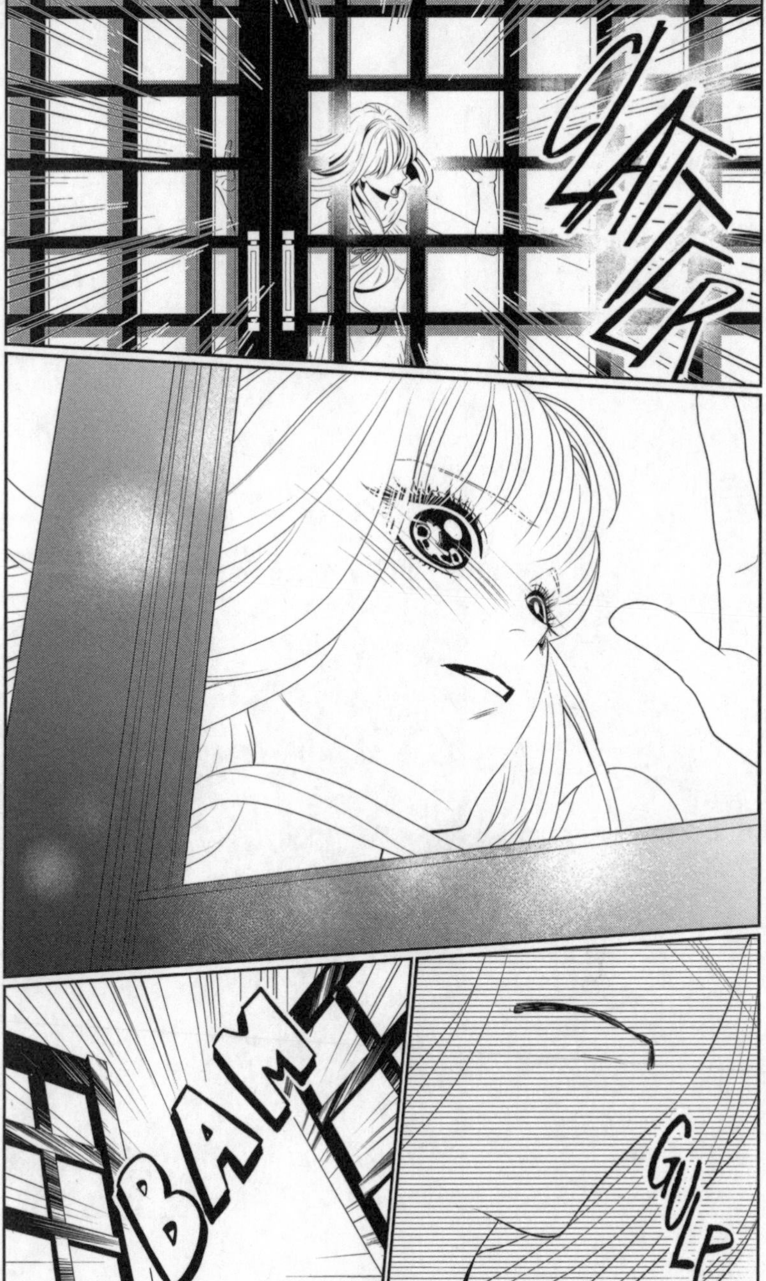
CLATTER
GULP
BAM

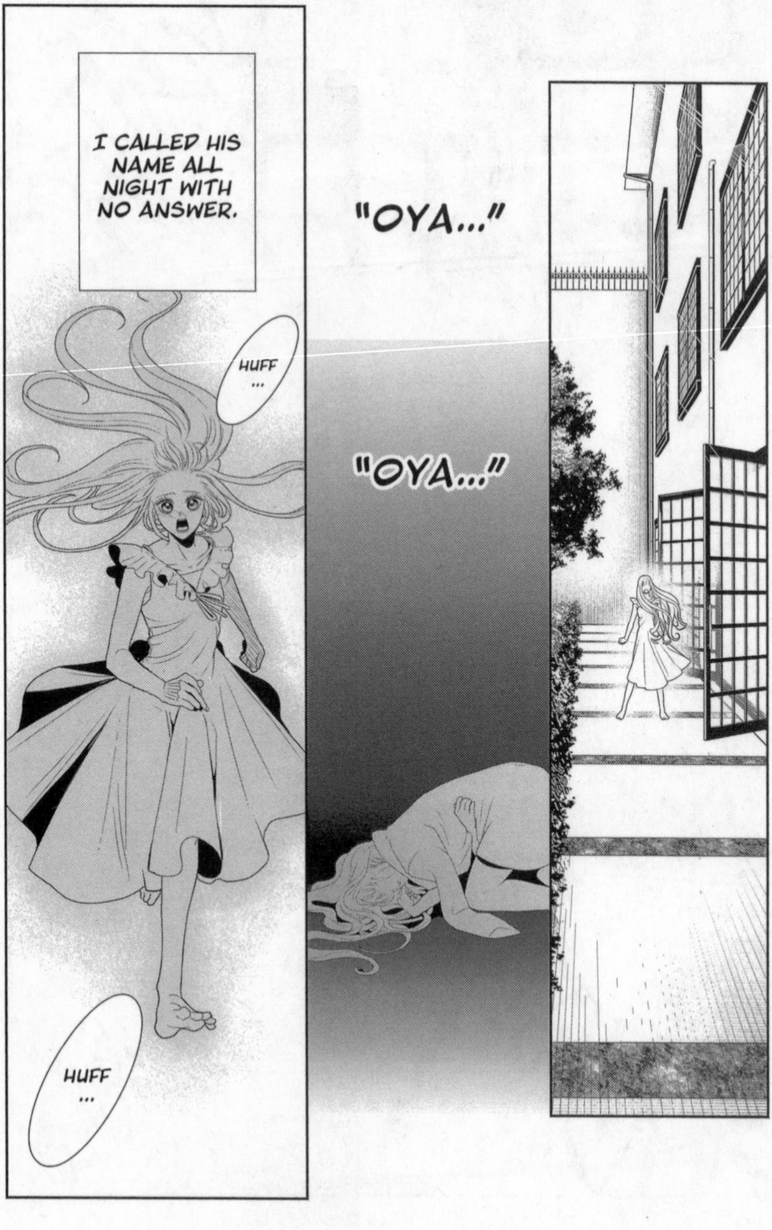
"OYA..."
"OYA..."
I CALLED HIS NAME ALL NIGHT WITH NO ANSWER.
HUFF...
HUFF...

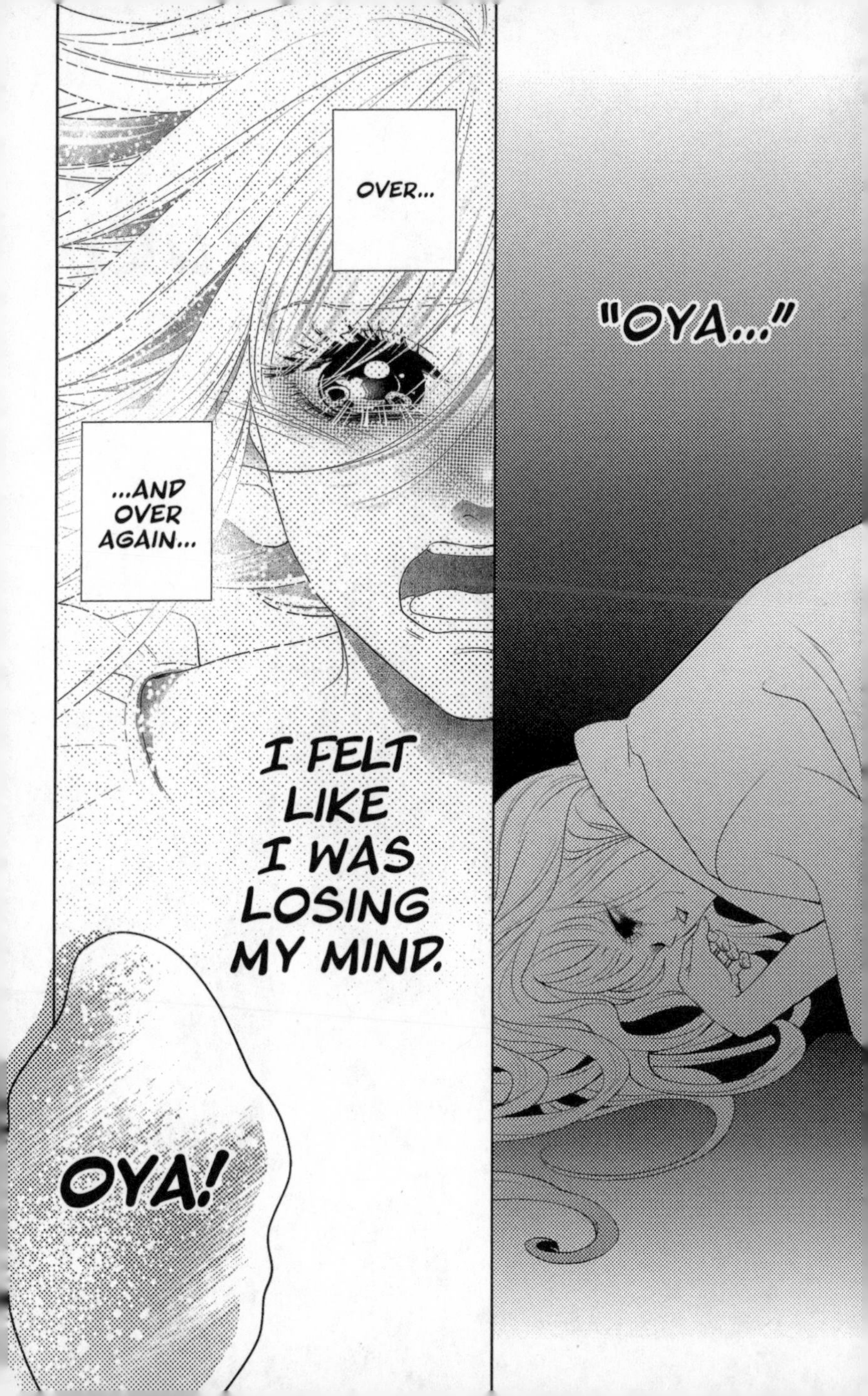
"OYA..."
OVER...
...AND OVER AGAIN...
I FELT LIKE I WAS LOSING MY MIND.
OYA!

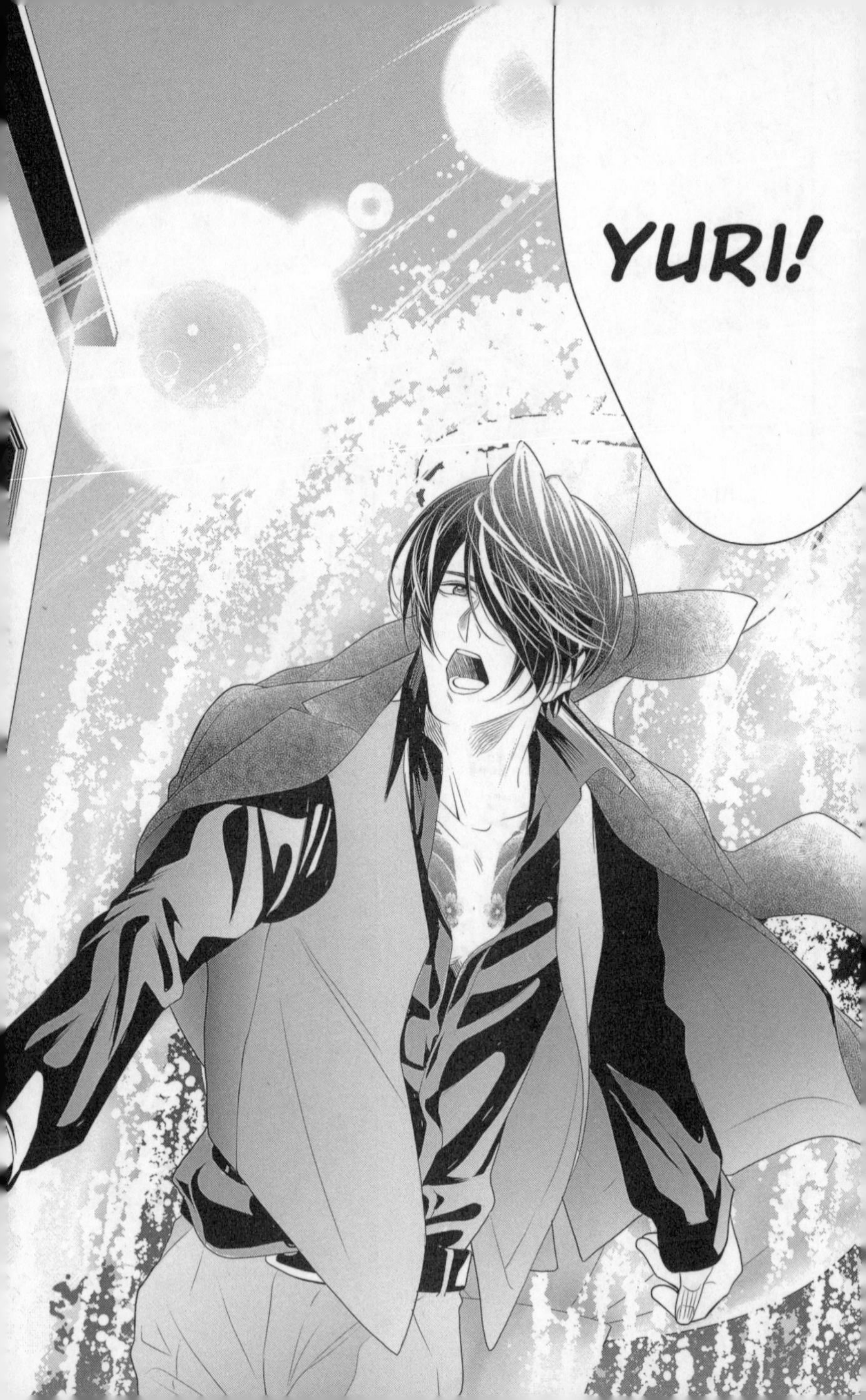
YURI!

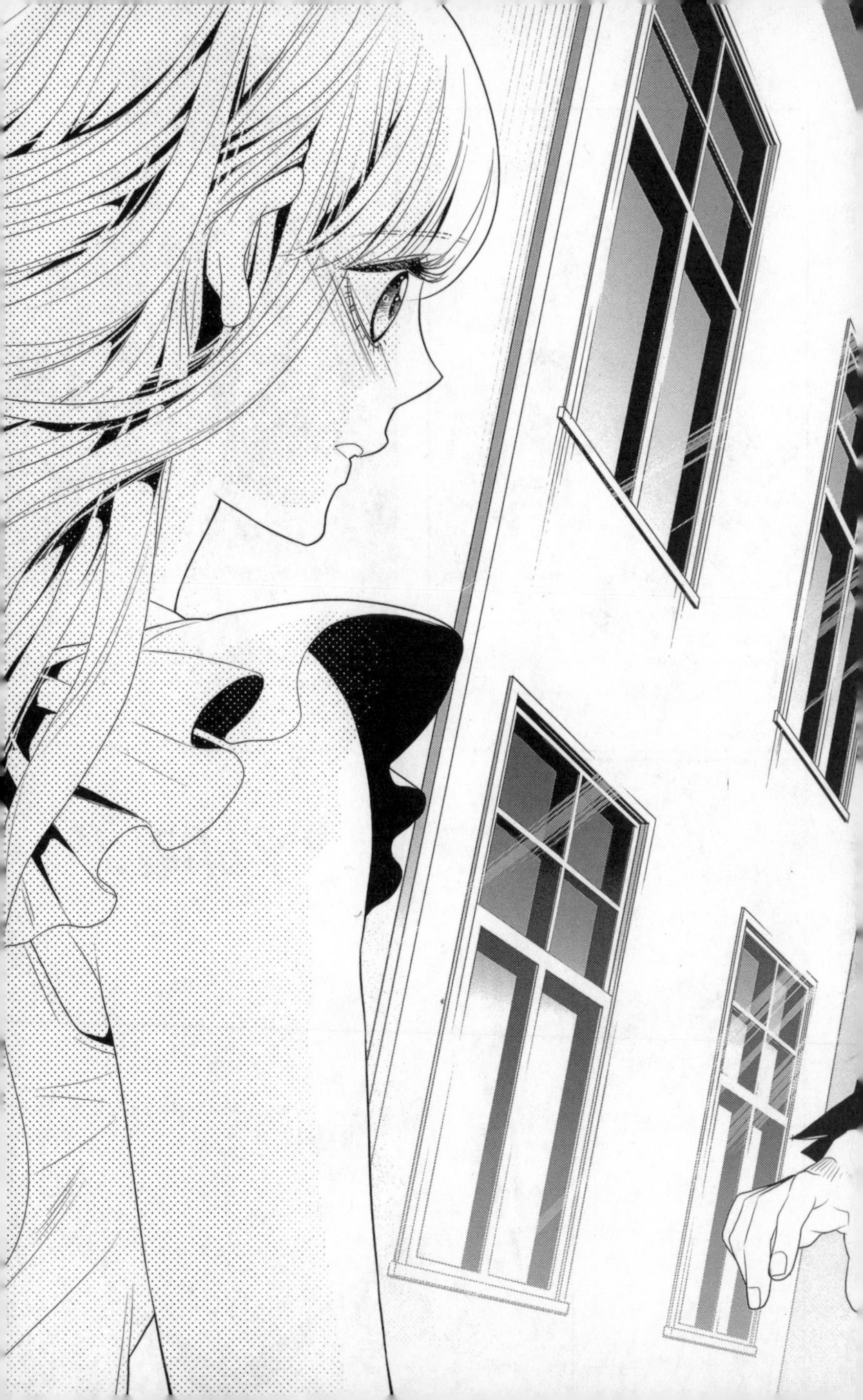

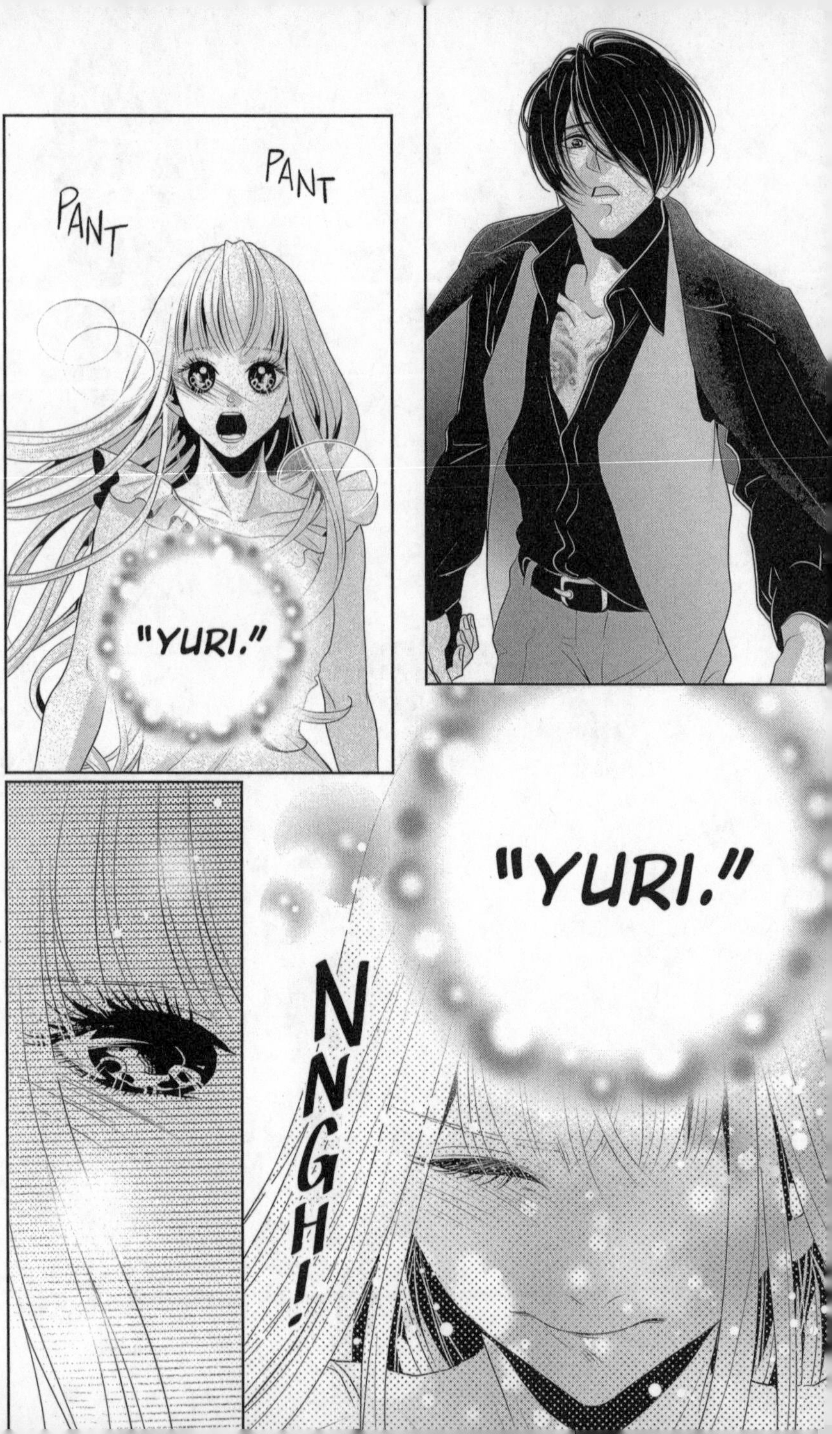
PANT
PANT
"YURI."
"YURI."
NNGH!

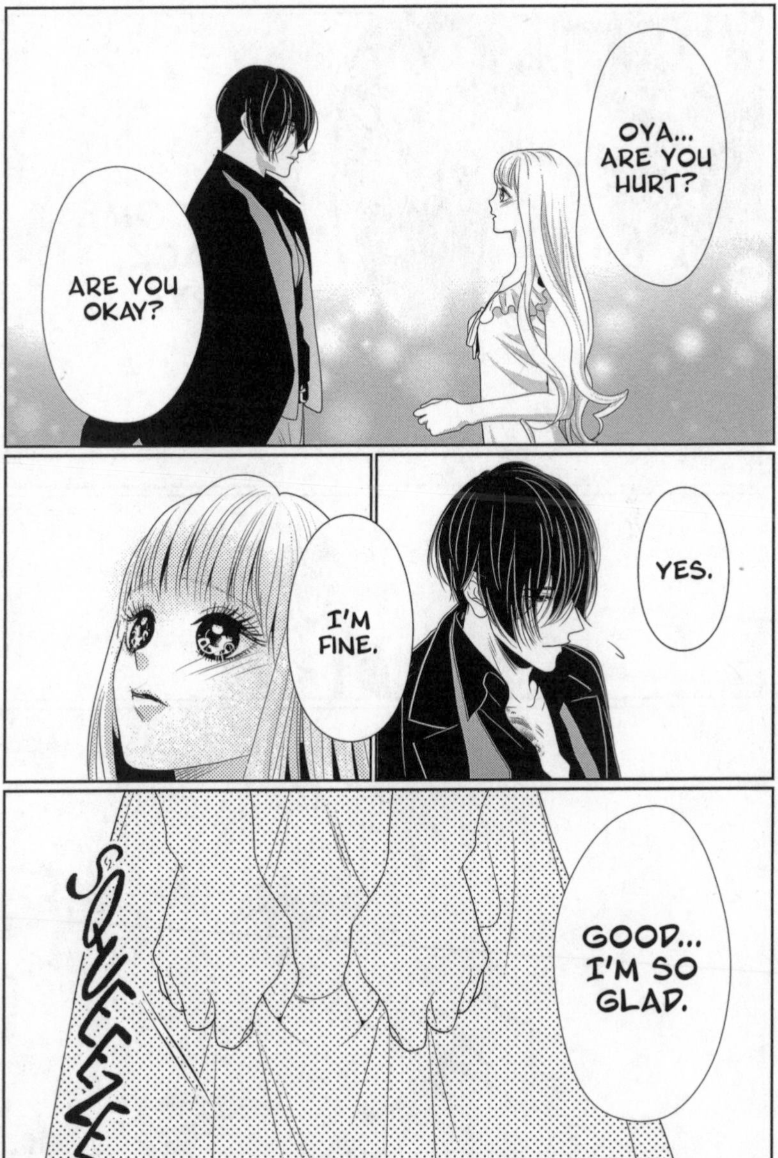
OYA... ARE YOU HURT?
ARE YOU OKAY?
YES.
I'M FINE.
GOOD... I'M SO GLAD.
SQUEEZE

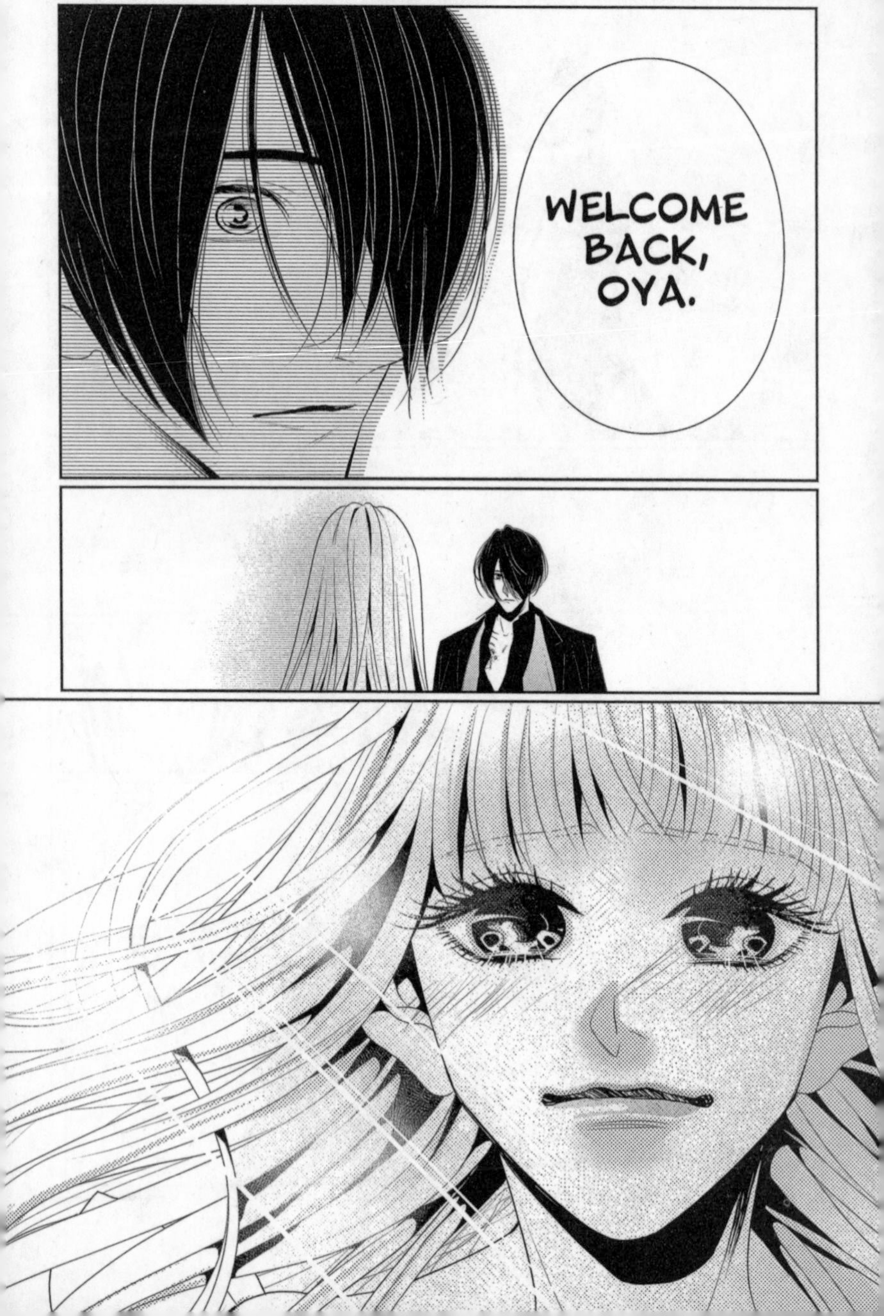
WELCOME BACK, OYA.

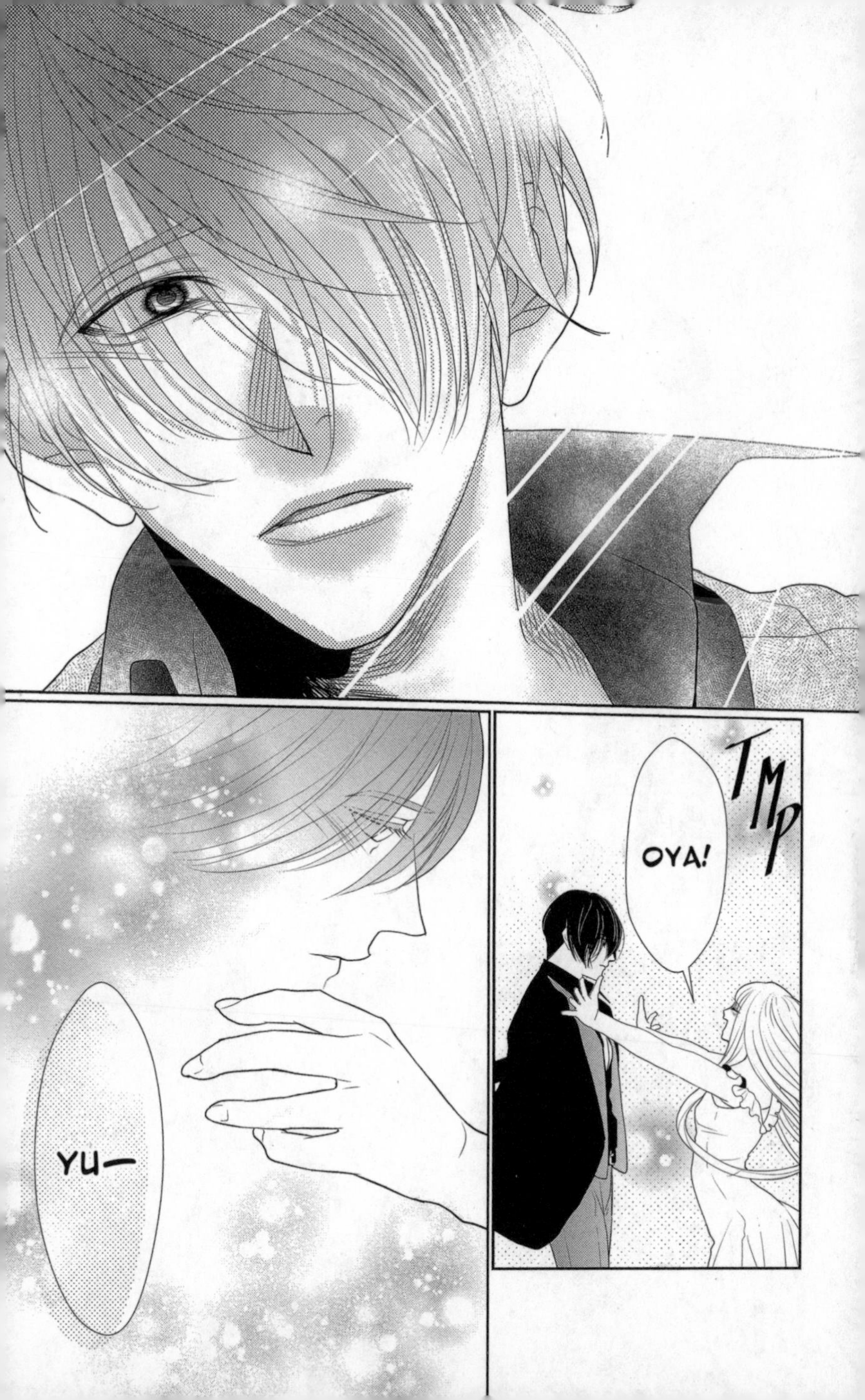
TMP
OYA!
YU—

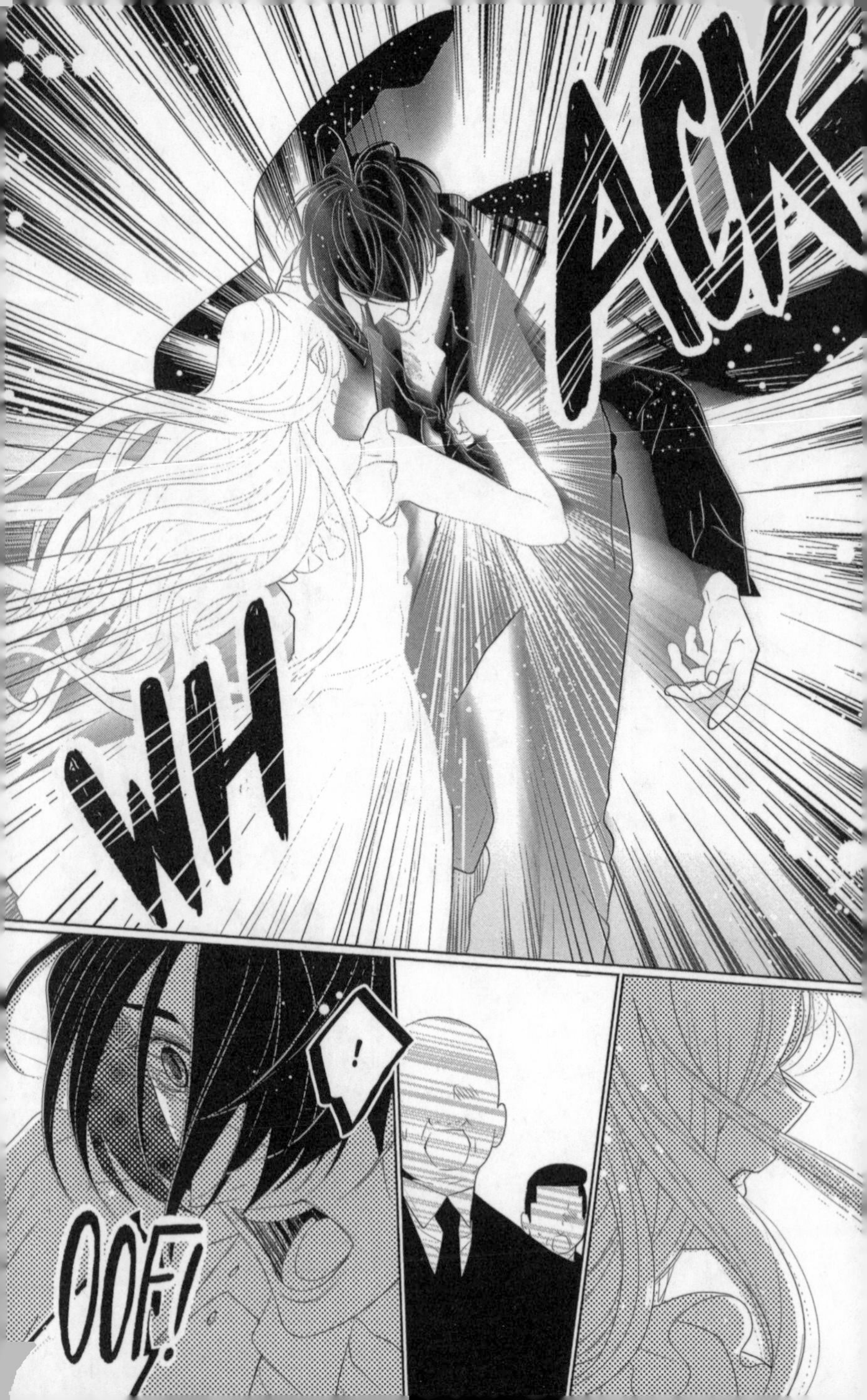
WHACK
!
OOF!

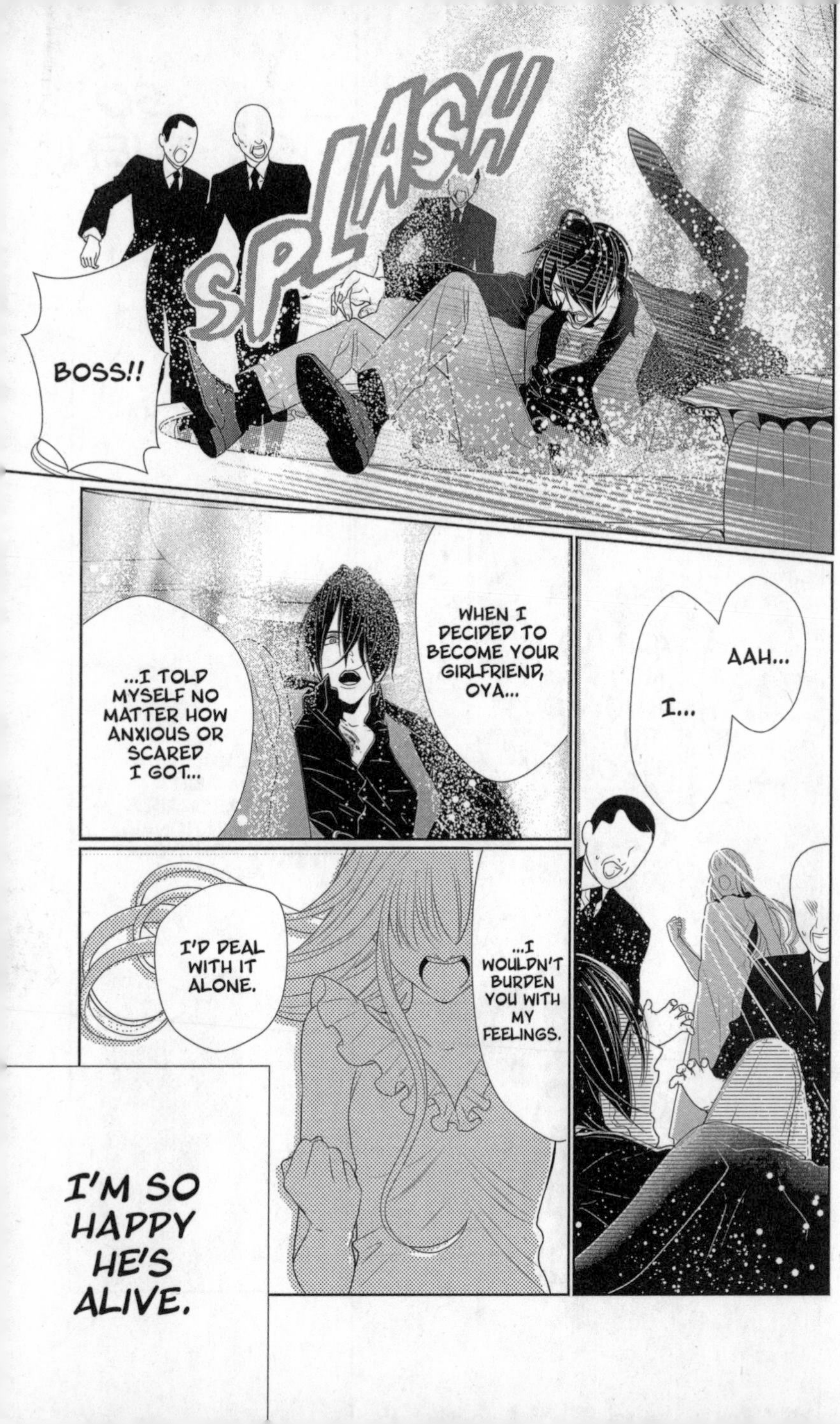
SPLASH
BOSS!!
AAH...
I...
WHEN I DECIDED TO BECOME YOUR GIRLFRIEND, OYA...
...I TOLD MYSELF NO MATTER HOW ANXIOUS OR SCARED I GOT...
...I WOULDN'T BURDEN YOU WITH MY FEELINGS.
I'D DEAL WITH IT ALONE.
I'M SO HAPPY HE'S ALIVE.

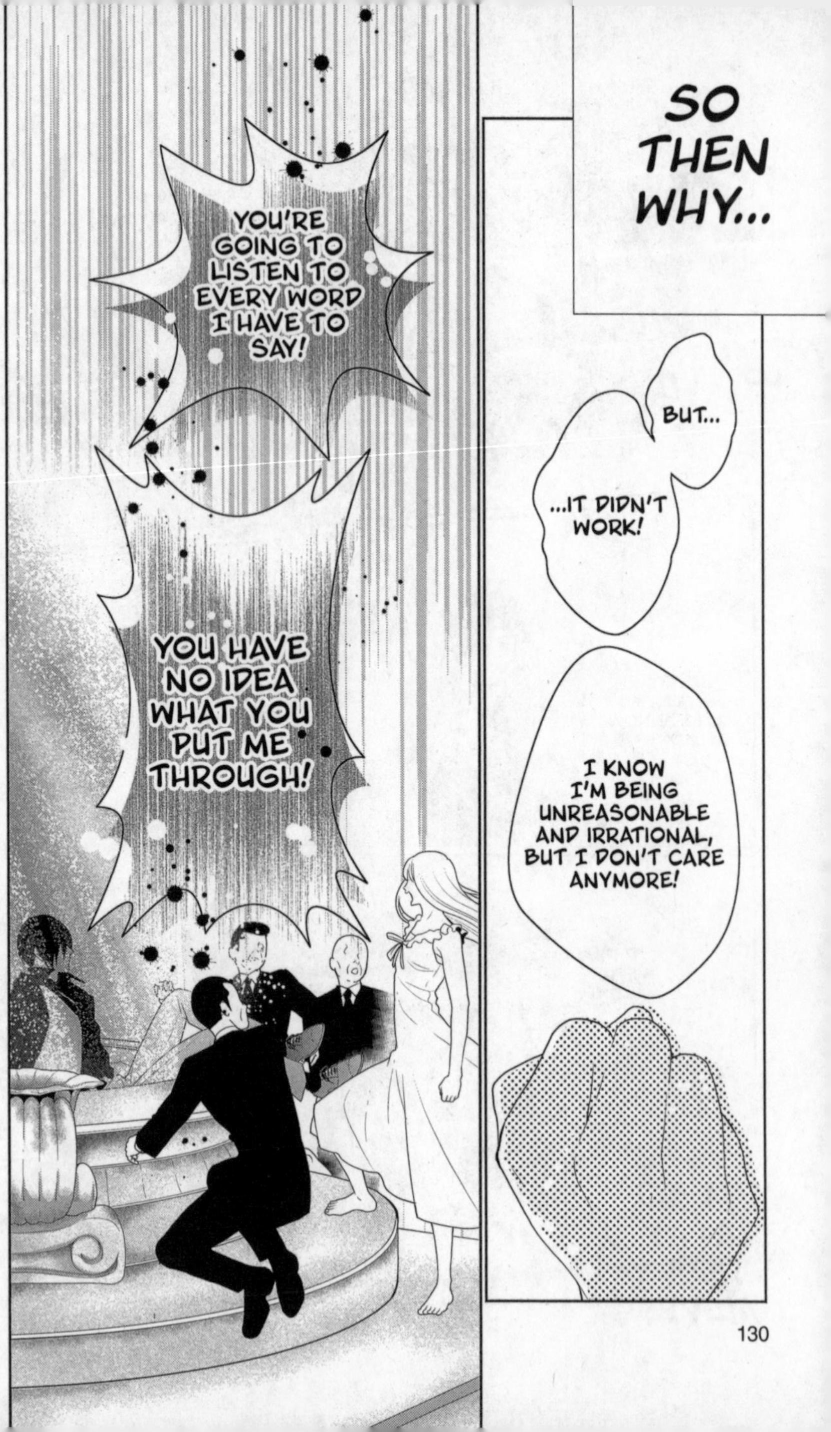
SO THEN WHY...
BUT...
...IT DIDN'T WORK!
I KNOW I'M BEING UNREASONABLE AND IRRATIONAL, BUT I DON'T CARE ANYMORE!
YOU'RE GOING TO LISTEN TO EVERY WORD I HAVE TO SAY!
YOU HAVE NO IDEA WHAT YOU PUT ME THROUGH!

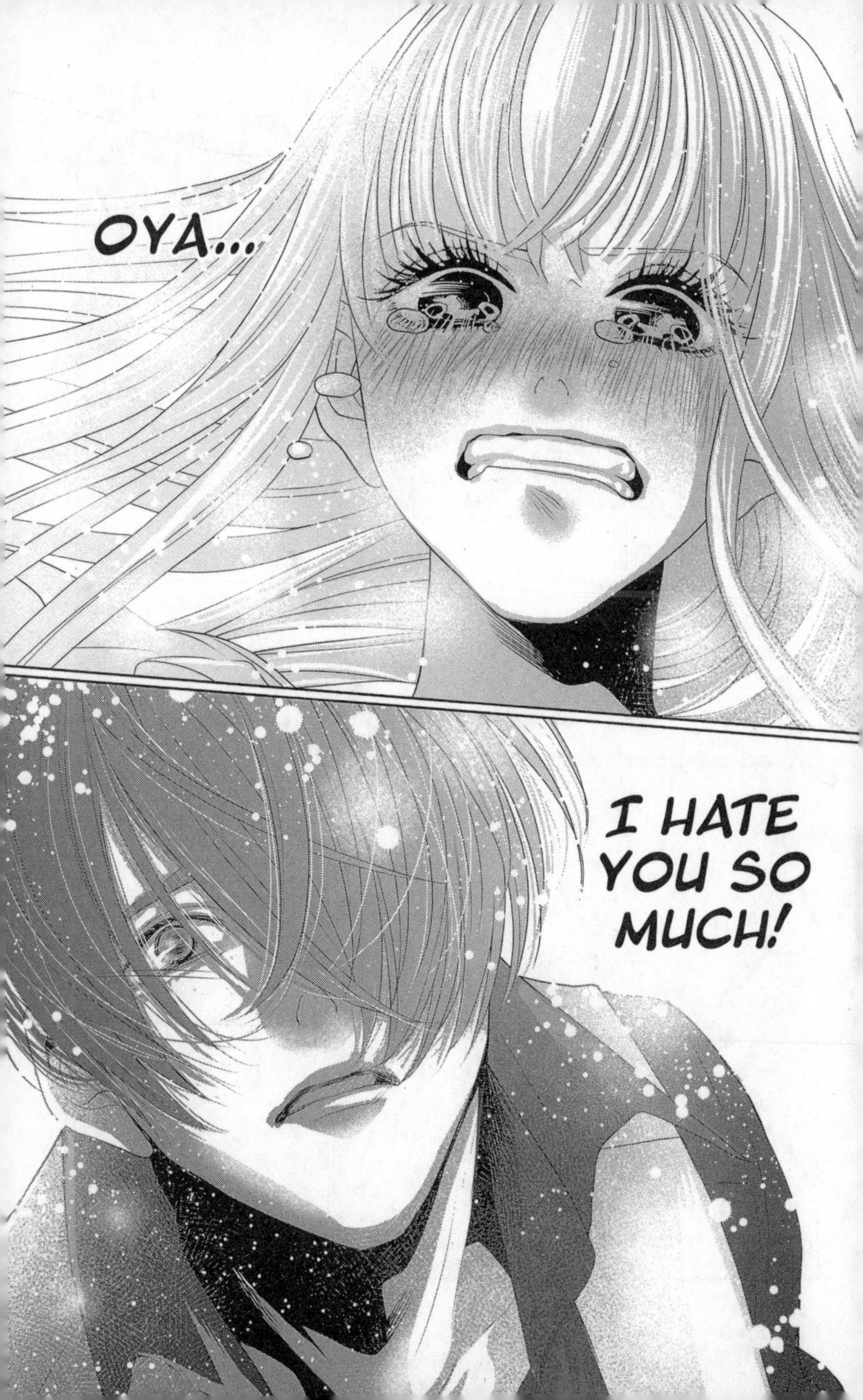
OYA...
I HATE YOU SO MUCH!

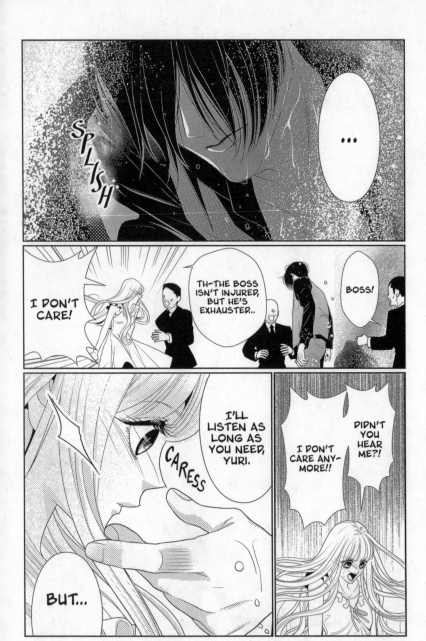

...
SPLISH
BOSS!
TH-THE BOSS ISN'T INJURED, BUT HE'S EXHAUSTED...
I DON'T CARE!
DIDN'T YOU HEAR ME?!
I DON'T CARE ANYMORE!!
I'LL LISTEN AS LONG AS YOU NEED, YURI.
CARESS
BUT...

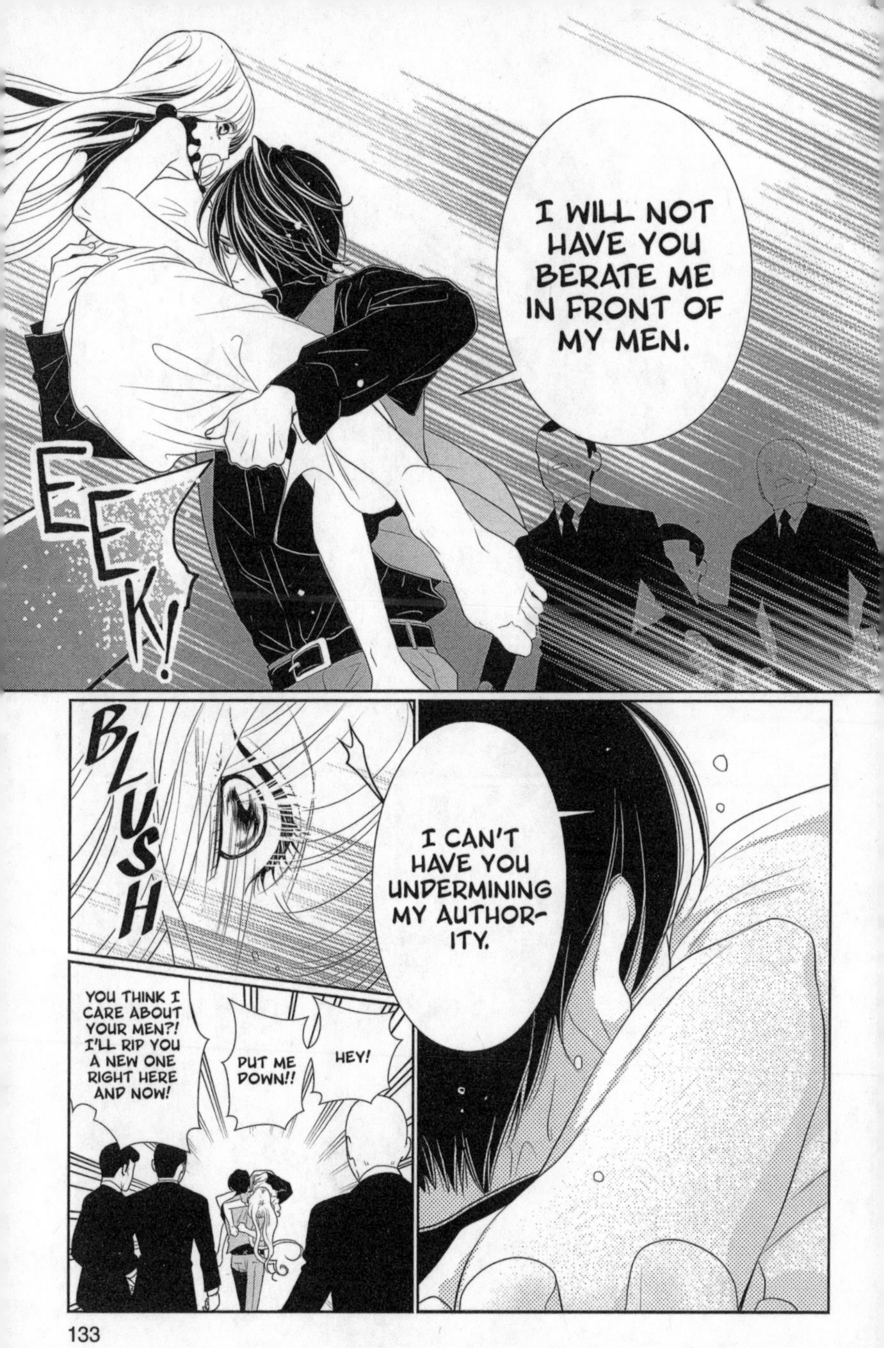
I WILL NOT HAVE YOU BERATE ME IN FRONT OF MY MEN.
EEEK!
I CAN'T HAVE YOU UNDERMINING MY AUTHOR-ITY.
BLUSH
HEY!
PUT ME DOWN!!
YOU THINK I CARE ABOUT YOUR MEN?! I'LL RIP YOU A NEW ONE RIGHT HERE AND NOW!

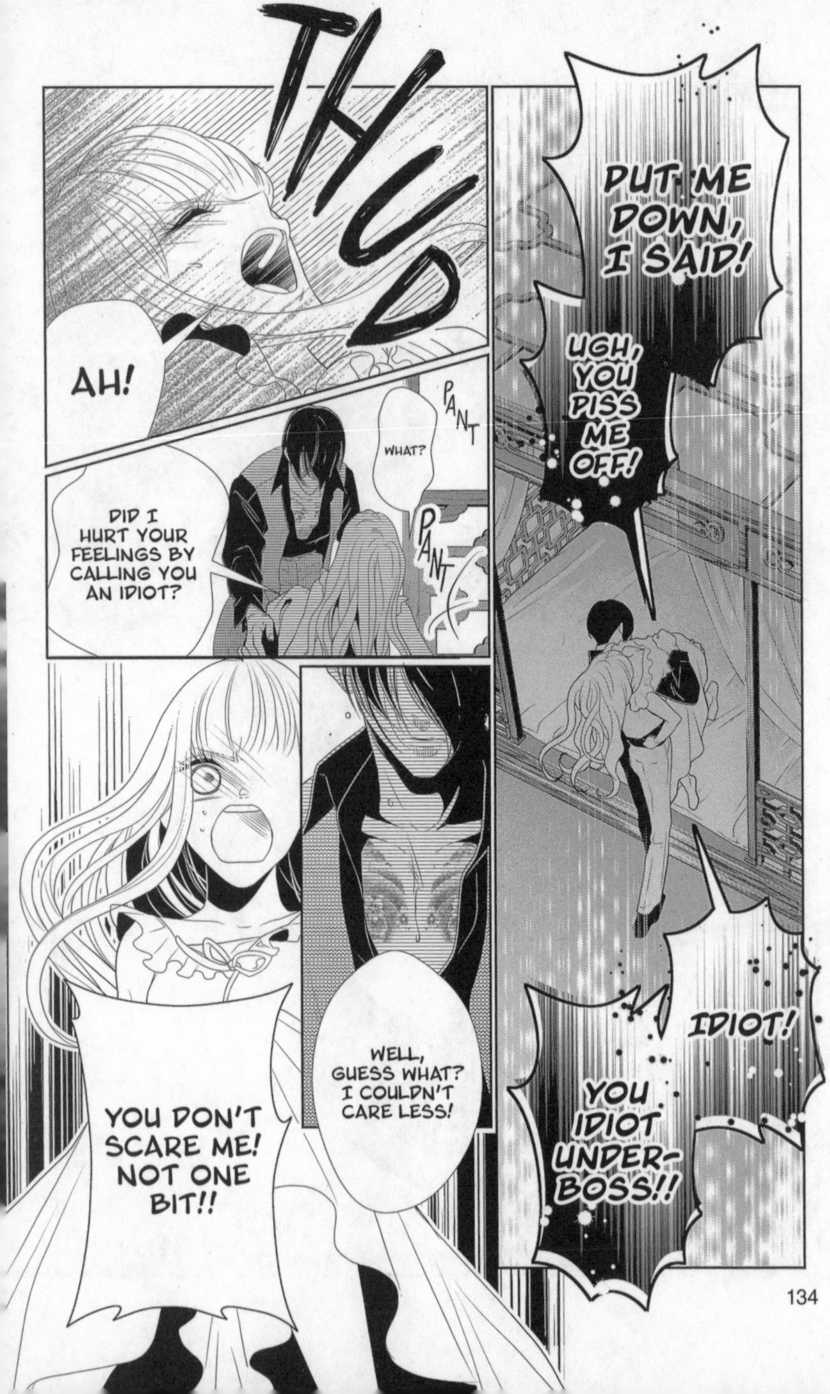
PUT ME DOWN, I SAID!
UGH, YOU PISS ME OFF!
IDIOT!
YOU IDIOT UNDER-BOSS!!
THUD
AH!
PANT
PANT
WHAT?
DID I HURT YOUR FEELINGS BY CALLING YOU AN IDIOT?
WELL, GUESS WHAT? I COULDN'T CARE LESS!
YOU DON'T SCARE ME! NOT ONE BIT!!

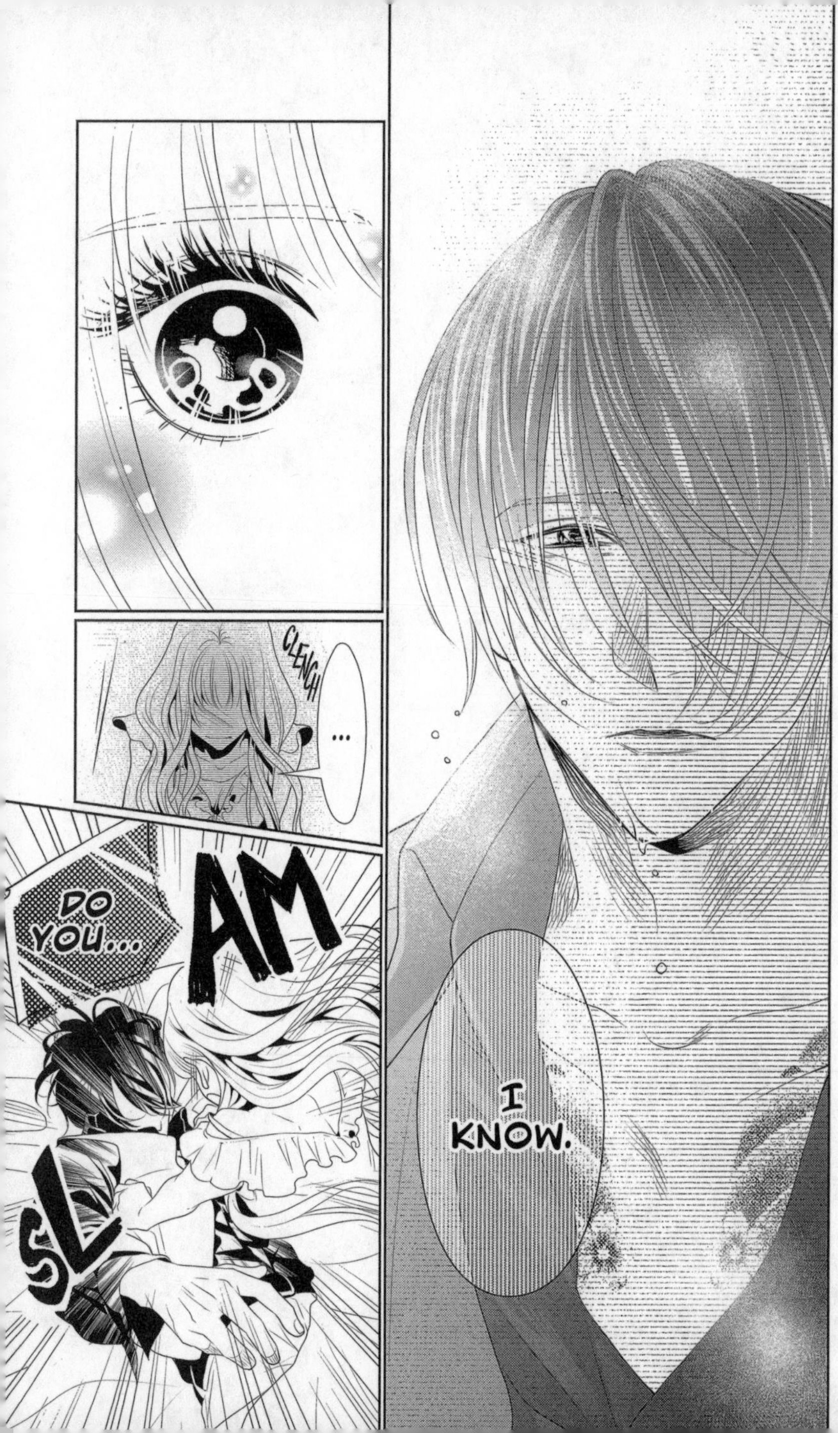
I KNOW.
CLENCH
...
DO YOU...
AM
SL

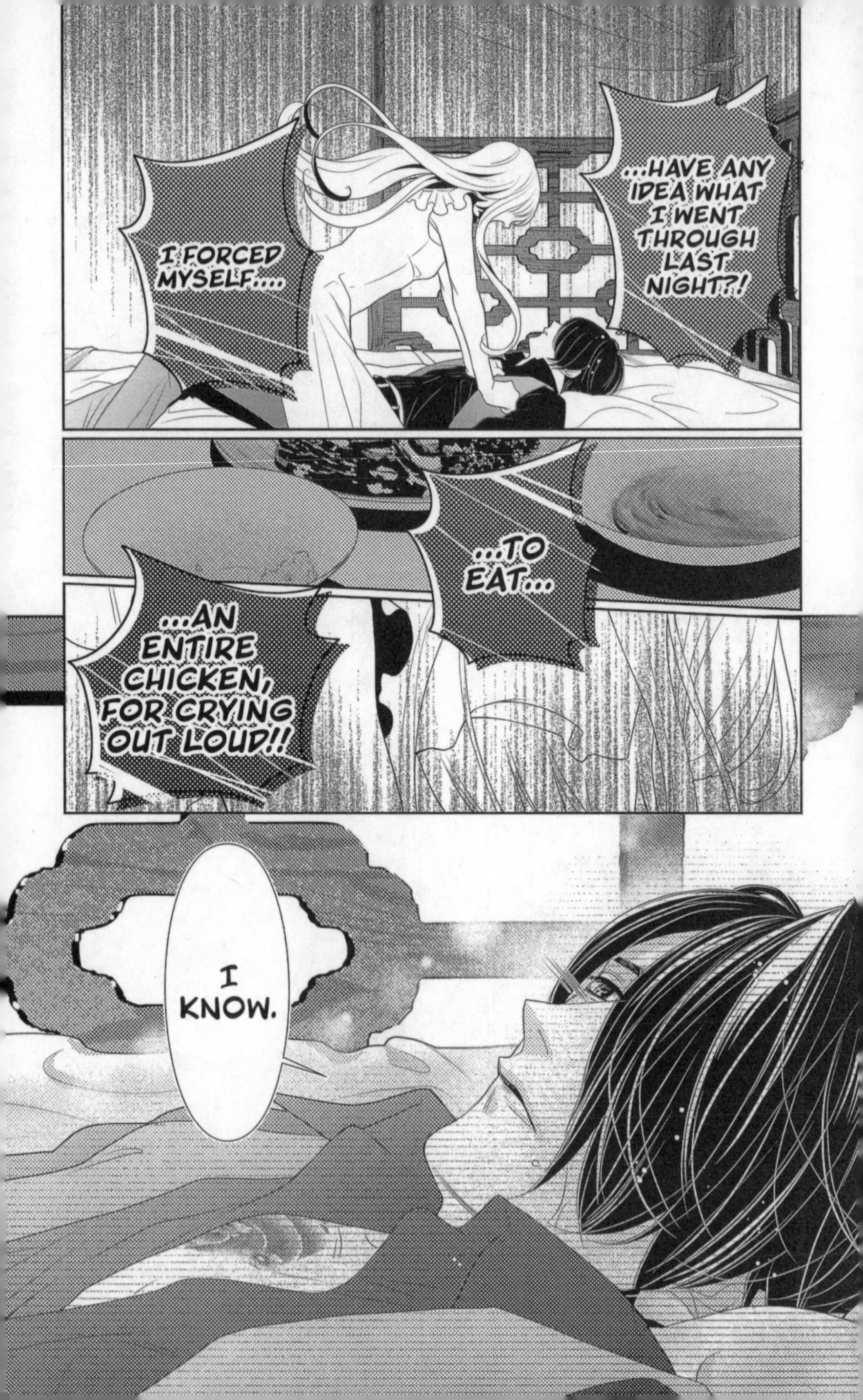
...HAVE ANY IDEA WHAT I WENT THROUGH LAST NIGHT?!
I FORCED MYSELF....
...TO EAT...
...AN ENTIRE CHICKEN, FOR CRYING OUT LOUD!!
I KNOW.

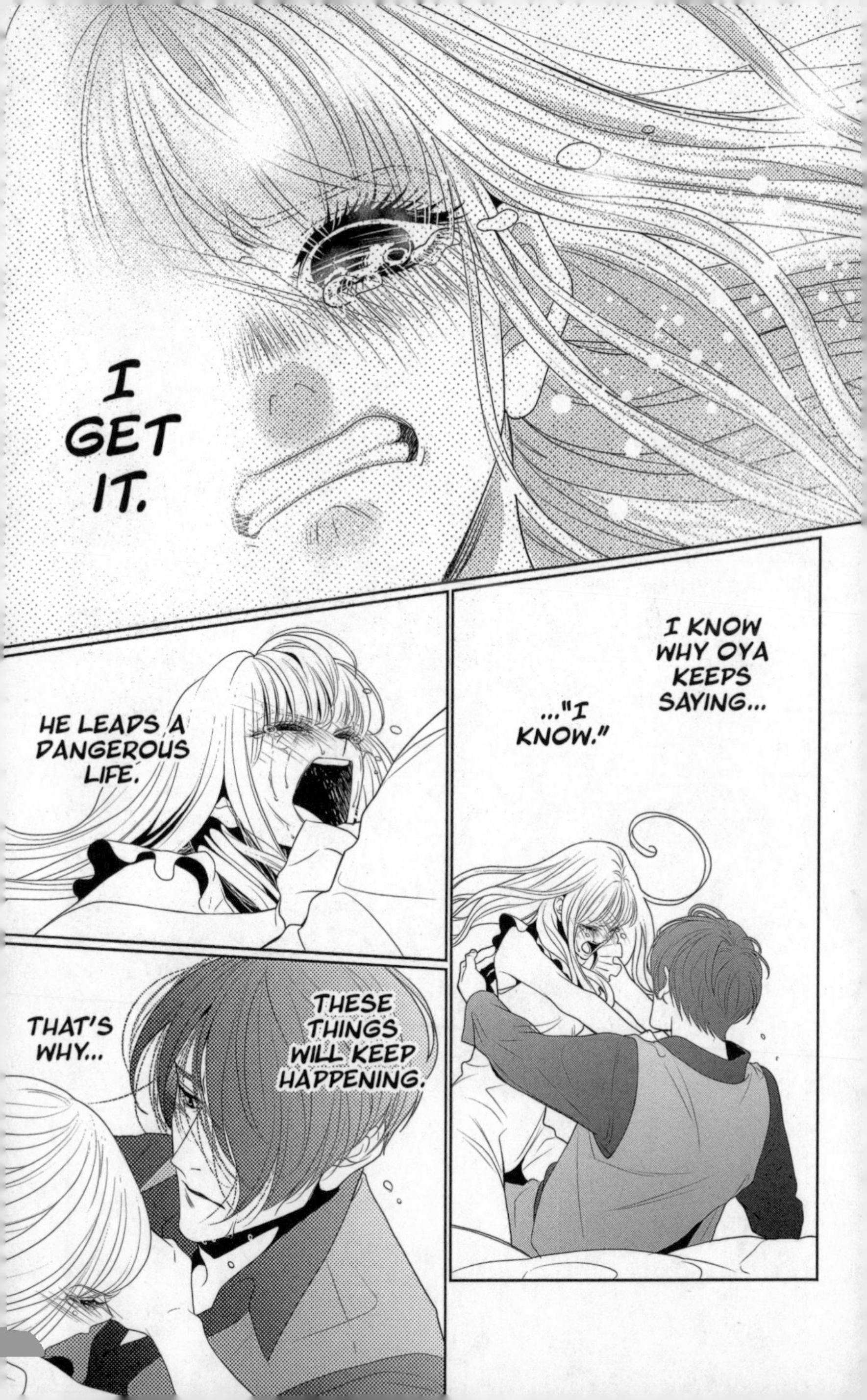
I GET IT.
I KNOW WHY OYA KEEPS SAYING...
..."I KNOW."
HE LEADS A DANGEROUS LIFE.
THESE THINGS WILL KEEP HAPPENING.
THAT'S WHY...

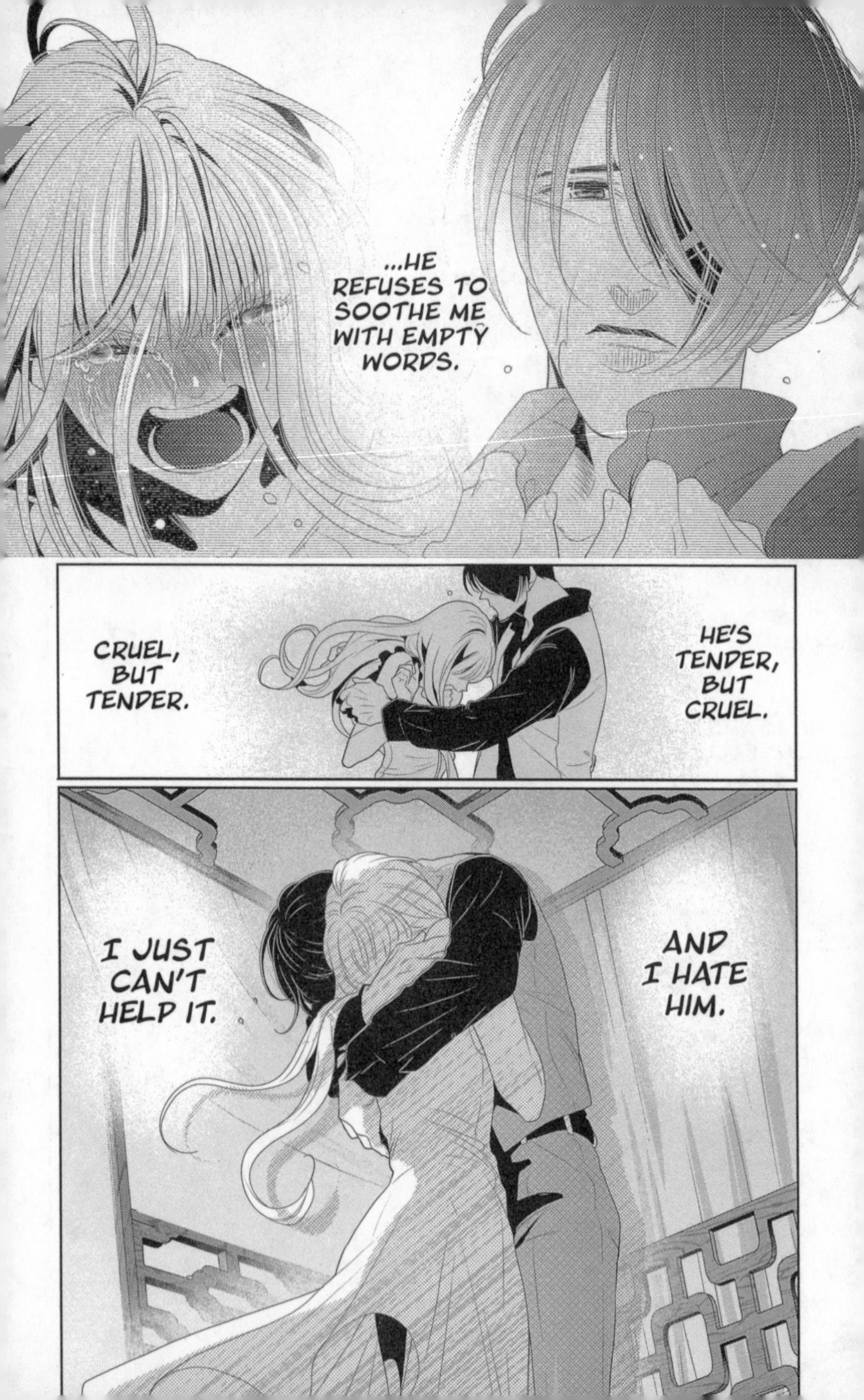
...HE REFUSES TO SOOTHE ME WITH EMPTY WORDS.
HE'S TENDER, BUT CRUEL.
CRUEL, BUT TENDER.
AND I HATE HIM.
I JUST CAN'T HELP IT.

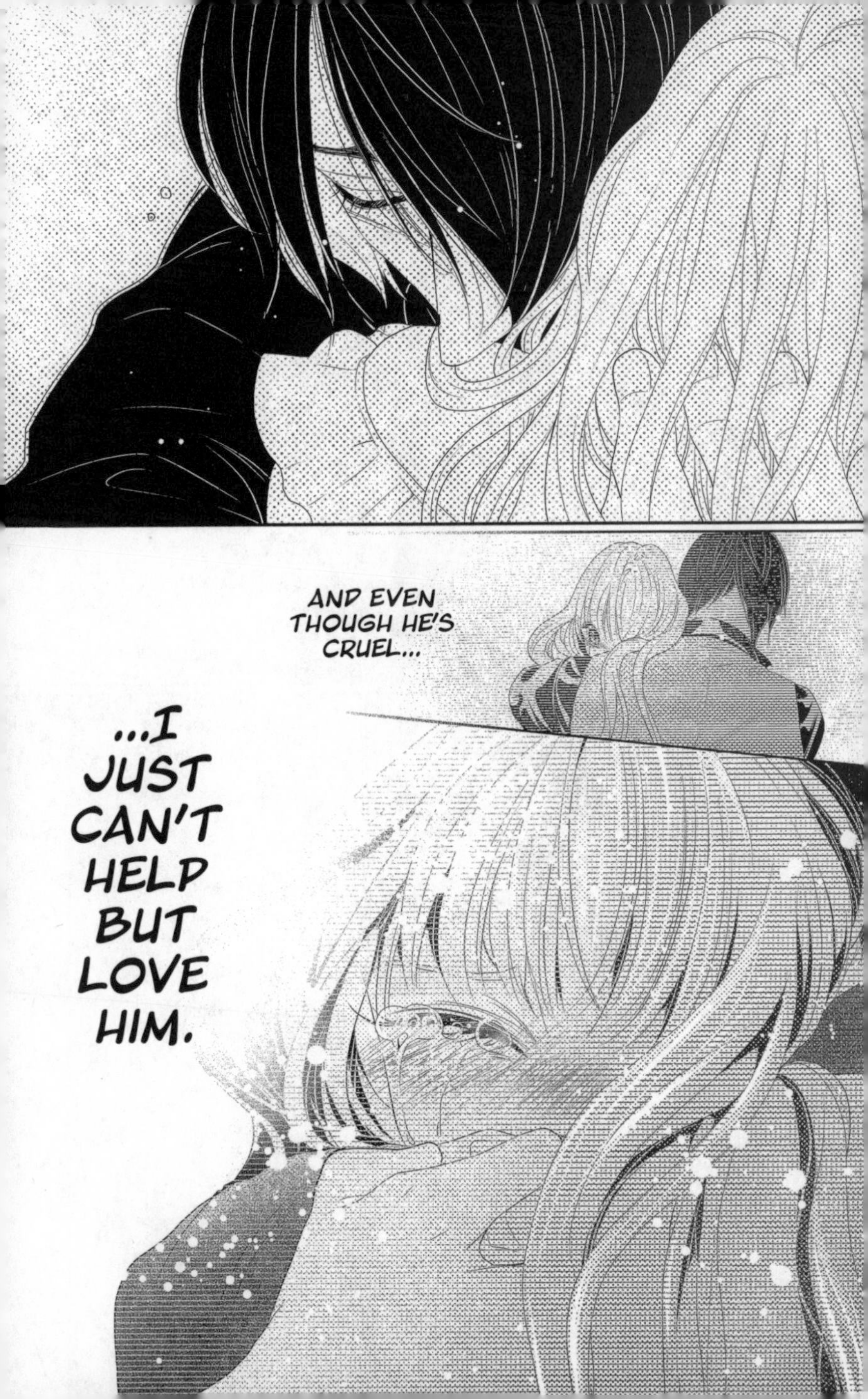
AND EVEN THOUGH HE'S CRUEL...
...I JUST CAN'T HELP BUT LOVE HIM.

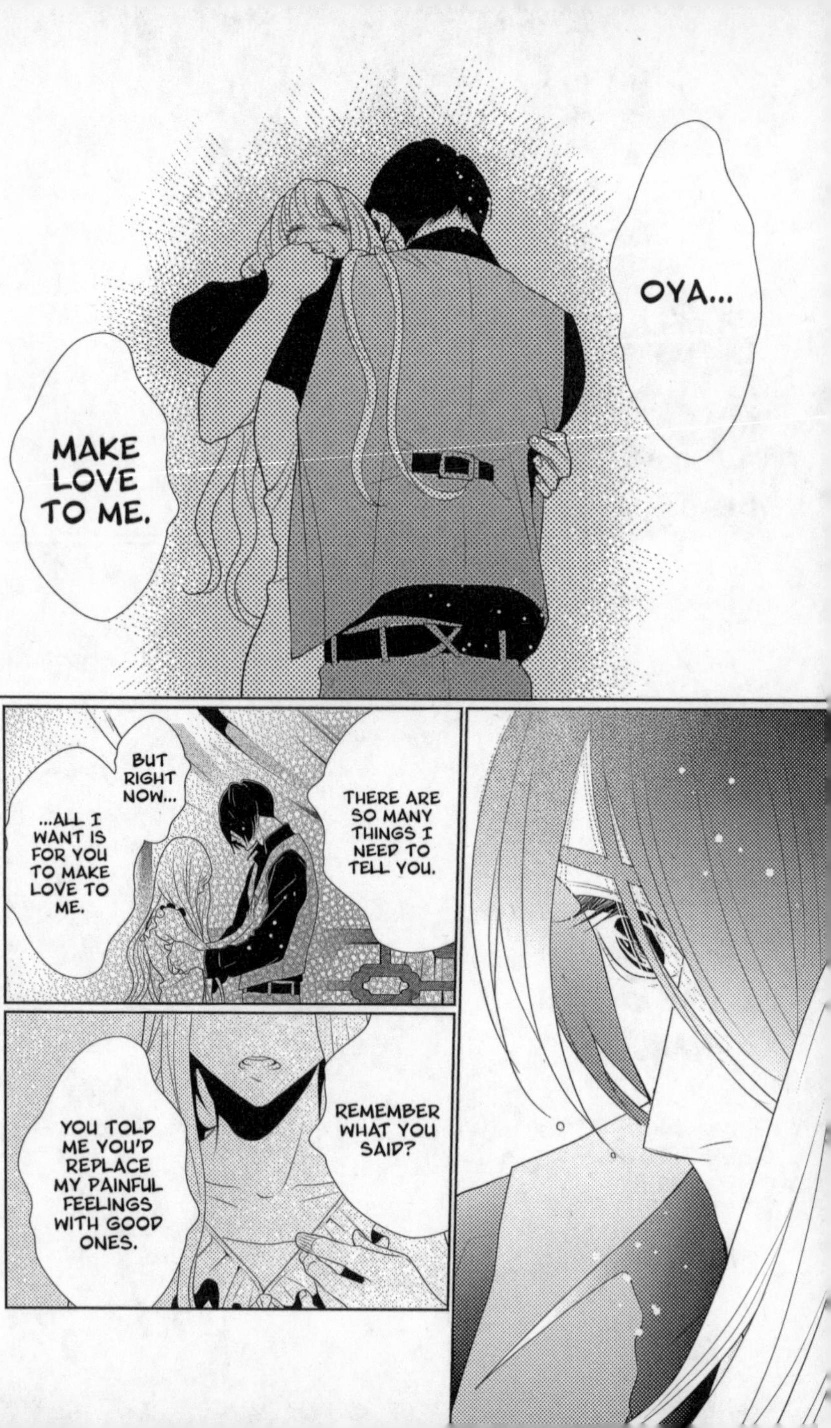
OYA...
MAKE LOVE TO ME.
THERE ARE SO MANY THINGS I NEED TO TELL YOU.
BUT RIGHT NOW...
...ALL I WANT IS FOR YOU TO MAKE LOVE TO ME.
REMEMBER WHAT YOU SAID?
YOU TOLD ME YOU'D REPLACE MY PAINFUL FEELINGS WITH GOOD ONES.

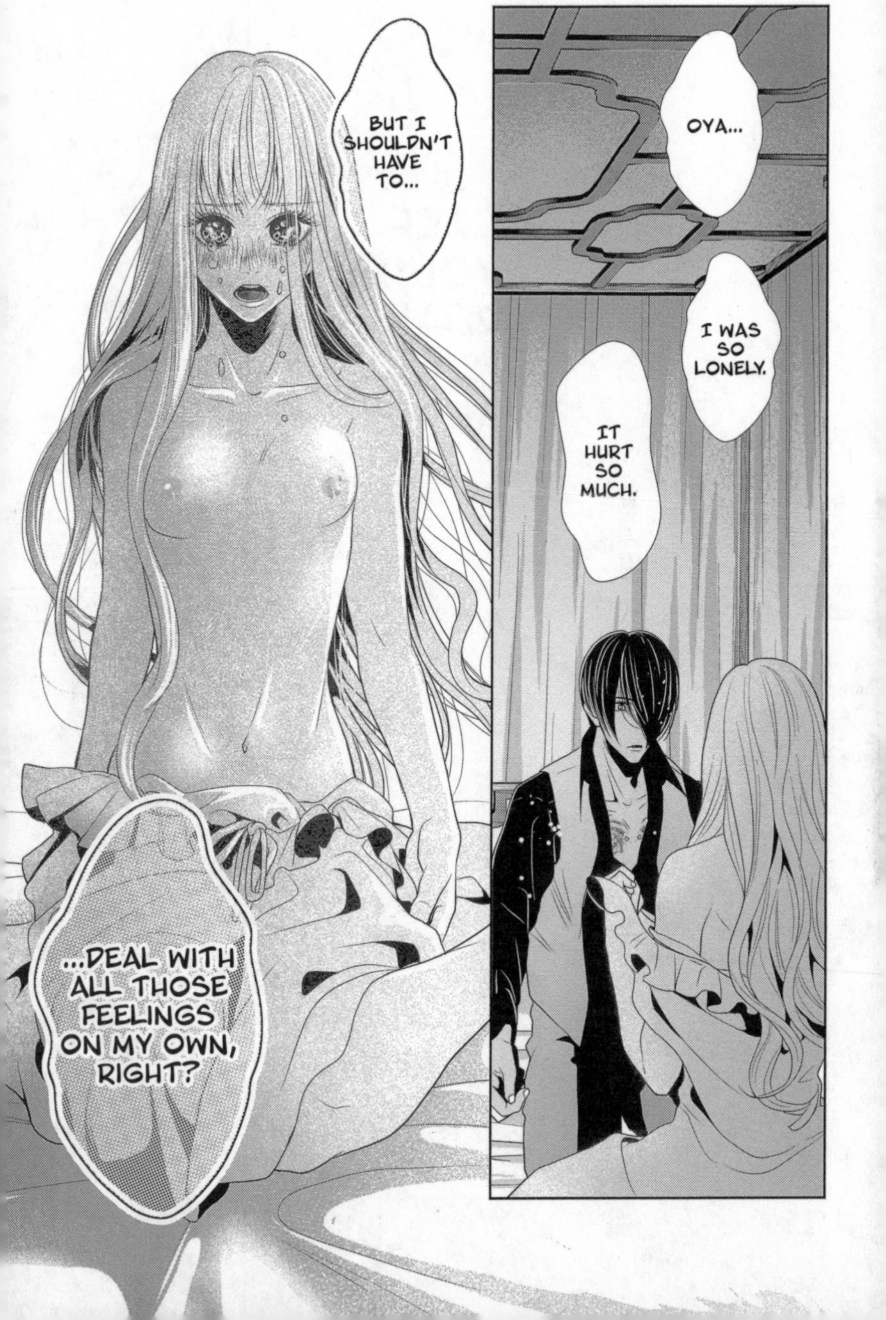
OYA...
I WAS SO LONELY.
IT HURT SO MUCH.
BUT I SHOULDN'T HAVE TO...
...DEAL WITH ALL THOSE FEELINGS ON MY OWN, RIGHT?

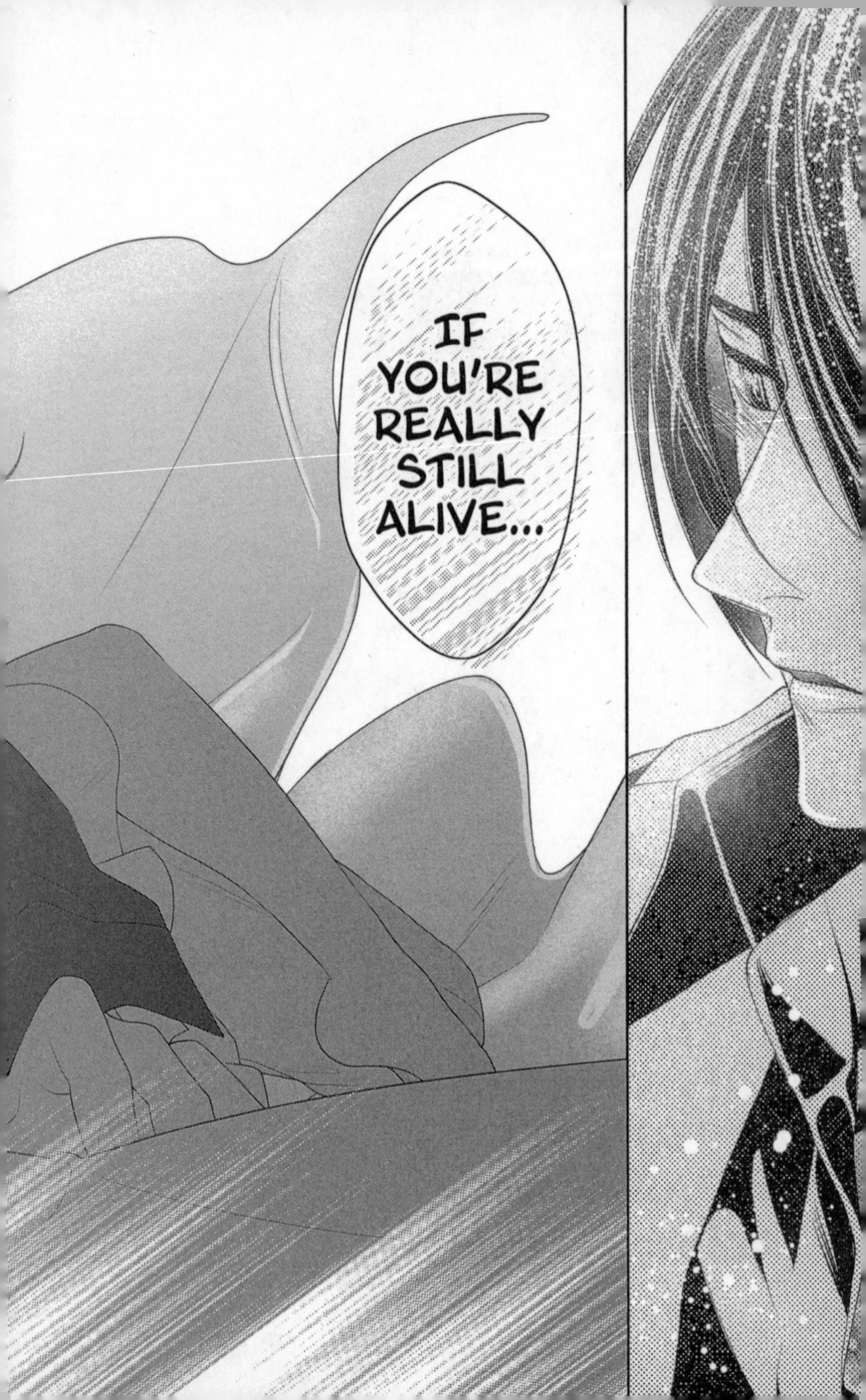
IF YOU'RE REALLY STILL ALIVE...

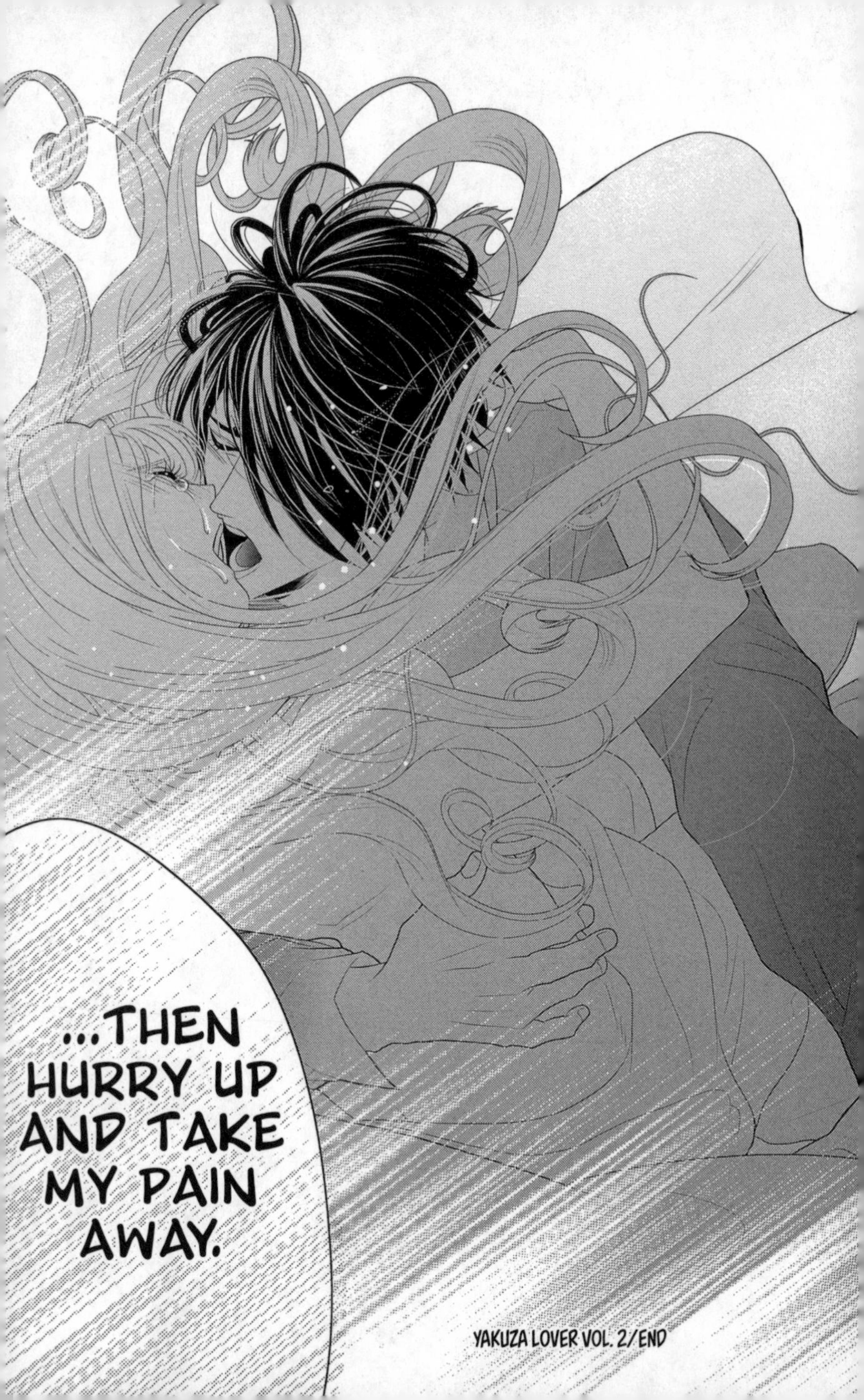
...THEN HURRY UP AND TAKE MY PAIN AWAY.
YAKUZA LOVER VOL. 2/END

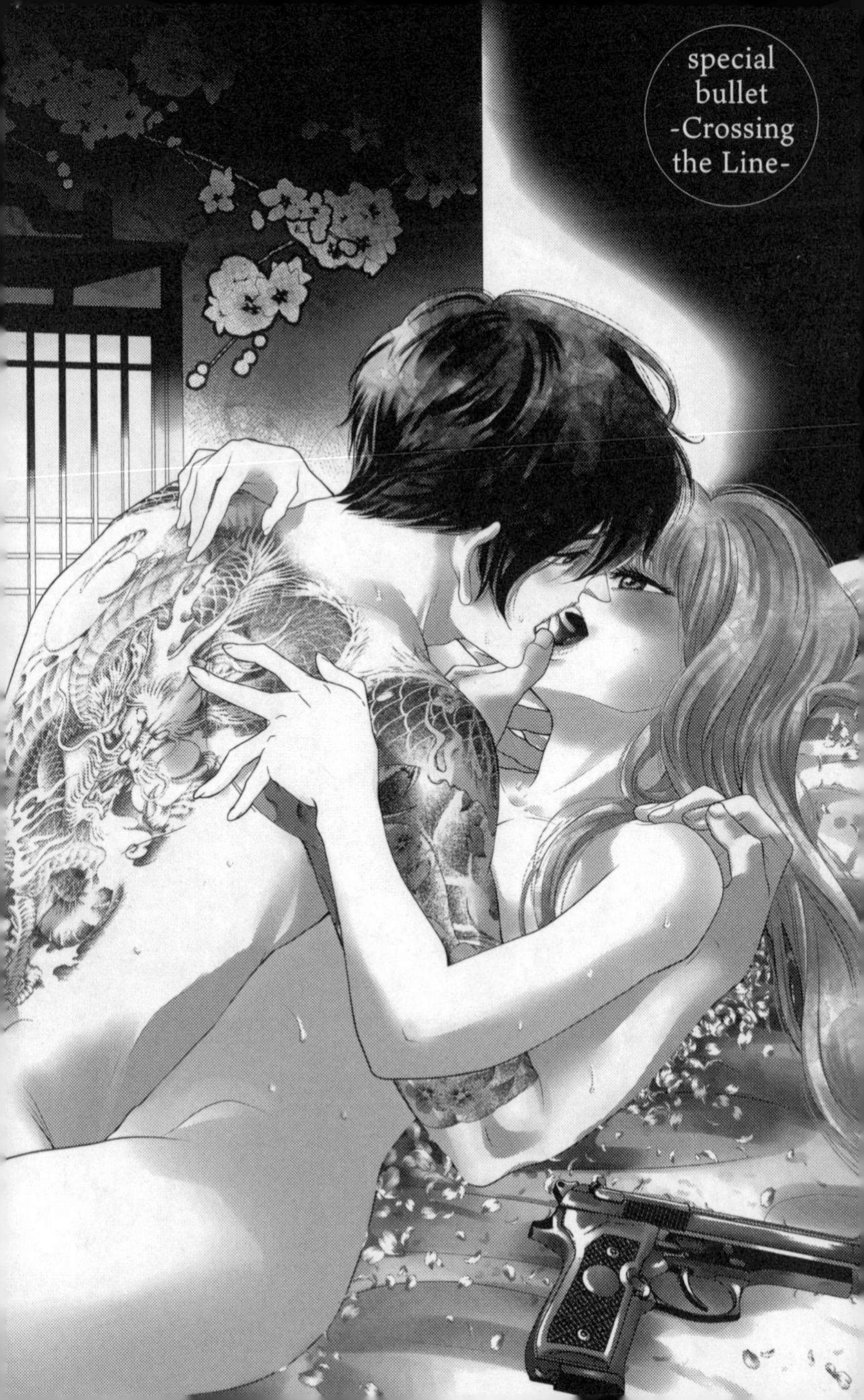
special
bullet
-Crossing
the Line-

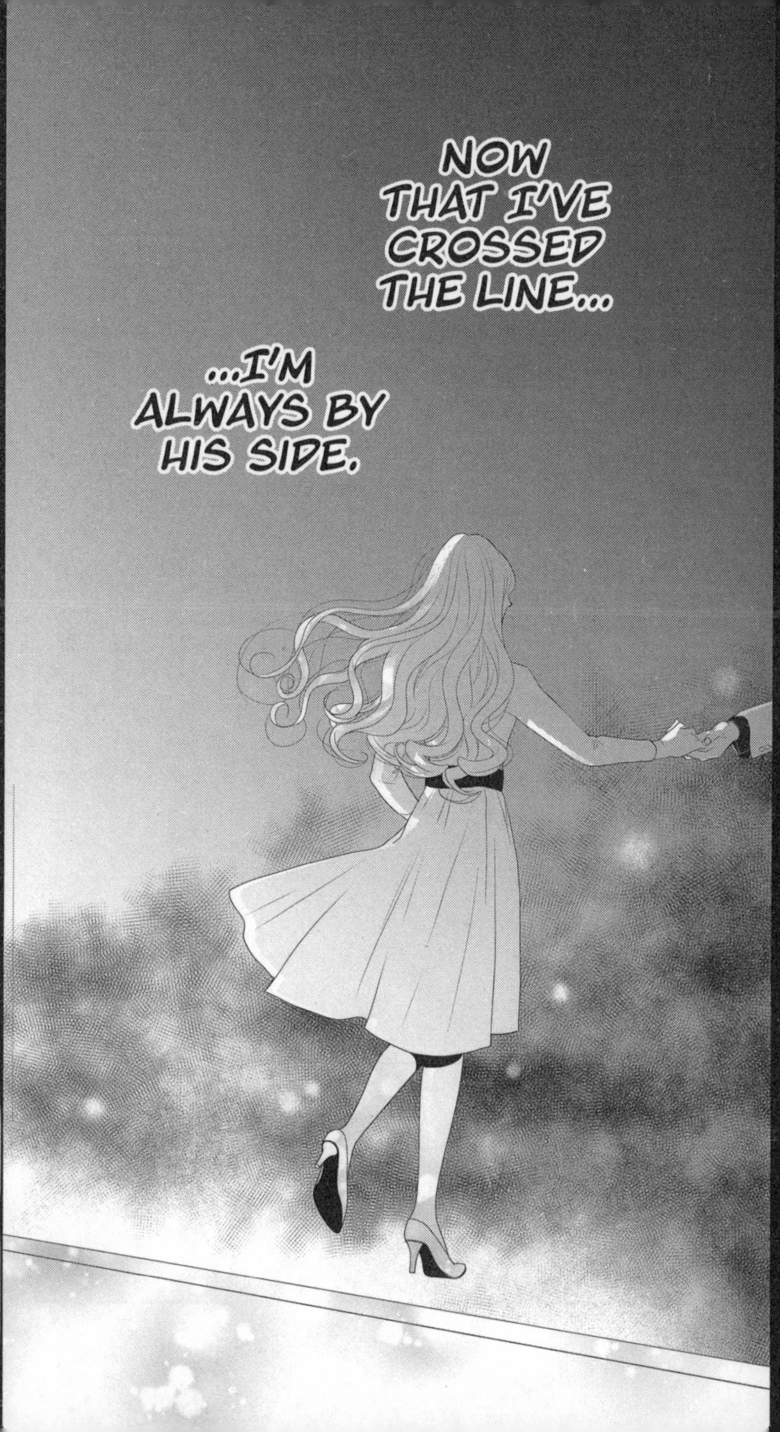
NOW THAT I'VE CROSSED THE LINE...
...I'M ALWAYS BY HIS SIDE.

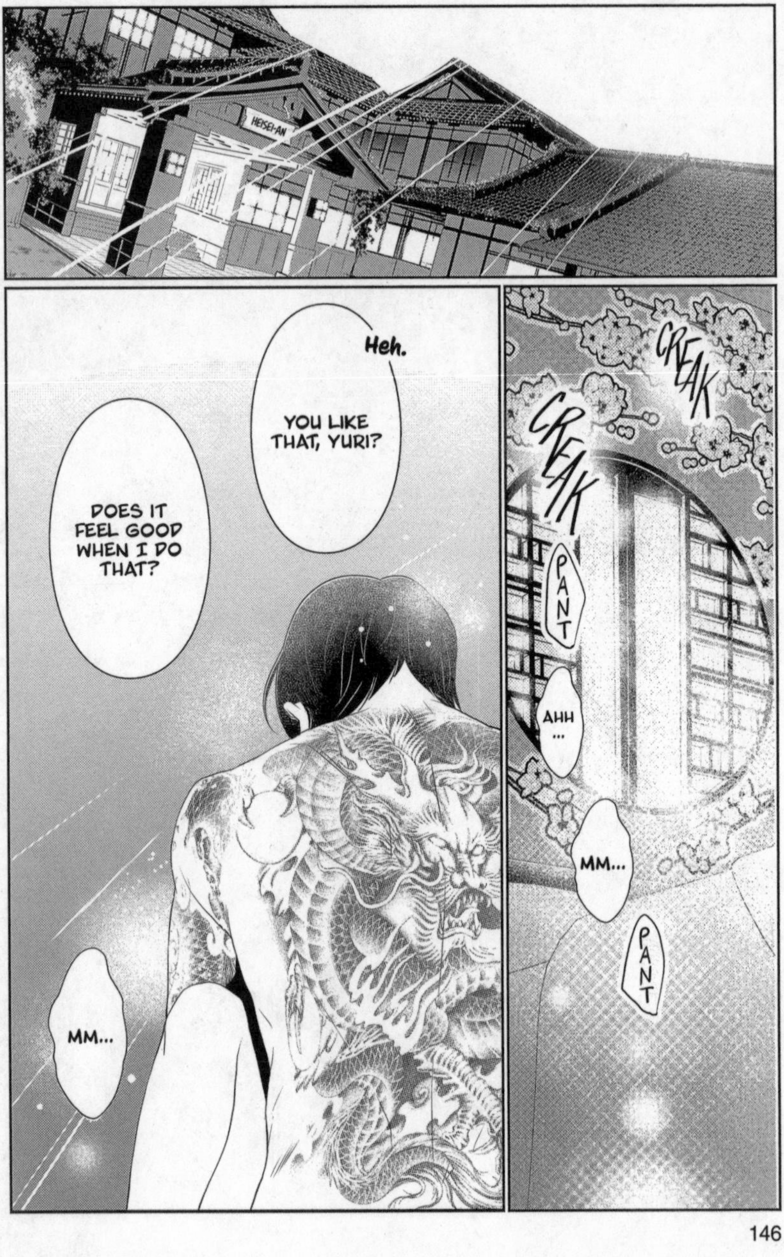
HEISEI-AN
CREAK
CREAK
PANT
AHH...
MM...
PANT
Heh.
YOU LIKE THAT, YURI?
DOES IT FEEL GOOD WHEN I DO THAT?
MM...

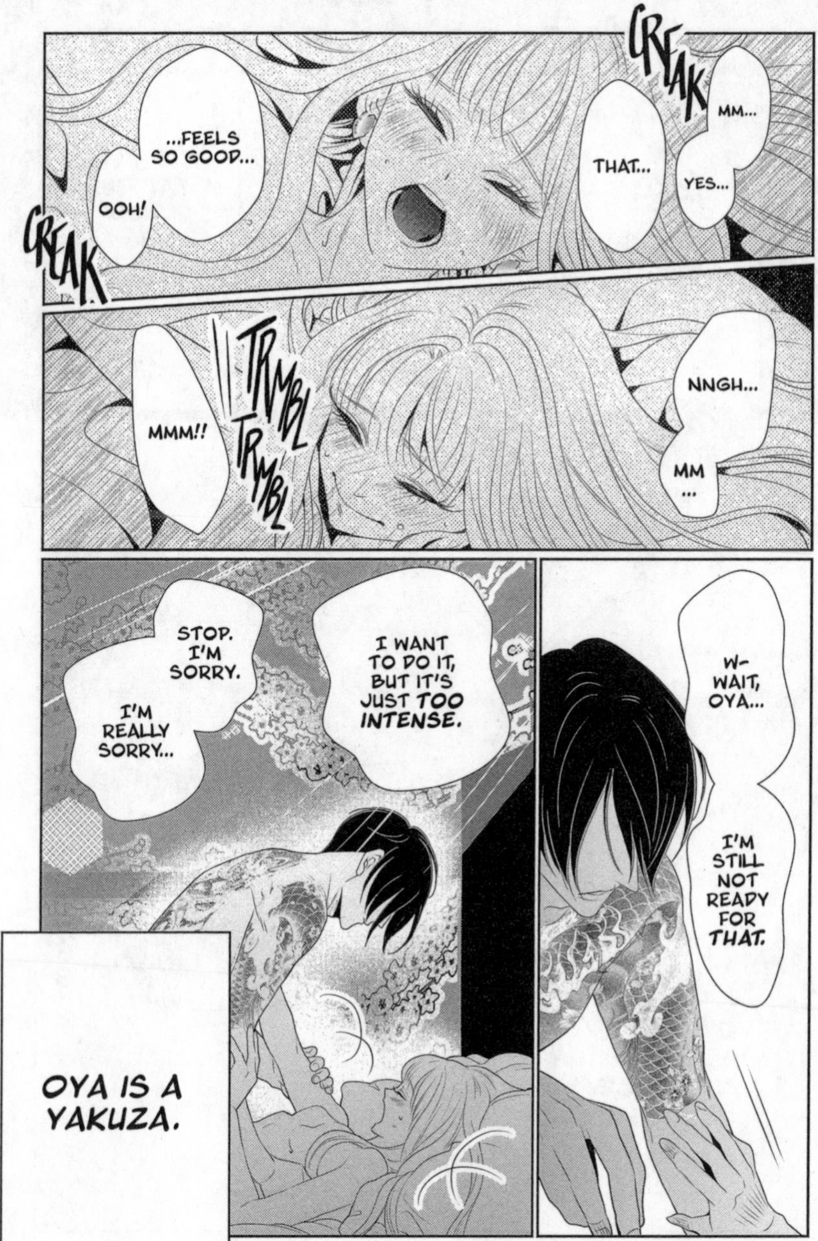
CREAK
MM...
YES...
THAT...
...FEELS SO GOOD...
OOH!
CREAK
NNGH...
MM ...
TRMBL TRMBL
MMM!!
W-WAIT, OYA...
I'M STILL NOT READY FOR THAT.
I WANT TO DO IT, BUT IT'S JUST TOO INTENSE.
STOP. I'M SORRY.
I'M REALLY SORRY...
OYA IS A YAKUZA.

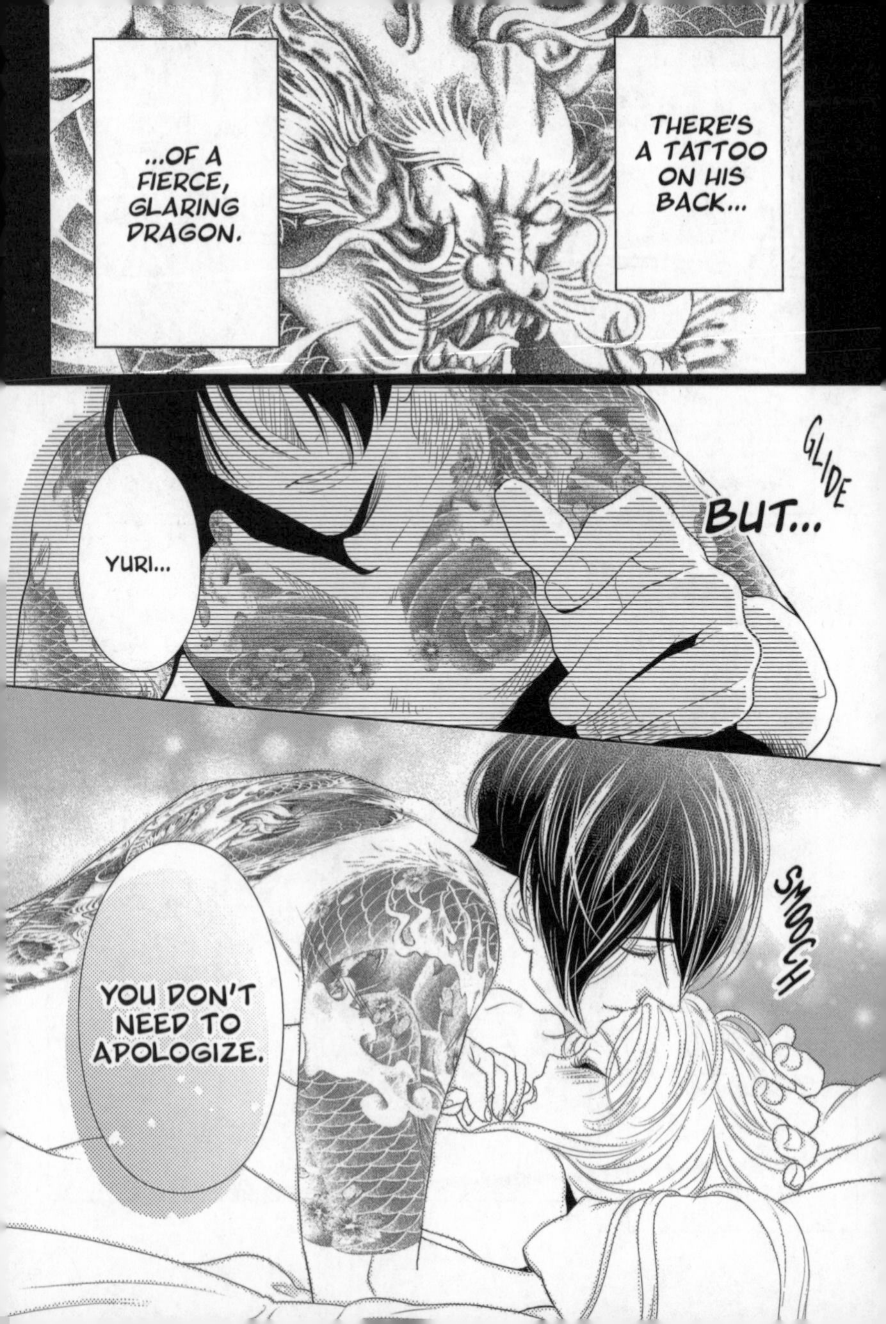
THERE'S A TATTOO ON HIS BACK...
...OF A FIERCE, GLARING DRAGON.
GLIDE
BUT...
YURI...
SMOOCH
YOU DON'T NEED TO APOLOGIZE.

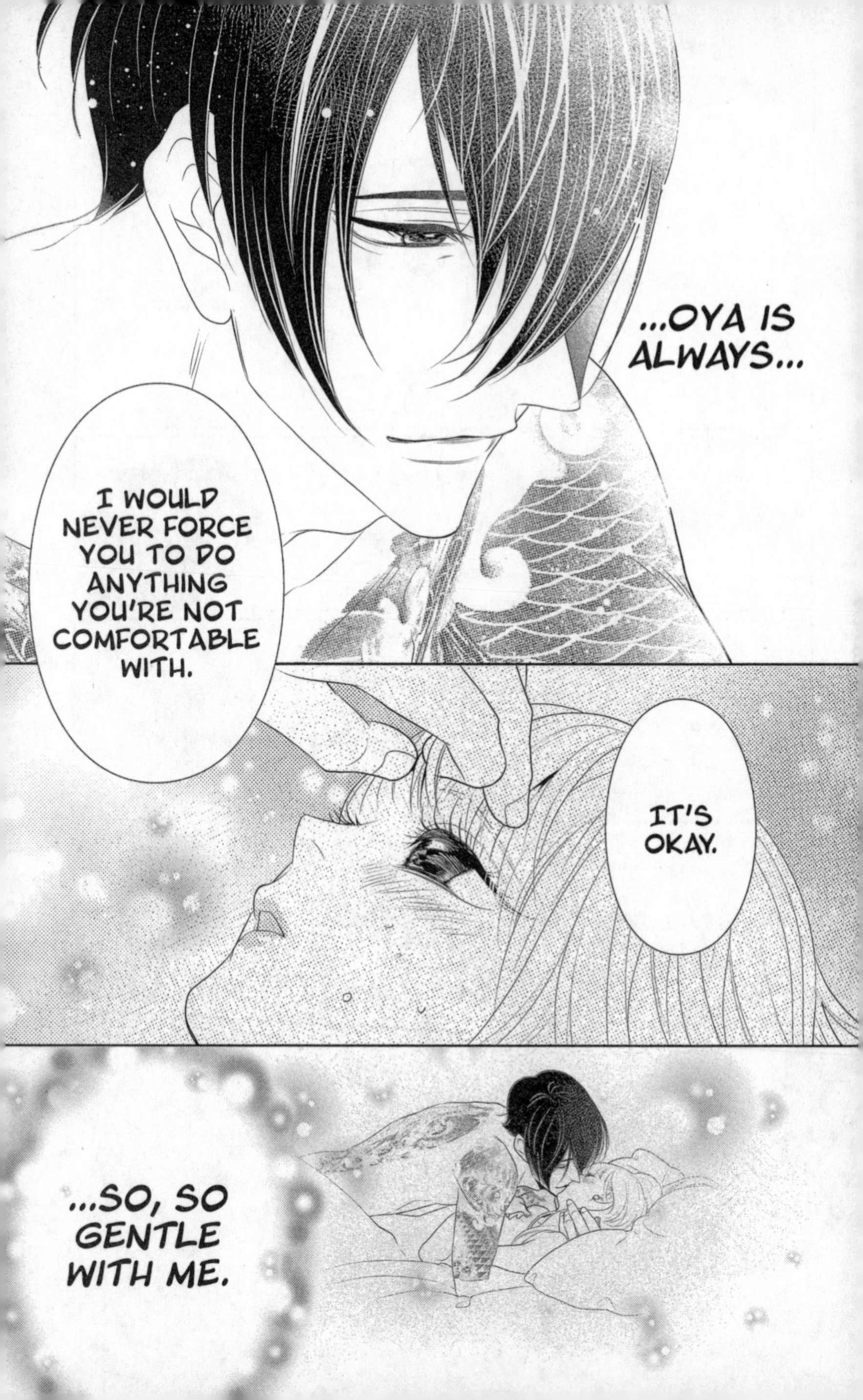
...OYA IS ALWAYS...
I WOULD NEVER FORCE YOU TO DO ANYTHING YOU'RE NOT COMFORTABLE WITH.
IT'S OKAY.
...SO, SO GENTLE WITH ME.

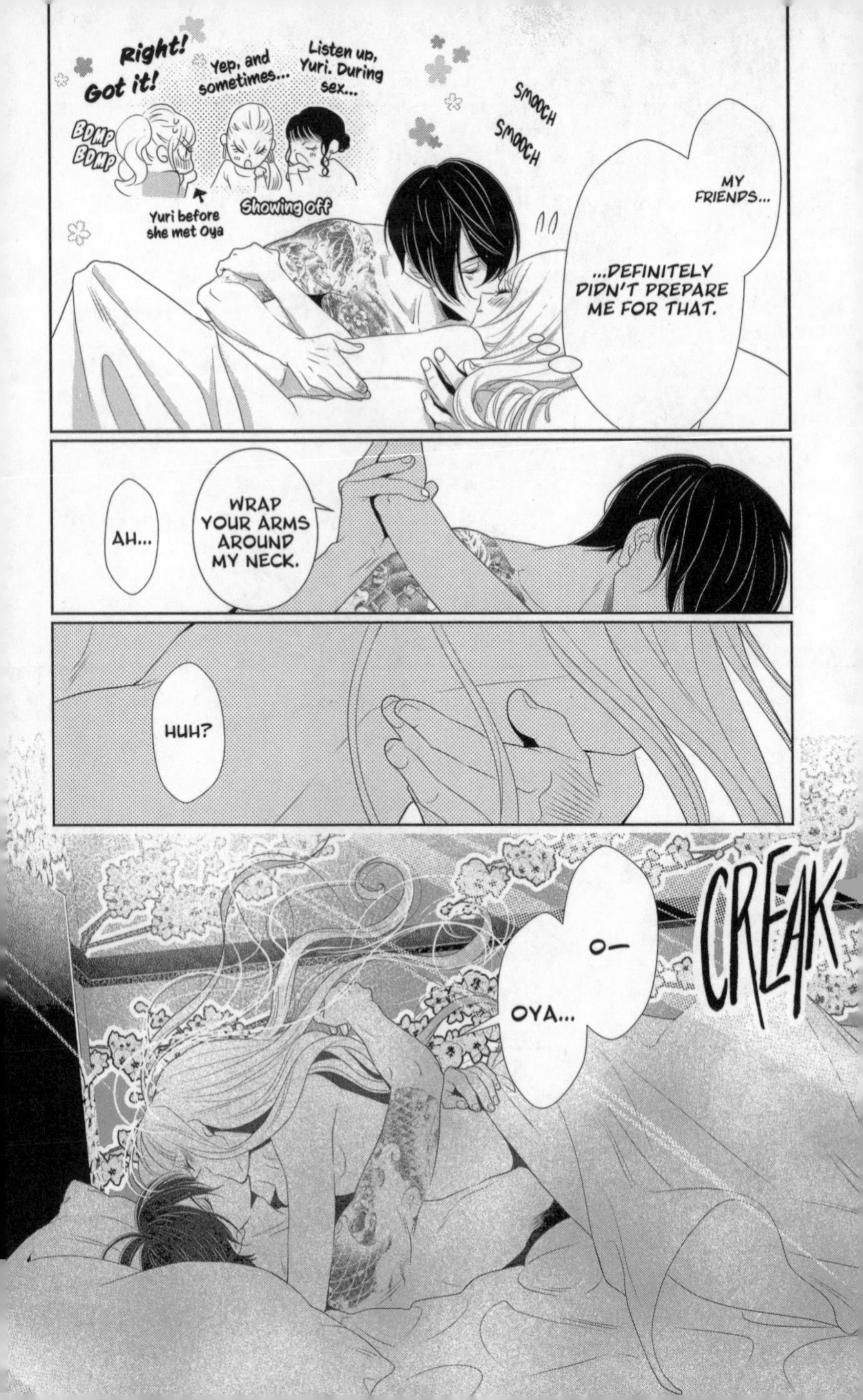
MY FRIENDS...
...DEFINITELY DIDN'T PREPARE ME FOR THAT.
SMOOCH
SMOOCH
Listen up, Yuri. During sex...
Yep, and sometimes...
Right! Got it!
BDMP BDMP
Showing off
Yuri before she met Oya
WRAP YOUR ARMS AROUND MY NECK.
AH...
HUH?
CREAK
O— OYA...

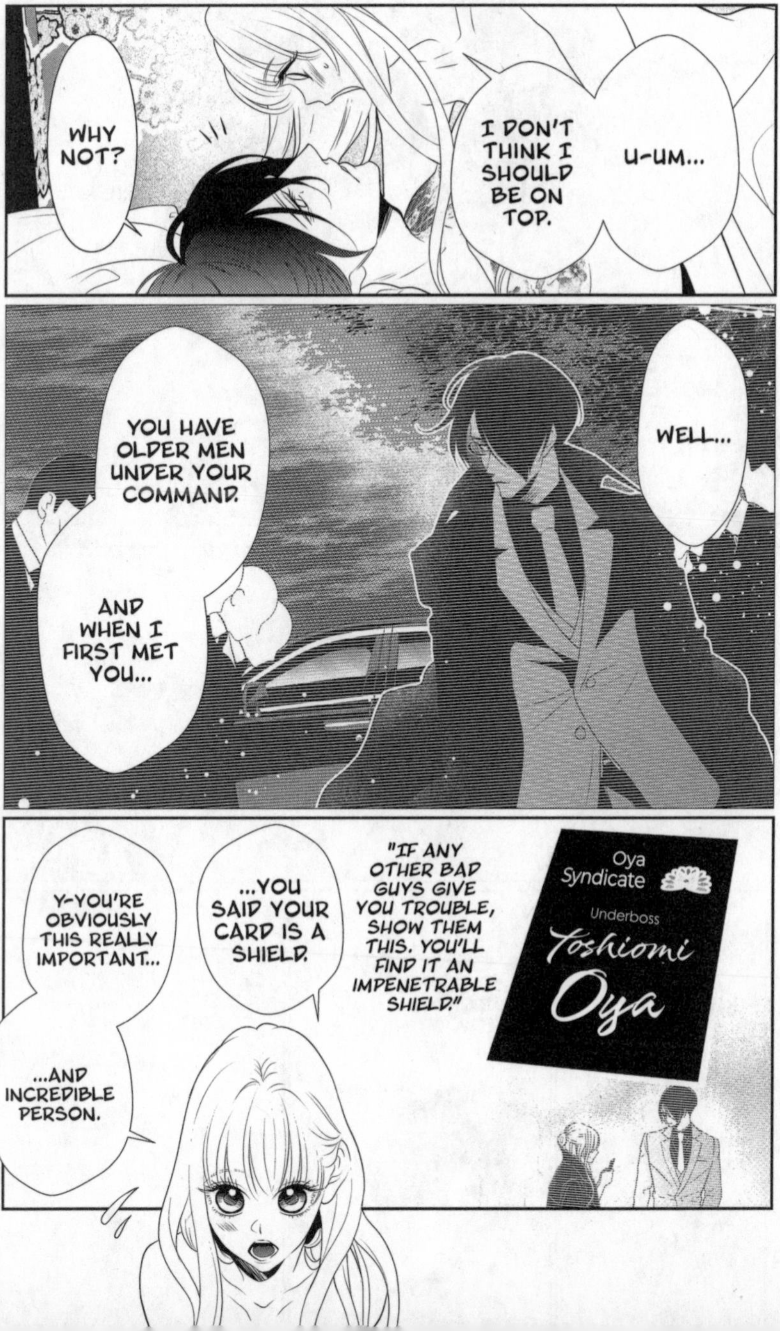
U-UM...
I DON'T THINK I SHOULD BE ON TOP.
WHY NOT?
WELL...
YOU HAVE OLDER MEN UNDER YOUR COMMAND.
AND WHEN I FIRST MET YOU...
Oya Syndicate
Underboss
Toshiomi Oya
"IF ANY OTHER BAD GUYS GIVE YOU TROUBLE, SHOW THEM THIS. YOU'LL FIND IT AN IMPENETRABLE SHIELD."
...YOU SAID YOUR CARD IS A SHIELD.
Y-YOU'RE OBVIOUSLY THIS REALLY IMPORTANT...
...AND INCREDIBLE PERSON.

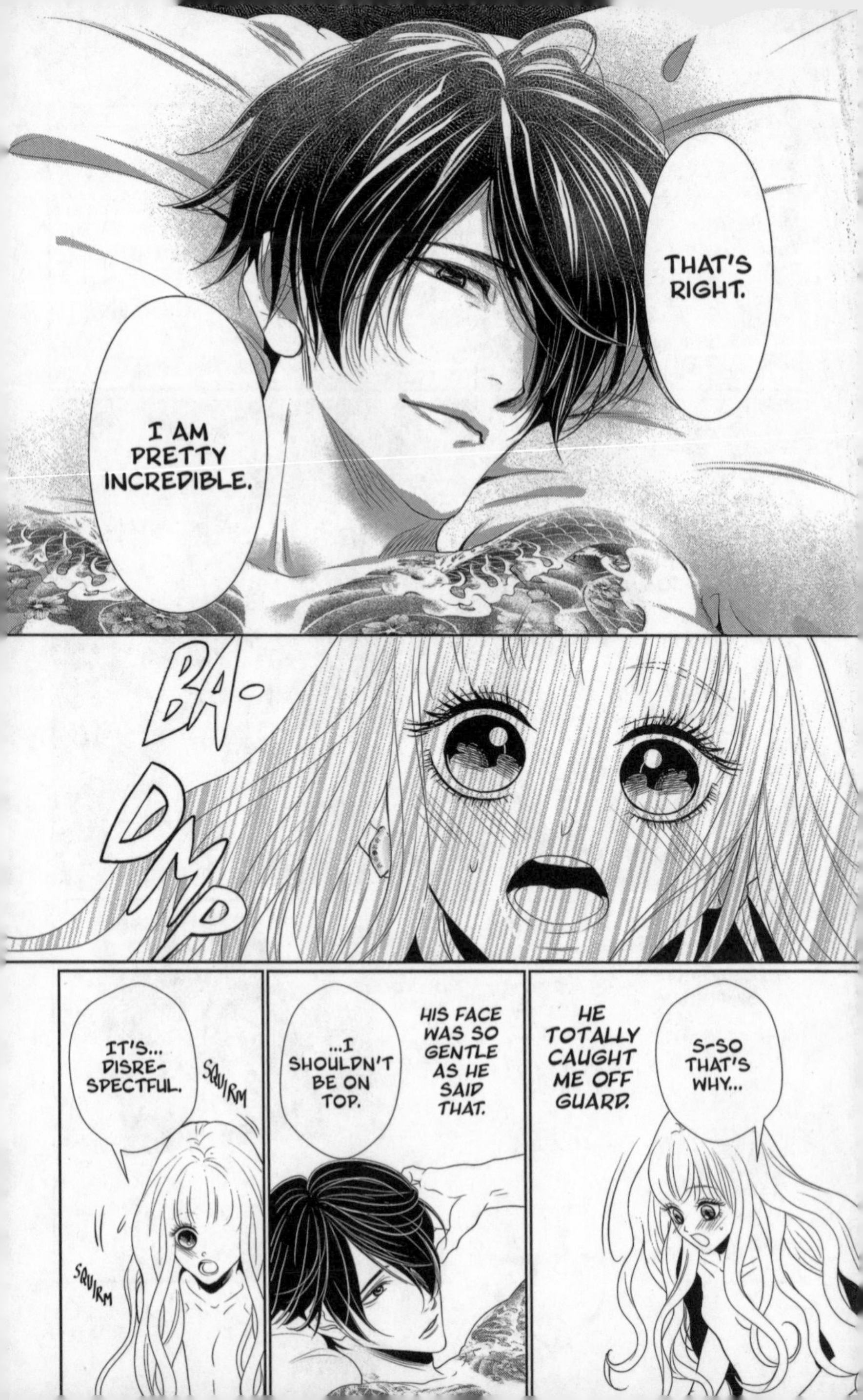
THAT'S RIGHT.
I AM PRETTY INCREDIBLE.
BA-DMP
S-SO THAT'S WHY...
HE TOTALLY CAUGHT ME OFF GUARD.
HIS FACE WAS SO GENTLE AS HE SAID THAT.
...I SHOULDN'T BE ON TOP.
IT'S... DISRE-SPECTFUL.
SQUIRM
SQUIRM

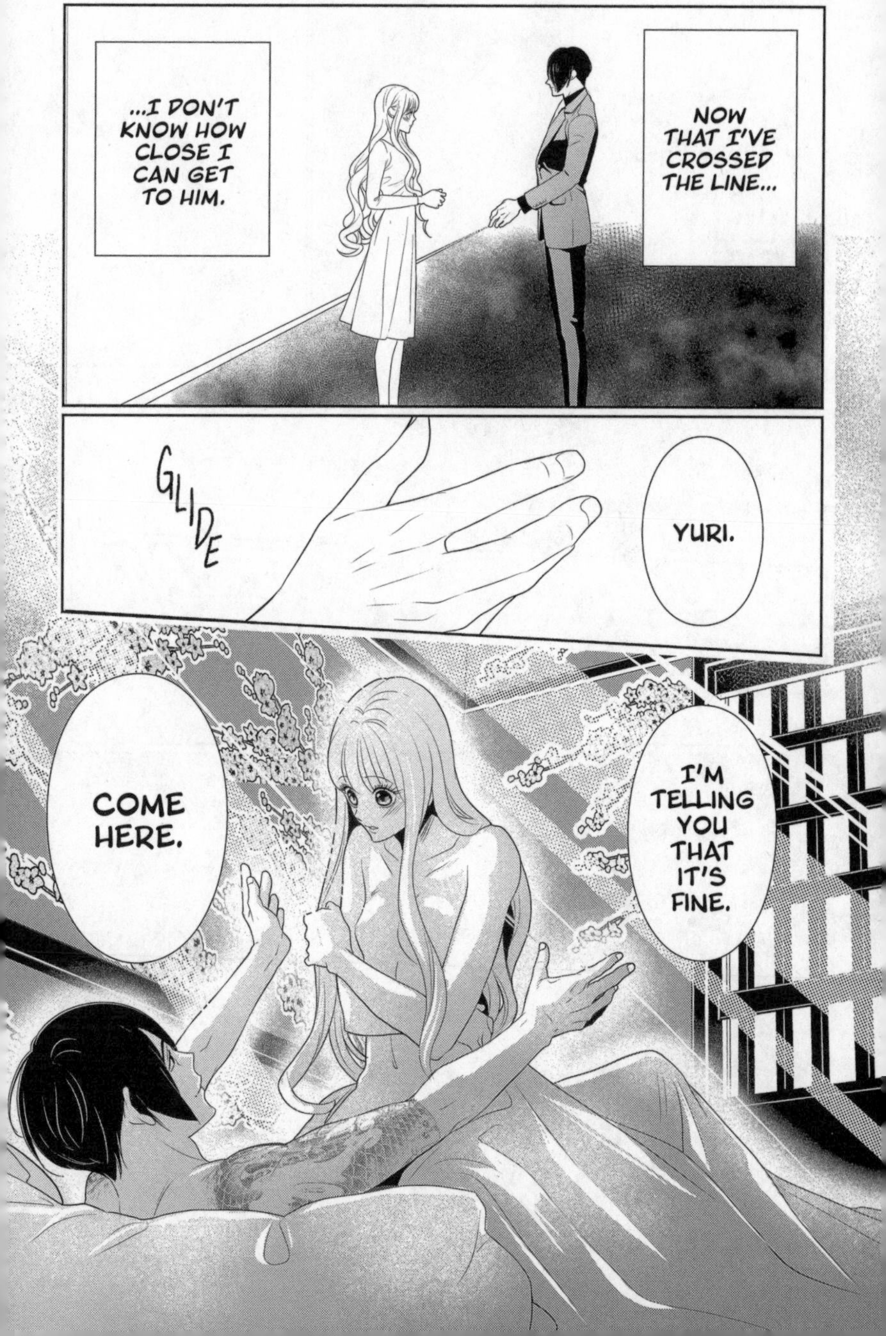
NOW THAT I'VE CROSSED THE LINE...
...I DON'T KNOW HOW CLOSE I CAN GET TO HIM.
YURI.
GLIDE
I'M TELLING YOU THAT IT'S FINE.
COME HERE.

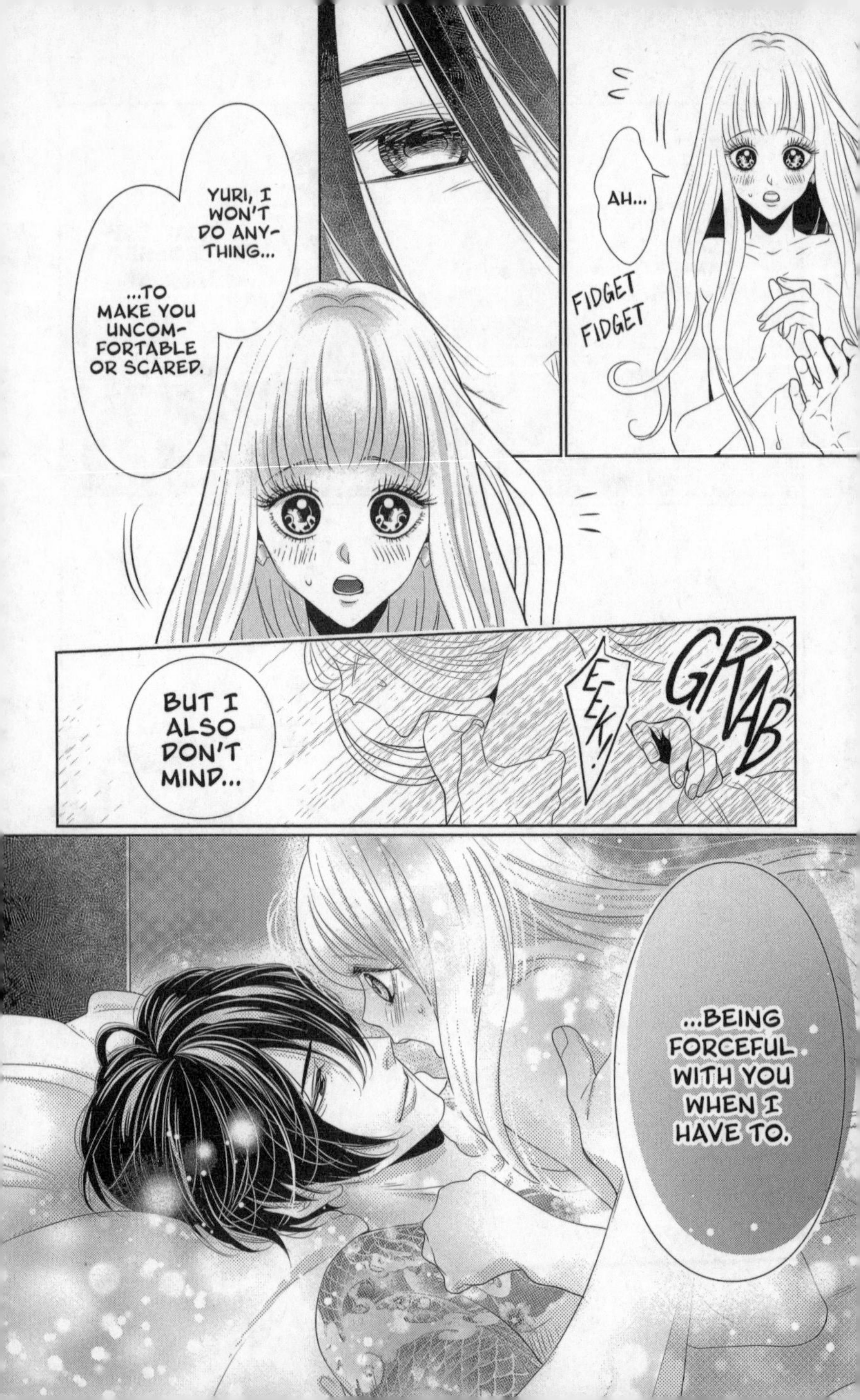
AH...
FIDGET FIDGET
YURI, I WON'T DO ANYTHING...
...TO MAKE YOU UNCOMFORTABLE OR SCARED.
GRAB
EEK!
BUT I ALSO DON'T MIND...
...BEING FORCEFUL WITH YOU WHEN I HAVE TO.

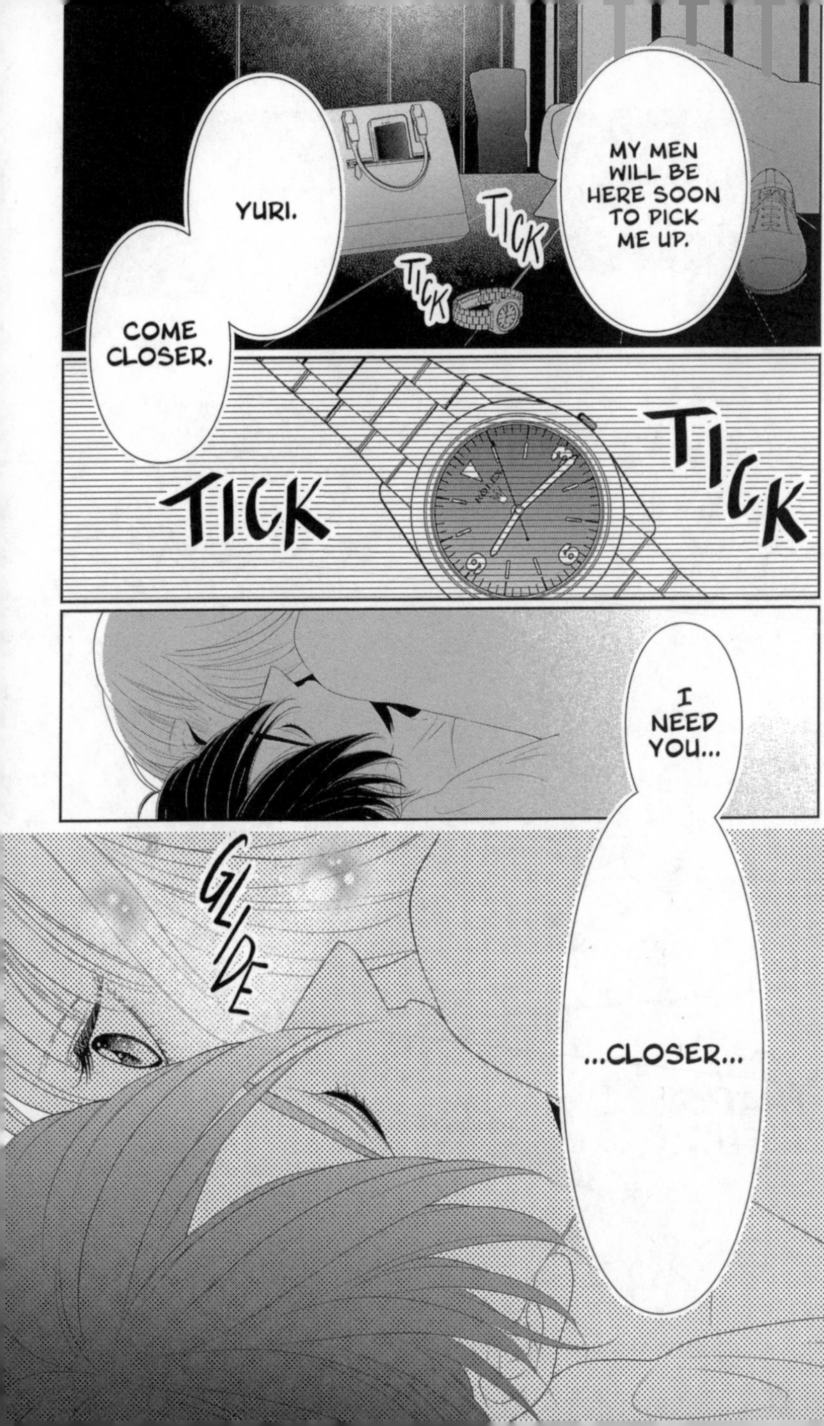
MY MEN WILL BE HERE SOON TO PICK ME UP.
TICK
TICK
YURI.
COME CLOSER.
TICK
TICK
I NEED YOU...
...CLOSER...
GLIDE

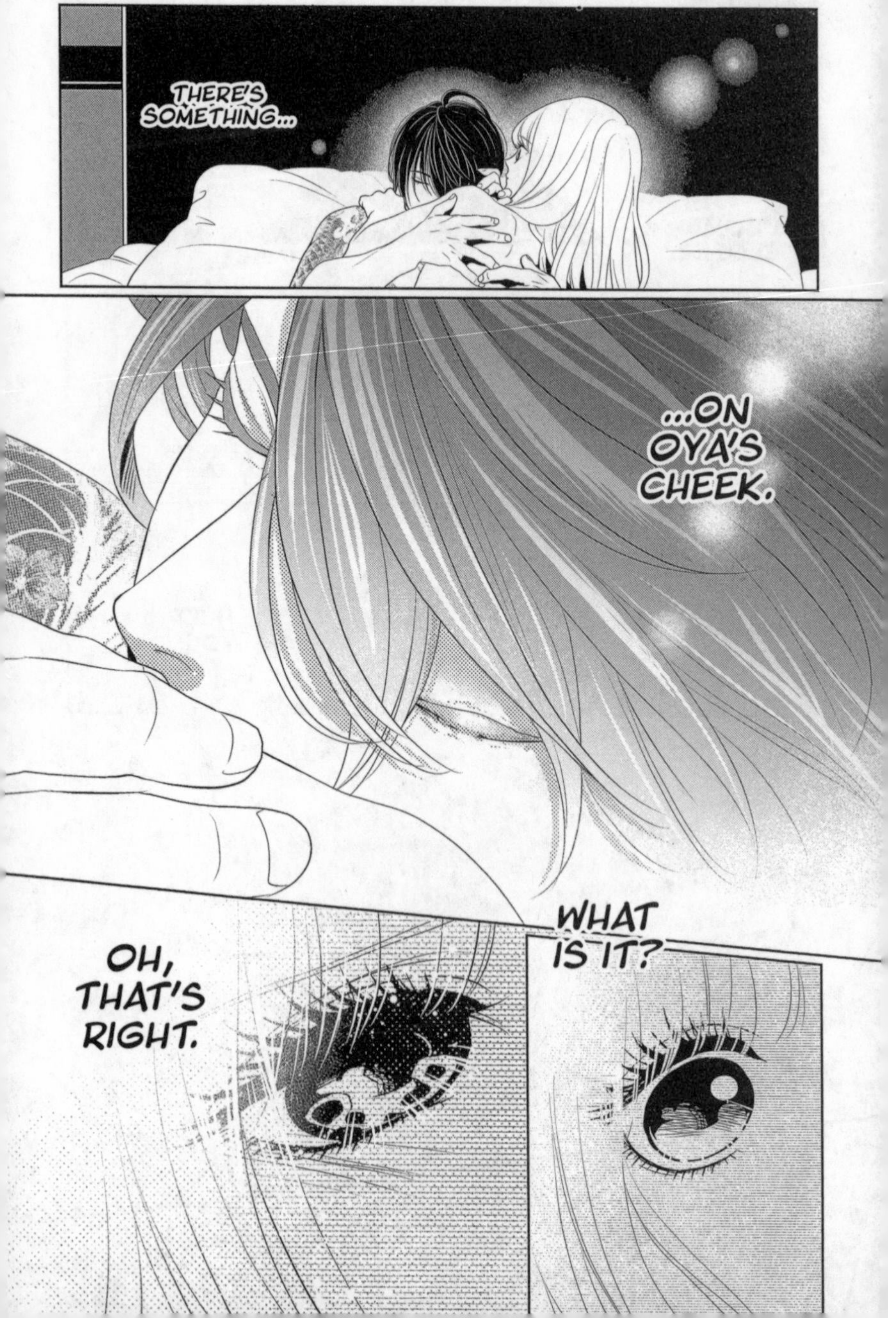
THERE'S SOMETHING...
...ON OYA'S CHEEK.
WHAT IS IT?
OH, THAT'S RIGHT.

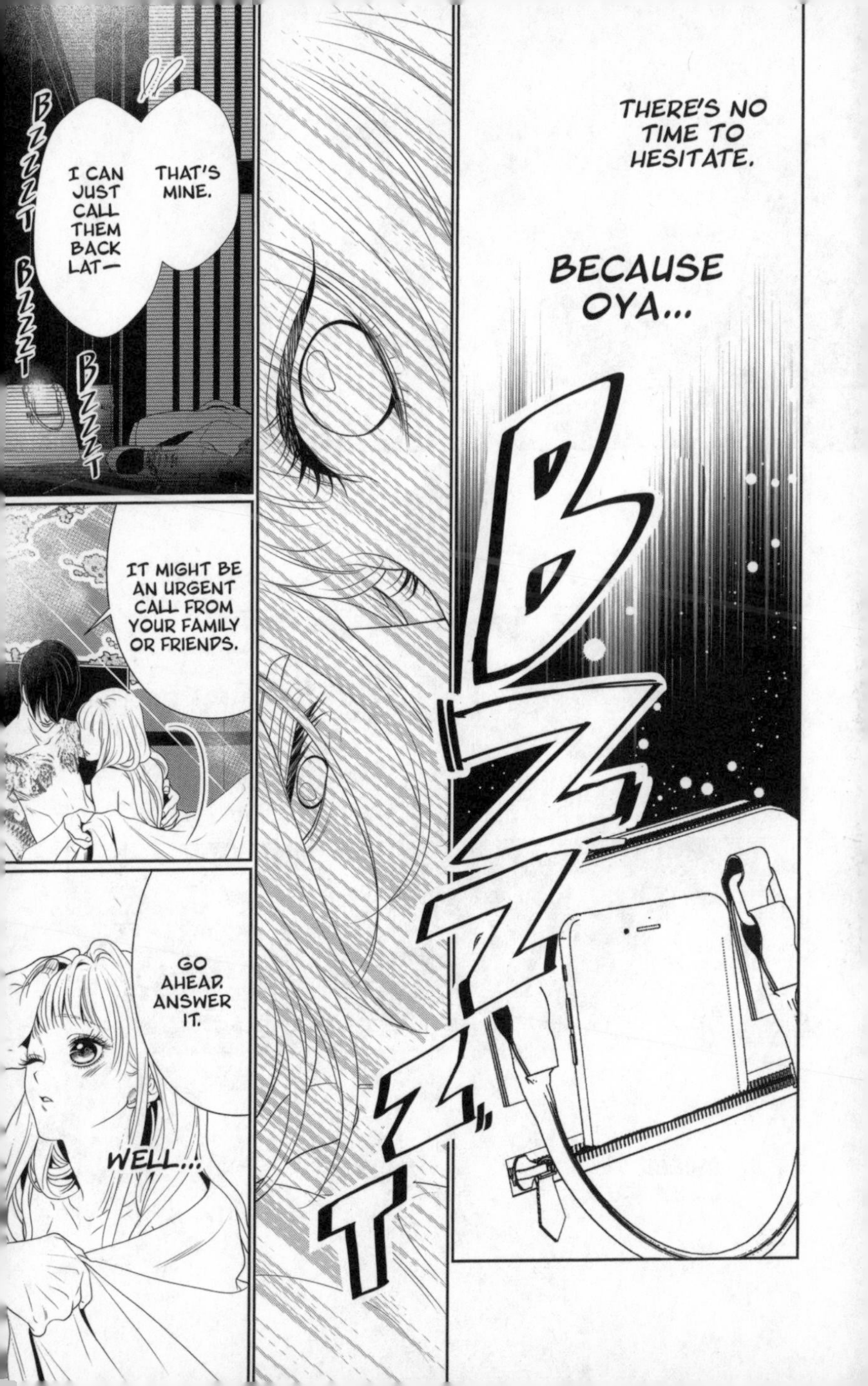
THERE'S NO TIME TO HESITATE.
BECAUSE OYA...
BZZZZT
THAT'S MINE.
I CAN JUST CALL THEM BACK LAT—
BZZZZT
BZZZZT
BZZZZT
IT MIGHT BE AN URGENT CALL FROM YOUR FAMILY OR FRIENDS.
GO AHEAD. ANSWER IT.
WELL...

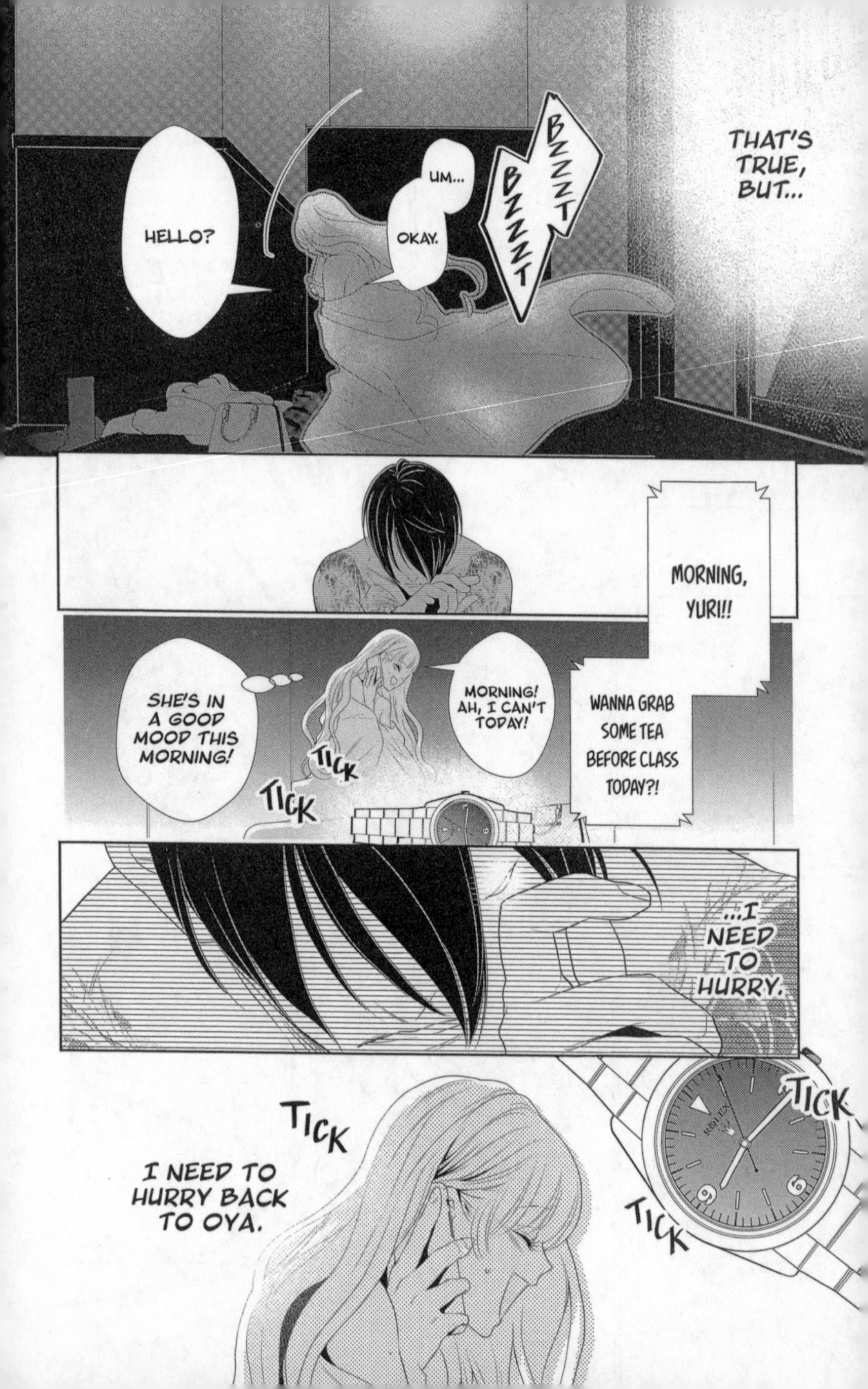
THAT'S TRUE, BUT...
BZZZT
BZZZT
UM...
OKAY.
HELLO?
MORNING, YURI!!
WANNA GRAB SOME TEA BEFORE CLASS TODAY?!
MORNING! AH, I CAN'T TODAY!
SHE'S IN A GOOD MOOD THIS MORNING!
TICK
TICK
...I NEED TO HURRY.
TICK
TICK
TICK
I NEED TO HURRY BACK TO OYA.

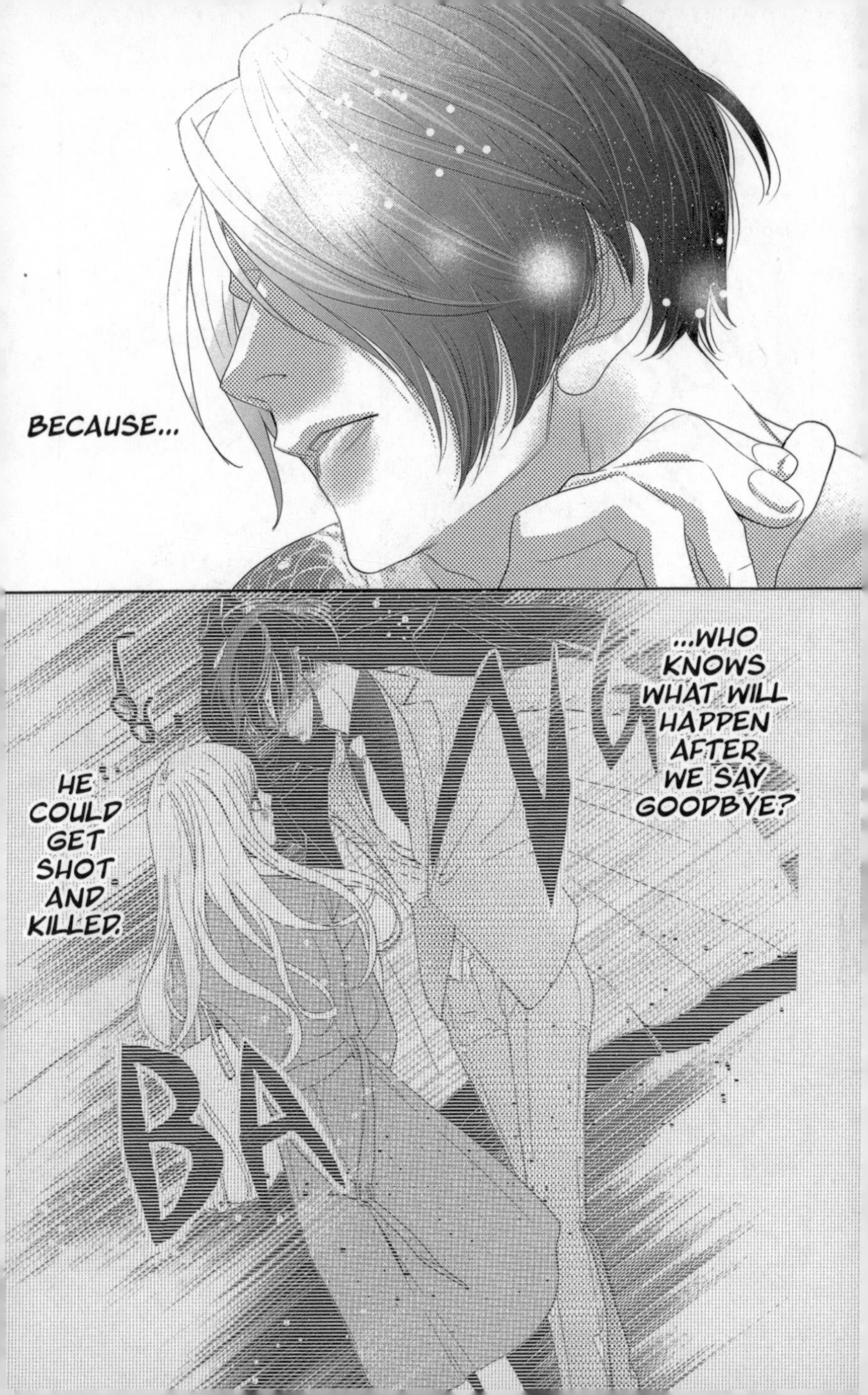
BECAUSE...
...WHO KNOWS WHAT WILL HAPPEN AFTER WE SAY GOODBYE?
BANG
HE COULD GET SHOT AND KILLED.

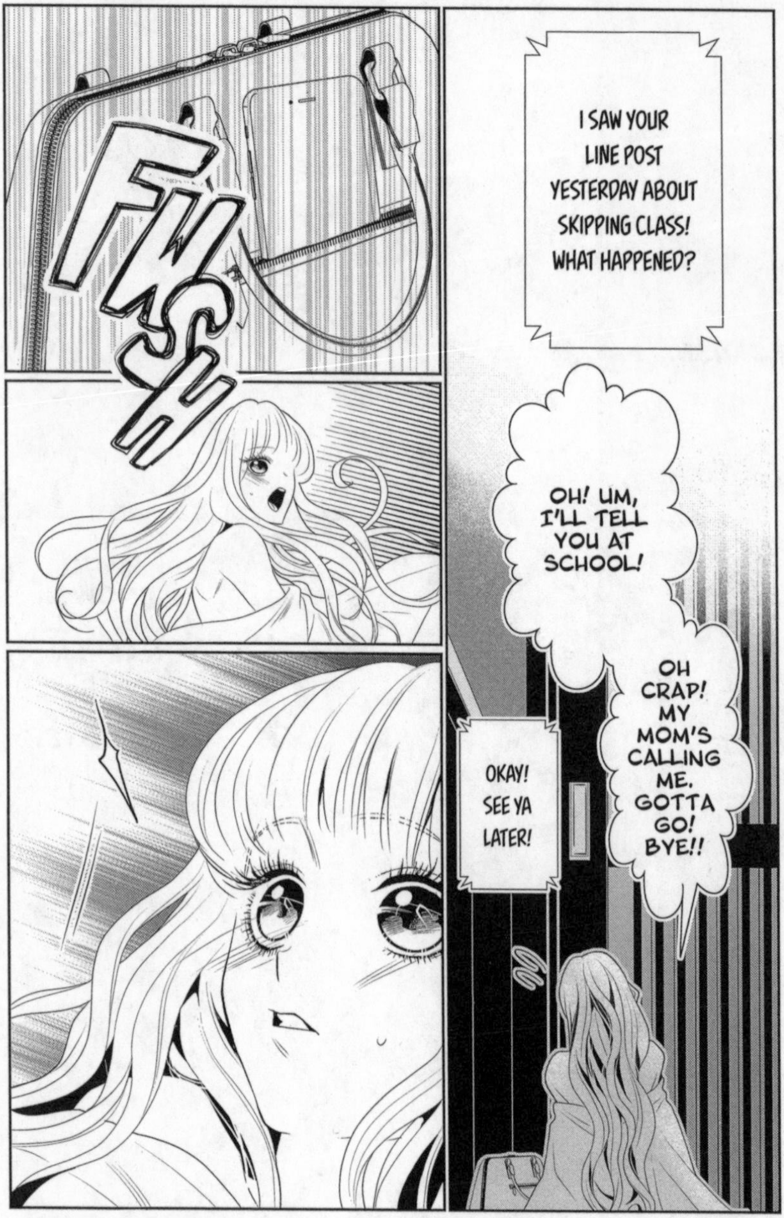
I SAW YOUR LINE POST YESTERDAY ABOUT SKIPPING CLASS! WHAT HAPPENED?
OH! UM, I'LL TELL YOU AT SCHOOL!
OH CRAP! MY MOM'S CALLING ME. GOTTA GO! BYE!!
OKAY! SEE YA LATER!
FWASH

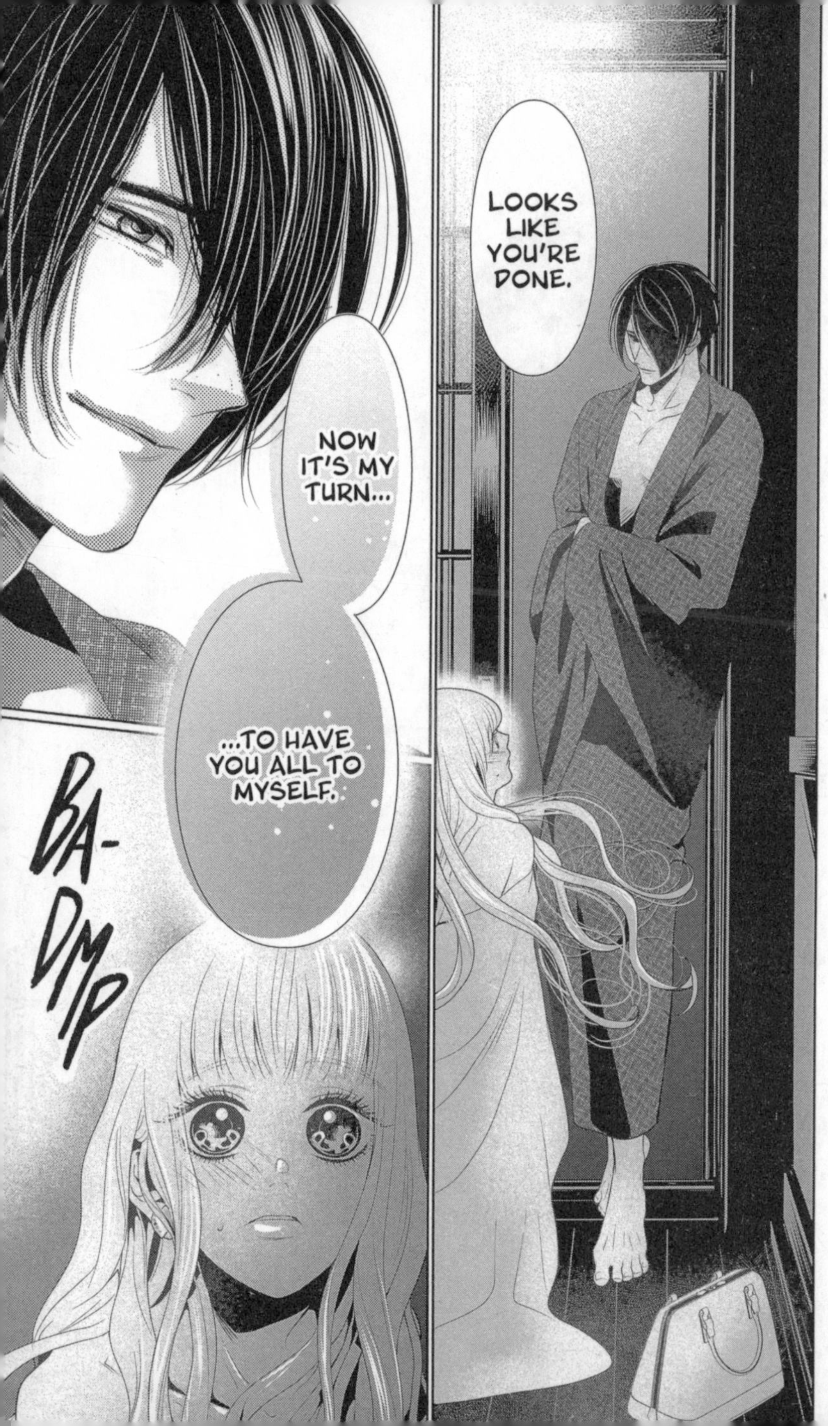
LOOKS LIKE YOU'RE DONE.
NOW IT'S MY TURN...
...TO HAVE YOU ALL TO MYSELF.
BA-DMP

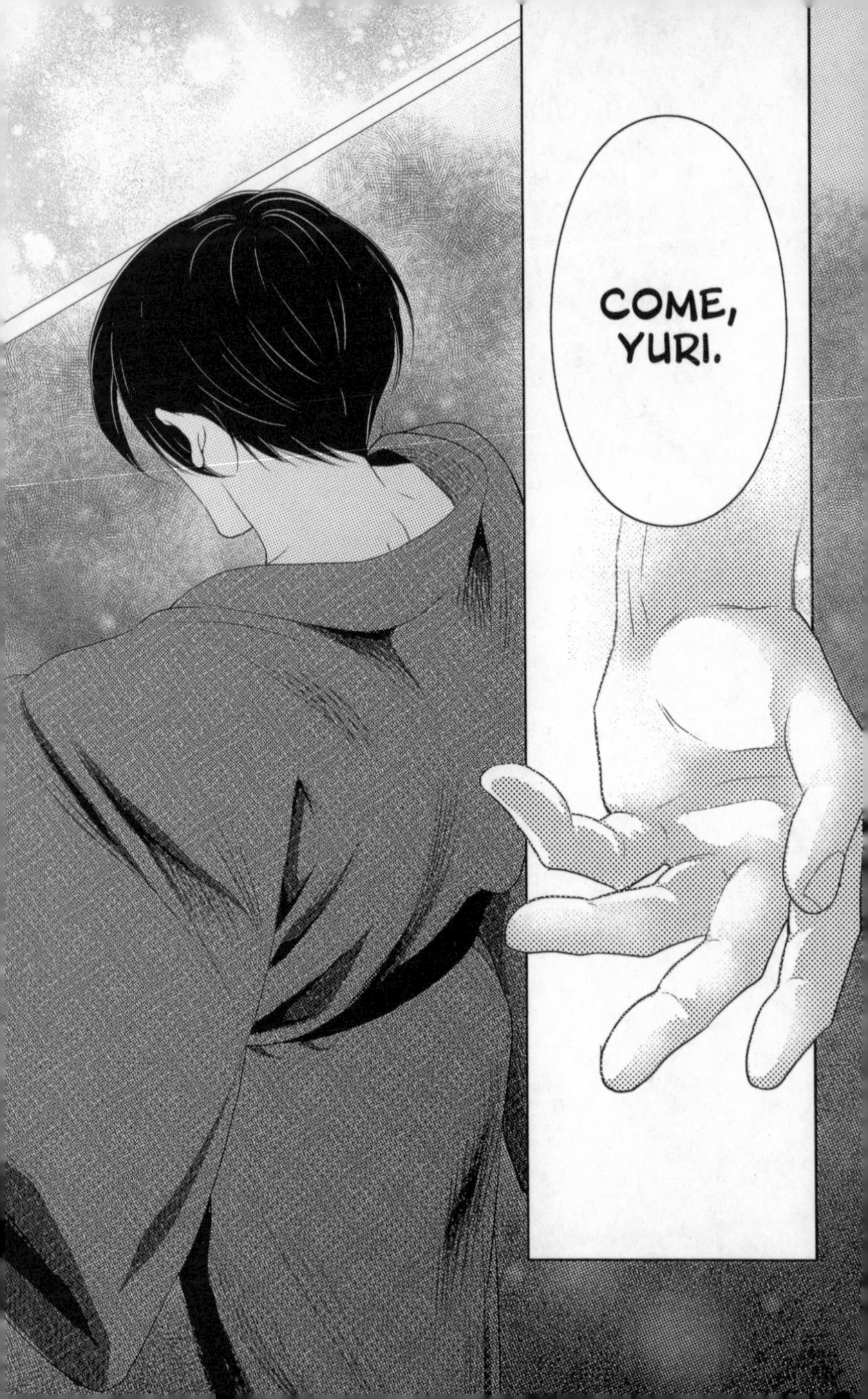
COME, YURI.

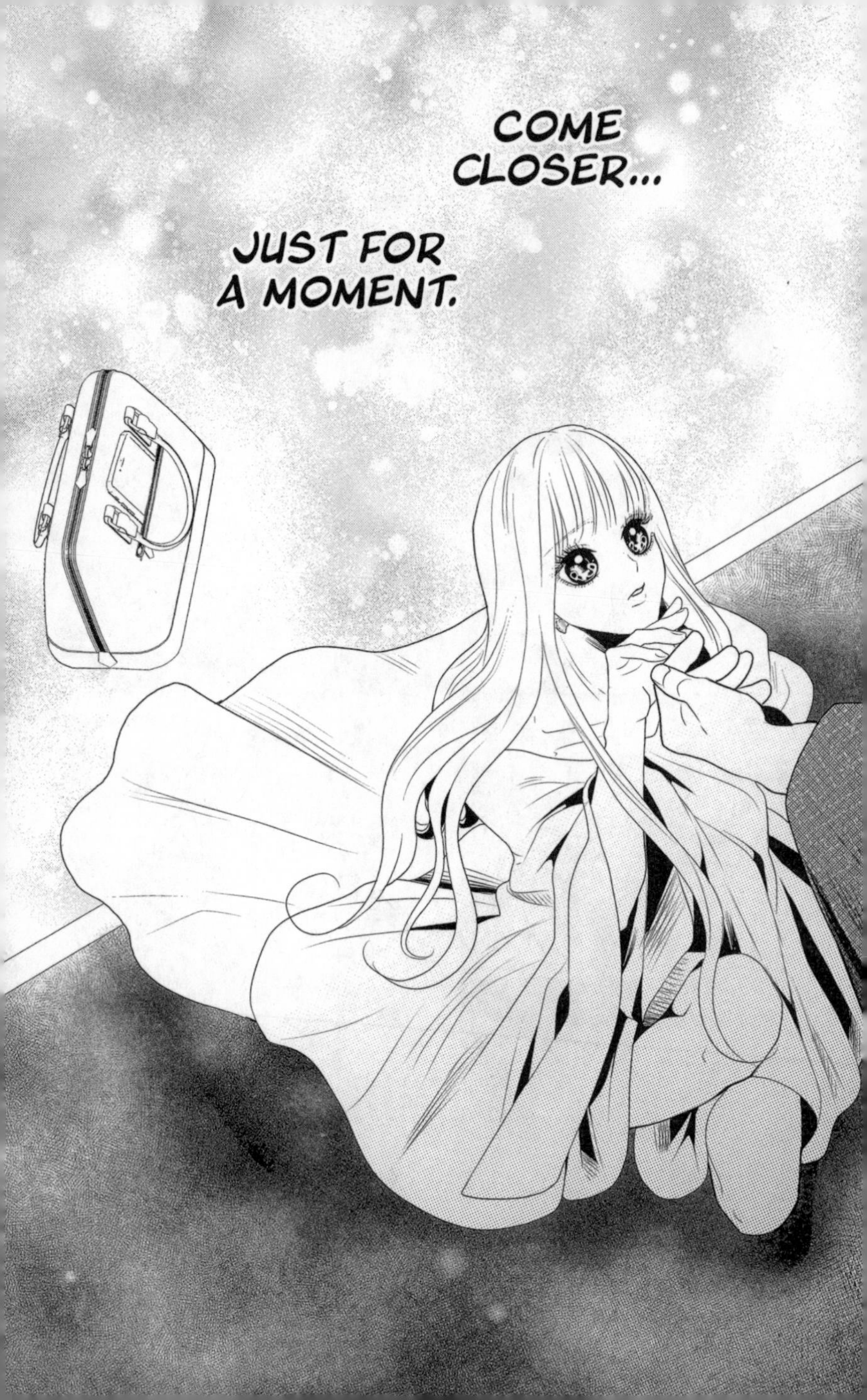
COME CLOSER...
JUST FOR A MOMENT.

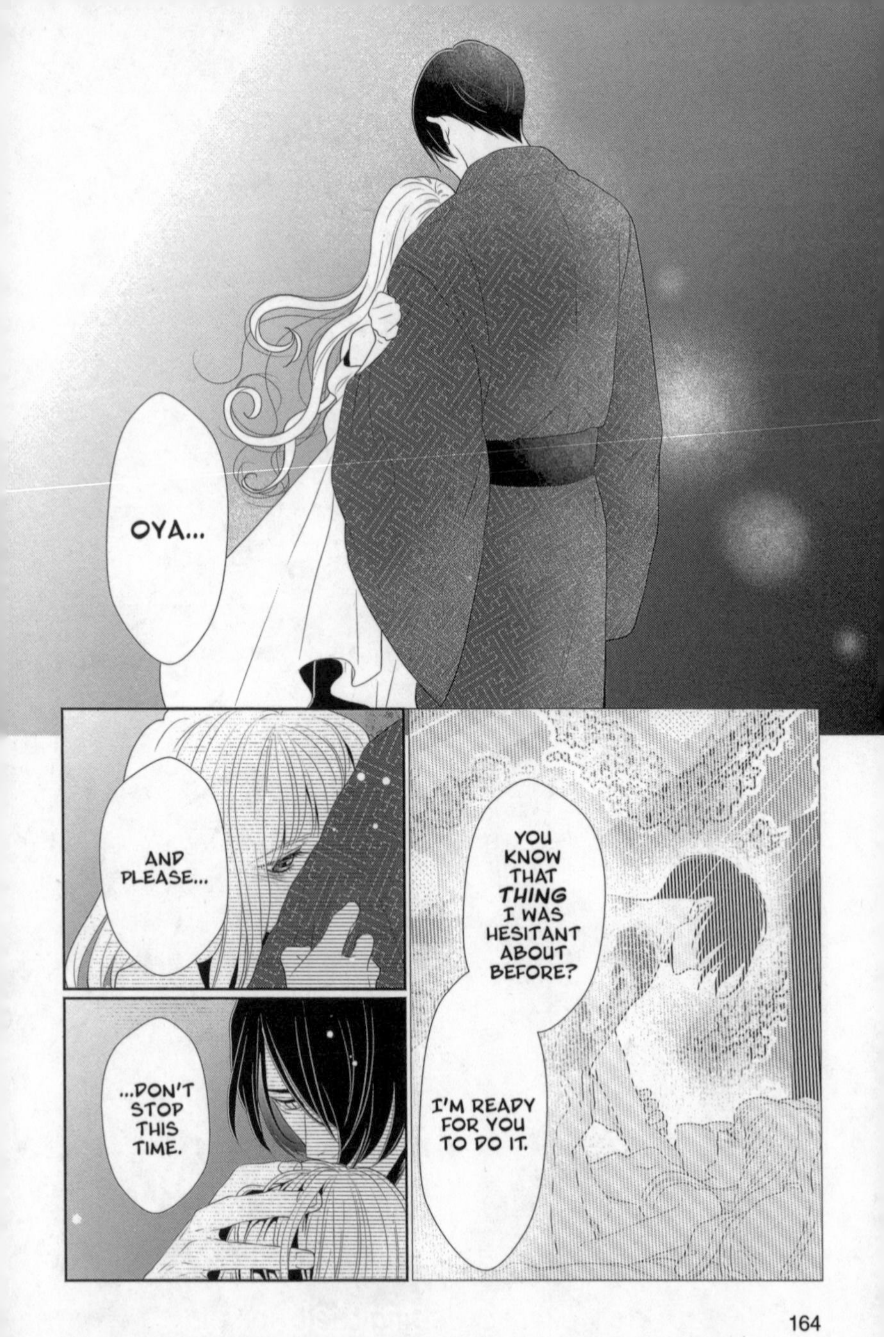
OYA...
YOU KNOW THAT *THING* I WAS HESITANT ABOUT BEFORE?
I'M READY FOR YOU TO DO IT.
AND PLEASE...
...DON'T STOP THIS TIME.

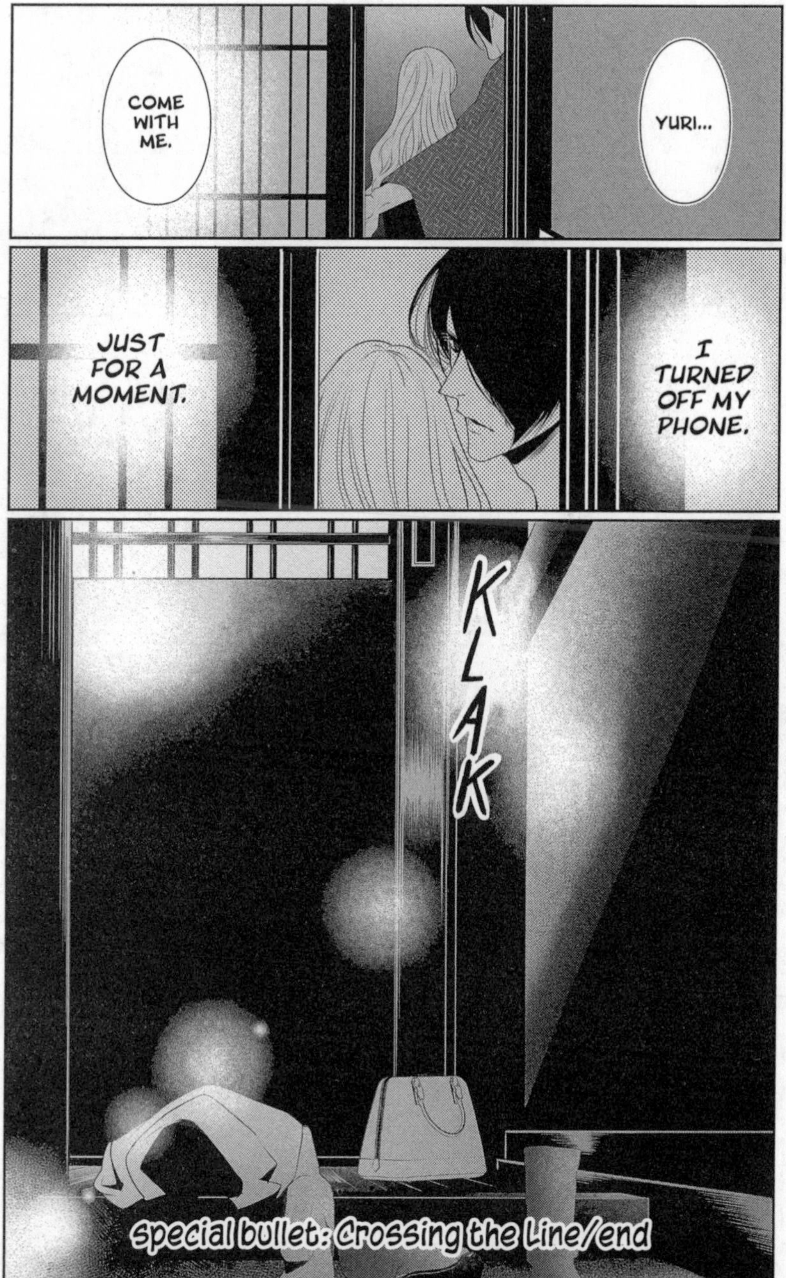
YURI...
COME WITH ME.
I TURNED OFF MY PHONE.
JUST FOR A MOMENT.
KLAK
Special bullet: Crossing the Line/end

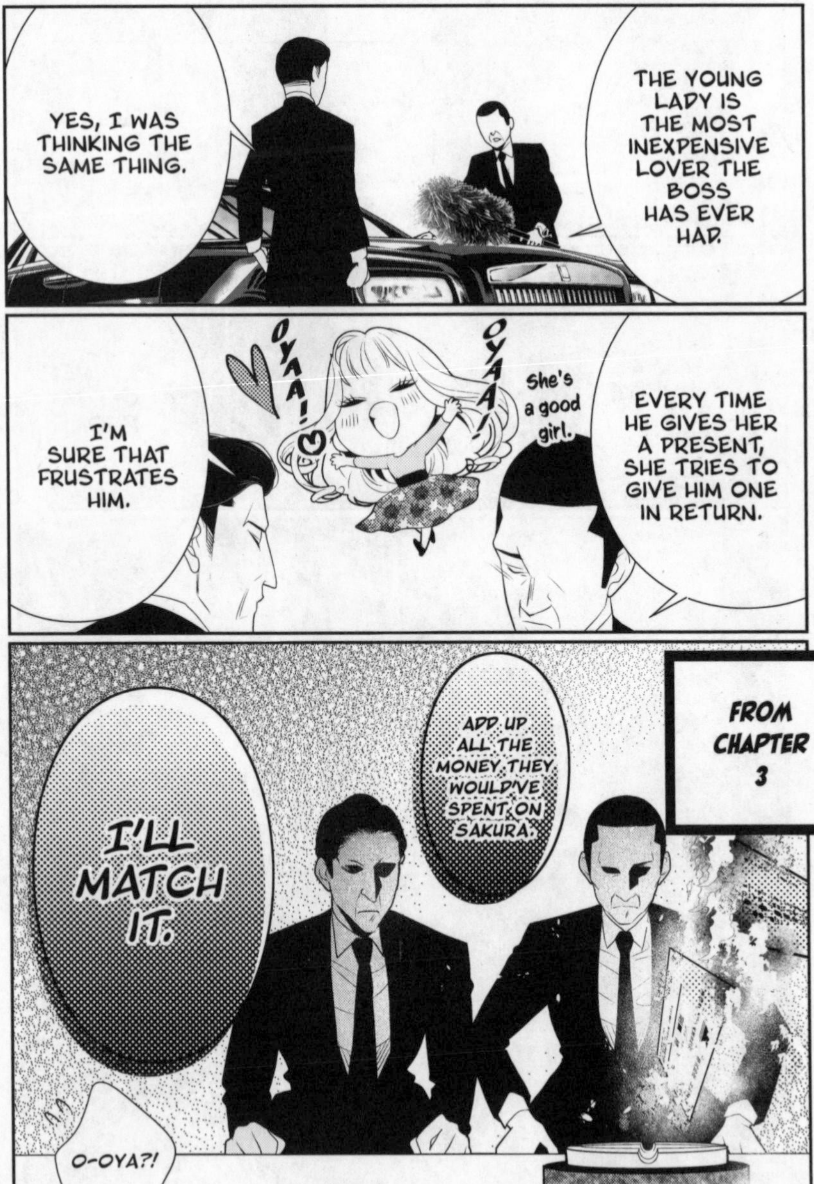
THE YOUNG LADY IS THE MOST INEXPENSIVE LOVER THE BOSS HAS EVER HAD.
YES, I WAS THINKING THE SAME THING.
EVERY TIME HE GIVES HER A PRESENT, SHE TRIES TO GIVE HIM ONE IN RETURN.
She's a good girl.
OYAA!
OYAA!
I'M SURE THAT FRUSTRATES HIM.
FROM CHAPTER 3
ADD UP ALL THE MONEY THEY WOULD'VE SPENT ON SAKURA.
I'LL MATCH IT.
O-OYA?!

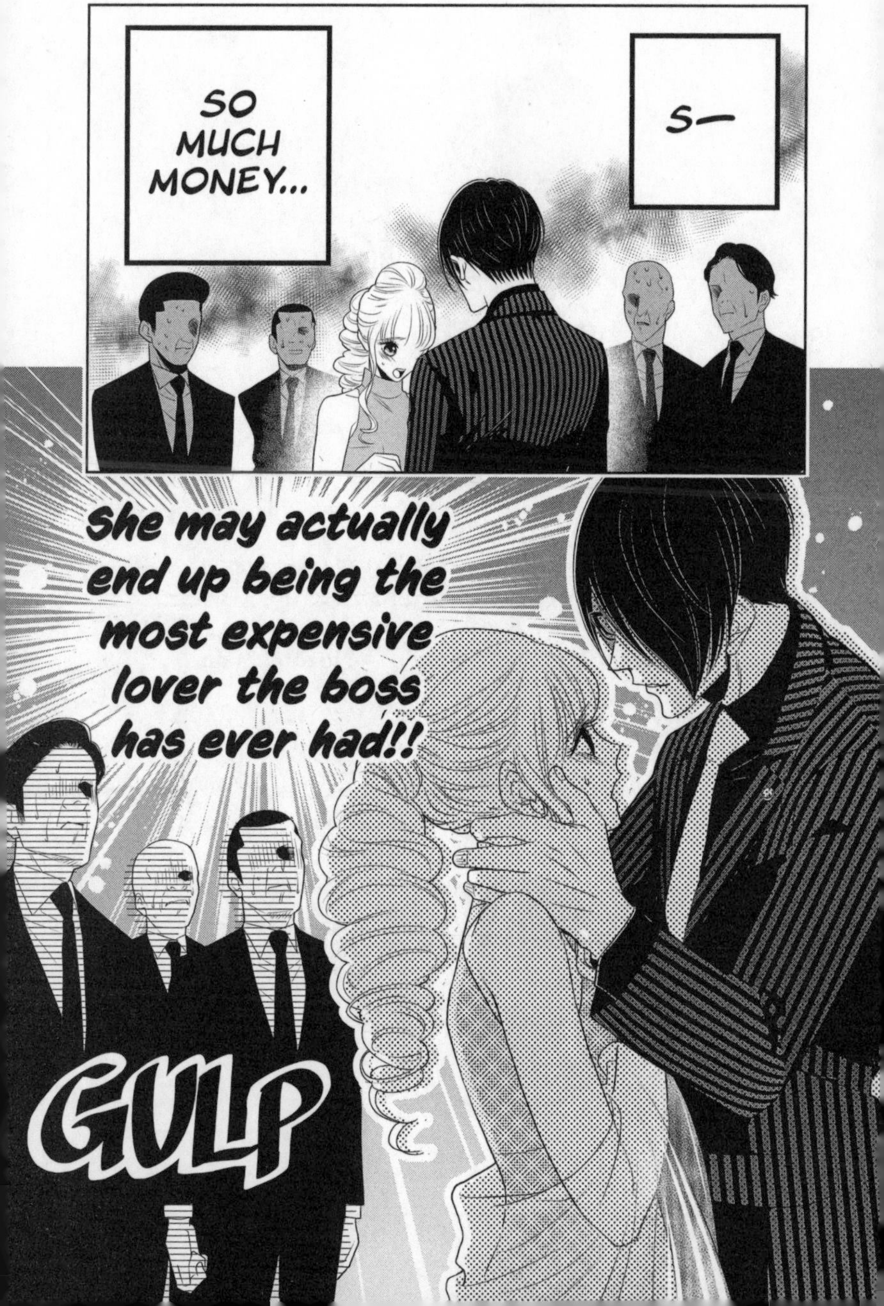
S—
SO MUCH MONEY...
She may actually end up being the most expensive lover the boss has ever had!!
GULP

ME OW

It's me.

Hello.

FLIP

(I'm bad at smiling.)

Thank you so much for reading *Yakuza Lover*. I hope
you enjoyed this volume's Shanghai-based story line.

—Nozomi Mino

• •

Nozomi Mino was born on February 12 in Himeji, Hyogo Prefecture,
in Japan, making her an Aquarius. She made her shojo manga debut in
the May 2006 issue of *Cheese!* with "LOVE MANTEN" (Love Perfect
Score). Since then, she has gone on to publish numerous works,
including *Sweet Marriage*, *Wagamama Otoko wa Ichizu ni Koisuru*
(Selfish Guys Love Hard) and *LOVE x PLACE.fam*. Her hobbies include
going on drives and visiting cafes.

YAKUZA LOVER

Vol. 2
Shojo Beat Edition

STORY AND ART BY
Nozomi Mino

Translation: Andria Cheng
Touch-Up Art & Lettering: Michelle Pang
Design: Yukiko Whitley
Editor: Karla Clark

KOI TO DANGAN Vol. 2
by Nozomi MINO
© 2019 Nozomi MINO
All rights reserved.
Original Japanese edition published by SHOGAKUKAN.
English translation rights in the United States of America, Canada, the United
Kingdom, Ireland, Australia and New Zealand arranged with SHOGAKUKAN.

Published by VIZ Media, LLC
P.O. Box 77010
San Francisco, CA 94107

10 9 8 7 6 5 4 3 2
First printing, September 2021
Second printing, June 2022

viz.com   shojobeat.com

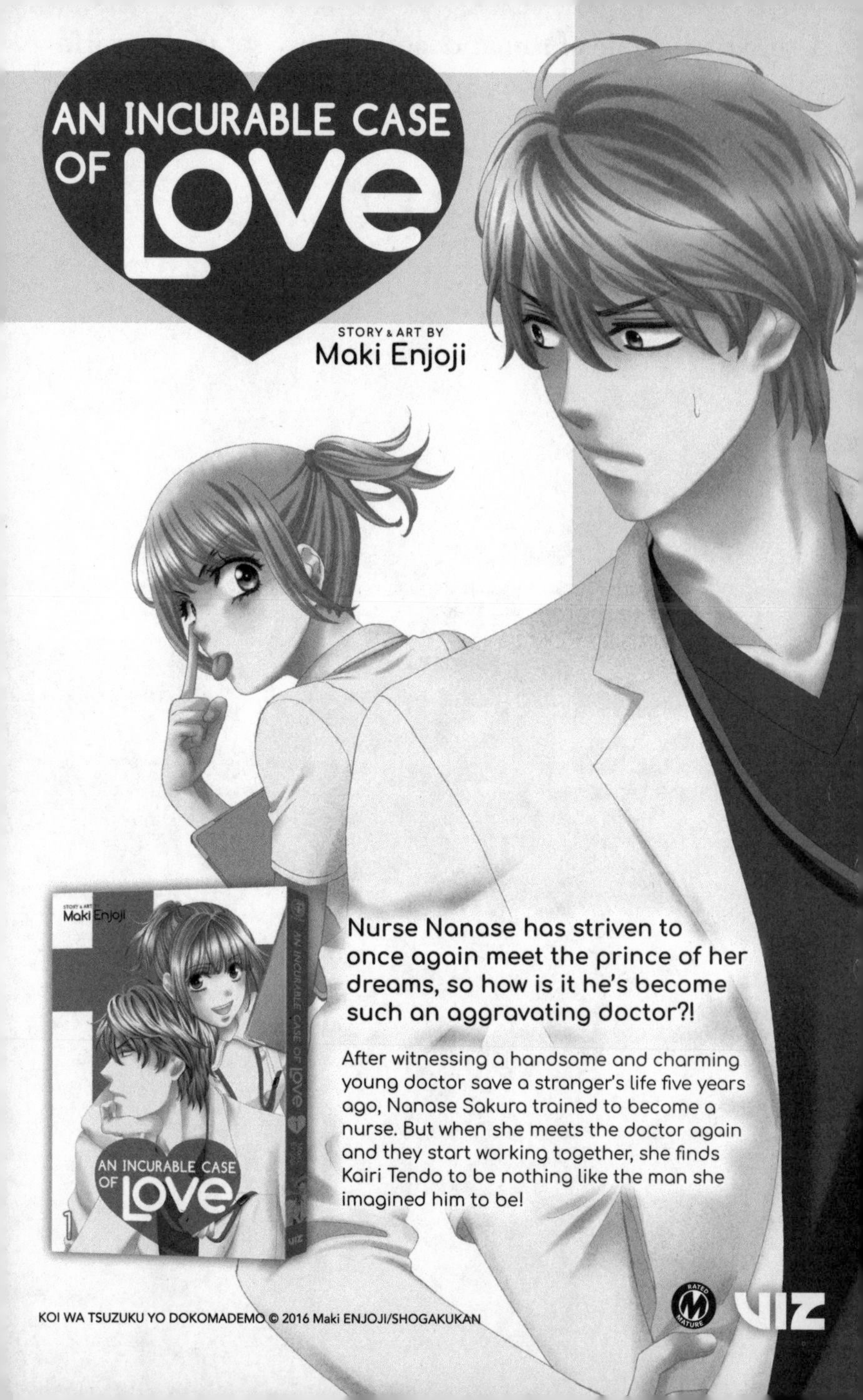
AN INCURABLE CASE OF LOVE
STORY & ART BY
Maki Enjoji
STORY & ART
Maki Enjoji
AN INCURABLE CASE OF LOVE
1
VIZ
Nurse Nanase has striven to once again meet the prince of her dreams, so how is it he's become such an aggravating doctor?!
After witnessing a handsome and charming young doctor save a stranger's life five years ago, Nanase Sakura trained to become a nurse. But when she meets the doctor again and they start working together, she finds Kairi Tendo to be nothing like the man she imagined him to be!
KOI WA TSUZUKU YO DOKOMADEMO © 2016 Maki ENJOJI/SHOGAKUKAN
RATED M MATURE
VIZ

A smoldering tale of romance and revenge set in the world of the *New York Times* best seller *Dawn of the Arcana!*

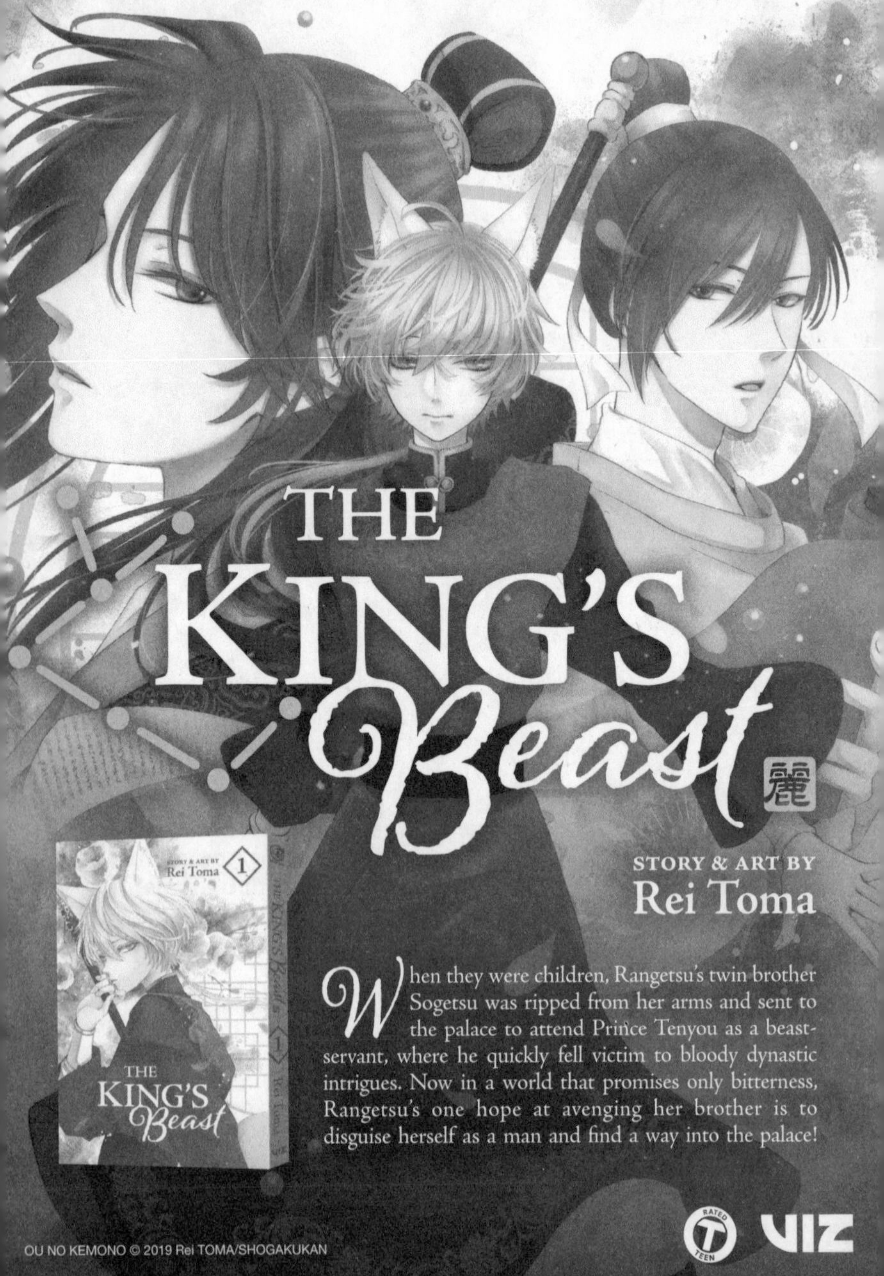

THE KING'S *Beast* 麗

STORY & ART BY
Rei Toma

STORY & ART BY
Rei Toma 1

THE KING'S *Beast*

When they were children, Rangetsu's twin brother Sogetsu was ripped from her arms and sent to the palace to attend Prince Tenyou as a beast-servant, where he quickly fell victim to bloody dynastic intrigues. Now in a world that promises only bitterness, Rangetsu's one hope at avenging her brother is to disguise herself as a man and find a way into the palace!

RATED TEEN · **VIZ**

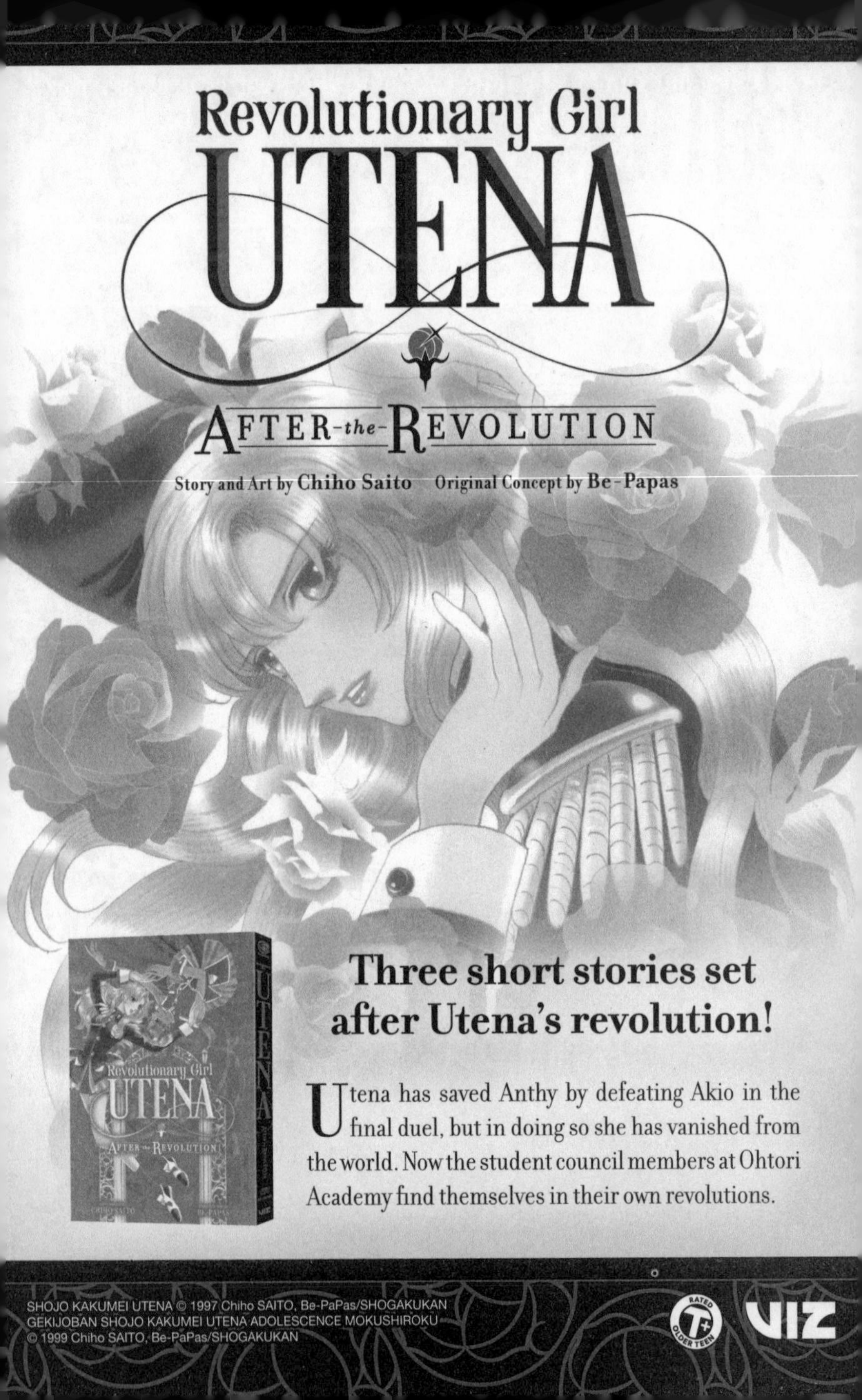

Revolutionary Girl
UTENA
AFTER-the-REVOLUTION
Story and Art by Chiho Saito Original Concept by Be-Papas
Three short stories set after Utena's revolution!
Utena has saved Anthy by defeating Akio in the final duel, but in doing so she has vanished from the world. Now the student council members at Ohtori Academy find themselves in their own revolutions.
SHOJO KAKUMEI UTENA © 1997 Chiho SAITO, Be-PaPas/SHOGAKUKAN
GEKIJOBAN SHOJO KAKUMEI UTENA ADOLESCENCE MOKUSHIROKU
© 1999 Chiho SAITO, Be-PaPas/SHOGAKUKAN
RATED T+ OLDER TEEN
VIZ

STOP RIGHT THERE!

You're reading the wrong way!

In keeping with the original Japanese comic format, *Yakuza Lover* reads from right to left, starting in the upper-right corner—so action, sound effects and word-balloon order are completely reversed to preserve the orientation of the original artwork.

So go ahead and flip the book over. You wouldn't want to spoil the ending for yourself now, would you?

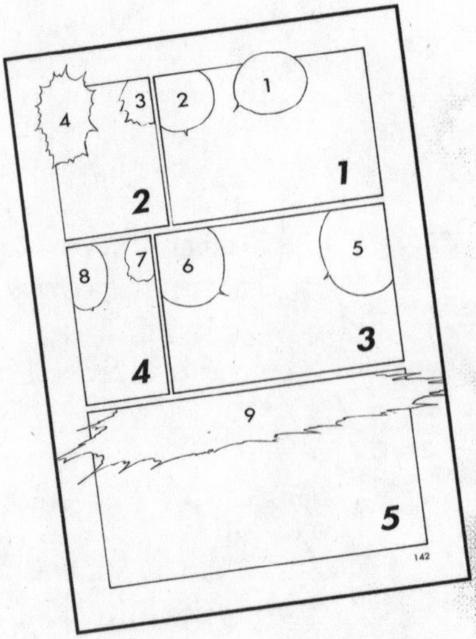
1
2
3
4
1
2
5
6
7
8
3
4
9
5
142

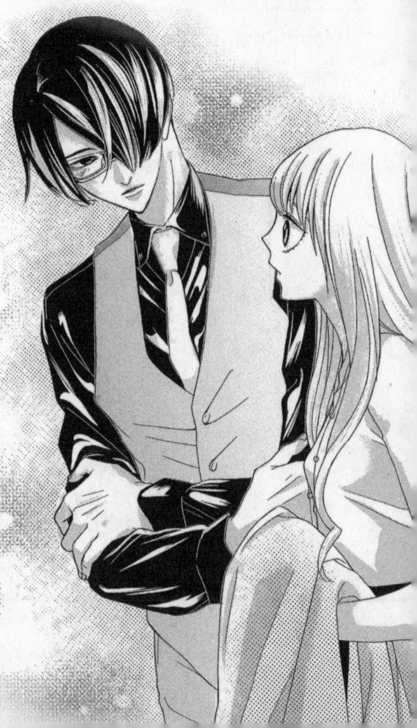